WIDSITH

CAMBRIDGE UNIVERSITY PRESS
London: FETTER LANE, E.C.
C. F. CLAY, Manager

Edinburgh: 100, PRINCES STREET
Berlin: A. ASHER AND CO.
Leipzig: F. A. BROCKHAUS
New York: G. P. PUTNAM'S SONS
Bombay and Calcutta: MACMILLAN AND CO., Ltd.

CAMBRIDGE LIBRARY COLLECTION

Books of enduring scholarly value

Literary Studies

This series provides a high-quality selection of early printings of literary works, textual editions, anthologies and literary criticism which are of lasting scholarly interest. Ranging from Old English to Shakespeare to early twentieth-century work from around the world, these books offer a valuable resource for scholars in reception history, textual editing, and literary studies.

Widsith

One of the few records of German heroic poetry, *Widsith* was found in the Exeter Book, a manuscript of Old English poetry compiled in the late tenth century. The tale, in which the wandering poet and narrator Widsith recounts his travels across northern Europe, is often seen as a catalogue of tribes, people and heroes who existed between the third and fifth centuries. Yet it is also, in Raymond Wilson Chambers' words, a rare and valuable 'record of lost heroic song'. Originally published in 1912, Chambers' study provides an introduction to the background of the German heroic tradition, as well as detailed analyses of specific aspects of *Widsith*, such as the metre, geography, and critical reception of the poem. This scholarly edition also includes an annotated version of the poem, and maps, as well as appendices which will be valuable to students and scholars of Old English literature.

Cambridge University Press has long been a pioneer in the reissuing of out-of-print titles from its own backlist, producing digital reprints of books that are still sought after by scholars and students but could not be reprinted economically using traditional technology. The Cambridge Library Collection extends this activity to a wider range of books which are still of importance to researchers and professionals, either for the source material they contain, or as landmarks in the history of their academic discipline.

Drawing from the world-renowned collections in the Cambridge University Library, and guided by the advice of experts in each subject area, Cambridge University Press is using state-of-the-art scanning machines in its own Printing House to capture the content of each book selected for inclusion. The files are processed to give a consistently clear, crisp image, and the books finished to the high quality standard for which the Press is recognised around the world. The latest print-on-demand technology ensures that the books will remain available indefinitely, and that orders for single or multiple copies can quickly be supplied.

The Cambridge Library Collection will bring back to life books of enduring scholarly value (including out-of-copyright works originally issued by other publishers) across a wide range of disciplines in the humanities and social sciences and in science and technology.

Widsith

A Study in Old English Heroic Legend

RAYMOND WILSON CHAMBERS

CAMBRIDGE UNIVERSITY PRESS

Cambridge, New York, Melbourne, Madrid, Cape Town, Singapore,
São Paolo, Delhi, Dubai, Tokyo, Mexico City

Published in the United States of America by Cambridge University Press, New York

www.cambridge.org
Information on this title: www.cambridge.org/9781108015271

© in this compilation Cambridge University Press 2010

This edition first published 1912
This digitally printed version 2010

ISBN 978-1-108-01527-1 Paperback

WIDSITH

A STUDY IN OLD ENGLISH HEROIC LEGEND

BY

R. W. CHAMBERS, M.A.

FELLOW AND LIBRARIAN OF UNIVERSITY COLLEGE, LONDON

Cambridge :
at the University Press
1912

Cambridge:

PRINTED BY JOHN CLAY, M.A.

AT THE UNIVERSITY PRESS

TO

W. P. KER

PREFACE

THE increasing interest shown during the last thirty years in *Beowulf* has, in England at least, not been extended to the other monuments of Old English heroic poetry : and that poetry has often, in consequence, been somewhat misjudged. The chief merit of *Widsith* is that it enables us to make a more correct estimate.

If *Widsith* had been, as some have thought it, an authentic record of a visit to the court of Ermanaric, it would have been valuable : though hardly so valuable as the account left by Priscus of his visit to the court of Attila, an account which nevertheless few trouble to read. But *Widsith* is more to us than any record of fourth or fifth century travel could have been : it is a record of lost heroic song. As one of its earliest editors said, with sound sense, if in questionable Latin, *Discimus ex eo, quot carmina temporum injuriâ nos amisimus.*

Another advantage to be drawn from a study of *Widsith* is that here we find the older scholars at their best. It is remarkable, considering the means at his disposal, how good are the comments even of the despised Conybeare, and still more is this true of those of Kemble, Leo, Lappenberg, Ettmüller, and in more recent days, of Möller, Ten Brink, and Müllenhoff. I hope that I have shown, both in dealing with the Harlung story and the Offa story, that my reverence for Müllenhoff is not a superstitious one. But it is time to protest against the undue depreciation of that great scholar, which has of late been prevalent, particularly in England and America. This depreciation is often not according to knowledge : indeed, we find later students, even the most scholarly, either ignorant of facts which were perfectly familiar to Kemble and Müllenhoff, or else hailing such facts as new discoveries.

Among the more recent students, I have to acknowledge indebtedness most frequently to Binz, Brandl, Bremer, Chadwick, Heusler, Holthausen, Heinzel, Jiriczek, Lawrence, Much, Olrik, Panzer, Symons. I have tried to express these and other obligations in the due place. Where there was general agreement on any point, I have been able to pass over it the more rapidly : where I had to differ from an opinion which has heavy critical authority behind it, I have felt bound to give my reasons at the greatest length space would permit. I regret that this tends to concentrate attention unduly upon points of difference.

The more the " literature of the subject " is studied, the less room does there seem to be for new views ; over and over again I have discovered that some observation which I was hoping to find new had been anticipated—by Brandl, Panzer, Olrik, Heinzel, or Rajna. But instances probably remain in which a view which has already been expressed by someone else is put forward as my own. I cannot hope to have run to earth every discussion of every hero or tribe recorded in *Widsith*.

And indeed, much has been published, especially during the past fifteen years, and in journals of high repute, which it is hardly necessary to put on record. I have therefore reserved the right of omitting references to comments which did not appear to lead us further : other omissions are no doubt the result of oversight. For the same reason, in the section on grammatical forms I have neglected spellings like *Moidum* for *Medum* (cf. *Oiddi* : *Eddi*) or *Amothingum* (*th* for þ) which, though interesting, could hardly be made the basis or support of any argument : and, in dealing with the metrical effect of the syncope of *u*, I have neglected lines like *On þam siex hund wæs*, where the loss of an earlier *u* might easily have been concealed by a slight rearrangement of the words.

Finally I have the pleasure of acknowledging the help in reading proofs very kindly given by Miss M. Eyre, Miss E. V.

Hitchcock, Mr L. A. Magnus, and, I should add, by the Cambridge Press reader. To Mr J. H. G. Grattan I am indebted for many corrections and suggestions, and to Professor Robert Priebsch for a constant advice which has been everywhere of service, but more particularly in the sections dealing with Ermanaric, Hama, and Heoden; to Professor W. P. Ker my debt is even heavier, and more difficult to define; it will be found, like the blow which Offa gave his adversary, *non unam partem sed totam transegisse compagem.*

R. W. CHAMBERS.

31 *December* 1911.

CONTENTS

CORRECTIONS AND ADDITIONAL NOTES

p. 7.   For a parallel to the 'Biblical interpolation' in *Widsith* see Matthew Arnold 'On the study of Celtic Literature,' p. 69 (1867 edit.).

p. 25.   For 'common grandfather Hrethel' read 'kinsman Hrethel.'

p. 172.   The assertion that l. 45 a, if we substitute for *Hroðgar* the earlier *Hroðgaru*, can still be paralleled in *Beowulf*, needs qualification.   For in half-lines like *sellice sædracan, fyrdsearu fuslicu*, the syllable *lic* should probably be read short (cf. Sievers, *P.B.B.* x, 504 ; xxix, 568).   Yet, for the other reasons given on p. 172, I do not think that *Hroðgaru* is impossible: and even if it were, there are three reasons, any one of which would prevent our basing upon this line an argument for dating the bulk of *Widsith* later than 700 A.D.   For, firstly, ll. 45 *etc.* are presumably a subsequent addition to the Catalogue of Kings (see pp. 135, 147) : secondly, a simple rearrangement of the words would make the line run satisfactorily : and thirdly, after a long syllable, bearing the subsidiary accent, *u* was lost earlier than after a long syllable bearing the main accent, and was certainly already lost before 700.

CHAPTER I.

The Heroic Poetry of the Germans.

OVER many great races an enthusiastic movement seems at a certain period to sweep, carrying them during a few years to success, alike in arms and song, till the stream sinks back into its old channel, and the nation continues a career, honourable, it may be, but wanting in the peculiar ardour of its great age. Such a spirit as came upon the Athens of Pericles, or the England of Elizabeth, seems to have animated the widely scattered Germanic tribes which, in the fifth and sixth centuries, plundered and drank and sang amid the ruins of imperial Rome.

To the cultured Roman provincial, trying to lead an elegant and lettered existence amid reminiscences of the great ages of Classical history, the drinking seemed immoderate, and the song dissonant. One such has told us how his soul was vexed at the barbarous songs of his long-haired Burgundian neighbours, how he had to suppress his disgust, and praise these German lays, though with a wry face. How gladly now would we give all his verses for ten lines of the songs in which these " long-haired, seven foot high, onion-eating barbarians " celebrated, it may be, the open-handedness of Gibica, or perhaps told how, in that last terrible battle, their fathers had fallen fighting around

C.   1

Gundahari[1]. But the Roman, far from caring to record these things, was anxious to shut his ears to them. The orthodox bishop of the fifth century, when compelled to listen to the songs of German tribesmen, seems to agree with the apostate emperor of the fourth, who thought these lays like the croaking of harsh-voiced birds[2]. So it has come to pass that, whilst the contemporary Latin verse has been only too abundantly preserved, the songs chanted at the feasts of Gothic and Burgundian, Frankish and Lombard, Danish and Anglian chiefs, in the fifth and sixth centuries, have been lost. The loss is among the most lamentable in the history of poetry.

Yet a few records have come down to us, for, as during centuries these songs passed, in the mouths of minstrels, from one branch to another of the Teutonic race[3], they often came to be written down. In later days Charles the Great caused the Frankish versions to be collected[4]. Upon the English poems Alfred the Great was educated[5]: upon them in turn he educated his children[6]; and he was wont to recommend to others the learning of "Saxon" lays by heart[7]. In this case, too, our authority makes mention of written books. It is

[1]
> Quid me, etsi valeam, parare carmen
> Fescenninicolæ jubes Diones
> inter crinigeras situm catervas
> et Germanica verba sustinentem,
> laudantem tetrico subinde vultu
> quod Burgundio cantat esculentus,
> infundens acido comam butyro?
> vis dicam tibi quid poema frangat?
> ex hoc barbaricis abacta plectris
> spernit senipedem stilum Thalia
> ex quo septipedes videt patronos, &c.
> > Sidonius Apollinaris, *Car.* xii, ed. Luetjohann,
> > p. 231 (in *M.G.H.*).

[2] ἐθεασάμην τοι καὶ τοὺς ὑπὲρ τὸν ʼΡῆνον βαρβάρους ἄγρια μέλη λέξει πεποιημένα παραπλησίᾳ τοῖς κρωγμοῖς τῶν τραχὺ βοώντων ὀρνίθων ᾅδοντας καὶ εὐφραινομένους ἐπὶ τοῖς μέλεσιν. (Μισοπώγων: Julian, ed. Hertlein, 1875–6, p. 434.)

[3] There is some evidence that not merely traditions, but complete lays passed from one Germanic nation to another. (Cf. Heusler, *L.u.E.* 4; Symons in *Z.f.d.Ph.* xxxviii, 164.)

[4] Einhard, *Vita Carol.* c. 29. In Pertz (fol.) *SS.* ii, 458.

[5] Asser, ed Stevenson, 1904, § 22 *Sed Saxonica poemata die noctuque solers auditor, relatu aliorum saepissime audiens, docibilis memoriter retinebat...23 Cum ergo quodam die mater sua...quendam Saxonicum poematicae artis librum... ostenderet...*

[6] § 75 *Eadwerd et Ælfthryth...et psalmos et Saxonicos libros et maxime Saxonica carmina studiose didicere.*

[7] § 76 *Interea tamen rex...et Saxonicos libros recitare, et maxime carmina Saxonica memoriter discere aliis imperare...non desinebat.*

likely, however, that, more often than not, these Germanic lays were not committed to writing at all. Of those that were, England has preserved a few, fragmentary but most precious, and continental Germany one.

Yet we can form but a poor idea of this old literature from the surviving fragments of the Songs of *Waldere* or *Hildebrand*, still less from *Beowulf*, the one poem which happens to have come down to us complete, but of which the plot is singularly poor. A better estimate of the value of these vanished songs can be made, partly from certain passages in the Latin chroniclers which are obviously founded upon lost lays, partly from the magnificent afterglow of the Old Norse heroic verse and prose saga; and not least from the glamour which an English poet, using the old motives and the old common-places, has been able to throw over the historic facts of the death, in battle against the heathen, of an Essex nobleman in the days of Ethelred the Unready.

So this world of high-spirited, chivalrous song has passed away, leaving fragments so scanty that it requires some sympathetic allowance before we can realise how great the loss has been :

hu seo þrag gewat
genap under nihthelm, swa heo no wære !

We cannot accept as compensation the remodelled stories in the thirteenth century High German garb in which they have come down to us. Sifrit, the horny-skinned wife-beater, Gunther hanging from a peg in his bedchamber[1], are but poor substitutes for the lost figures of the old Teutonic hero-song, Gundahari the Burgundian, Offa the Angle, Ermanaric the tyrant or the noble Theodoric. The *Nibelungen Lied* is beyond dispute one of the world's greatest things. Inferior as it is in detail to the Greek epic, yet, when all is drawing to an end, and the terrible Hagene has been overcome by the perfect knight, Dietrich von Bern, we are left with a deep awe akin to what we feel when we see Priam at the knees of Achilles. The *Nibelungen Lied* is glorious, but its glory, like its metre, is not that of the ancient lays.

---

[1] *Der Nibelunge Not* (Lachmann, 590*, 837* ; Bartsch, 640, 894).

It is our duty then to gather up reverently such fragments of the old Teutonic epic as fortune has preserved in our English tongue, and to learn from them all we can of that collection of stories of which these fragments are the earliest vernacular record

Widsith.

The weightiest vernacular document bearing upon the old German hero-cycles is a poem found in the *Exeter Book,* that collection of English religious verse, transcribed in the late tenth or early eleventh century, which was given to his cathedral church by Leofric, first Bishop of Exeter (died 1072).

Widsith and *Deor*, which stand respectively eleventh and twentieth in the collection, differ remarkably from the other poems in the volume. They are relics of heathendom embedded in a Christian anthology. Both are lyrics founded upon epic tradition: in each a gleeman tells a tale of himself, adorning his song by copious allusions to the stories he loves.

Widsith—"Farway"—the ideal wandering minstrel, tells of all the tribes among which he has sojourned, all the chieftains he has known. The first English students[1] of the poem regarded it as autobiographical, as the actual record of his wanderings written by a real *scóp*; and were inclined to dismiss as interpolations passages mentioning princes whom it was chronologically impossible for a man who had met Ermanaric to have known. This view was reduced to an absurdity by Haigh, who pointed out that a certain hero, Hama, is mentioned last. But what reason can have led to his being mentioned last? Clearly only one; the Traveller

---

[1] For example: Conybeare, *Illustrations,* 1826, p. 28: Kemble, *Preface to Beowulf,* 1833, p. xvii: Guest, *Rhythms,* 1838, vol. ii, pp. 76, *etc.*

Stopford Brooke (*English Literature from the beginning to the Norman Conquest,* 1898, pp. 46–8) and Garnett (*English Literature,* i, pp. 7–8) have, more recently, been inclined to regard the poem in this light, though with considerable hesitation; and so, with perhaps less hesitation, have Anderson (pp. 5, 23) and Chadwick (*Camb. Hist.* i, 36).

Brandl, too, speaks of *Widsith* as autobiographical (*Berl. Sitzungsberichte,* xxxv, 1908); a view which is disputed by Schücking (*Engl. Stud.* xlii, 111). But I take Brandl to mean merely that *Widsith* is cast in an autobiographical form, not that the travels narrated are historic; this last view would not be consistent with what Brandl has said elsewhere about *Widsith* (*Pauls Grdr.* (2) ii, 1, 968).

himself, Haigh urged, was Hama, and was moved by motives of modesty[1].

The temptation to attribute historic value to poetry in which the names of historic chiefs often meet us is, of course, strong; and, giving way to it, the early chroniclers of many nations have incorporated heroic tradition into their histories. But it is an essential characteristic of heroic poetry that, whilst it preserves many historic names, it gives the story modified almost past recognition by generations of poetic tradition. Accurate chronology too is, in the absence of written records, impossible: all the great historic chieftains become contemporaries: their deeds are confused: only their names, and sometimes their characters, remain.

The more we study the growth of German heroic tradition, the more clear does it become that *Widsith* and *Deor* reflect that tradition. They are not the outpourings of actual poets at the court of Ermanaric or the Heodenings. What the poems sung in the hall of Ermanaric were like we shall never know: but we can safely say that they were unlike *Widsith*. The mere excision of a name here and there will not put our poem back to the date of Ermanaric, any more than the excision of a few late features will make Mallory's Morte d'Arthur a correct account of the court of a sixth century British king[2].

The reasons which prevent us from regarding *Widsith* as the itinerary of a real *scóp* have been stated fully and convincingly by a recent critic[3]. To suppose that the author, in his own person, claims to have come into contact with Ermanaric is indeed to misunderstand the spirit of the poem. The Traveller's tale is a phantasy of some man, keenly interested in the old

---

[1] Haigh, *Sagas*, p. 148.

[2] I cannot agree with Mr Chadwick's attempt to draw historic and even chronological data from *Widsith*. See *Origin of the English Nation*, 135. How limited is the historic element in German heroic tradition has been well shown by Heusler, *Berl. Sitzungsberichte*, xxxvii, 1909.

[3] Lawrence in *Mod. Philol.* iv, 355, *etc.*, 367, *etc.* The careful and measured statement of Dr Lawrence appears to me to be conclusive. But the view that the Traveller's wanderings are at least in part historic is still so prevalent among English scholars that I have thought it better to summarize below the considerations which, as it appears to me, make it impossible so to regard them, from an investigation first of heroic legend (pp. 142–3) and then of geography (pp. 163–5).

stories, who depicts an ideal wandering singer, and makes him move hither and thither among the tribes and the heroes whose stories he loves. In the names of its chiefs, in the names of its tribes, but above all in its spirit, *Widsith* reflects the heroic age of the migrations, an age which had hardly begun in the days of Ermanaric.

Catalogues of this kind are peculiarly liable to interpolation, especially during a period of oral tradition. There is a natural tendency for each gleeman through whose hands the poem passes to corrupt the names of clans and heroes with which he is not familiar, and to add the names of others which his tribal prejudices lead him to think should not have been left without honourable mention. Hence catalogues, from those in the second book of the *Iliad* or the eleventh book of the *Odyssey* downwards, are always to be suspected[1].

But in *Widsith* we have a catalogue of some seventy tribes[2]; and of sixty-nine heroes, many of whom can be proved to have existed in the third, fourth and fifth centuries of our era, and the latest of whom belong to the sixth century. Yet, although every chief whom we can date lived prior, not only to the conversion of the English to Christianity, but even to the completion of their settlement in Britain, this thoroughly heathen poem has come down to us in a transcript which some English monk made about the year 1000. Clearly it will require patience to disentangle its history, and fix its approximate date and place of origin.

---

[1] A comparison of *Widsith* with the Greek heroic catalogues would be helpful: it has been indicated, without details, by Meyer (*Altgermanische Poesie*, 1889, p. 4). We might also compare later mediaeval lists of romances such as those given in Skelton's *Philip Sparrow*, those quoted in the appendix to Ker's *Epic and Romance*, or those Italian catalogues printed by Pio Rajna (*Zeitschrift f. Romanische Philologie*, II, 1878, pp. 138 *etc.*, 222 *etc.*). The likeness of these latter to *Widsith* was noted by Rajna himself (*Origini*, p. 40). But the closest parallel of all is found in the Icelandic name lists, as given in the heroic muster rolls, in the *Thulor*, and in poems like *Grimnismál*, *Hyndloljóþ*, the opening lines of the *Angantyr lay* (cf. *C.P.B.* I, 565), or the enumeration of dwarfs in *Volospá*. For later Icelandic lists see Kölbing, *Beiträge zur vergleichenden Geschichte der romantischen Poesie*, 1876, pp. 154–5, and *C.P.B.* I, pp. xviii, cxi.

[2] Including twenty-two referred to only in the doubtful passage.

General Impressions of the Poem.   Obvious Interpolations.
Age of the subject-matter.

Whilst the general consensus of opinion would make our poem one of the oldest, if not quite the oldest, in Germanic literature, one critic of repute has, on the strength of certain Biblical and Oriental names occurring in it, placed it as late as the early ninth century[1].

Such a view has, however, been justly condemned by Müllenhoff as superficial[2]. It neglects the fact, so obvious even to a casual observer, that these Biblical and Oriental names are confined to one brief passage, and are alien to the spirit of the poem as a whole. The author was clearly a man steeped in all the lore of the Teutonic races : he makes his Widsith visit Swedes and Burgundians, Angles and Danes, Lombards and Goths : he is interested in the national heroes of all these folk : he knows something too of the peoples across the mark : Widsith has visited the Finns of the North and the Wends of the East, has heard tell of the Caesar of the East and has been in Italy. He is skilled in traditional and genealogical lore, in those " old unhappy far off things and battles long ago " which are so highly rated in the heroic age of any people. But we may safely say of the poet that his study was but little on the Bible. The student who reads *Widsith* for the first time passes therefore, with a feeling of surprise, from a list of tribes with whose stories any gleeman of the heroic age would be familiar, to a series of supposititious travels among Medes and Persians, Israelites and Hebrews. Accordingly this passage was, at a very early stage in the criticism of *Widsith*, condemned as spurious[3]; and for a critic,

[1] K. Maurer in Zacher's *Z.f.d.Ph.* II (1870), 447.
[2] *D.A.* v, 65–6.
[3] By Kemble. "More than one circumstance, however, compels us to conclude that later transcribers added to the work of Hermanaric's contemporary. Not only is the insertion of several nations only known in Europe through the Bible, and the distinction between Hebrews and Israelites suspicious, but the mention of Theodoric the king of the Franks, if by this prince the son of Chlodowic be meant, places the poem in which his name occurs later at least than A.D. 480." *Preface to Beowulf*, 1833, p. xvii. Leo, *Sprachproben*, 82, endorsed this view.

in trying to fix the date of the poem, to overlook its doubtful nature and to base his theories upon it, is, as Müllenhoff has stated, uncritical.

It is true that the certainty with which a German scholar will sometimes fix upon this or that passage as interpolated is apt to arouse scepticism in English students[1]. But here the evidence is peculiarly strong, and we are compelled to endorse the judgment of Müllenhoff, that a critic will hardly recognise any passage as interpolated, if he does not so recognise this[2].

Exactly how long is the interpolated passage, it is more difficult to say. The four lines of Oriental adventure (75, 82–4) must certainly go:

> Mid Sercingum ic wæs and mid Seringum, ...
> Mid Israhelum ic wæs and mid Exsyringum,
> Mid Ebreum and mid Indeum and mid Egyptum.
> Mid Moidum ic wæs and mid Persum, and mid Myrgingum.

Müllenhoff is perhaps right in condemning the whole thirteen lines, 75—87, and in including in the same condemnation lines 14—17 (Alexandreas) and lines 131—134. Our judgment must depend upon our interpretation of certain puzzling individual words. As an example of this, line 87 may be taken,

> And mid Eolum and mid Istum and Idumingum.

What tribe can be signified under the name *Eolum* is unknown; and if we are to attach any meaning to the word, we must alter the text. *Istum* in all probability refers to the Esths, whatever race may have been designated by that name, but our judgment of the verse must depend upon the interpretation of *Idumingum*.

If these are the Idumæans of the Bible, then the verse must be attributed to our late monkish interpolator. But it is at least possible that we have here a record of a Baltic tribe, neighbours and near of kin to the Esths, the *Ydumaei*, whose unruly doings are recorded by a Livonian chronicler of a later period[3]. If this be so, we have in the juxtaposition of Esths and Ydumaei a piece of geographical information of the kind which the author or authors of the original poem would be

---

[1] Cf. Jebb, *Oedipus Coloneus*, 1885, p. lii; Morley's *English Writers*, II, 31.
[2] *Z.f.d.A.* XI, 291.
[3] See Appendix G, *Idumingas*.

likely to possess, but which would appear to be quite beyond
the reach of the tenth century English monk whom we suppose
to have interpolated lines 82—84; and we must in that case
pronounce the lines genuine.

If, however, we place on one side the four lines 72, 82—4
as interpolated, and the other lines rejected by Müllenhoff as
suspect, the poem leaves upon us a very definite impression.
It is a catalogue of the tribes and heroes of Germany, and
many of these heroes, though they may have been half legendary
already to the writer of the poem, are historic characters who
can be dated with accuracy.   Widsith has been at the court of
the most powerful of all the Gothic kings, Eormanric, who
died A.D. 375; and of Guthhere (Gundahari) the Burgundian,
who ruled at Worms from 413 to 437.   He knows of Ætla
(Attila), who reigned from 433 to 453, and of the Frankish
Theodoric, who reigned from 511 to 534.   He even mentions
being in Italy with Ælfwine (Alboin) who invaded Italy in 568
and died in 572 or 573[1].

On the other hand, scholars have, with few exceptions,
assumed that no mention is made of the Ostrogothic Theodoric,
the conqueror of Italy, who reigned from 474 to 526, and whose
fame was to eclipse that of all the chiefs just mentioned, till
Eormanric (Ermenrich), Guthhere (Gunther), and Ætla (Etzel)
came to be mere foils to the heroic figure of the mirror of
knighthood, Theodoric of Verona: Dietrich von Bern.

The assumption that Dietrich von Bern does not appear in
Widsith was made too hastily, as can be proved; but certainly
the figure of the great Ostrogothic king had not yet assumed
its gigantic proportions when our poem was written.   If
mentioned at all, Theodoric is thought of as a retainer of
Eormanric: later poets would have thought of Eormanric only
as the uncle and foe of Theodoric.

Our poem then reflects a definitely marked period: that of
those barbarian invasions of the Roman Empire, which began
when the Goths first swarmed across the frontier, and ended
with Alboin's falling upon an Italy worn by famine, pestilence

---

[1] See Hodgkin, *Italy*, v, 168 (footnote).

and the sword of Visigoth, Hun, Vandal and Ostrogoth. Whether *Widsith* is to be regarded as the work of one man, or as a cento of several heroic catalogues, need not for the moment trouble us; for, though the various sections of the poem may show minor idiosyncrasies, they all reflect the same heroic age. Excluding the lines of Biblical lore, we are left with a poem recording the tribes and chiefs of the German migrations, from the middle of the third to the middle of the sixth century: from Ostrogotha to Alboin.

Alboin gives us then a limit to the age of the poem in its present form. It must be later than 568, not *necessarily* much later, for we need not scrupulously allot a term of years to allow of Ælfwine receding into the legendary plane of the earlier Eormanric and Ætla: to the far-off dwellers on the North Sea, both might perhaps soon seem equally distant.

How much later, we can only guess after a rather minute examination of the stories of the chiefs and peoples recorded in *Widsith*. If we find the poet constantly referring to a state of things which had passed out of existence by the seventh century, this, together with his silence on all matters later than the year 568, will incline us to regard the matter of the poem, approximately, as belonging to the last decades of the sixth century or the first of the seventh.

In the sixth century each of the innumerable tribes into which each of the five great branches of the German people was subdivided was an independent nation, with its own laws, traditions and policy; and these nations were scattered over all Europe and part of Northern Africa. No man could know them all, and it is quite easy to see wherein the interests of the poet of *Widsith* lay. That poem does not belie the English dress in which it has come down to us. It is in the countries bordering on the Baltic and the North Sea, *be sǽm tweonum*, that we must locate the tales which interest him: the stories of Sceaf, Hagena and Heoden, Finn Folcwalding, Offa the Angle, Breca of the Brondings, Hrothgar and Ingeld.

But one branch of the German people had done and suffered so much that their heroes became household names throughout all Germania. The Gothic champions, Eastgota and Eormanric, Wudga and Hama, and the Huns who, first as the enemies, then as the allies, and again as the enemies of the Goths, are inextricably entangled in their history and saga: these are as familiar to the poet of *Widsith* as his own sea-heroes.

Widsith visits many people: but he starts from amid the sea-folk, and his objective is the Gothic court. We shall find it easy to get order out of the apparent chaos of his tradition and ethnology, if we divide the stories he loves into (1) Gothic saga and (2) the tales of the sea-folk.

At the outset, this is summed up in seven words when it is said of the minstrel:

> Hreðcyninges ham gesohte,
> eastan of Ongle, Eormanrices.

NOTE. When a Germanic hero is spoken of without reference to any particular version of his story, I give the name in the current historical form; but when referring particularly to any version, in the form proper to that version. Thus *Ermanaric* is the form generally used, *Eormanric* and *Jormunrekk* being reserved respectively for the king of Old English and of Scandinavian legend. Similarly *Gundahari* is used for the historic king: O.E. *Guthhere*, O.N. *Gunnar*, M.H.G. *Gunther* for the hero of particular traditions.

A difficulty arises in the case of heroes who have no known historical prototype. Here the Old English name (e.g. *Hama*) has to be used both generally, and also as the specifically O.E. form; a form like *Heimir* is left for the champion as depicted in the *Thidreks saga*.

When Scandinavian names are transliterated ð is represented by *th*, not by *d*: *v* by *v*, not by *w*. But where a form seems to be definitely established with *d* or *w*, it is retained: *Swanhild, Swein, Sigurd, Thidreks saga*. The *r* of the nominative is kept after vowels, but not after consonants: *Heimir, Jormunrekk, Thithrek*.

CHAPTER II.

THE STORIES KNOWN TO WIDSITH: GOTHIC AND BURGUNDIAN HEROES.

The beginnings of Heroic Song in Germany.

TACITUS[1] mentions the ancient songs in which the Germans celebrated Tuisco, the earth-sprung god, and his son Mannus, the authors and founders of their race. Whether these poems were narrative or choric we do not know. That not gods alone but also historical and semi-historical heroes were commemorated, is proved however by the further remark of Tacitus concerning the old poems "quod unum apud illos memoriæ et annalium genus est." One other precious scrap of information Tacitus has preserved. When making his last mention of Arminius, and telling how Tiberius refused to compass by poison the death of the enemy of the Roman people, he sums up thus the further history of the liberator of Germany: "dolo propinquorum cecidit...septem et triginta annos vitæ, duodecim potentiæ explevit, *caniturque adhuc barbaras apud gentes*[2]."

It is not strange that this notice of a chief, cut off in the flower of his age by the treachery of those closest to him, has reminded modern critics of the story of Sigurd the Volsung, and that some have seen in the story of Sigurd's death by the wiles of his sworn brethren the last traditional echo of this treacherous onslaught upon Arminius, and of the songs in which his deeds and his death were celebrated. No evidence however is forthcoming to support such a theory, and there is much which tells directly against it.

[1] *Germania*, 2.

[2] *Annals*, ii, 88.

Not till some three centuries later, and among the Goths, do we find the first German heroes whose stories told in German speech have lasted through the ages.

It may even be that the development of epic poetry, as opposed to the choric poem of a more primitive age, was the work of Gothic minstrels. But there is no proof of this. Those critics[1] who would see evidence of the preeminence of the Goths in epic song in the fact that Clovis the Frank requested the gift of a harper from Theodoric the Goth, as recorded in the correspondence of Theodoric's minister, Cassiodorus[2], have overlooked the context. For in the preceding letter, a florid effusion treating of the Lydian and Phrygian measures, the Sirens, Orpheus, and the Psalms of David, the selection of this harper is deputed to Boethius the Patrician. The *citharoedus* was, then, no Gothic minstrel, but an Italian or Greek performer; and the letter to Clovis, so far from marking the first spread of epic poetry from the Goths to the Franks, proves nothing at all[3]. It is necessary to emphasize this, because theories as to the date of *Widsith* have been based upon the argument that the gleeman's visit to Eormanric reflects that preeminence of the Gothic court in heroic song which is inferred from the letter to Clovis[4].

Eastgota.

But there is no need to exaggerate the part played by the Goths in the development of Germanic song, for in any case it is important enough.

Jordanes mentions songs which dealt with the wanderings of the Goths after they had left their old home on the shores of the Baltic, and were migrating across the steppes of Russia to

---

[1] e.g. Koegel, *Ltg.* I, 1, 130.   [2] *Variæ*, II, 40, 41.

[3] Since writing this I have noticed that it was pointed out nearly thirty years ago by an Italian scholar (Rajna, *Origini*, p. 36) and more recently by an English one (Chambers, *The Mediaeval Stage*, 1903, p. 34) that the letter to Boethius indicates that the *citharoedus* was sent to the Franks to replace barbaric by civilized music. Yet he is still quoted as evidence for Germanic heroic song, even by those who do not accept the whole of Koegel's deductions (e.g. Symons in *Pauls Grdr.*(2) III, 622; Chadwick in *Camb. Hist.* I. p. 20).

[4] See Bojunga in *P.B.B.* XVI, 548.

the Black Sea[1]. It is not however till the third century, with the irruption of the Goths into the Roman Empire, that we come to a king—Ostrogotha—whose name became part of the common stock of Germanic story.

Towards the end of *Widsith* a list is given of chieftains at the court of Eormanric, king of the Goths. The list is a long one, and, as we should expect, it includes the names of Goths of a much earlier date, who have been attracted into the circle of the later and greater king. Thus, amongst Eormanric's followers mention is made of—

East-Gotan,
frodne and godne, fæder Unwenes.

Eastgota, far from being a follower of Eormanric, was apparently his great-great-grandfather. But his fame paled before that of younger heroes, and his story was forgotten, amid the exciting events which crowded one upon another during the centuries following his reign. He is otherwise unremembered in extant Germanic heroic poetry, but some hint of his story is given by Cassiodorus (c. 480—575), and by Jordanes, whose *De Origine Actibusque Getarum* (written between 550 and 552) has preserved the substance of the lost books of Cassiodorus, on the History of the Goths.

Enituit enim Ostrogotha patientia wrote Cassiodorus in a famous passage on the characteristics of the kings of Gothic story[2]: and this patience, followed in the end by hard hitting, seems to be the essential feature of the story of Ostrogotha, as told by Jordanes[3].

Stirred by the injustice of the Emperor Philip (A.D. 244—249) who refuses to pay to the Goths their due subsidies,

---

[1] *ad extremam Scythiæ partem, que Ponto [Pontico] mari vicina est, properant; quemadmodum et in priscis eorum carminibus pene storicu [historico] ritu in commune recolitur.* *Getica*, IV, (28).

[2] Cassiodorus, *Variæ*, XI, 1.

[3] Whatever may be the etymology of *Ostrogotha* (see Streitberg in *I.F.* IV, 300–9), it is not disputed that at a very early period it was understood to mean 'East-Goth.' For Hunuil-Unwen see note to l. 114. The equation of Eastgota and Ostrogotha rests then upon the identity of name, and the close resemblance of the son's name. We might also compare *frod and god* with Cassiodorus' *enituit patientia* and Jordanes' *ut erat solidi animi* (XVII, 99). The evidence for the identification seems satisfactory, and there is nothing to be said for the other suggested interpretations of the name, as Angantyr (Rafn in *Antiquités Russes*, I, 111), Eckehart (Heinzel, *Ostgotische Heldensage*, 67) or as "ein dritter sonst unbekannter Hereling" (Boer, *Ermanarich*, 67, 79).

Ostrogotha, king of the united Gothic nation, Ostrogoths and
Visigoths alike, crosses the Danube, and wastes Mœsia and
Thrace : on the occasion of a second invasion the Goths put the
town of Marcianopolis to ransom, and return with the plunder
to their land. Hereupon the nation of the Gepidae, closely
related to the Goths, is moved to envy. The Gepidae, and their
king Fastida, have been elated by a recent victory, in which
they have almost annihilated the Burgundians; they accordingly
send envoys to Ostrogotha, and demand that he shall either
meet them in battle, or surrender to them a portion of the
Gothic territory. Ostrogotha replies that he abhors such a
war ; that they are kinsmen, and should not strive; nevertheless, that he will not yield his land. A stubbornly fought
contest follows : but the superiority of the Gothic cause and
the Gothic spirit to that of the "dull" Gepidae gives the victory
to Ostrogotha, and the Gepidae flee back to their country.
During the rest of Ostrogotha's reign the Goths enjoy peace,
till, at his death, Cniva succeeds and again invades Roman
territory[1].

How much of this is history, and how much saga, it is not
easy to say. But there seems no sufficient reason to doubt
that Ostrogotha is a real person[2]. His invasion was fruitless,
and his fame was crowded out by that of later and more
popular Gothic heroes, Widigauja, Ermanaric, Theodoric. But
Ostrogotha's name is the first that meets us in the record of
two among the great things of the world—the Gothic invasion
of the Roman Empire, and the Gothic heroic stories which were
to be the delight of Europe for a thousand years.

Ermanaric and Sonhild.

And ic wæs mid Eormanrice ealle þrage.

Very different was the fortune of Ostrogotha's successor in
the fourth generation, King Ermanaric[3], who died about the
year 375, and whose fame remained in the memory of German-

---

[1] Jordanes, *Getica* xvi, xvii, (89–100).   [2] See Appendix C, *Eastgota*.
[3] *Airmanareiks according to the scribal usage of the Gothic Bible.

speaking people for at least twelve centuries[1]. It was, however, as the "colossal type of a ferocious and covetous ruler, raging against his own kin," a character which he already bears in *Widsith*, that Ermanaric was remembered.

The historic fact of Ermanaric's reign is certified by the contemporary and reliable evidence of Ammianus Marcellinus[2], who records how Ermanaric by his warlike deeds made himself formidable to his neighbours, how the Huns and Alans broke in upon his extensive and prosperous empire and ravaged it, and how Ermanaric, after vain attempts to rally against the even greater disasters which rumour threatened, sought refuge in a voluntary death. A death so unprecedented in the annals of German kings naturally lent itself to romantic explanation and comment; and the story, as given by Jordanes almost two centuries later, may perhaps contain a considerable element of fiction.

Jordanes tells of the great power attained by Ermanaric *nobilissimus Amalorum, quem merito nonnulli Alexandro Magno conparavere maiores,* and how he ruled, not only over the German races and the Esths of the coast, but also over the Wends and the Sclaves, "tribes who, although now, thanks to our sins, they are raging round us on every side, were yet at that time all subject to Ermanaric[3]."

This empire, stretching from the Black Sea to the Baltic, seems to have been as loosely organized as it was widely spread, and it fell to pieces on the advent of the Huns, of whose diabolical origin and "bestial ferocity" Jordanes gives an account, tinged with all the gusto of racial antipathy. Whilst Ermanaric was brooding over the appearance of the Huns, the faithless race of the Rosomoni, which, amongst others, was at

---

[1] A Low German poem was printed in 1560, which told how "Dirick van dem Bërne [Theodoric] he sülff twölffte" slew "den Köninck van Armentriken, mit veerde halff hundert man." Reprinted by Goedeke, Hanover, 1851. A reprint is also given by Abeling in *Teutonia*, vii, *Supplementheft*. This very corrupt version shows some evidence of being ultimately derived from the same original as the *Hamðismál*. (See Symons in *Z.f.d.Ph.* xxxviii, 145-166.) The poem keeps the old tradition as to Ermanaric's ferocity. Dirick says,

'De Kœninck van Armentriken de ys uns suluen gram,
He wil vns Heren all twœlue yn den Galgen hengen laen.'

[2] xxxi, 3, 1 (recens. v. Gardthausen, Vol. ii, Lipsiæ, 1875).

[3] *Getica*, xxiii, (119).

that time tributary to him, took occasion to betray him. For the king, moved with fury, had caused a certain woman of this race, named Sunilda, to be torn asunder by wild horses on account of the treacherous revolt of her husband; her brothers, Sarus and Ammius, in vengeance for the death of their sister, attacked Ermanaric and wounded him in the side, so that he became sick and infirm. Balamber, king of the Huns, took advantage of this sickness to move his battle array against the Ostrogoths, from whom the Visigoths were now, owing to some dispute, separated.

In the midst of these troubles, Ermanaric, overcome by his wounds, and the incursions of the Huns, died, full of days, at the age of one hundred and ten years[1].

Jordanes' story has been accepted by the historians as history[2]; as a more detailed account of events only partially known to the contemporary Ammianus. The mythologists, on the other hand, are convinced that it is myth[3], a legendary

---

[1] Nam Hermanaricus, rex Gothorum, licet, ut superius retulimus, multarum gentium extiterat triumphator, de Hunnorum tamen adventu dum cogitat, Rosomonorum (Rosomanorum, Rosomorum, Rosimanorum) gens infida, quæ tunc inter alias illi famulatum exhibebat, tali eum nanciscitur occasione decipere. dum enim quandam mulierem Sunilda (Sunielh, Sunihil; Suani-hildam, *Holder*) nomine ex gente memorata pro mariti fraudulento discessu rex furore commotus equis ferocibus inligatam incitatisque cursibus per diversa divelli præcipisset, fratres ejus Sarus et Ammius (Ammus, Aminus, Iammius) germanæ obitum vindicantes, Hermanarici latus ferro petierunt; quo vulnere saucius egram vitam corporis imbecillitate contraxit. quam adversam ejus valitudinem captans Balamber rex Hunnorum in Ostrogotharum parte movit procinctum, a quorum societate iam Vesegothæ quadam inter se intentione (contentione, *Holder*) seiuncti habebantur. inter hæc Hermanaricus tam vulneris dolore quam etiam Hunnorum incursionibus non ferens, grandevus et plenus dierum centesimo decimo anno vitæ suæ defunctus est.

Jordanes, *Getica* ed. Mommsen, cap. xxiv (129–30). For the interpretation of difficult words: *gens* = nation, not family: *famulatum exhibebat* = was subject, of a whole tribe, not referring to the personal service of a retainer: *discessus* = revolt, not flight, see Mommsen's Index (IV) and Jiriczek (2) 57–59.

[2] Gibbon, ed. Bury, 1897, III, 57, 91–2; Hodgkin's *Italy*, I, 246 (but cf. III, 4).

[3] That the story is fictitious has been argued from the name *Sunilda*, which is the form found in the best MSS of Jordanes. This, it is said, is the Gothic **Sonahildi* or **Sonihilds*, 'the woman who atones'; clearly therefore a feigned name, like the names of the brothers *Sarus* and *Ammius*—'the armed ones.' See Müllenhoff in Index to Mommsen's Jordanes; Symons in *Pauls Grdr.* (2) III, 683; Jiriczek (2) 63; Roediger, *Die Sage von Ermenrich*, 248. Roediger would make Jordanes' story purely mythical in origin; a story of the god Irmin-tiu, otherwise Ermanarikaz, which was later, he thinks, connected with the story of the historic Ermanaric in order to explain that king's mysterious death. But this is more than doubtful. Roediger lays weight upon the names *Sarus* and *Ammius*, "Solche einfachen Namen deuten immer auf mythische Träger." But *Sarus*, so far from being a fictitious name, was borne by a chief in historic

amplification of the fact recorded by the Roman historian. There is no conclusive evidence in either direction. The story of Ermanaric's suicide, as told by Ammianus, is strange and unaccountable, but it rests on the word of a peculiarly truthful historian : if it *is* true, then its very strangeness only gives all the more reason why a saga should have been invented to account for Ermanaric's death.

Unfortunately, true or not, Jordanes' account leaves much unsettled. All attempts to identify and explain the *Rosomonorum gens infida* have proved inconclusive, though a stream of conjectures is forthcoming, beginning with the attempt, uusuccessful though supported by the great names of Gibbon and of Grimm, to identify them with the Russians[1], down to the more recent interpretations of the word as the "red-haired" or "red-skinned," a symbol of perfidy[2], or the "doughty[3]" or "the men of the ice[4]."

Jordanes' tale, at best, is obscure, and the difficulty has been rather increased by attempts to force his words so as to read into them the version of the Swanhild story, which we know to have been current in Scandinavia three centuries after

times (Hodgkin's *Italy* I, 733 ; cf. Jordanes, *Romana*, 321, with Müllenhoff's note). As to the name *Sunilda*, the mss of Jordanes vary greatly. *Sunielh, Sunihil,* are found. The oldest record of the name, in Germany, the charter of 786, gives the ambiguous form *Suanailta* ; the Icelandic gives *Svanhildr*. So that argument from the form of the name seems perilous; and indeed there are reasons for connecting the first element in the name rather with *sunja* (truth) than *sōn* (atonement) ; see Boer, *Ermánarich*, 8. Even if the name does mean ' the woman who atones ' this would not involve its having been invented to fit the story, for Sunilda's death does not lead to any atonement, but rather is the cause of further feud (Panzer, *H.i.B.* 41, 77).

[1] Gibbon, ed. Bury III, 92 ; Grimm, *G.D.S.* 747-8. Heinzel, *Hervararsaga* (*W.S.B.* cxiv, 102), thinks the Rosomoni were probably Slavs. For a more recent identification with the *Ruotsi* of the Baltic see Aspelin (J. R.) *La Rosomonorum gens et le Ruotsi*, Helsingfors, 1884 ; and cf. Grotenfelt, *Die Sagen von Hermanarich u. Kullervo* in *Finnisch-Ugrische Forschungen*, II, 50 (1903).

[2] This not very probable suggestion is made by Bugge (*Á.f.n.F.* I, 1-20). He suggests an original form **Rusmunans,* and points out that the treacherous Sibech, Sifka, who in the later versions of the story fills the place earlier occupied by the treacherous Rosomoni, and their chief, as the evil genius of Ermanaric, has red hair. See *Thidreks saga,* cap. 186.

Bugge (p. 9) assumes in his argument that the deserter was chief of the Rosomoni ; this however does not necessarily follow from the words of Jordanes, who states only that *his* wife belonged to that race. The treachery of the Rosomoni is the attack by Sarus and Ammius.

[3] Koegel, *Ltg.* I, 1, 148.

[4] **Hrusamans,* suggested as a possible alternative to Bugge's interpretation by Grienberger (*Z.f.d.A.* xxxix, p. 159. The whole article, on the races noted by Jordanes as subject to Ermanaric, is important).

his day[1]. With this interpretation Sunilda would be the wife
of Ermanaric and *pro mariti fraudulento discessu* would mean
" on account of her dishonest desertion of her husband ; viz.
Ermanaric." But this rendering, in addition to doing violence
to Jordanes' Latin[2], is, from the context, impossible: if Jordanes
had regarded Sunilda as Ermanaric's unfaithful wife, he would
hardly have introduced her without explanation simply as
quandam mulierem Sunilda nomine.

Except in making Ermanaric's victim his wife, this
Scandinavian version keeps fairly near the original story.
Jormunrekk sends his son, and a treacherous councillor
Bikki, to woo on his behalf, and to escort to the Gothic
court, the maiden Swanhild. Bikki first urges the son to
woo the maiden for himself, and then betrays him to his father.
Jormunrekk in wrath causes his son to be hanged, and has
Swanhild bound in the town gate, that she may be trodden to
death by horses. But she is so fair that no horse will trample
on her, till Bikki counsels that her eyes be bound[3]. So she
dies, but her brothers Hamthir and Sorli, clothed in enchanted
armour given them by Guthrun their mother, attack Jormunrekk in his hall and smite off his hands and feet, before they
are overwhelmed by numbers and stoned to death.

The Norse poets do not trouble to make the action of
Bikki the traitor intelligible: no motive is given for his be-
traying Swanhild and Jormunrekk's son to death[4]. Saxo

---

[1] Koegel, *Ltg.* i, 1, 147. This interpretation was earlier suggested by
W. Müller in his *Mythologie der deutschen Heldensage*, Heilbronn, 1886, 163-4.

[2] Jiriczek(2) 58-9.

[3] The account given by Snorri differs in some details from that given in
the *Vǫlsunga saga*, and chiefly in this, that the murder of Swanhild is not
deliberate, but the result of a sudden impulse. Jormunrekk, as he rides
from hunting in the forest, sees Swanhild dressing her hair; and he and his
men tread her to death under their horses' feet: Sn. *Edda*, udg. Jónsson,
p. 189.

[4] A portion of the story forms the subject of two poems at the end of the
Elder Edda, the *Hamðismál* and *Guðrúnarhvǫt*, which have been attributed to
the tenth century (see Ranisch, *Zur Kritik u. Metrik der Hamþismál*, Berlin
dissertation, 1888, 29, 74), and it is told by Snorri early in the thirteenth
century, and again in the *Vǫlsunga saga* somewhat after the middle of that
century. All these versions differ slightly, and their mutual relations are by
no means clear. Still more important, by reason of their early date, are the
allusions in the *Ragnars drápa* of Bragi the Old. In this the poet describes the
shield which he has received from Ragnar Lodbrok. This shield is covered,

Grammaticus tells us that Bicco, before he became the servant of Iarmericus, was a Livonian prince, whose brothers had been slain by that king, and who thus wreaks his vengeance by causing the king to slay his dearest; but this is clearly a subsequent addition to the story, reflecting as it does the racial quarrels of a later age.

Such was the tale, as it was current in Scandinavian lands from at least the ninth century throughout the Middle Ages. But both in England and in continental Germany this portion of the Ermanaric story seems soon to have died out. In England the names Swanilda and Sorli occur in charters; but very late, whilst their form makes it probable that they are Scandinavian introductions, not witnesses to native English tradition: Serlo too is found, but this again is a foreign form[1]. But the occurrence of the name of Bicca or Becca fixed to different English localities, *Biccanhlew, Biccanpol, Beccanleah, Beccanford*, seems to show that his part in the story was at one time known in England; and this is rendered the more probable by *Widsith*, which not only numbers Becca among the retainers of Ermanaric, but mentions the tribe subject to him— the Baningas.

like that of Achilles, with images; the figures on Bragi's shield, however, refer to specific stories, and the allusions show that the Swanhild story was known in the North, in the first half of the ninth century, in substantially the same form as we have it in the *Vǫlsunga saga*, some four and a half centuries later. The authenticity of Bragi's song, which forms an important landmark in the history of German heroic tradition, has been disputed by Bugge, on the ground of grammatical forms, vocabulary, metre, style and subject matter. (*Bidrag til den eldste skalde-digtnings historie*, 1894.) These arguments have been weighed at great length by F. Jónsson (*Aarbøger f. nord. Oldk.* II, 10, 4, 1895 *De ældste skjalde og deres kvad*), and more briefly by Gering (*Z.f.d.Ph.* XXVIII, 111), Kahle (*Litteraturbl. f. Philol.*, 1895, Sept.), Mogk (*Lit.-Centralblatt*, 1895, 15, 540), Panzer (*H.G.* 155–7), Jiriczek (₂84), with the unanimous verdict that the case against the authenticity of the *Ragnars drápa* has not been made out.

The version of the story given by Saxo Grammaticus may be regarded as a compromise between the Norse and the (mainly lost) Low German versions. The different elements have been separated by Olrik, *Sakses Oldhistorie*, II, 1894, 252–3; in the imperfect state of our evidence it is hardly possible to say which element predominates. For different views on this subject see Symons in *Pauls Grdr.*₍₂₎ III, 688; Jiriczek₍₂₎ 115. Ermanaric's son is called Randvér in the Norse versions, Broderus in Saxo.

[1] Binz in *P.B.B.* XX, 209 thinks it Frankish. If the references in the Quedlinburg and Würzburg chronicles to the death of Ermanaric are really derived, as Schroeder has argued (*Z.f.d.A.* XLI, 24–32) from an English source, then the story of Sarus and Ammius must have been still known in England in the ninth century. But see below, p. 30 (footnote).

Eormanric and Ealhhild in Widsith.

That Ermanaric was well known in England is proved by the references in Old English heroic poetry.

In *Beowulf* there is mention of the "wily hatred[1]" of Eormenric. Not dissimilar is the reference in *Deor's Lament*:

We have heard of Eormanric's wolfish mind : far and wide he ruled the folk of the kingdom of the Goths : a grim king was he.

But the fullest and clearest reference to Eormanric is in the central passage of our poem :

And I was with Eormanric all the time, there the king of the Goths was bounteous unto me. Lord of cities and their folk, he gave me an armlet, of pure gold, worth six hundred shillings. This I gave into the possession of my lord and protector Eadgils, when I came home : a gift unto my beloved prince, because he, lord of the Myrgings, gave me my land, the home of my father. A second ring then Ealhhild gave unto me, noble queen of chivalry, daughter of Eadwine. Through many lands her praise extended, when I must tell in song, where under the heavens I best knew a queen adorned with gold giving forth treasure ; when Scilling and I with clear voice raised the song before our noble lord (loud to the harp the words made melody) what time many cunning men said they had never heard a better song. Thence I wandered through all the land of the Goths...

It is remarkable that whilst certain points in the criticism of *Widsith* have been scrutinized and canvassed with almost excessive keenness, others have been taken on trust from the days of the first editors. Since Ealhhild is here mentioned immediately after Eadgils, and since Widsith the Myrging owes obligations to both, Leo conjectured that Ealhhild was queen of the Myrgings and wife of Eadgils[2]. In this he was followed by Lappenberg[3]. Both brought forward this relationship as a mere inference. Later scholars[4] have followed them, but often without any expression of doubt. Yet there is nothing in the poem which points at all conclusively to this relationship. All we know about Ealhhild is that she is a daughter of Eadwine, who is apparently the same Eadwine, king of the Lombards, who is mentioned as Ælfwine's father.

---

[1] *searoniþas.* The word, however, need not necessarily have a bad sense, cf. *Beowulf*, 582.

[2] durch Ealhhilden...die (*wie es scheint*) Fürstin der Mýrgingen (*wohl* Eadgils Gemahlin), p. 75.

[3] Ealhhilde wird erwähnt, *wie es scheint*, als Fürstin der Myrgingen, Gemahlin oder Mutter des Königes derselben Eadgils, p. 175.

[4] e.g. Thorpe (510), Ettmüller [1] 12, Müllenhoff, *Beovulf*, 98 ; Ten Brink in *Pauls Grdr.* [1] II, 1, 544 ; Koegel, *Ltg.* I, 1, 139 ; Stopford Brooke, I, 2.

It was left for Richard Heinzel, who was not dealing primarily with our poem at all, and who consequently approached it without any prepossessions, to suggest that Ealhhild is the wife, not of Eadgils, but of Eormanric: and that we have a reference to a form of the story in which Ealhhild had been substituted for Swanhild, and the Lombard dynasty for the "treacherous Rosomoni." Heinzel threw out this suggestion cursorily, without discussing it at length, and it has not yet been sufficiently scrutinized[1]. Yet the interpretation of *Widsith* depends upon it. It is remarkable how many of the theories of previous critics have been built upon the assumption that Ealhhild is the wife of Eadgils.

The discrepancy in the names Swanhild and Ealhhild ought not to weigh too heavily against Heinzel's view. Alike in epic song and in everyday conversation, Swanhild would be abbreviated to Hild. In song, an abbreviated Hild might easily be expanded to Ealhhild. Both changes can be exactly paralleled. Thus, in the saga of Olaf Tryggvason, Jarl Eystein has a daughter named Hild *or* Swanhild[2]. The change by which Hild(ico) may have become Grimhild (Kriemhild) is a commonplace of the history of the development of the Niblung story[3]. So that there would be nothing unprecedented in Swanhild being first abbreviated to Hild and then expanded to Ealhhild[4]. But we have seen that it is quite uncertain what the first element of the name originally was.

---

[1] *Ueber die Hervararsaga*, p. 102 in the *W.S.B.* cxiv, 11. Heinzel's view has been accepted by Jiriczek(2) 73, Lawrence in *Mod. Philol.* iv, 351-3, Holthausen, ii, 164, and, with some doubt, by Gummere(2) 199; it has been developed by Boer (*Ermanarich*, 15-18).

[2] "Móðir þeirra var Hildr eðr Svanhildr, dóttir Eysteins jarls," *Fornmanna Sögur*, 1825, i, 5. For abbreviations of names see Franz Stark, *Die Kosenamen der Germanen*, Wien, 1868; and a note by Olsen in the *Aarbøger for Nordisk Oldkyndighed*, 1905, p. 72.

[3] See Symons, *Sigfrid u. Brunhild* in Zachers *Z.f.d.Ph.* xxiv, 29 ; and, to the contrary, Boer in *Z.f.d.Ph.* xxxvii, 484. Cf., too, Abeling, 206.

[4] Although compound names in *Ealh-* are not uncommon in Old English, the name *Ealhhild* does not seem to have been current in England in historic times. It is found on the continent, though rarely. In the ninth century revenue book of the Abbey of St Remi at Reims the name occurs twice (*Polyptique de l'Abbaye de Saint Remi*, par B. E. Guérard, Paris, 1853. *Alchildis ingenua*, p. 69 ; *Algildis ingenua, cum infantibus*, p. 86). In 819 a serf named *Alachilt* is granted, with many others, to the Abbey of Fulda (*Codex Diplomaticus Fuldensis*, herausg. Dronke, Cassel, 1850). The name *Alachilt, Alahilt* occurs also in the Books of the Confraternity of St Gall (ed. Piper in *M.G.H.* Berlin, 1884). See Förstemann, i, pp. 53, 75.

Probably it was *Son-* or *Sun-*, and only later, when it became unintelligible, was this corrupted into *Swan*. *Hild* is the fixed element in the name; and there is no reason why in some versions of the story *Sunhild* should not have been altered to *Ealhhild*. We constantly find the compound names of heroes thus changed in one of their elements. The Hrothgar of *Beowulf* is the Roe, Hroar of Scandinavian tradition, forms which would correspond to an Old English *Hrothhere*. So the Eanmund of *Beowulf* appears in Saxo as Hömothus (i.e. *Eymothr* instead of *Eymundr*)[1]. The Sîfrît of the South is the Sigurd of the North. If even so great a hero as Sigfrid could not keep his name intact in passing from one end of Germania to the other, there is no inherent improbability in the name *Sonhild—Sunhild—Swanhild* having been corrupted.

It becomes then a question of what evidence we have in favour of identifying the Ealhhild of our poem with Swanhild. At least five points, some of them not strong in themselves, deserve to be weighed:

(1) Ealhhild is daughter of Eadwine, apparently the famous Lombard king who is mentioned elsewhere (1. 74) in *Widsith*; and quite apart from Heinzel's theory, it is thought that in *Widsith* the Lombard story has, in some way or other, been linked on to the Gothic. How this took place we cannot say, but that Lombard heroes are enumerated among Eormanric's household was pointed out half a century ago by Müllenhoff[2], and seems quite possible. Now this contamination of two distinct traditions would be explicable if the English version of the story gave Eormanric a Lombard princess to wife. And this might easily happen. The Rosomoni, to whom Sunhild originally belonged, had long been forgotten. Yet Eormanric's wife must belong to some great race. To whom rather than to the Lombards, who had just established themselves as successors of the Goths in the lands of Italy? There was more reason to turn Eormanric's luckless queen into a Lombard than into a

---

[1] Cf. Olrik, *Sakses Oldhistorie*, 191. For other changes in names of heroes of tradition see Heusler in *Z.f.d.A.* LII, 97, *etc.*: *Heldennamen in mehrfacher Lautgestalt.*

[2] *Z.f.d.A.* XI, 278.

Hellespontine, which she is in Saxo[1], or a Volsung, which she is in the *Vǫlsunga saga*.

Yet we must not place too much weight upon this argument: for it is not absolutely certain that our poet regarded Ealhhild as a Lombard princess, whilst the supposed list of Lombard heroes inserted into the catalogue of Eormanric's household is far too doubtful for us safely to argue from it. The supposed combination of Gothic with Lombard legend does not, then, go very far towards proving Heinzel's hypothesis.

(2) This hypothesis makes it easier to explain why our poet, whilst he makes Eormanric give to Widsith a ring of very high price, yet calls him a *wraþ wœrloga*. Remembering how highly generosity to retainers in general, and to singers in particular, ranks among the kingly virtues in Old English heroic poetry, it is likely that some *specific* evil act lies in the background in order to justify this epithet in this context.

The Ermanaric of tradition certainly was a "treacherous tyrant": but it seems hardly fair that he should be called so in the poem celebrating that Widsith whom he had treated so well. But if Widsith owed obligations to Ermanaric's murdered wife, then the epithet becomes appropriate enough.

(3) A detailed examination of the passage dealing with Eormanric's gift to Widsith favours the interpretation that Ealhhild is the queen of Eormanric, who, after the bountiful act of her lord, gives Widsith a second ring in the Gothic hall, rather than the queen of Eadgils, who gives him the ring on his return home, in compensation for that which he presents to her husband. The episode deserves consideration for the light it throws on the manners and ideals of ancient Germania.

When trade, or fortune in the gift hall or on the battlefield, had put into the hands of a "thegn" treasures too great for a private gentleman to possess—an armlet or necklace of surpassing value, a king's panoply, a tame bear—custom approved of his presenting it to a great chief: if he had one, to his own chief. But it was not usual for the chief to acknowledge this gift by presenting in return things like in kind but inferior in

[1] Ed. Holder, viii, 279–81.

quality. The prince makes the donor his personal servant, or gives him a landed estate, or weds him to his daughter. It is not so much an exchange as a recognition of mutual dependence. The winnings of the retainer fall to the chief: the chief values wealth only as he may share it with his retainers[1]. Thus Beowulf receives from Hrothgar rich gifts for his service at Heorot, sword, armour, horses[2]; jewels, and a glorious necklace from Hrothgar's queen[3]: on his return he gives armour, sword and horses to his lord Hygelac, and the necklace to Hygd, Hygelac's wife. On his part, Hygelac gives Beowulf feudal domains, placing, as he does so, in Beowulf's bosom the sword of their common grandfather Hrethel[4]. Again, when Eofor the Geat slays the Swedish king Ongentheow, he presents the spoils to Hygelac, who gives him in return land and wealth, and the hand of his only daughter[5].

A not dissimilar episode comes in the Saga of Harold Hardrada[6]. Authun, an Icelander, comes to the court of Harold with a bear which the king covets. However, Authun will neither sell nor give the beast to the king, but declares his intention of taking it to Swein of Denmark, with whom King Harold is at war. Harold allows him free passage; but on his way back he is to come and tell what King Swein has given in return. This Authun does,

The king took his greeting well. "Sit down," he said, "and drink here with us," and Authun did so. Then Harold asked, "How did King Swein requite thee for the bear?" Authun replied, "In that he accepted it, Sir, from me." "I would have requited thee so," said the king, "what more reward did he give thee?" Authun replied, "He gave me silver to go South" (on a pilgrimage to Rome). Then said King Harold, "To many men does King Swein give silver, though they have not brought him treasures. What more?" "He offered," said Authun, "to make me his page and do me much honour." "That was a good offer," said the king, "but he surely did more." "He gave me," said Authun, "a big ship with a cargo of the best." "That was magnificently done," said the king, "but so would I have requited thee. Did he give thee more?" Authun said, "He gave me a leather bag full of silver, and said that then I should not be destitute, if I kept that, though my ship were wrecked off Iceland." "That was an excellent precaution to take," said the king, "and more than I should have done. I should have thought we were quits when I had given thee the ship and cargo: did he requite thee yet more?" "Of

---

[1] Cf. Tacitus, *Germania* xiv.   [2] 1020–49.
[3] 1192, *etc.*   [4] 2152–2199.   [5] 2990.
[6] *Fornmanna Sögur*, Kaupmannahøfn, 1831, vi, 297–307: Wimmer, *Oldnordisk Læsebog*, 1877, 55–60. The two texts differ in detail.

a truth, Sir," said Authun, "he did : he gave me this ring which I have on my hand, and said it might happen that I lost all my wealth and the ship : that then I should not be destitute if I had the ring. And he bade me not part with it, unless I owed so much to some great man that I wished to give it him. And now I have met such a man : for thou mightest have taken from me both the bear and my life : but thou didst give me free passage when others obtained it not." The king received the gift graciously and gave Authun in return good gifts before they parted.

But if Queen Ellisif had stepped down from the dais and offered Authun an inferior ring in exchange for the gift he had just made to King Harold—Authun would no doubt have accepted it with his usual tact : but I think every retainer in the hall would have felt that a mistake had been made. Nor would Queen Hygd have given Beowulf another necklace in exchange for the glorious one which he gave her.

Now the armlet given by Eormanric is of extraordinary value : for Eormanric was the richest and the most generous of tyrants. It is valued at six hundred shillings[1]. It would probably have been held ostentatious, and it would certainly have been imprudent, for a minstrel to wear treasure worth the price of his own life. Nobody but Eormanric, the possessor of fabulous wealth[2], could afford to give such an armlet to a singer.

In giving this present to his lord, the reward Widsith would expect would be, as Authun said, "that he should accept it." He certainly would not expect an inferior ring in return. It is turning a gracious act of love and loyalty into a matter of mere barter if we are to read the lines as Ten Brink and the rest read them :

Eadgils' Gemahlin aber, Ealhhild, *entschädigte* den Sänger für das verschenkte Kleinod durch einen andern Ring[3].

On the other hand, if Ealhhild is the Gothic queen, her action is in accordance with the laws of Germanic courtesy. She follows up the magnificent present of Ermanaric, her lord, by offering the poet a second ring : one of less value, naturally ; but which he is to keep for her sake, in memory of the service

---

[1] See Appendix N, *On the beag given by Eormanric.*
[2] See Saxo, Book viii (ed. Holder, p. 278), for an account of the treasure house of Iarmericus : cf. too *Dietrichs Flucht*, 7854–7862.
[3] Ten Brink in *Pauls Grdr.*(1) ii, 542. So Lawrence speaks of it as a "business transaction" (*Mod. Philol.* iv, 369).

he has done her in escorting her to the hall of the Goth. And this ring Widsith does keep.

An argument which postulates gentlemanly feeling among sixth century barbarians may seem to some fantastic. But it can be further urged:

(4) That only by this interpretation does the whole passage yield consistent sense. "Eormanric gave me a ring, which, when I came home, I gave to Eadgils my lord (*minum hleodryhtne*). Ealhhild gave me another ring. Whenever I had to sing, I sang her praises through many lands as the most generous queen: when Scilling and I sang before our lord (*uncrum sigedryhtne*), many men said they never heard a better song. Thence I fared through the whole land of the Goths."

If the poet rewards his benefactress by spreading her fame through many lands, then Eadgils' land, which is instanced, can hardly have been hers[1]. Nor can we understand the transition to the next sentence, "*Thence* I fared through all the land of the Goths," if Ealhhild's gift takes place, not in the heart of the Gothic land, but after Widsith has returned home to the far-distant Myrging court[2].

How, if we make Ealhhild the wife of Eadgils, are we to interpret the second reference to Widsith's lord (*uncrum sigedryhtne*)? It is inapplicable to Eormanric; for Widsith is giving an example of how he rewarded his patroness for her gift by spreading the fame of her generosity. He cannot sing, in the hall of Eormanric, of a generosity which he does not experience till he returns home to Eadgils' hall. Besides, the word *dryhten* in Old English poetry always implies a distinct tie of subjection. In the mouth of Widsith *dryhten* should refer to his feudal chief Eadgils, not to Eormanric. But this it can hardly do, if Ealhhild is the wife of Eadgils. For as we have seen, Widsith is giving an example of how he spread her fame through many lands, and he cannot have done this by singing, in her presence, in her lord's hall.

(5) Finally, and this is the heavy evidence, the introduction

---

[1] This struck Ten Brink. The transition, he says, is abrupt (p. 543).
[2] This difficulty had before been felt by Möller (*V.E.* 2, 3), who, assuming Ealhhild to be Eadgils' wife, found it necessary to rearrange the text.

tells us that Ealhhild accompanied Widsith to the house
(not of Eadgils the Myrging, but) of Eormanric the Goth:
and for what purpose except to become his bride, is not
clear[1]. It has been suggested that she went as a hostage[2].
But this does not fit in with the theory of those who hold
that she is wife of Eadgils; for, if Widsith escorted her as a
hostage to the court of Eormanric, how does she come to be in
Eadgils' hall, when he returns home, to present him with
another armlet? And, though we know from Tacitus that
the daughters of great houses[3] were often sent as hostages,
we may well doubt whether a self-respecting prince, such as
we may suppose Eadgils to be, would have sent his *wife*.

True, many critics have regarded the introduction as a later
addition; and almost certainly they have been right in so
regarding it[4]. But in any case the introduction dates from
a time when Old English verse and legend were living; the
poet who prefixed it had our poem before him in a form
certainly much purer and possibly much fuller than that
in which it has come down to us; and the fact that he
evidently regarded Ealhhild as wife of Eormanric is strong
evidence that the original poem implied that she was so.

For these reasons it seems best to regard Ealhhild as the
murdered wife of Eormanric, the Anglian equivalent of the
Gothic Sunilda and the Northern Swanhild. Perhaps however
we ought to discriminate. That Ealhhild is Eormanric's wife
appears to me to be demonstrable: that legend attributed to
her the same tragic story as to Swanhild is probable enough,
but not equally demonstrable.

Ermanaric and the Harlungs.

Herelingas,
Emercan sohte ic and Fridlan.

That the story of Ermanaric and Swanhild was still current
in the eighth century in continental Germany is rendered
probable by the occurrence of the name Suanailta, in connection with other names of the Ermanaric cycle, in a charter

---

[1] See note to l. 6. [2] Chadwick (138).
[3] *puellæ nobiles. Ger.* VIII. [4] See below: Chap. iv, end.

of the year 786. Unless a very striking series of coincidences has taken place, the story must have been in the minds of the god-parents who gave the names[1]. Yet, alike in High and Low German tradition, Swanhild was soon forgotten, and with her the motive for the death of Ermanaric's son[2]. But another evil deed was attributed to Ermanaric: the murder of his two nephews, the young Harlungs, brought about by the evil counsel, perhaps in the earliest stories, certainly in the later ones, of his henchman Sibeche.

From the tenth century onwards there are several references to this Ermanaric story in the Latin chronicles of Germany: of these the most important is one which is found, with only slight variations, in the chronicles of Quedlinburg and of Würzburg[3], and which introduces the names of three important actors in the story who are known to us from *Widsith*, Freotheric and the Harlung brethren (Herelingas) Emerca and Fridla. These two chronicles date, the first a few years before, the second a few years after the year 1000—and the story they tell is this:

At that time Ermanaric ruled over all the Goths, more cunning than all in guile, more generous in gifts; who after the death of Frederic his only son, brought about by his own wish, hanged from the gallows his nephews, Embrica and Fritla. He drove likewise from Verona Theodoric his nephew at the instigation of his nephew Odoacer, and compelled him to dwell with Attila in exile...Ermanaric, King of the Goths, was slain in shameful wise, as was fit, by the brethren Hamido, Sarilo and Odoacer, whose father he had killed, after they had first cut off his hands and his feet[4].

[1] See Müllenhoff in *Z.f.d.A.* xii, 302-6. On the other hand, it might be argued that, without postulating anything more than the ordinary working of the laws of chance, an occasional combination recalling the grouping of heroic story might be expected, in view of the fact that the records of proper names which have come down to us from the 'Dark Ages' are comparatively numerous.

[2] Yet different forms of the names *Sonhild* and *Swanhild* continue in frequent use. See Pertz *passim*, especially *SS.* t. vi; and Langebek iv, 83.

[3] *Chronicon Wirziburgense* in Pertz, fol. *SS.* t. vi, 1844, p. 23.

[4] *Eo tempore Ermenricus super omnes Gothos regnavit, astutior omnibus in dolo, largior in dono; qui post mortem Friderici filii sui unici, sua perpetratam voluntate, patrueles suos Embricam et Frithlam patibulo suspendit. Theodericum similiter patruelem suum, instimulante Odoacro patruele suo, de Verona pulsum apud Attilam exulare coegit....Ermenricus rex Gothorum a fratribus Hamido et Sarilo et Odoacro, quorum patrem interfecerat, amputatis manibus et pedibus, turpiter, uti dignus erat, occisus est.* We cannot be certain whether this exactly represents a current version, or is the chronicler's attempt at harmonizing different stories known to him.

The *Würzburg Chronicle* is quoted in preference to the *Quedlinburg Annals*, because it tells the story more clearly than does the extant text of *Quedlinburg*;

This gives a very rough summary of the story, as current in continental Germany during the Middle Ages. Though Swanhild has gone, it is still remembered that Ermanaric, intentionally or unintentionally, caused the death of his son, or sons[1]. But it is more as the betrayer of his nephews, the " Harlungen," and still more as the foe of his nephew Theodoric or Dietrich, that Ermanaric is remembered.

In one of the papers which Müllenhoff left behind him, unpublished and indeed hardly legible, the origin of the Harlung story, in the light of comparative mythology, is discussed with a marvellous erudition. The paper, deciphered by the pious care of a disciple, was published in 1886[2]: it is one of the most valuable of Müllenhoff's many contributions to the history of German heroic song. According to Müllenhoff the Harlungen were originally twin divinities, comparable to the Castor and Pollux of Grecian story. They are sent by the Heaven-God, Irmin-tiu, the Germanic equivalent of Zeus or Jupiter[3], to woo for the God the sun-maiden, bedecked with

---

although it is quite possible that the entry in *Würzburg* is derived from an earlier MS of *Quedlinburg*. (See H. Bresslau, *Die Quellen des Chronicon Wirziburgense* in the *Neues Archiv der Gesell. f. ältere deut. Geschichtskunde*, xxv, 1900, pp. 32–3.)

Schroeder has argued (*Z.f.d.A.* XLI, 27, *etc.*), from the forms of the proper names, that this reference to the Ermanaric story was derived from an English source. I cannot agree with this view. The form *Adaccaro*, found in *Quedlinburg* for *Odoacro*, is hardly English. Schroeder argues that the use of the contracted form *Frithlam* points to England. But we are not certain that the original form in the source of *Quedlinburg* and *Würzburg was* contracted: the Bamberg Codex of *Würzburg* gives *Frithelam* (see Bresslau). And in any case it is not clear that the contracted form was peculiarly English: against *Fridla* in *Widsith* we have *Friþela* in the charter (Birch, 1002: see below, p. 34).

[1] Cf. *Dietrichs Flucht* 2457, etc.

> *Ez gewan der Künic Ermrich*
> *einen sun, der hiez Friderich,*
> *den er sit versande*
> *hin ze der Wilzen lande.*
> *dar an man sin untriuwe sach:*
> *nu seht wie er sin triuwe brach*
> *an sinem liebem kinde!*

Cf. also *Thidreks saga* c. 278–80, 303, 307.

[2] *Z.f.d.A.* xxx, 217– *Frija und der Halsbandmythus.*

[3] That Tiu was equivalent to Zeus, phonetically and mythologically, was, when Müllenhoff wrote, regarded as one of the few pieces of firm land in the mythological quagmire (cf. Noreen, *Altisländische Grammatik*, Halle, 1892, § 68, 7). That the two names do not exactly correspond phonetically has been pointed out, however, by Streitberg (*I.F.* I, 514). But Streitberg cites parallels for the phonetic variation, and adheres to the identification on mythological

jewels, chief among which is the "Brisingo meni." They are, however, false to their trust, woo the maiden for themselves, and fall victims to the wrath of the god whom they have deceived. Müllenhoff argued that the likeness of this story of the vengeance of Irmin-tiu upon the Harlungs to the story of the vengeance of Ermanaric upon his wife and son, and the similarity of the name of the avenger in each case, caused the two to be confused : and the Gothic king came to be credited with having slain, not only his son, but also his nephews, the two young Harlungs.

The glamour which must always surround the posthumous work of a great scholar, and the learning and skill displayed by Müllenhoff in piecing together his materials, disarmed criticism for the moment; and in the best recent surveys of Germanic heroic story and mythology Müllenhoff's mosaic of myth has been accepted[1]. Yet it is pure conjecture[2]. We have no proof that the "Brisingo meni" was ever in the hands of the Harlungs, or that its possession by Ermanaric is in any way connected with their death. Indeed it is quite conceivable that the Harlungs are derived not from any mythical figures, but from some historic tribe or princely house, perhaps actually overthrown by Ermanaric, perhaps supposed in later story to have been so overthrown[3].

Now whether Ermanaric was from the beginning the typical tyrant and oppressor of heroic legend is not clear. We cannot be certain whether his evil fame is due to the attribution to him of the murder of the Harlungs[4], or whether this attribution is due to his evil fame[5]. But even the blackest of tyrants needs

---

grounds. Bremer (*I.F.* iii, 301-2) regards the phonetic difficulties as insuperable, and points out that the German Tîwaz is the war-god, and not the Heaven-Father. Yet the identification seems fairly certain. Cf. Mogk in *Pauls Grdr.*(2) iii, 313; R. Meyer, 178; Golther, 200, *etc.*

[1] Symons in *Grdr.*(2) iii, 685; Jiriczek(1) 100; R. Meyer, 218-9 (broadly).

[2] Cf. Panzer, *H.i.B.* 84, *etc.* 89, *etc.*; Boer, *Ermanarich*, 66.

[3] Cf. Boer, *Ermanarich*, 80. The Harlungs cannot be derived from the Heruli, as suggested by Grimm (*G.D.S.* 472) and recently urged by Matthaei (*Z.f.d.A.* xliii, 319, *etc.*). *Harlung* and *Erl* are too different linguistically to be easily identified, and there is no evidence demanding such identification. See note to l. 87.

[4] Jiriczek(2) 66, 103; Bojunga in *P.B.B.* xvi, 548.

[5] Symons in *Pauls Grdr.*(2) iii, 685.

some motive for his evil acts, and this motive was given by the evil counsellor Sibich [Sifka in the *Thidreks saga*] who, together with his antagonist and foil Eckehart, the typical faithful retainer, may have belonged to the Harlung story even from the beginning[1]. Sibich, like Iago, does evil for the love of it: but his actions in the North German story, as recorded in the *Thidreks saga*, are made more plausible by the motive of revenge: his wife has been seduced during his absence from the country by Erminrek: and he sets to work to bring about, by his evil counsels, the downfall of the tyrant. By the advice of Sifka and of Sifka's wife, Erminrek causes the death of his sons; of two unintentionally, and of the third deliberately[2]; he then compasses the death of his two nephews from Harlung land[3], and finally is persuaded to attack his nephew Thithrek —Theodoric of Verona.

There is an obvious parallel between the original Harlung myth of the faithless wooers, as it has been reconstructed by Müllenhoff, and the Norse story of the prince who, sent to woo Swanhild, betrays his trust. It is quite possible that Norse tradition, though it does not record the Harlung myth[4], derives from a version which has nevertheless been influenced by it, and that the modifications of the story which make Swanhild the wife of the tyrant, and his own son the object of that tyrant's jealousy, are due to the influence of the Harlung story. The difficulty of this supposition is that it leaves us nothing but the likeness of the names Irmin-tiu and Ermanaric to account for the contamination of the two stories[5]. Should the jealousy motive of the Norse story be simply a reflection of the Harlung myth it might follow that Bikki is merely a

---

[1] This however is doubtful, especially in view of the absence of Ecgheard from *Widsith*. See Binz in *P.B.B.* xx, 209–10; Panzer, *H.i.B.* 85; Boer, *Ermanarich*, 72, etc.

[2] Erminrek has in this version three sons, Frithrek, Reginballd, and Samson (*Thidreks saga*, 277–80).

[3] *af Aurlungalandi* (*Thidreks saga*, 281).

[4] Saxo's reference to the Harlung story is due, no doubt, to Low German influence.

[5] See, however, Roediger in *Weinholds Zeitschrift* i, 247. Roediger's suggestion that *Ermanarikaz* was an old title of Tiwaz would make the contamination of his story with that of the historic king more intelligible. But any evidence that this title ever belonged to Tiwaz is wanting.

duplicate, a reproduction, of the faithless Sibich[1]. On the other hand, it is more likely that they are independent figures, Bikki the traitor proper to the Swanhild story, Sibich to the Harlung story[2]; and this is supported by the mention in our poem of both figures, Becca and Sifeca.

Eormanric and the "Herelingas" in Widsith.

The mention of the Harlungs in *Widsith* is important, as showing that already their story formed a part of the Ermanaric cycle. In this connection it may be noted that, in *Beowulf*, the *Brosinga mene* is in the hands of Eormenric, and is carried off by Hama. Whether there was any relation between this and the Harlung story we cannot tell.

From the absence of further references in Old English literature, and of persons named after the characters of the story, Eormanric, Emerca, and Fridla, it has been argued that this story of Eormanric died out early in England. A Kentish King Iurmenric[3] is recorded; elsewhere the name does not meet us. But it may well have been that these names were regarded as too ill-omened. We need to be careful in deducing arguments as to survival of legend from personal names.

That the Harlung story had at one time a footing in England is proved by the occurrence of *Herling*, principally in place names[4]. We cannot draw conclusions from the fact that we find no Englishman with the name *Sifeca* or *Seofeca*: perhaps his story was known too well for any father to give the traitor's name to his son. It is noteworthy that in the topography of Saxon Berkshire we find the name of the traitor not far from that of one of his victims, *Seofocan wyrð* near

---

[1] Jiriczek(2) 112.

[2] Symons in *Pauls Grdr.* (2) III, 686. In the earlier edition of the Grundriss Symons had hazarded the guess that Bikka was the unrecorded name of the husband of Swanhild, *Grdr.*(1) II, 41. In this he had been partly anticipated by Bugge (*Arkiv f. Nordisk Filologi*, I, 8, 1883), "Der synes...at være god Grund til at gjenfinde denne troløse Raadgiver i Suniïdas af Jordanes omtalte Mand."

[3] He was father of Ethelberht of Kent (see the early ninth century genealogies in Sweet's *Oldest Eng. Texts*, 171, and cf. Florence of Worcester, ed. Thorpe, 1848, I, 12).

[4] Binz in *P.B.B.* xx, 209.

Friþela byrig[1]. There is then no reason to doubt that the Sifeca mentioned in *Widsith* is the traitor of the Harlung story[2].

Do these two stories of Swanhild and of the Harlungs involve a different view of Ermanaric: and, if so, can we trace in *Widsith* different strata, different views of the character of the great Gothic tyrant?

It has been asserted with some confidence that we can[3]: that in the oldest Gothic story Ermanaric was a national hero, who only slowly, and especially through the murder of the Harlungs— a story which had originally, as these critics suppose, nothing to do with him—passed into the typical tyrant, the murderer of his kin. Thus it has been argued by Bojunga that:

"This darkening of Ermanaric's character has not yet taken place in the older parts of *Widsith*, although the Harlung story appears to be already known. In *v.* 88 ff. Ermanaric appears as a generous patron of the arts, whilst in the late introduction (*v.* 8—9) he is, in accordance with later story, characterized as *wráþ wǽrloga.*"

Here again, the deductions hardly seem warranted by the facts. There is nothing inconsistent in a tyrant being a generous patron of the arts: and *Widsith* is not alone in asserting the open-handedness of Ermanaric[4]. It was his essential feature in story to be at one and the same time "more cunning than all in guile, more generous in gifts[5]."

---

[1] Müllenhoff in *Z.f.d.A.* xxx, 225; Birch, *Cart. Sax.* iii, 201 (No. 1002).

[2] This has been disputed by Binz, *P.B.B.* xx, 207–8. Heinzel has shown, conclusively, that two of the champions mentioned as retainers of Eormenric are characters of the *Hervarar saga.* Binz would go further, and identify Sifeca with Sifka, the Hunnish mistress of the Gothic king Heithrek of the *Hervarar saga.* But phonetically this has no advantage over the old identification of Sifeca with the traitor, whilst in other respects it is inferior: for the name occurs in *Widsith* as that of a retainer of Ermanaric, which Sifeca the traitor was, but Sifka the Hunnish concubine certainly was not. The conjecture of Binz has, however, been supported by Jiriczek(2) 73; Panzer, *H.i.B.* 84; Boer, *Ermanarich*, 60 (with some hesitation).

[3] Bojunga in *P.B.B.* xvi, 548. Similarly Möller has seen between ll. 8, 9 and 89 a discrepancy pointing to difference of authorship (*V.E.* 33). Thorpe in his edition tried to account for the supposed inconsistency by assuming a gap in the text. See note to l. 9 of text.

[4] Compare, for example, *Alpharts Tod*, 207: *Thidreks saga*, 322.

[5] *Astutior omnibus in dolo, largior in dono.* *Chronicon Wirziburgense* in Pertz, *SS.* t. vi, 1844, p. 23.

Nor can we be at all certain that any such distinction as Bojunga assumes, differentiated the Ermanaric of sixth century tradition from the Ermanaric of, say, eighth century tradition.

No doubt as time went on Ermanaric became more and more the typical tyrant, and was made responsible for one evil deed after another. The murder of his wife and the treachery towards his nephews are clearly not historical : we can trace the different accretions of tradition by which these crimes come to be attributed to the great Gothic king. But already in the sixth century Ermanaric had probably the reputation of a cruel tyrant. For Cassiodorus, in summing up the characteristic virtues of all the Amal kings, as mirrors in which the princess Amalasuintha may perceive her own merits, makes no mention of him[1]. Nor is it quite the case, as has been urged, that this omission can be accounted for by the fact that there was no *tertium comparationis* between the victorious Ermanaric and the daughter of Theodoric ; no virtue belonging to Ermanaric which could be attributed to a woman[2]. His open-handedness might certainly have been quoted, the more so as *largitas*, the most essential of royal virtues to the Germanic mind, has no representative in Cassiodorus' list.

The omission, then, of the greatest name in the whole list of Amalasuintha's ancestors can only be the result, either of a fault in our text[3], or of a feeling that the great conqueror was, after all, not quite a credit to the family. If then Ermanaric left behind him a doubtful fame, even among those Goths whose mightiest monarch he had been, we can the more easily understand how readily, later, the slaughter of the Harlungs came to be attributed to the typical tyrant king, and how this slaughter ceased to be the righteous retribution of an outraged god, and became the act of a grasping and avaricious tyrant.

---

[1] *Enituit enim Hamalus felicitate, Ostrogotha patientia, Athala mansuetudine, Winitarius æquitate, Unimundus forma, Thorismuth castitate, Walamer fide, Theudimer pietate.* Cassiodori *Variæ* xi, 1 ; ed. Th. Mommsen.

[2] Roediger in *Weinholds Zeitschrift*, i, 243 ; Jiriczek (2) i, 67.

[3] Mommsen in a note to his Jordanes (p. 76) suggests that the name of Athala has been inserted in the text of Cassiodorus, by error, for that of Ermanaric. But this seems unlikely, for Athala's virtue *mansuetudo* would hardly have been chosen as the conqueror's strong point. Athal is vouched for by Jordanes' genealogy (xiv, 79) ; he is grandson of Ostrogotha.

The fact, therefore, that in the introduction to *Widsith* Eormanric is roundly denounced is not enough to prove that introduction a later addition. It probably is so: but we shall need more evidence than this.

Theodoric of Verona.

Last and longest remembered of the evil deeds of the Ermanaric of story was his tyranny and treachery towards his nephew Theodoric.

As a matter of history Theodoric was born on the day when the news reached his father's house of the final victory which liberated the Goths from that subservience to the Huns into which they had fallen on the death of Ermanaric eighty years before. But this liberty only meant, during the whole of Theodoric's boyhood and youth, a state, half of dependence upon the Eastern empire, half of hostility to it, always of penury. At the age of twenty Theodoric became, by the death of his father Theodemer[1], leader of this little nation of soldiers out of employ. In 488 he received from the Eastern emperor permission to try his fortune in Italy, then ruled by Odoacer and a miscellaneous host of German mercenaries. So Theodoric invaded Italy with the whole Ostrogothic nation, taking with him remnants of the Rugian people under their king Frederic, who had a blood feud to avenge upon Odoacer. After a four years struggle, marked by his great victories of the Isonzo, of Verona and of the Adda, prolonged by the treachery of his allies, first of Tufa and then of Frederic, Theodoric at last slew Odoacer in his palace at Ravenna on March 15th, 493. Then followed his thirty-three years of just and peaceful rule. "He cared for justice above all things, and was a true king[2]."

But Theodoric had not been dead ten years when a spasmodic revival of the strength of the Eastern empire led to a war between the Gothic nation and their Rugian allies on the one hand, and, on the other, the "Roman" army of mercenaries drawn from three continents, and led by two great military

---

[1] M.H.G. *Dietmâr;* O.N. þioðmarr.   [2] Procopius, *Bell. Gott.,* I, 1.

geniuses, first Belisarius, then Narses. Eighteen years of incessant fighting followed. The Goths were hampered at the outset by the incompetence of their leaders: and all the heroism of later chiefs, when war had brought the right men to the front, failed to redress the balance. Five times was Rome taken and retaken: twice the Goths wore out their strength in unsuccessful attacks upon the massive Aurelian walls, before the last great pitched battle took place at the foot of Mount Vesuvius. The Byzantine historian's account of this reminds us of the Old English lay of Maldon. The Goths dismounted for the fight, and the last Gothic king placed himself, with his shield-bearers, in the forefront of the battle, changing his shield as often as it became too heavy, from the weight of the enemy's javelins fixed in it. When at last he was slain, in the moment of so changing his shield, the Goths did not cease from fighting. All that day and the next the battle continued: on the third day the survivors asked and received permission to leave Italy, and settle in some barbarian land, far from the power of Rome[1].

But it took two years more to root out the isolated Gothic settlements and garrisons scattered throughout Italy, and this last struggle was lengthened by an intervention in favour of the Goths made by the Alamanni. The Alamanni were bound by ancestral ties of gratitude to Theodoric[2], and now they left their homes around the Lake of Constance to aid the Goths[3] and to share in the plunder of Italy. Their intervention failed: as so often later, both sword and plague wasted the German invaders: but it is a very probable conjecture that the last remnants of the Goths accompanying their allies took refuge in the land of the Alamanni. Certainly it is there that we find some of the earliest and most frequent traces of Gothic saga[4], and it is probably not too bold to regard the constant occurrence of the name *Amalunc* around the Lake of Constance, in the books of the Confraternities of St Gall and Reichenau, as a trace of an actual Gothic element in the population.

---

[1] Procopius, *Bell. Gott.* IV, 35; cf. Dahn, II, 176–242.
[2] See Cassiodori *Variæ*, II, 41 (letter of Theodoric to Clovis interceding for the Alamanni).
[3] See Agathias, II, 6–7.
[4] See Uhland's Essay on Dietrich von Bern (esp. p. 379, note 1), in the *Schriften zur Geschichte der Dichtung*, VIII, 334, *etc.*, Stuttgart, 1873.

From these highlands of South Germany the story of
Theodoric spread gradually to the coast tribes of the North[1],
but as it passed from tribe to tribe it became strangely altered.
For Theodoric's work was, as we have seen, undone within a
lifetime, his countrymen driven out of the land he had won for
them, and Italy, which he had ruled and protected so well, left
a prey to the ferocious Alboin and his robber dukes. Poetry
seized upon this tragic aspect of Theodoric's career. He is the
greatest of warriors, yet fortune always robs him of the fruits of
victory : so that the traditions of North Germany and the epics
of South Germany represent the conqueror of Italy as a fugitive
who only enters into his kingdom after thirty years' exile, after
having lost all save one of his vassals.

So one of the most successful figures in all history came to
be the type of endurance under consistent and undeserved
misfortune. Dietrich's lament for his fallen vassals is one of the
most pathetic things in the literature of the Middle Ages :

> Owe daz vor leide niemen sterben ne mac ![2]

A northern poet brought together Guthrun and Thiothrek
as the most sorely tried of men and of women :

Never, says Guthrun when falsely accused to her husband Atli of
unfaithfulness with Thiothrek, Never did I embrace the king of hosts,
the blameless prince; all other were our words as we two bent our heads
together, bewailing.

> Né ek halsaþa herja stille,
> jǫfor óneisan eino sinne:
> aþrar vǫ́ro okrar spekjor,
> es vit hǫrmog tvau hnigom at rúnom[3].

Indeed, so unlike is the career of Dietrich von Bern to that
of the historic Theodoric that W. Grimm went so far as to deny
their identity[4]: two originally quite distinct figures had, he
thought, been confused. Yet the transition from the hero of
history to the hero of story is quite intelligible, if we do not
allow ourselves to forget the later fortunes of the Gothic race.

[1] The spreading of tradition must have been facilitated by the intercommunication of mercenary bands. We meet members of North-Sea coast tribes
serving in Italy a generation after Theodoric's death (Agathias, i, 21).
[2] *Nibelungenlied*, ed. Bartsch, 2323.
[3] *Guþrúnarkviþa* iii, 4 (Symons, *Edda*, i, 410).
[4] *Heldensage*, 344. The mythical theory of the Dietrich story was elaborated
by Hahn, *Sagenwissenschaftliche Studien*, Jena, 1876, pp. 66, *etc.*

It is true that popular poetry does not deal in the "abstractions and generalizations of philosophical world history," and to suppose that in the misfortunes of the Theodoric of saga the poets consciously sought to allegorize the subsequent misfortunes of his people is to misunderstand the spirit of German heroic poetry, which did not work things out in this way[1]. But the Gothic stories were probably in the first place carried beyond the confines of Italy by Gothic refugees. It would be natural for these men to emphasize the tragic side of Theodoric's story, and, exiles themselves, to represent their national hero as an exile. Tradition never preserves an accurate chronology, and Theodoric's many years of struggle, followed by thirty years of peace, might easily become thirty years' disaster, followed by a few years of belated victory. And so the story of Dietrich von Bern might grow quite naturally from that of the historic Theodoric.

On the other hand, if the events of his life are distorted, the character of the Theodoric of history—just, sometimes stern, on rare occasions ferocious, is reflected by later tradition with considerable accuracy. Contemporary Roman historians, and those of the next generation, had every reason to bear hard upon the memory of the Arian barbarian, at the overthrow of whose kingdom they rejoiced. Yet they agree in representing him as one who loved justice, and held the laws sacred: who, though he would not take the title of Roman Emperor, and was content to be called *reiks* as the Barbarians call their chiefs, was second to none of the best in the line of Emperors—a terror to his foes, loved and regretted by his subjects, Goths and Italians alike[2].

The main features of Dietrich von Bern are here.

To a certain extent we can trace the development of the historic Theodoric into Dietrich von Bern. The earliest tradition must have followed fact in representing Odoacer as

---

[1] Compare W. Müller, *Myth.* 183, "In der Sage bekam das Andenken an die letzten Geschicke der Goten natürlich das Übergewicht...." Against this it is urged by Jiriczek(₂) 130, "mit allgemeinen blassen Abstractionen operiert die Sagenbildung nicht." Jiriczek is undoubtedly right: yet national history must unconsciously colour national tradition.

[2] Procopius, *Bell. Gott.* I, 1.

Theodoric's adversary. A record of this stage of the story is
preserved in the *Hildebrand Lay.* "He (Hildebrand) fled
from the enmity of Odoacer with Theodoric, and his warriors
many[1]." But tradition tends to make all its heroes contemporary, and so Theodoric became the nephew of the tyrant king
Ermanaric, whilst Odoacer first remained in the background as
the instigator of trouble[2] and finally disappeared altogether.
Sifeca, Sifka or Sibech, the evil genius of Ermanaric in the
murder of the Harlungs, is made responsible for Ermanaric's
cruelty to Theodoric also.

Theodric in Widsith.

The author of *Deor*, to judge from the way in which he
introduces their names, knew of Eormanric as the foe of
Theodric. On the other hand, it has come to be a dogma that
Theodoric of Verona is unknown to *Widsith*, and that the
Theodric who is twice mentioned in the poem, first in the
catalogue of kings, and then among the champions of
Ermanaric, is that Theodoric the Frank, the son of Chlodowech,
who grew to be a hero of story second only to Dietrich von
Bern.

This Theodoric the Frank was an illegitimate son: there
were difficulties about the succession and quarrels with his
kin, followed by a victorious reign[3]. Not dissimilar was the
history of Theodebert his son[4]. From these events grew the
great Middle High German stories of Hug-Dietrich and his
son Wolf-Dietrich, stories which turn upon the reproach of
illegitimate birth attaching to Wolf-Dietrich, the jealousy of his
half-brothers, stirred up by the wicked Sabene, the allegiance
of the faithful Berchtung and his sons: Sabene and Berchtung
being contrasted much as are the false Sibech and the true
Ekkehart in the story of the Harlungs.

[1] flôh her Ôtachres nîd,
hina miti Theotrîhhe, enti sînero degano filu.
See Koegel *Ltg.* I, 1, 216.
[2] As in the *Würzburg Chronicle.* Yet perhaps this reflects a confused
tradition. On the other hand it is *conceivable* that, in the *Hildebrand Lay*,
Odoacer is not the tyrant, but the tyrant's counsellor.
[3] See below, Chap. iii: *Theodoric the Frank.*
[4] For Theodebert see Agathias, I, 4; Gregory of Tours, *Hist. Franc., passim.*

There can be no doubt that in *Widsith* 1. 24 (*þeodric weold Froncum*) the reference is to Theodoric the Frank, the son of Chlodowech. It has been too readily assumed that the later allusion to a Theodoric in l. 115 refers also to the Frankish king, and that Theodoric the Goth is left without mention in *Widsith*[1]; from which it has been argued that Theodoric's connection with the Ermanaric story is later, and dates from the eighth century. Yet the assumption that the Theodric of l. 24 is identical with the Theodric of l. 115 is a perilous one. The first mentioned Theodric is king of the Franks; the latter Theodric is a champion at the court of Eormanric. Besides, it is dangerous to argue from one section of *Widsith* to the other: the two sections *may* have been originally independent poems[2]. The only reason for identifying the Theodric of l. 115 with Hug-Dietrich or Wolf-Dietrich is the fact that his name is coupled with that of Seafola, in whom Müllenhoff saw the Old English equivalent of the treacherous Sabene of Middle High German story. But it was overlooked that there are two heroes of the name Sabene: the one a faithless retainer of Hug-Dietrich, the other—Sabene of Ravenna—the faithful retainer of Dietrich von Bern, often referred to in *Dietrichs Flucht*[3]. The coupling of Seafola with Theodric is then equally appropriate, whether that Theodric be the Goth or the Frank, and gives no evidence as to which of the two heroes the poet had in mind. But the balance of probability is in favour of the Ostrogoth, for several reasons:

(1) Tradition would easily make Ermanaric's kinsman Theodoric into one of his retainers, and we know that it ultimately did so: but no satisfactory explanation has been given which would account for the mention of Theodoric the Frank among Ermanaric's household[4].

(2) The omission of the name of Theodoric the Ostrogoth from a list of Gothic champions would in any case be strange.

---

[1] Koegel, *Ltg.* I, 1, 149–51; Symons in *Pauls Grdr.* (2) III, 691; Jiriczek (2) 74.

[2] I hope to show below (Chap. iv: end), that they almost certainly were.

[3] *Dietrichs Flucht* is a late poem: but Sabene's name probably represents an early tradition; for after the name had become current as that of a traitor it would hardly have been chosen by a poet adding new characters to his story, for a faithful retainer.

[4] See note to l. 115.

(3) Although the Angles certainly knew something of the conquests of Theodoric the Frank, we have no evidence that the romantic story of Hug-Dietrich, Wolf-Dietrich and Sabene ever became a part of the Anglian stock of tales. The stories of Theodoric the Ostrogoth, however, did form part of this stock.

For there is sufficient evidence that Theodoric the Ostrogoth was known, and well known, to the Anglian poets. "Theodric held for thirty winters the city of the Mærings: to many was that known" says *Deor*.

The reference is obscure: we should expect rather "was exiled from" than "held": but the very allusiveness of the poet seems to show that he expected his hearers to know the story well. In the *Waldere* fragment[1] we have another reference to Theodric, this time in the character which he plays so largely both in High and Low German story : that of the foe of monsters and giants. A speaker, probably Guthhere, is referring to a famous sword, perhaps "Mimming":

> I wot that Theodric thought to send it to Widia himself, together with much treasure...forasmuch as Widia, the son of Weland, kinsman of Nithhad, released him from sore straits : through the domain of the giants he hastened forth.

In the Anglo-Saxon *Martyrology* we are told how Theodericus was hurled to torment down a crater of the Lipari Isles—a story which is doubtless due to ecclesiastical hatred of Theodoric as an Arian heretic, the slayer of Boethius, and as a hero of secular song : the same hatred to which we owe the conclusion of the *Thidreks saga*, where the Fiend, in the form of a black horse, runs off with Thithrek. When the Anglo-Saxon compiler adds *þæt wæs Theodoricus se cyning þone we nemnað þeodric*[2], this seems conclusive evidence for the existence of vernacular traditions respecting Theodoric in England at the date when the *Martyrology* was written; that is to say the ninth century.

---

[1] The evidence of this would of course be worthless if, as Koegel (*Ltg.* I, 1, 235–41) and Binz (*P.B.B.* xx, 217) suppose, the *Waldere* is merely a literal transliteration from the O.H.G. But Binz himself has shown how insufficient is the evidence brought forward by Koegel to support this theory.

[2] *Old English Martyrology*, ed. Herzfeld, *E.E.T.S.*, p. 84.

It has further been pointed out[1] that Ida of Bernicia named two of his sons Theodric and Theodhere: Theodhere (Diether) was, in story, the name of Theodric's young brother, whose premature death at the hands of Theodric's former friend and follower, Widia (Wittich), was the most cruel of the blows which fell upon Dietrich von Bern. Perhaps this combination of names in the Northumbrian genealogy is a mere coincidence: if Ida had the story in mind in naming his sons it must have spread north very early; for Ida was ruling in Bernicia barely a generation after the death of Theodoric the Great, and some years before the last of the Ostrogoths were expelled from Italy.

But other personal names seem to confirm a knowledge of the Theodric story in England[2], and when we find the information volunteered in the Alfredian translation of Boethius, *se þeodric wæs Amulinga*, we can hardly hesitate to attribute this to epic tradition. Add the fact that Theodric's henchmen, the Wylfingas—the Wülfinge of High German tradition—are also well known in English story[3], and it seems ultra-scepticism to doubt, as does Binz[4], that the mighty figure of Theodoric played a considerable part in the Anglian lays. Indeed the evidence for the popularity of Theodoric the Goth is far better than the evidence for the popularity of Beowulf the Geat. For a passing allusion, which the poet evidently expects his readers to understand, is better evidence of popularity than a story told at full length: and we have not one allusion only, but several.

When then, in *Widsith*, we find the name Theodric in a place where Theodoric the Goth is wanted, and where

---

[1] Brandl in *Pauls Grdr.*(2) II, 1, 953. It is so natural for kinsmen to bear names containing the same element that this may well be a mere coincidence.

[2] *Lib. Vitae*, ed. Sweet in *Oldest Eng. Texts*, p. 159, line 212. A collection of the early allusions to Theodoric in England will be found in Müllenhoff's *Zeugnisse u. Excurse*, v, 1, in the *Z.f.d.A.* XII, 261-2. Müllenhoff notes the occurrence of the name *Omolincg*, *Omulung* in two very early charters. The signatures are respectively of the years 692 and 706, or perhaps some years later, for the name occurs in the endorsement (see Birch I, 76 and 116). The signatory Omolincg, Omulung is clearly one and the same, the abbot of some monastery presumably in the district of Worcester. It is conceivable that Omulung is a foreign cleric, an immigrant from the great abbeys of St Gall or Reichenau, where we know the name to have been common.

[3] See note to l. 29.   [4] *P.B.B.* xx, 212-214.

Theodoric the Frank would be a most unwelcome intruder, there is surely no reason why we should abstain from the obvious interpretation of *Seafola ond þeodric* as Theodoric the Goth and his retainer Sabene of Ravenna[1].

Whether Anglian story at this date represented Ermanaric as the relentless foe of Theodoric is another question. Probably not: for since in *Widsith* Ermanaric is not yet thought of as ruler of Italy, but governs the Goths in their old home by the Vistula, there is no reason why Theodoric's invasion of Italy should be regarded as directed against him. In *Deor* the mention of the tyranny of Eormanric immediately after the reference to Theodric probably points to a connection in story between the two: but of this we cannot be certain.

Attila.

Ætla weold Hunum.

No very considerable lapse of time would be needed before tradition brought together Ermanaric and Theodoric as contemporaries. For the intervening years had been a blank in the history of the East-Goths; years spent in the service of their Hunnish overlords; and the great deeds which had been achieved during this time had gone to the credit, not of the Gothic name, but of Attila, king of the Huns.

Two distinct traditions concerning Attila can be traced among the German races. On the one hand South German tradition represents him as a great and hospitable king, the holder of a court frequented by valiant knights. Like Arthur in a similar position, he is overshadowed by his knights and by his queen, till he becomes a commonplace, and sometimes a

---

[1] See Heinzel, *Osgotische Heldensage*, 8. Heinzel has noticed the double occurrence of Sabene: he and Holthausen (*Beowulf*, p. 125) are, I believe, the only critics who interpret the *þeodric* of l. 115 as Theodoric of Verona. At an earlier date (*Hervararsaga* in *W.S.B.* cxiv, 50) Heinzel had given his adhesion to the common belief that the reference was to Hug- or Wolf-Dietrich. Of course, if the hypothesis of Bugge (*H.D.* 71, 167–8; *P.B.B.* xxxv, 267) and Müller (202) is correct, that Wolf-Dietrich and Sabene are originally figures of Ostrogothic tradition, this would account for the way in which they are introduced into *Widsith*. But this theory has not been proved.

weak figure. But he is always kindly and hospitable[1]. On the other hand there is the Atli of Scandinavian story, grim, covetous, terrible, who murders the Niblungs, the brethren of his wife, and perishes at length through the vengeance of that wife.

When we remember that in the great battle on the Mauriac plain almost the whole inland Teutonic world was ranged, the one half as Attila's foes and the other half as his henchmen, we can understand how this double tradition grew up in German lands. To the Rugian, the Gepid, the Thuringian and the Eastern Frank, but above all to the Ostrogoth, Attila would be the great king in whose hall their chiefs feasted, and following whose banners they had gained all that a German warrior most loved—

> sweord and swatigne helm, swylce eac side byrnan
> gerenode readum golde.

To them Attila would be indeed the "little father."

To the Visigoth on the other hand, the Salian Frank, and the Burgundian, Attila would be the grasping "tyrant of the world, making war without a quarrel and thinking any crime allowed him[2]." The Atli of the North seems to be derived, through various stages of Low German saga, from the point of view of the Salian Franks and other nations who fought against Attila in the great battle[3], whilst in the South German Etzel we can trace quite clearly the benevolent overlord of Ostrogothic tradition. Not that the old hostility of Goth and Hun was forgotten in this South German tradition[4]: on the contrary we shall see that in the person of the old national hero Widigoja (the Wittich of High German story, the Wudga or Widia of Anglo-Saxon tradition) recollections of the old struggle with the Huns in the days of Ermanaric were mingled with a vague remembrance of the death of Attila's sons in the war of liberation eighty years after Ermanaric's death. But in Southern story the Gothic cause grew to be identified with the tyrant

---

[1] See Vogt, *Z.f.d.Ph.* xxv, 414; Koegel, *Ltg.* I, 2, 283; Hodgkin's *Italy*, II, 176; Thierry, *Histoire d'Attila*, 1864, II, 224, *etc.*

[2] Jordanes, ed. Mommsen, xxxvi (187). The words are put into the mouth of the Roman envoys at the Visigothic court.

[3] *Pauls Grdr.*(2) III, 700.

[4] See Appendix (I), *Ermanaric as the foe of the Huns.*

Ermanaric, whilst Attila, Etzel, was glorified as the patron and helper of Dietrich von Bern—no very strange part for him to play, when we remember that Attila actually was the leader and friend of Theodemer, Theodoric's father. So that in that very South German tradition which was most closely in touch with Ostrogothic story, the sympathy of the poets was rather with the Huns than with the Goths. In Low German tradition, on the other hand, Attila was the tyrant foe: and the form which his name takes in *Widsith*—Ætla, not Etla—points conclusively to Low German tradition[1]. In *Widsith*, therefore, the struggle between Goth and Hun is looked upon from the Gothic side: the scene of the conflict is the old home of the Goths by the Vistula, where Ætla, as the typical Hunnish chief, is, despite chronology, opposed to Eormanric and his men. Chronology has been also disregarded in the list of Ermanaric's champions: earlier heroes like Eastgota or Wudga have been drawn into the great conflict with the Huns.

The tradition of this conflict has also been preserved to us in the Icelandic: in the prose of the *Hervarar saga* and in the verse lay of Hloth and Angantyr: a fine poem, but so allusive and so corrupt that without the help of the prose saga we should hardly be able to understand it. The *Hervarar saga* is the life story of a sword "Tyrfing," the work of dwarfs, which is fated, every time it is drawn, to be the death of a man. The tale of the race of heroes through whose hands the sword passes is traced from generation to generation till we come to Angantyr, third of the name, who has inherited the lordship of the Goths and the sword Tyrfing from his father, the grim king Heithrek. As Angantyr is drinking the funeral feast over his father, Hloth, a bastard son of Heithrek by the daughter of Humli, king of the Huns, comes riding from the East to claim one half of the inheritance. He speaks in the poem:

"Half will I have of all that Heithrek owned—cow, calf, humming hand mill...half the war gear, the land, and the shining rings."

"The white shield must be cloven," Angantyr replies, "and cruel spear clash with spear and many a man fall on the grass, ere I will halve mine inheritance with the son of Humli, or divide Tyrfing in twain."

[1] See note to l. 18.

Yet Angantyr offers mighty treasures to Hloth, men, horses, maids, necklaces, silver and gold, "and the third part of the Gothic folk shalt thou rule alone." At this old Gizur, the foster father of Angantyr, is wroth and grumbles "That is an offer meet to be accepted by the son of a bondwoman, the son of a bondwoman though born to a king": and with this taunt all thought of peace is gone. Humli calls out the Hunnish host, from the boy of twelve winters and the foal of two winters, in order to vindicate his grandson's right, and they fall upon the Gothic borders, and first upon the amazon sister of Angantyr, Hervor. Hervor is slain, and Ormar the master of her host comes with the news to Angantyr, "drenched is all Gothland with the blood of men." Angantyr sends Gizur to challenge the Huns to battle at Dunheath; the challenge is delivered and Gizur is allowed to ride away in safety, to tell to Angantyr the vast numbers of the Hunnish hordes[1]. From the prose saga we get a lengthy account of the battle, waged for ten days[2]. But the poem omits all account of this, and passes at once to the last scene of all, as Angantyr stands over his dying half-brother: "Ill is the doom of the Fates."

The connection between this story and the Ermanaric catalogue in *Widsith* was noticed by C. C. Rafn in his edition of the *Hervarar saga*[3] half a century or more ago. A few years later another scholar[4] pointed out that the *Hliþe and Incgenþeow* of our poem were Hloth and Angantyr.

It seems clear that the *Hervarar saga* and the Ermanaric catalogue in *Widsith* go back to a common tradition, which had its roots in the early history of the Huns and the Goths. Whether we can fix any precise event in that early history as the origin of the story is another matter. Heinzel has tried to do this, and has drawn attention to a number of remarkable parallels between the incidents preceding the battle on the Mauriac plain, and

---

[1] This part of the story Saxo knew, and incorporated into his History of the Danes (ed. Holder, 154–5).

[2] *Fornaldar Sǫgur*, 1829, I, 503–8. The *Lied von der Hunnenschlacht* will be found in the *Eddica Minora* of Heusler and Ranisch, Dortmund, 1903; also in the text of the *Hervarar saga*.

[3] In the *Antiquités russes* Rafn identified Ormar and Wyrmhere: his other attempts at identification (e.g. Angantyr and Eastgota) were less fortunate. See notes to *Wyrmhere* (l. 116) and *Hliþe* (l. 119) below.

[4] See note to l. 116.

the incidents in the closing chapter of the *Hervarar saga*[1]. But in all probability no one specific battle gave rise to the tradition. Into the ten days' battle of Dunheath Norse poetry has probably compressed the century long struggle of Goth and Hun: and *Widsith* is probably right in pointing to a succession of fights rather than any one pitched battle. For popular tradition will easily turn a desultory conflict into a single dramatic encounter, but hardly the reverse[2].

And the fact that in the Norse story Atli is not the leader of the Huns, is strong evidence that the tradition does not derive from Attila's great reverse on the Mauriac plain. For to Teutonic tradition Attila is essentially *the* Hun. That he should be introduced into *Widsith* is therefore natural, even if the fighting on the Vistula reflects those ancient battles which preceded the fall of Ermanaric, long before Attila's days. But when in the *Hervarar saga* we find that the Hunnish leader is not Atli but Humli, we may be sure that this is an original trait of the story. Attila could hardly have lost his place as Hunnish leader in the battle of Dunheath, had he ever rightly possessed it[3].

Wudga and Hama.

Ne wæran þæt gesiþa þa sæmestan,
þeahþe ic hy anihst nemnan sceolde...
Wræccan þær weoldan wundnan golde,
werum and wifum, Wudga and Hama.

To two heroes, met during his wanderings, Wudga and Hama, our poet does special honour. The word *wræcca*, which is applied to them, comes later, in High German, to signify simply champion, or warrior. But in Old English it has not lost its significance of "exile"; and in this representation of Wudga and Hama as strangers within the Gothic borders we have perhaps an indication that, at the time when *Widsith* was

---

[1] *Hervararsaga*, esp. pp. 50, *etc.* Heinzel's theory is discussed and rejected by Veselovsky in the Russian *Journal of the Ministry of Public Instruction*, May, 1888, pp. 74–90, "Short notes on the Byliny." See summary by V. Jagič in the *Archiv für Slavische Philologie*, Berlin, 1888, XI, 307.

[2] See Jagič, p. 308.

[3] For reasons to the contrary see, however, Heinzel, *Hervararsaga* in *W.S.B.* CXIV, 79.

written, it was still felt that they did not rightly belong to the Ermanaric cycle : much as Sir Tristram, though he visits the court of Arthur and is enrolled a knight of the Table Round, is never quite at his ease there, but betrays that he has stepped out of a story originally distinct. It is probable however that *wrœccan* means more than this, and that in the stories known to *Widsith*, Wudga and Hama were outlaws.

Wudga is probably a more ancient figure of Gothic tradition than even Ermanaric.

Vidigoia[1] is mentioned by Jordanes as one of the Gothic heroes whose memories were preserved in popular song[2]: in a later chapter a locality is mentioned " where of old Vidigoia, the bravest of the Goths, fell by the wiles of the Sarmatians[3]." In the course of generations the Huns, as the historic foes of the Goths, naturally took the place of the Sarmatians, whilst Widigauja came to be drawn into the cycle of two distinct Gothic kings, whose fame eclipsed his own. As the foe of the Huns he was naturally connected with Ermanaric[4], whilst tales of adventures with giants and monsters made him the associate of Theodoric. These tales are preserved both in the Middle High German and in the *Thidreks Saga* : we have seen that the Old English *Waldere* alludes to the reward Widia received for releasing Theodric from straits, presumably among the giants and monsters. Thus Widigauja, Wittich, owes fealty to two kings ; and when later tradition made these kings deadly foes, his position became a difficult one. True, story represented him as having entered the service of Ermanaric, with the consent of his former lord, Theodoric, before their quarrel[5]. But,

---

[1] Corresponding to a presumed Gothic * *Widigauja*.

[2] *Ante quos etiam cantu maiorum facta modulationibus citharisque canebant, Eterpamara, Hanale, Fridigerni, Vidigoiæ et aliorum, quorum in hac gente magna opinio est, quales vix heroas fuisse miranda iactat antiquitas.* Cap. v (43) ed. Mommsen.

[3] *ingentia si quidem flumina, id est Tisia, Tibisiaque et Dricca, transientes venimus in loco illo ubi dudum Vidigoia Gothorum fortissimus Sarmatum dolo occubuit; indeque non longe ad vicum, in quo rex Attila morabatur, accessimus.* xxxiv, (178). The spot is probably in the centre of what is now Hungary. The rivers mentioned are not easy to identify, but one of them is apparently the Theiss. See Wietersheim, *Geschichte der Völkerwanderung*, 2 Aufl. herausg. Dahn, ii, 230–31.

[4] See Müllenhoff, *Z.f.d.A.* xii, 256.

[5] *Alpharts Tod*, 26 ; cf. Jiriczek[(2)] 307.

even so, his honour was not, in the High German versions, saved, and *Vidigoia Gothorum fortissimus* becomes "Wittich the untrue[1]."

One of the worst checks received by the historic Theodoric in the long struggle which made him master of Italy was due to his having first received into his service, and having then been deserted by, a general of his adversary's, Tufa. Perhaps this double treason came to be ascribed to Wittich[2]. Even his valiant deeds against the old enemies, the Huns, stood Wittich in little stead. The legend which made him the slayer of the sons of Attila is probably, as Heinzel has pointed out, an echo of the two great battles in which the Goths threw off the yoke of the Huns, defeated the sons of Attila, and slew one of them; the battle of the river Nedao in the year 454[3], and the subsequent and final victory, probably of the same year. The historic victors in these battles were the father and uncles of Theodoric, but, as the national champion against the Huns, it was impossible to keep Widigauja out of the business. When, however, later story made Attila Theodoric's refuge from the treachery of his uncle Ermanaric, the slaying of the children of Attila became one of the worst of the many evil acts of Wittich. But only one out of many; for Wittich came to be a sinister figure: the merciless slayer of youthful princes. The death of one of these, Nuodunc, is referred to several times in the *Nibelungen Lied*: it is one of the old sorrows lying in the background, when the Burgundians are hospitably entertained

---

[1]　　　　　　　*da nâmen si den ende*
　　　　　　　von des ungetriuwen Witegen hende.
　　　　　　　　　　　　　Rabenschlacht, stanza 364.

[2] *Dietrichs Flucht*, 7133 etc., 7712 etc., cf. Max Rieger in *Z.f.d.M.* I, 233. The connection between the treason of Wittich and that of the historic Tufa is often spoken of as certain (e.g. by Jiriczek(1) 133 ; (2) 136). But there are serious difficulties: cf. Boer, *Ermanarich*, 88; Müller, 160. Apparently it is only in the latest versions of his story that Wittich becomes a traitor. We should have to assume, either that a tradition of Tufa's treachery survived independently to a late date, and was transferred to Wittich after his degradation; or that, under learned influence, the historic fact of Tufa's treachery was attributed to the traditional Wittich, by some such combination of history and legend as has been suggested for the old French epic by Bédier (*Les légendes épiques*, 108 etc., 399 etc.).
　　　The connection sometimes suggested with the historic Witigis (e.g. by Abeling, *Das Nibelungenlied*, 1907, p. 221; Matthaei in *Z.f.d.A.* xlvi, 51 etc.) seems very doubtful.

[3] Hodgkin's *Italy*, ii, 192; iii, 14.

by the Margrave Rüdiger[1] and his lady. But the story is not told at length in any extant High German poem: for in High German story the place of Nuodunc was taken by the young Alphart, whom Wittich does to death with the help of his friend Heime, and that too by a foul stroke[2]. As well as Nuodunc, Alphart and the sons of Attila, Wittich slays the young brother of Dietrich, *Diether der vürste wolgetân*[3]. But vengeance is at hand in the person of Dietrich himself. He gives chase to Wittich, whom neither taunts, nor the example of his uncle Reinolt, can persuade to stand his ground. But Dietrich gains on him, and the sea is in front. Wittich has already rushed into the sea when "at that moment came a mermaid....She took the mighty warrior, and carried him with her, horse and all...with her, down to the bottom of the sea[4]."

It is unusual for the god in the machine to appear in order to save the traitor from the vengeance of the hero: and may we not safely see in Wittich's end a survival from the story of the valiant champion of earlier date[5]?

We have no reason to think that degradation overtook Wudga in any of the English stories: for even the continental Saxon versions, as translated in the *Thidreks saga*, kept his honour unimpaired. In the *Thidreks saga* Vithga passes, with Thithrek's consent, into the service of Erminrek, whilst these heroes are yet friends. He warns his old master of the evil which is compassed against him by Sifka's wiles: but when Thithrek tries to regain his own by force Vithga has, against his will[6], to bring up his liegemen to fight under Erminrek's banners. Deserted by Sifka, he rallies the host, slays first Nauthung, then the sons of Attila, and at last, after warning him in vain, Thithrek's young brother; and falls a victim to Thithrek's revenge. The interest to the Saxon poet lay in the

---

[1] *Der Nibelunge Not*, ed. Bartsch, 1699: cf. also 1903, 1906, 1927. For other references see Grimm, *H.S.* 101 (third edit. 112).
[2] *Alpharts Tod*, 289. The version is confused, fragmentary and interpolated.
[3] *Rabenschlacht*, stanza 453, etc.
[4] *Rabenschlacht*, stanza 964–5; cf. 966–974.
[5] As is noted by Grimm, *H.S.* 360 (third edit. 408) there are noble features even about the High German Wittich, such as his lament after he has smitten Diether.
[6] Cap. 323.

4—2

story of the good knight compelled to fight those who are dear to him; the pathos is that of the Margrave Rüdiger, in the *Nibelungen Lied*, or of the closing chapters of Mallory, where Lancelot and his men wage war against King Arthur. This feeling receives fine expression in the preceding scene, where the old friends, Master Hildebrand and Reinald, meet in the moonlight by the river between the two hosts: "Then said Hildebrand, 'Where is Vithga, our beloved friend, with his host?' Then Reinald answered, 'You can see the green tent, with the silver knob on the top of the pole. There Vithga sleeps, and many Amlungs. And they have vowed that to-morrow they will cleave many a helm[1].'"

"In Witege and Heime later heroic story has personified, in duplicate, the faithless, venal, cold-hearted and sinister champion[2]." We have seen that, with regard to Witege, this must be understood with limitations: and equally is this the case with regard to Heime.

There is no historical incident with which we can associate Hama's name. The earliest references are in *Widsith*, where Hama is Wudga's comrade; the already mentioned St Gall document of 786, in which a *Heimo* and his daughter *Suanailta* occur; and the puzzling passage in *Beowulf*:

> syþðan Hama ætwæg
> to þære byrhtan byrig Brosinga mene,
> sigle and sincfæt, searoniðas fealh [*Grundtvig*, *Leo*, fleah]
> Eormenrices, geceas ecne ræd.

Since Hama carried off to the bright town the necklace of the Brisings, jewel and precious work: penetrated [*better*, fled] the wiles of Ermanaric, chose the eternal welfare[3].

---

[1] Cap. 326. Vithga overshadows his master, and is the real hero of much of the *Thidreks saga*, as Launcelot of the *Morte Arthur*. Vithga takes a robbers' castle which has defied Thithrek (cap. 84), and it is only by borrowing Vithga's sword Mimung that Thithrek is able to accomplish his greatest triumph, and vanquish Sigurd (cap. 222).

[2] Symons in *Paul's Grdr.*(2) III, 694.

[3] Bugge (*P.B.B.* XII, 70) takes *geceas ecne ræd* to be a reference to Heime's retirement to the monastery. But this, though a motive common enough in the later romances, seems out of place in *Beowulf*. It is much more probable that it means "he died" (Müll. in *Z.f.d.A.* XII, 304). It is possible that the retirement into the monastery which we find in the *Thidreks saga* is a weakening of some more tragic end in the earlier story, just as the vengeance which Dietrich works upon Elsân (*Rabenschlacht*, stanza 1120) is ultimately commuted into retirement to a monastery. Cf. Jiriczek(2) 318. Or does the phrase simply mean "he did right" (in harrying Ermanaric)?

From these last documents Müllenhoff hazarded the guess that Hama was the name of the treacherous retainer whose desertion of Ermanaric is recorded by Jordanes, and that the *fraudulentus discessus* was the robbing Ermanaric of his treasure[1]. This seems improbable. The evidence of the charter, far from supporting it, is against it. Is it likely that a man named *Heimo*, if this had been the name of the legendary chief who did the deed, and left his wife to bear the punishment, would have given to his daughter the name of that hapless wife?

It has generally been assumed that the reference to Hama in *Widsith* points to him as still a retainer of Eormanric. But the passage needs careful examination. Widsith travels through the land of the Goths and visits the company of Eormanric: then follows a long list of names, concluding with a reference to combats with the people of Attila. Then comes a second list of names, and it is in this second list that the names of Wudga and Hama occur. Of them it is said that as exiles (*wræccan*) they ruled by means of twisted gold over men and women.

Now a comparison of the more than twenty places in which the word *wræcca* occurs in Old English poetry shows it to have a distinct and emphatic meaning: "exile," "outlaw," even "outcast." Of course Wudga and Hama may be outlaws who have taken refuge at the court of Eormanric, as suggested above: but this is not the most obvious interpretation of the lines, nor does it explain why the group to which Wudga and Hama belong should form a separate list distinct from the other followers of Eormanric. It seems more natural to read the passage thus:—the poet traverses the Gothic land, visiting first of all the court of Eormanric; then, after leaving that court, he visits (still in or near the Gothic land) other heroes, imagined as dwelling in exile on the outskirts of the kingdom of Eormanric. This interpretation derives some support from the phrase used of Wudga and Hama: "they ruled there by means of twisted gold over men and women." To rule by means of gold, to give gold, is in Old Germanic poetry the

---

[1] *Z.E.* xiii in *Z.f.d.A.* xii, 302–6.

peculiar prerogative of the independent or semi-independent chief. It is a phrase hardly appropriate to a retainer.

Turning to the *Thidreks saga* we find Heimir essentially an outlaw champion. Whilst still a lad, he takes service with Thithrek; but he is exiled for a fault. He lives as a robber and, once at least, has to save himself by flight. "Then did Heimir say that which many men have since found to be true, that no iron is so true to its lord as is the spur[1]." At length Thithrek pardons him, and he returns to his allegiance. But he plays only a subordinate part till the time comes when Thithrek himself is exiled, when Heimir denounces Erminrek to his face, escapes, thanks to Vithga's timely aid, from pursuit, and lives thenceforth as an outlaw, harrying Erminrek's land[2]. It is to be noted that he is not represented as *accompanying* Thithrek in his exile, and he takes no part in Thithrek's subsequent attempts to win back his own by force. He lives his outlaw life for twenty or thirty years, burning and slaying by day and by night, till at length he repents of the evil, and enters a monastery. Here Thithrek finds him, after all his other knights have been lost, and a fine scene ensues between the two grey-headed men, as Thithrek slowly breaks down Heimir's resolve, and draws him forth again into the world[3].

Our sources are, then, consistent in the view they take of Hama. In *Beowulf* he is a fugitive, possessed of treasure, robbed, apparently, from Ermanaric: in *Widsith* he is an exile, possessed of treasure, and standing to Ermanaric in some relation no further defined: in the *Thidreks saga* he is an outlaw, and gains treasure by plundering Erminrek's land.

From these references one critic[4] has argued that Wudga and Hama were originally figures connected, not with Ermanaric, but with Theodoric, friends who follow him into exile when he flees before Ermanaric. But in no version of the story are they so represented: not in the High German, nor in the *Thidreks saga*, where Vithga and Heimir, though friendly to Thithrek, expressly do *not* follow him into exile. That Heimir

---

[1] Cap. 116.　　　[2] Cap. 288, 429.　　　[3] Cap. 434.
[4] Boer, *Ermanarich*, 185.

especially should not do so is strange; for Heimir is in the *Thidreks saga* the Bedivere of Thithrek's company: "first made and latest left of all the knights." That he should not be with his master in his greatest need, but should choose to live as a solitary outlaw harrying Erminrek, is not what we should expect any story-teller to invent. Such an extraordinary trait can only be accounted for in one way: it must be part of an original tradition which represented Hama as thus harrying Ermanaric on his own account, and which probably goes back to a period before any tradition of hostility between Ermanaric and Theodoric had grown up.

And this is confirmed by the references to Hama in Old English poetry. In *Beowulf* there is no mention of Theodoric: this indeed cannot count for much, for the allusion to Hama's story is hasty, and no details are given. But in *Widsith* also it is quite clear that Hama's exile is not connected with that of Theodoric. For the visit of Widsith to the land of the Goths, in which he meets with the *wræccan*, Wudga and Hama, is imagined as taking place before the evil deeds of Eormanric have occurred. Amongst the household of Eormanric Widsith meets the Harlung brethren, and apparently Theodoric himself.

The exile of Hama in *Widsith* is, then, independent of any quarrel between Eormanric and Theodoric. More probably, Hama is the typical outlaw of early Germanic tradition; the forerunner of those bandit heroes whom we meet later in Icelandic saga and English ballad. This would account for certain rough features which characterize the Heimir of the *Thidreks saga*, a slayer of merchants[1] and burner of monasteries[2], of whom it is said that "had he had never so much gold and silver, the monks would not have received him had they known he was Heimir Studasson[3]." Heimir is contrasted with the more chivalrous Vithga[4]: in the High German, on the other hand, Heime is more noble than Wittich. In *Alpharts Tod* a clear distinction is drawn between him and Wittich. Heime is placed in a difficult position, but that man must be indeed a censorious judge, who, after reading the poem through, feels

[1] Cap. 110.   [2] Cap. 435.   [3] Cap. 429.   [4] Cap. 87, 108, 207.

that *his* honour is besmirched[1]. It is Wittich who, after Heime has stepped in to rescue him, takes an unfair advantage.

One of the best of all the old stories told in the *Thidreks saga* is that of how Heimir betook himself, in his old age, to the monastery, to atone for his sins; surrendering to the abbot all his wealth, his weapons, his horse and store of gold and silver, but concealing his name. The monastery is harried by a giant, who challenges the monks to fight out the quarrel. The monks can find no champion, though they promise a mansion in paradise to their representative in case of defeat. Heimir learns the trouble from his fellow monks in the chapter house, and volunteers to meet the giant; rather to the distress of the abbot, who does not approve of a monk of his being a fighting man. Heimir asks for his weapons back: the abbot answers falsely:

"Thou shalt not have thy sword: it was broken asunder and a door hinge made of it here in the monastery. And the rest of thine armour was sold in the market-place." Then spake Heimir "Ye monks know much of books, but little of chivalry: had ye known how good these weapons were, ye had never parted with them." And he sprang towards the abbot, and took his cowl in both hands, and said "Verily thou wast a fool, if no iron would suit thee to furnish thy church doors, but my good sword Naglhring, which has cut asunder many a helm, like cloth, and made many a son of the giants headless: and thou shalt pay for it." And he shook the cowl, with the head inside, so hard that four of the abbot's teeth fell out; three on to the floor, and the fourth down his throat. And when the monks heard mention of Naglhring, then they knew that it was Heimir Studasson, of whom they had oft heard tell. And they were sore afraid, and took the keys, and went to the great chest where all his weapons were stored. One took his sword Naglhring, the second his hauberk, the third his helm, the fourth his shield, and the fifth his spear. And all these weapons had been so well stored that they were no whit worse than when he parted with them.

And Heimir took Naglhring, and saw how fairly its edges and its gold ornaments shone: and it came into his mind what trust he had had in its edges each time that he should fight. And as he thought of many a happy day, and how he had ridden out with his fellows, he was first red as blood, and then pale as a corpse. And he kept silence for a time. After that he asked where was his horse Rispa. And the abbot made answer "Thy horse used to draw stones to the church: he has been dead many a year[2]."

In this picture of Hama become a monk, standing before the abbot and the assembled chapter, dreaming of the old days when he rode out with Ermanaric and Theodoric, there is

---

[1] Cf. especially stanzas 280, 287.　　　　　　[2] *Thidreks saga*, 431.

something typical of the decline and end of the Gothic stories. The old heroic world disappeared before the mediaeval church and mediaeval chivalry[1].

In England there is evidence that even before the Norman conquest the heathen heroes were being forgotten; whilst we can trace in the Latin chroniclers[2] indications that a new heroic world, the heroes of which were the Christian kings of England, was gradually displacing the old. In France Charlemagne, the champion of Christendom, supplanted those older heroes whose songs had been chanted in the halls of Karl the Great. In Scandinavian lands, it is true, the old stories survived: but passing through the Viking age they developed into something different in spirit from the songs of the earlier migrations. Still more was this the case in continental Germany. The old names survived, and some fragments of the old stories, but the spirit that breathed through them was different.

[1] For the last English reference to Wudga and Hama see Appendix K.
[2] Especially William of Malmesbury, and, to a less degree, Henry of Huntingdon.

Burgundian heroes: The Burgundians at Worms.

The Burgundians originally dwelt in Eastern Germany[1]. Broken, about the middle of the third century, in a quarrel with the Gepidae, they made their way across Germany to the banks of the Rhine, and before the end of the century they were threatening the Roman frontier from across the river: if we can believe Orosius,—which we cannot—they had, by the year 374, so far recovered from their early disasters as to number 80,000 fighting men[2]. Shortly after Alaric and his Goths had sacked Rome, Gundahari, King of the Burgundians, claimed his share in the plunder of the empire by setting up a sham emperor, Jovinus. " Every circumstance," says Gibbon, " is dark and extraordinary in the short history of the reign of Jovinus[3]." The all-powerful Goths seem to have supported him. But he proved unsatisfactory, and we find Attawulf, the successor of Alaric in the leadership of the Goths, undertaking "if fair and honourable terms were offered" to send in the head of the pretender. We must hope that Gundahari—"the glorious Gunnar"—was no party to this buying and selling of the emperor he had made: but it looks suspicious that the same year saw the destruction of Jovinus, and the apparently peaceable acquisition by the Burgundian chief of the long-coveted territory on the left bank of the Rhine[4]. So Gundahari ruled at Worms[5], *ze Wormez ûf den sant,* and this obscure incident of the puppet emperor[6]

---

[1] See note to l. 19.

[2] Orosius VII, 32 (A.U.C. MCXVIII, *Burgundionum quoque, novorum hostium, novum nomen, qui plusquam octoginta millia (ut ferunt) armatorum, ripæ Rheni fluminis insederunt* (see Migne (1846) XXXI, 1144). This is a misrepresentation, both as to the numbers of the Burgundians and as to the novelty of their appearance, of the entry in Jerome's continuation of the Chronicle of Eusebius, A.D. 377 (374) *Burgundiorum 80 ferme millia, quot numquam antea, ad Rhenum descenderunt.* (Jerome in Migne (1846) XXVII, 698.)

[3] Gibbon, ed. Bury, III, 343–4. Cf. Hodgkin's *Italy*, I, 829–30.

[4] *Burgundiones partem Galliæ propinquantem Rheno obtinuerunt. Jovinus et Sebastianus fratres in Galliis regno arrepto interempti.* Prosper Aquitanus, *Chron. Integrum* in Migne (1846) LI, p. 591.

[5] There is still a Guntersbluhm between Worms and Mainz (Jahn, 329–30).

[6] It is through a fragment of Olympiodorus that we know of Gundahari's share in the business: Ἰοβῖνος ἐν Μουνδιακῷ [read Μογουντιακῷ] τῆς ἑτέρας Γερμανίας, κατὰ σπουδὴν Γωὰρ τοῦ Ἀλανοῦ καὶ Γυντιαρίου ὃς φύλαρχος ἐχρημάτιζε τῶν Βουργουντιόνων τύραννος ἀνηγορεύθη. Müller, *Fragmenta Historicorum Græcorum* (1851) vol. IV, p. 61. Probably this happened in the year 411.

would have been all history had to tell of him, had he not, more than a score of years later, fought two pitched battles, in the second of which he and all his warriors were slain.

Chief and Retainer in German Story.

Gundahari's death was an incident of the type which most appealed to the poets and warriors of the ancient German world[1]. How some great lord, attacked by hopeless odds, is defended by a small group of faithful followers, who keep up a desperate fight after their lord is slain, doggedly determined not to leave the field on which he lies dead: this is a tale which, in historic prose or heroic verse, in bombastic Latin or Greek periods, or in simple vernacular dialects, is told over and over again throughout the "Dark Ages[2]."

Long before, Tacitus had mentioned this loyalty of the retainer to his lord as one of the essential features of German character. "It is a lifelong disgrace and reproach for the retainer to have left the field when his chief has fallen. To defend and protect his lord, and to assign to him the honour of his own brave deeds, is the retainer's essential pledge of loyalty[3]." But the loyalty of the retainer does not as a rule appeal very strongly to the Roman or Byzantine writer. When the bodyguard of Odoacer all fell around their lord in the palace hall of Ravenna, the chronicler is satisfied with the dry entry *occisus est Odoacar rex a rege Theodorico in palatio cum commilitibus suis*[4], words which may record a struggle as heroic as those in the halls of Atli and Rolf and Finn. It is

---

[1] Cf. the section *Hirdmandsdǿd og eftermæle* in Axel Olrik's *Danmarks Heltedigtning*, 1903.

[2] Compare especially the episode of Cynewulf and Cyneheard in the *Anglo-Saxon Chronicle*: the *Battle of Maldon*: and several passages in Saxo Grammaticus, especially those in Book ıı founded on the lost *Bjarkamal*:

> Ad caput extincti moriar ducis obrutus, ac [better at] tu
> Ejusdem pedibus moriendo allabere pronus,
> Vt videat quisquis congesta cadavera lustrat
> Qualiter acceptum domino pensavimus [pensarimus] aurum.
>
> (Saxo, ed. Holder, 1886, p. 66.)

Almost exactly the same phrases occur in *Maldon*; e.g. ll. 290–294 and 317–319.

[3] *Germania*, xıv.

[4] *Fasti Vind. priores*, in Mommsen's *Chronica Minora*, ı, 320 (*M.G.H.*). *Interfecti sunt quivis ubi potuit reperiri* says the *Anon. Valesii*.

without much enthusiasm, though fortunately more at length, that Agathias records the heroic death of Phulcaris—Folchere— and his thegns. Folchere, a leader of Herulan allies, had allowed his men to be ambushed by a picked body of Franks, concealed in a Roman amphitheatre:

> So the army was scattered: but Folchere, left behind with his body-guard, would not deign thus to take to flight...He made stand as best he could, with his back to a tomb, and slew many of the enemy, now rushing upon them, now drawing back gradually with his face to the foe. And while he might still have escaped easily, and his followers were urging him to do so, "How," said he, "could I bear the tongue of Narses blaming me for my recklessness?"...So he stood his ground and held out to the last, till he fell forward upon his shield, his breast pierced with many darts, and his head broken by an axe. Upon his body his followers fell, to a man, perhaps voluntarily, perhaps because they were cut off[1].

The Roman or Greek is separated from his heroic age by too many centuries. Court intrigues, theological councils, miracles wrought by the corpses of saints, are of more interest to him. With the German it is different; after he has been converted to Christianity the feeling remains as strong as ever. For it is not only in the secular literature, in the Old English *Chronicle*, in *Maldon*, or in Saxo that we find it. It fires equally the Christian poetry, so that whenever the motive of loyalty is touched, the gospel stories of the *Heliand,* or the legends of apostles, become for the moment war-songs. It is thus that, when St Andrew's disciples are bidden to leave him, as he goes on a desperate errand, they reply:

> Whither shall we, then, go? Outcast, dishonoured, when men reckon who best did to his lord war-service, what time in the field of battle hand and shield endured hardship, smitten by the sword[2].

Guthhere.

It is easy then to understand why the story of the fall of Gundahari and his men in battle against the Huns was of interest not merely to the Burgundian, but to all his neighbours, till, as the centuries passed on, it became known from end to end of Germania. Eight centuries after his fight Gundahari was still remembered from Iceland to Austria, and

---

[1] Agathias, I, 15.
[2] *Andreas*, 405–414: cf. Wiglaf's speech in *Beowulf* (ed. Holder), 2864–91: cf. also 2633–60.

three elaborate collections of the stories which had been woven round his name have come down to us. In the *Nibelungen Lied* we have the version which some Austrian poet or poets put together, about the year 1200. The Saxon versions, as current in Bremen or Münster[1], were put together in the form of a prose saga—the *Thidreks saga*—by a Norseman, writing perhaps not much later than the Southern poet[2]. Later still, a little after the middle of the thirteenth century, the Norse lays which had been sung during centuries in Iceland, Norway, and Greenland, and which are still in great part extant, were paraphrased and codified in the *Vǫlsunga saga*.

In all three cases another story, originally quite distinct, is blended with that of the Burgundian downfall: the tale of Sigfrid the Volsung, which told how Sigfrid slew a dragon and won a mighty hoard of gold, and a maiden to be his bride, whom he wakened from an enchanted sleep: and how the Niblungs, his treacherous comrades, robbed Sigfrid of bride, and gold, and life. Gundahari the Burgundian comes to be identified with the Niblung king: at what date we cannot exactly tell; but apparently *Widsith* does not know this version of the story. Gundahari's violent death thus becomes a just retribution for his sin. And so "the best tale pity ever wrought" was formed around the historic figure of the Rhine-land chief: "the Great Story of the North, which should be to all our race what the Tale of Troy was to the Greeks—to all our race first, and afterwards, when the change of the world has made our race nothing more than a name of what has been—a story too—then should it be to those that come after us no less than the Tale of Troy has been to us[3]."

And thus Gundahari has been sung by the poets of fourteen centuries: but on the other hand the historians have treated him but shabbily. Gibbon ignores him, except for the mention of his name in the Jovinus business: and so also do more recent writers. Yet the overthrow of Gundahari is mentioned,

---

[1] *Thidreks saga*, cap. 394.

[2] "Sagaen er rimeligviis bleven til under Kong Haakon Haakonssöns Reg-jering."—C. R. Unger, in his introduction to the *Thidreks saga*, p. iv.

[3] William Morris: Introduction to his version of the *Vǫlsunga saga*.

briefly, by two contemporaries and by several later historians: and the scanty, but quite reliable information which we thus have from a number of Latin sources was pieced together by Müllenhoff fifty years ago[1]. Combining the accounts of Prosper of Aquitaine, and of Hydatius, Bishop of Chaves[2], we have this result. That in 435 or 436, a quarter of a century, that is, after they had gained their footing in and around Worms, Gundahari and his Burgundians again became restive, and tried to press into Belgic Gaul: that they were met by the Roman general Aetius, overwhelmed, and forced to beg for peace. That within two years of this defeat Gundahari had to face an onslaught of the Huns, who slew him, *cum populo atque stirpe sua* to the number of twenty thousand.

Whether the later saga is true to history in representing the Hunnish foemen as having been led by Attila, we cannot tell. Paul the Deacon says it was so: but three centuries of heroic song separate him from the historic battle. Paul is obviously following an inaccurate popular account when he connects this battle with the great invasion of Gaul twenty years later, which resulted in Attila's repulse upon the Mauriac plain[3]. Elsewhere

---

[1] *Zur Geschichte der Nibelungensage* in *Z.f.d.A.* x, 148–9.

[2] [436] *Burgundiones, qui rebellaverant, a Romanis duce Aetio debellantur.* [437] *Burgundionum cæsa xx millia.* Hydatii *Continuatio Chronicorum* in Mommsen's *Chronica Minora*, vol. ii, pp. 22, 23 (*M.G.H.*).

[435] *Eodem tempore Gundicarium Burgundionum regem intra Gallias habitantem Aetius bello obtinuit* [read *obtrivit*] *pacemque ei supplicanti dedit: qua non diu potitus est; siquidem illum Hunni cum populo atque stirpe sua deleverunt.* Prosper Aquitanus, in Migne, li (1846), 596–7.

435. *Gundicharium Burgundionum regem Aetius bello subegit, pacemque ei reddidit supplicanti, quem non multo post Hunni peremerunt.* Cassiodori *Chronica* in Mommsen's *Chronica Minora*, ii, 156 (*M.G.H.*).

It is Sidonius Apollinaris who tells us that the occasion was an incursion into Belgica, in his Panegyric addressed to Avitus, c. 455 and therefore twenty years after the event.

Aetium interea, Scythico quia sæpe duello est
edoctus, sequeris; qui, quamquam celsus in armis,
nil sine te gessit, cum plurima tute sine illo.
nam post Iuthungos et Norica bella subacto
victor Vindelico Belgam, Burgundio quem trux
presserat, absolvit iunctus tibi.

Sidonii *Carminum* vii, 230–235. Ed. Luetjohann in *M.G.H.*

[3] *Historia Miscella*, recens. Franc. Eyssenhardt, Berolini, 1869, pp. 323, 332, *His etiam temporibus Gundicarium Burgundionum regem intra Gallias habitantem Aetius patricius bello optrivit pacemque ei supplicanti concessit* (Bk xiv, cap. 11). *Attila itaque primo impetu mox ut Gallias introgressus est, Gundicarium, Burgundionum regem, sibi occurrentem protrivit* (xv, 4).

he more accurately distinguishes between the two events[1].
Paul's account is chiefly to be valued as a witness to the
tradition of his day: Attila does not fall upon the Burgundians in their town of Worms; Gundahari marches eastward to meet his death, "postquam *sibi occurrentem* Attila
protriverat." This has ever been an essential feature of the
story, whether told in High German, Icelandic, or English :

We will go and look on Atli, though the Gods and the Goths forbid;
Nought worse than death meseemeth on the Niblungs' path is hid,
And this shall the high Gods see to, but I to the Niblung name,
And the day of deeds to accomplish, and the gathering-in of fame[2].

The statement that Gundahari was cut off with his race and
people is an exaggeration. A remnant was left, and some eight
or nine years after the disaster was settled in a new home in
Savoy. Burgundians played their part in the great battle
against Attila[3]. The nucleus (dwelling between the modern
Geneva and the modern Lyon) gradually extended their borders
till they again became a mighty nation. It was in these days
that, with their abundant animal spirits, their astonishing
appetites, and their more astonishing thirst, they vexed
Sidonius Apollinaris. The Burgundian code of laws, drawn
up before 516, under King Gundobad, contains a valuable
reference to "our ancestors of royal memory, Gibica, Gundo-
mar, Gislahari, Gundahari, our father and our uncle[4]."

---

[1] *Attila rex Hunorum, omnibus belluis crudelior, habens multas barbaras
nationes suo subjectas dominio, postquam Gundigarium, Burgundionum regem,
sibi occurrentem protriverat, ad universas deprimendas Gallias suæ sævitiæ
relaxavit habenas.*
    De episcopis Mettensibus, in Pertz (fol.), *SS.* t. II (1829), p. 262.
[2] William Morris—*Story of Sigurd the Volsung.*
[3] Jordanes, ed. Mommsen, xxxvi (191).
[4] *Si quos apud regiæ memoriæ auctores nostros, id est: Gibicam, Gundo-
marem* [or *Godomarem*], *Gislaharium, Gundaharium, patrem quoque nostrum
et patruum liberos liberasve fuisse constiterit, in eadem libertate permaneant.
Lex Burg.* p. 43, ed. L. R. de Salis, in *M.G.H.* Leges I, ii, 1. The correct
rendering of *auctores* has been disputed. Binding and Waitz translate "predecessors." Gundobad, they think, was not a descendant of the old reigning
house. Jahn on the other hand (pp. 300, 301, footnote) argues pretty conclusively that *auctores* here must mean ancestors. Müllenhoff and Bluhme
would make the new race of kings descendants of the old, and the fact that
their names are compounded out of the same elements tells in favour of this
(*Z.f.d.A.* x, 153–4; VII, 527).

Gifica and Gislhere.

The Gibica who thus stands at the head of the Burgundian line is clearly the Gifica of our poem, the Gibeche of High German, the Giuki of Scandinavian story. Whether he ever had any historic existence is uncertain. The name, for the founder of a dynasty, is suspicious, in view of the frequency of the terms *beaggifa, goldgifa, maððumgifa* as synonyms for "King[1]." No argument can be drawn from the occurrence of this name along with those of historical kings, in the Burgundian laws: the Burgundian of the sixth century had, of course, no doubts as to the historic existence of the ancestor of his kings. In any case Gifica's reign, whether actual or mythical, must be dated back to the old days when the Burgundians dwelt in the East, and were neighbours of the Ostrogoths in the forests of the Vistula. After the Burgundians were settled in the West there would be a natural tendency either to make him a king of the Burgundians in their new home; or, keeping him in the East, to forget his connection with the Burgundians altogether, and to make him a Hun or Goth. And, in different branches of the old tradition, we find both these things happening. In the Norse versions Giuki is father of Gunnar; and sometimes too in the High German stories Gibeche is the father of Gunter, and rules at Worms[2]. But in the *Nibelungen Lied*, Dankrat[3] is Gunter's father, while Gibeche is a champion of the Hunnish court[4].

Now it is noteworthy that when, in *Widsith*, Gifica is mentioned as ruling the Burgundians, it is in immediate connection with Ætla and the Huns, with Eormanric the Goth and Becca his liegeman, with the Kaiser who rules the Greeks, and with

---

[1] Wackernagel, *Sprachdenkmäler der Burgunden*, p. 389 (in C. Binding). Grimm (*Z.f.d.Ä.* I, 572–5) argues that the name, mythical in origin, ultimately came to signify a Giver half or entirely divine.

[2] As, for example, in the *Rosegarden at Worms*. In the *Waltarius* also, Gibicho is father of Guntharius.

[3] Grimm pointed out that Dankrat is possibly originally synonymous with Gibica (*Z.f.d.A.* II, 573). See also Jahn, 126.

[4] *Der Nibelunge Not*, ed. Bartsch, st. 1343, 1880. Compare *Dietrichs Flucht*, 7114, where Gibeche is a counsellor of Ermrich.

Cælic of the Finns. The poet who drew up these lines had learnt to think of Gifica as an Eastland hero: he probably knew lays which represented Burgundian and Goth as neighbours: he felt no difficulty at any rate in grouping them together[1].

The Gislhere who is mentioned subsequently in our poem with other heroes, presumably Gothic, is almost certainly to be identified with the King Gislaharius of the Burgundian laws. Later German tradition represents this prince as the chivalrous younger brother of Gunther, *Gîselher daz kint*[2]. But his place in the list, as given in the Burgundian laws, would make him a predecessor or ancestor; and this is borne out by the way in which his name occurs in *Widsith*. Ruling over the Burgundians whilst they were still close neighbours of the Goths, having dealings, whether in peace or war, with Gothic kings and champions, he has been drawn into the Gothic cycle exactly as has the Gibeche of *Dietrichs Flucht*, and like him is thought of as a retainer of Ermanaric, or at any rate as a hero of the Gothic cycle. That he was ever a Burgundian has apparently been forgotten.

---

[1] See note to l. 19.
[2] So in the *Thidreks saga* he is a younger brother (cap. 169). The part played by Gîselher in the *Nibelungen Lied* and *Thidreks saga* may, of course, be due not to continuous tradition but to subsequent learned influence. See Wilmanns *Untergang der Nibelunge*, 1903, pp. 23–4. Yet this seems improbable.

CHAPTER III.

THE STORIES KNOWN TO WIDSITH. TALES OF THE SEA-FOLK, OF THE FRANKS AND OF THE LOMBARDS.

The North-Sea tribes in the time of Tacitus. The Frisians and Finn.

HITHERTO we have been following the stories of those chiefs, Ermanaric, Attila, Gundahari, who led their German hordes within ken of the historians of the Roman Empire, and concerning whose historical existence we therefore have definite, if scanty, information. To turn from these stories to those of the North-Sea folk, the native stuff of our English heroic poets, is like moving from a room lighted by the occasional flash of a dying fire to one where we have to grope in absolute darkness. For to the Romans these Northern tribes were little known, and that chiefly during the struggle under Tiberius and Germanicus. It is one great merit of Tacitus' *Germania* that it preserves to us fragments of that information concerning our forefathers, which was acquired during this struggle. For by the time of Tacitus himself the Romans had withdrawn west of the Zuider Zee and of the Rhine: and these coast tribes had passed out of their sight[1].

The name *Ingaevones* which these coast tribes possessed in common rested, Tacitus tells us, upon a belief that they were all sprung from one eponymous ancestor Ing[2]. Most westerly

---

[1] Exactly to what extent the Romans came into contact with the Frisians is not certain. That the Frisian fisheries, on what is now the north coast of Holland, were at one time worked by Roman publicans has been proved by an inscription found near Leeuwarden. See *Mnemosyne*, xvi, 439, *De inscriptione romana apud Frisios reperta*, by U. Ph. Boissevain. There were Frisian contingents, too, in the Roman army.

[2] *Germania*, cap. ii.

of all these maritime peoples dwelt the Frisians, amid those
'vast lakes navigated by Roman fleets[1],' which have since become
the Zuider Zee. Tacitus recognises two groups of Frisians—
the Lesser Frisians, dwelling apparently to the west of these
lakes, near the Roman frontier, and the Greater Frisians,
dwelling in the unexplored marshes of the North and East.
Five or six centuries later, the same distinction seems to be
recognised by the poets of *Beowulf* and *Widsith*[2]. There are
the Western people, always associated with the Franks, against
whom Hygelac's raid was directed: and the main body of the
Frisians, whose traditional hero is Finn Folcwalding.

The tale of Finn must have been one of the best known
stories in seventh century England: of our five extant heroic
poems, or fragments of poems, three refer to it. The task of
harmonizing these references into one story is not an easy one.
But to investigate the Finn story in detail would take us too
far afield. The object of the present study is to see what we
can discover from *Widsith* about the lost Old English lays ; the
lay of Finnsburg is fortunately not all lost, and its reconstruction
demands a separate study[3]. The popularity of the story in
England is not to be attributed to Frisian immigrants[4]. In the
great fight in Finn's hall, most of the North-Sea tribes seem to
have claimed their share, and the tale was probably common at
an early date to them all, and was brought across the North
Sea by gleemen of Saxon and of Jutish race[5].

Chauci and Saxons.

The Frisians were divided from their next neighbours, the
Chauci, by much the same boundary as now separates the north
coast of Holland from that of Germany. All the space up to

---

[1] Cap. xxxiv. [2] See note to l. 68.

[3] References will be found in Brandl, in *Pauls Grdr.*(2) II, i, 986 and in Heyne-
Schücking, 112. For Finn Folcwalding see also Rieger, *Z.f.d.A.* xi, 200; Grimm,
D.M. 218; transl. Stallybrass, I. 219.

[4] Βριττίαν δὲ τὴν νῆσον ἔθνη τρία πολυανθρωπότατα ἔχουσι...Ἀγγίλοι τε καὶ
Φρίσσονες καὶ οἱ τῇ νήσῳ ὁμώνυμοι Βρίττωνες. Procopius, *Bell. Gott.* iv, 20.
But this statement as to Frisian immigrants lacks confirmation, and is
probably due to a confusion of Frisians and Saxons.

[5] Binz in *P.B.B.* xx, 179–186. Binz points out that men and places bearing
the names of heroes of the Finn story are found chiefly in Essex, and in that
part of Wessex which had originally a "Jutish" population: but not, oddly
enough, in Kent.

the Elbe was occupied by the Chauci, of whom Tacitus draws an idyllic picture. *Populus inter Germanos nobilissimus, quique magnitudinem suam malit justitia tueri. Sine cupiditate, sine impotentia quieti secretique nulla provocant bella*[1]. Beyond the Elbe, in Holstein, dwelt the Saxons, who, though they are strangely enough passed over in silence by Tacitus, are located by Ptolemy's reference to them as dwelling "upon the neck of the Cimbrian Peninsula."

By the fourth century the name of the Chauci has disappeared, and the whole district from Holstein to the Frisian border is apparently filled with people calling themselves Saxons[2]. Clearly some confederation, whether friendly or forcible, has taken place, by which the Saxon name has come to be applied to both people. The Saxons who colonized England include, then, the Chauci of Tacitus, in addition to the little tribe in Holstein which originally bore the Saxon name[3], but which clearly would not have sufficed to settle Essex, Middlesex, Sussex, Wessex, and the lands by the Severn.

The main body of the Saxons remained in Germany, but by constant conquest and assimilation of Frankish and Thuringian tribes, they became a great people, and at the same time lost their distinctively Anglo-Frisian character. Consequently the modern dialects of North-West Germany are not "Anglo-

---

[1] *Germania*, xxxv. The Chauci are classed by Pliny among the *Ingaevones, Nat. Hist.* iv, 14 (28) "*Ingyaeones quorum pars...Chaucorum gentes.*"

[2] Probably the change took place in the third century, when the Saxon name again meets us for the first time since Ptolemy, whilst the name Chauci disappears (see Weiland, 26–7). Hence there is no mention of the Chauci in *Widsith*, unless we are to accept the exceedingly doubtful conjecture of Müllenhoff (see note to l. 63). Grimm (*G.D.S.*, 675, on which see Rieger,'*Z.f.d.A.* xi, 186–7) would see possible survivals of the name Chauci in the *Hugas* of Beowulf and the *Hôcingas* of *Widsith*. In the latter conjecture Grimm had been anticipated by Müllenhoff, *Nordalb. Stud.* i, 157; in the former by Ettmüller[1] 16. Neither conjecture seems likely. It has been urged in support that the district near the modern Groningen was of old called *Hugmerke*, which has been interpreted "the border of the Hugas" (Chauci). But the support to be derived from this is weak geographically, for there is no evidence that the Chauci ever extended so far west; and weak etymologically, for other interpretations of *Hugmerke* need to be considered. See Richthofen, *Untersuchungen über Friesische Rechtsgeschichte*, Berlin, 1882, Th. ii, Bd 2, pp. 754–5; and cf. Weiland, 29. That *Hugas* is equivalent to *Chauci* has been maintained by Much (94); for reasons to the contrary cf. Loewe in *I. F., Beiblatt*, xiv, 22.

[3] Möller, *V.E.* 84; Weiland, 31.

Frisian[1]," and the *Heliand,* or the Old Saxon *Genesis,* though
they perhaps show "Anglo-Frisian" peculiarities, are not
written in an "Anglo-Frisian" dialect. These poems, though
Christian in subject matter, are in style and spirit closely akin
to the old heroic poetry[2]: whilst the old tales of Ermanaric and
Gundahari, Weland and Wade, must have lived on side by side
with the religious poetry, till they were woven by a Norwegian
of the 13th century into a more or less continuous story around
the figure of Theodoric of Verona. This *Thidreks saga,* Norse
in diction but Saxon in origin, gives as we have seen the most
valuable sidelights upon the English, as well as upon the Norse
and High German versions of the old tales.

The Worshippers of Nerthus.

East and north of the Saxons and Chauci dwelt, in the days
of Tacitus, a confederation of tribes[3]. Unfortunately, no common
name has been preserved, but we know from Tacitus that the
Reudigni, Aviones, Angli, Varini, Eudoses, Suardones, Nuithones,
dwelt among fastnesses of wood and water and worshipped in
common Nerthus—that is, Mother Earth—believing her to
intervene in human affairs.

There is a sacred grove in an island of the ocean, and in the grove a
car, dedicated and veiled. One priest alone has access to it. He can
tell when the goddess is present, and he attends her as she is drawn by
a team of cows in reverent procession. Then there is holiday wherever
the goddess condescends to visit as a guest: they do not go forth to
war; they do not take up arms; all weapons are laid aside: then and
then only peace is known and loved, till the same priest brings back the

---

[1] See Bremer in *Pauls Grdr.* (2) III, 850, 860–73.

[2] Nowhere is the loyalty of the *gesith* to his lord shown better than in the
relation between Satan and his followers in the Old Saxon Genesis, as represented in the so-called *Cædmon,* or the relation of Thomas to his Lord, as shown
in the *Heliand* (3993–4002). Cf. Olrik, *Heltedigtning,* 81.

[3] Tacitus mentions these peoples among the Suevic tribes, who often have
been considered as more or less equivalent to the "inland" Herminones. Yet
these seven tribes certainly dwelt *proximi Oceano,* and should therefore rather
be classed among the Ingaevones. They were certainly "Anglo-Frisian."
Tacitus has been enumerating the inland people, and as he goes north he
continues to enumerate among the Suevic peoples first the Lombards, then the
Angles (note, however, that *Widsith* distinguishes Engle and Swæfe whilst
grouping them together). But Tacitus admits ignorance: *Et hæc quidem pars
Suevorum in secretiora Germaniæ porrigitur. Propior, ut...Danubium sequar,
Hermundurorum civitas.* Accordingly he proceeds to trace the Suevi along the
more familiar border lands of the Danube.

goddess to her grove, tired of human converse. Car, draperies and, if you will believe it, the very divinity are washed in a secret lake, in which lake the slaves who do the work are forthwith drowned. Hence a mystic terror and a pious ignorance of what that may be which is seen only by those destined to die.

Strange has been the history of this goddess Nerthus in modern times. Sixteenth century scholars[1] found irresistible the temptation to emend the name of "Mother Earth" into *Herthum*, which nineteenth century scholars further improved into *Hertham, Ertham*. For many years this false goddess drove out the rightful deity from the fortieth chapter of the *Germania*[2]. Antiquaries identified the "island of the ocean" with Rügen, which happened to possess a convenient lake, and diligent enquiries as to Hertha in that locality succeeded at last in inoculating the inhabitants with a tradition regarding her. According to one assertion, she even found her way into the proverbs of the Pomeranian peasantry[3]. And so an early Teutonic goddess Hertha was turned loose into the field of comparative mythology. Without wishing to trespass on that field, or rather

> Serbonian bog
> Where armies whole have sunk,

it is enough to state that there can be no doubt that the correct reading in the *Germania* is *Nerthus*, and that no goddess Hertha was ever worshipped by the ancient Angles. The Scandinavian form corresponding to *Nerthus* would be *Njǫrthr*, and such a god[4] was worshipped with his son Ingvifreyr at old Uppsala, with rites resembling those which Tacitus describes as rendered

---

[1] Perhaps we might say fifteenth century scribes: for some transcripts of the *Germania* of that period read *Herthum*, and one even *nisi quod mammenerthū* (see *Germania*, ed. Massmann, 1847, pp. 18, 118). It must have been upon this reading that Holder based his *Mammum Erthum*—Mother Earth (*Germania*, ed. Holder, 1882).

[2] Amongst editors who have bowed the knee to Hertha may be mentioned Oberlin (1801), Bekker (1825), Walther (1833), Ritter (1834, 1836), Kritz (1860, *Ertham*). The Aldine edition of 1534 reads *Herthum*, following the reading of Beatus Rhenanus in his edition of the preceding year.

[3] Grimm, trans. Stallybrass, I, 256; Müllenhoff, *D.A.*, IV, 470–1.

[4] The change in sex would be rendered easier by the fact that the u-stems were always, in the main, masculine, and in Norse became exclusively so. A stage at which a male and a female Nerthus were venerated side by side seems to be indicated by *Heimskringla*, I, 4; *Lokasenna*, 36. For Njǫrth, see Mogk in *Pauls Grdr.*(2) III, 323 *etc.*, 367 *etc.*; R. Meyer, 204 *etc.*; Golther, 218 *etc.*, 456 *etc.* For the change from Feminine to Masculine see Kock in *Z.f.d.A.* XXVIII, 289, *Historisk Tidskrift* (Stockholm) 1895, 166, *note*.

to Nerthus. The coupling of Ingvifreyr with Njǫrth suggests the question whether Ing—otherwise known as Frea, the lord—may not have been coupled with Nerthus in the worship upon the isle of the ocean.

The island centre of this Nerthus-worship we might at first sight be tempted to identify with Heligoland—the "Holy Island" of the North Sea[1]. But that little rock, with its grass-crowned red cliffs, and its stretches of white sand, could never have given root to the sacred grove of the goddess[2]. We must rather place this in one of the (now Danish) islands near the Great Belt: perhaps in Zealand[3], from which the spreading of the cult across the Sound to the Scandinavian lands can have most easily taken place. It is highly probable, at any rate, that the sanctuary was situated in one of the islands of the Baltic. For there is hardly room to locate the seven tribes of Tacitus all upon the mainland; some of them must have occupied the adjacent Baltic islands.

The limits of Angel.

Offa weold Ongle...
ac Offa geslog ærest monna
cnihtwesende cynerica mæst.

The best of all possible evidence that the Angles and their kindred tribes once held the islands adjoining is given by a passage added to the old English translation of Orosius, in which Ohthere describes to his lord, King Alfred, his voyage from *Sciringesheal* (in the Bay of Christiania) to *æt Haethum*

---

[1] The identity of Heligoland and of the island sacred to Nerthus has been maintained by Schade (*Die Sage von der heiligen Ursula*, Hannover, 1854, pp. 113–118). Beyond the fact of Heligoland having been in later times a sacred island, and having possessed a sacred spring, there is little to be said in favour of the identification, and much against it. Tacitus' description seems to demand either an island large enough for the processions of the goddess, or sufficiently near to the mainland to allow the chariot and its team of cattle to be ferried across. Cf. also Müllenhoff in *Nordalb. Stud.* I, 128. Weiland in 1889 thought it "no longer open to doubt that the sacred island of Nerthus was in the North Sea, not in the Baltic" (*Die Angeln*, 9). Recent criticism has tended to reverse this judgement.

[2] *habet arborem nullam.* Adam of Bremen, IV, 3, in Pertz (fol.) *SS.* VII, p. 369.

[3] Much in *P.B.B.* XVII, 195–8.

(Haddeby, the modern Schleswig). The voyage takes five days. For the first three he sails south down the Cattegatt. "Then was Denmark" [the original home of the Danes in Southern Sweden, which till many years later was an essential part of Denmark] "Then was Denmark to his left, and the open sea to his right, three days." [Here Ohthere reaches the Sound.] "And then, two days before he came to Haddeby, was Jutland to his right, and Sillende [? Zealand¹], and many islands. *In those lands dwelt the Angles, before they came hither to this land.*" [Having passed the Sound, Ohthere has to turn to the right, and steers his way amid the islands, keeping Zealand (and Jutland) still on his right, but having to his left the smaller islands Falster and Laaland, which are mentioned just below as belonging to the Danes.] "And then for two days he had on his left the islands which belong to Denmark."

The importance of this passage can hardly be exaggerated. King Alfred, we have seen, was deeply versed in old English poetry, and must have known dozens of lays, lost to us, dealing with the old kings of Angel, their tributary kings, their feuds and alliances with other Baltic-Sea folk. And here we have an authority which we can hardly regard (in this part, at any rate, of the Orosius) as other than that of Alfred himself, making not merely Jutland, but also many islands, part of the original Anglian home.

The whole of this territory was probably, in the first century, occupied by the Nerthus-worshipping people. Exactly how we locate or identify the seven tribes mentioned by Tacitus does not really much matter. Tacitus has been enumerating tribes from south to north—first the Semnones, then the Langobardi—

---

¹ Sillende is probably Zealand (O.N. *Selund,* or *Silund,* called sometimes *Siellendia, Sjalendia,* in Latin-Danish documents). The difficulties which have been raised with respect to this passage are quite gratuitous. It is unnecessary to apologize for taking the "Denmark" on Ohthere's left as Southern Sweden, by the plea that "Southern Sweden was then in the hands of Denmark" (*M.L.R.* IV, 273). This district was *then* as much a part of Denmark as Jutland is now: and Alfred, like Adam of Bremen, calls it by its name. The Sweden of this date was a most restricted area. The difficulty arises only if we insist upon understanding Alfred's terms in their twentieth century meaning. The alteration of the text suggested by Schück (*Folknamnet Geatas,* p. 19) is unnecessary. See Appendix L, *The geography of the Orosius compared with that of Widsith.*

and the use of the word *deinde* implies that he is still enumerating them in this order: and so far as we can check him we find that he is. The Reudigni, then, would be most to the south, in Holstein. But on this "neck of the Peninsula" Ptolemy placed the Saxons. One critic therefore supposes "Reudigni" to be a nickname of the Saxons[1]. The arguments in favour of this identification are exceedingly inconclusive, but there is nothing to be said against it; and as it enables us to find a home for the Reudigni, who would otherwise be destitute, and at the same time accounts for the extraordinary omission of the Saxons by Tacitus, it seems convenient to accept it as a possible hypothesis[1]. Then come, in Tacitus' enumeration, the Aviones and the Angli. The modern *Angeln* enables us to locate the Angli *proper* in *and around* southern Schleswig: the Aviones, as neighbours both of the Saxons and of the Angles, are most easily placed in Fünen and the other islands. Following a hint of J. Grimm[2], Much[3] would interpret the name with great probability as the "island folk," and this interpretation supports the theory of their home in the Baltic Isles. The Aviones are, in all probability[4], to be identified with the Eowan, who are mentioned, together with a number of these sea-folk, and their heroes, in *Widsith*.

> Breoca [weold] Brondingum, Billing Wernum;
> Oswine weold Eowum, and Ytum Gefwulf,
> Fin Folcwalding Fresna cynne.
> Sigehere lengest Sæ-Denum weold.

The Varini are certainly[4] the Wernas of *Widsith*: following Tacitus, we should expect to find them just north of the Angles in northern Schleswig: and traces of their name are still to be found there. With less certainty, though still with some probability[4], we can identify the Eudoses with the Ytas of our poem and with the Jutae, who, according to Bede, colonized Kent and the Isle of Wight. Following Tacitus, we should put them

---

[1] Much in *P.B.B.* XVII, 191-5. Müllenhoff hazarded the guess that the name Reudigni was that of a small people subsequently merged in the more comprehensive Saxons (*Nordalb. Stud.* I, 119). See also Weiland, p. 27.

[2] *G.D.S.* (first ed.) 472, (fourth ed.) 330. But Müllenhoff had anticipated Grimm, *Nordalb. Stud.* I, 118 (1844).

[3] *P.B.B.* XVII, 195.

[4] See the footnotes to *Wernum, Eowum* (ll. 25, 26) and note on *Ytum* (Appendix D, *The Jutes*).

in southern Jutland, the more so as this agrees with Bede's information about the Jutes. There is still territory left in the north of Jutland in which to settle the Suardones [or Suarines] and Nuithones—the former conceivably identical with the Sweordweras of our poem[1].

Most, then, of what is now Denmark and Schleswig-Holstein was in the days of Tacitus held by the Nerthus-tribes, with the Angles dwelling in the centre, and probably, at any rate at a later date, giving their name to the whole confederation. For it is not likely that Britain, from the Forth to the Stour, and the Wash to the Severn, was conquered and settled by the little central people alone: and, though we cannot trace in English place-names any of the minor tribes except the Varini and the Jutes, the evidence of Alfred, who brings the *Engle* from Jutland and the islands, shows that *he* at least believed that all joined in the settlement of England. It is of particular importance to the study of *Widsith* to observe clearly what Alfred says. For several eminent scholars[2], assuming that King Alfred and Bede state that the Angles came from Angel, and that the ancient Angel must necessarily have been coterminous with the modern Angeln, have argued: that Angeln cannot have been the home of the ancient Angles, because it is too small to have held them all: that therefore King Alfred and Bede are wrong, and that the home of the Angles was somewhere far inland, on the banks of the middle and upper Elbe. This view cannot be passed over in silence by a student of *Widsith*, since our poem definitely localizes Offa, King of the Angles, in Angel. If, then, the connection between the Angles and Angeln rests, as Zeuss thought, upon a piece of false etymology of Bede's time or a little earlier, we must not attribute *Widsith*, in its present form, to a period much earlier than Bede. The assumption that the ancient Angel was no larger than the modern Angeln is, however, a gratuitous one: on the contrary, we have only to think of Cumberland, Northumberland, Lombardy, Burgundy, Servia to see that when a national name remains, while the nation, as such, is passing

---

[1] Although the two names do not correspond phonetically. See note to l. 62.
[2] E.g. Zeuss, 496; Steenstrup in *Danmarks Riges Historie*, I, 76-77.

away, the waning of the nation is naturally accompanied by a shrinkage in the application of the name. Alfred's statement as to the wide extent of the territory occupied by the Angles before their emigration to Britain may be taken as indicating that here, as everywhere else in Germany, a confederation of the smaller tribes of Tacitus' day had taken place, and that the name Angli had come to be applicable to the whole or a great portion of the Nerthus-worshipping tribes.

The Danes.

The immediate neighbours of the Angles (using the term in the broad sense) were the Danes, dwelling originally on what is now the southern coast of Sweden[1]. These two seafaring people, separated only by the narrow seas, must have been emphatically either friends or enemies. Especially must this have been the case after the Angles began to migrate to Britain and the Danes began to settle in the vacant lands— two events which followed hard upon one another. The emigration of the Angles, we know, lasted through the latter half of the fifth century and great part of the sixth. Already by the beginning of the sixth century, Danes had probably occupied most of Jutland as well as Zealand[2]. By the end of the sixth century, it is asserted, they were in possession up to the Eider[3]. Now this Danish settlement may have been a hostile one ; but, on the other hand, it may have taken place by a friendly arrangement, an understanding that Danish immigrants might claim any vacant land, but must not disturb such of the old inhabitants as chose to remain behind. A friendly settlement

---

[1] It must be noted that although Tacitus, Pliny and Ptolemy know the Cimbric Chersonnese, and Ptolemy knows it well, none of them know of the Danes, unless the Danes are to be identified with the Δαυκίωνες of Ptolemy II, 11, 16. The Daukiones are neighbours of the Goutai in the south of Skandia. Jordanes (cap. III, 23) mentions the Danes, and the context would lead us to suppose that he placed them in Scandinavia. From a passage in Procopius (*Bell. Gott.* II, 15) we should gather that there were Danes in Jutland about the year 510, and from this time onward mention of the Danes is fairly frequent. As the Angles pass into Britain, the Danes, stepping into their places, come within the view of the Roman and Greek writers.

[2] See Moller *V.E.* 5 (footnote).

[3] Bremer in *Pauls Grdr.*(2) III, 837.

seems quite likely on *a priori* grounds. It is true that we hear
little of such arrangements during these centuries, because the
historians are only concerned with territorial squabbles just
when they lead to big battles and wholesale slaughter; yet
the constant migrations would have been impossible without
some mutual understandings. The battles we hear of spring
from those cases where rival claims could not be harmonized[1].
Beowulf shows that the northern courts of the sixth or seventh
century were not ignorant of diplomacy. And in the case we
are considering there would be no cause for quarrel. Danish
settlers would find enough vacant land, and more than enough,
for Angel proper remained desert till Bede's time. The waning
Anglian folk, deprived of their best warriors, and left with more
old men, women, children and cattle than they could well
protect, would live in fear of sea-raids of Vikings, whether
Heruli or Heathobards, or land raids from the Suevic folk to
the south, who had ancient grudges to pay off dating from the
time of Offa. The remaining Angles would see with satisfac-
tion stalwart Danes coming, not to plunder, but to settle and to
take up land in neighbourhoods which had been left naked and
defenceless[2]. The newcomers would soon, and all the more
quickly if they started with a common ancestral hatred for
Heathobard plunderers, be united to the old inhabitants by
their common interest in defending the country. There is a
good deal of circumstantial evidence that things happened in
this way.

Saxo Grammaticus begins his Danish history with the
brothers Dan and Angul[3]. He describes them as the joint
founders and rulers of the Danish race: from Dan sprang the
royal line of Denmark; whilst Angul gave his name to the

---

[1] Cf. Gregory of Tours, *Historia Francorum*, v, 15. A quarrel arises from
the unexpected return of a tribe to territories which they had vacated, and
which they find occupied by new settlers. Negociations take place, which
break down owing to the excessive claims of the original owners. Definite
agreements between tribes who invaded new lands and those who occupied their
old homes are mentioned by Procopius, *Bell. Vand.* I, and Paul the Deacon, II, 7.

[2] The Danes in *Widsith* and *Beowulf* are not a sea-roving people, but are
rather busied in defending their own borders from pirates.

[3] *Dan igitur et Angul, a quibus Danorum cepit origo...non solum conditores
gentis nostre, verum eciam rectores fuere* (Saxo, I, 1). See also Bremer in *Pauls
Grdr.*(2) III, 853.

province he ruled, and his successors, when they obtained possession of Britain, changed its name to a new one derived from their fatherland. Now the Danes must have been quite aware that the English, with their widely-differing dialect, were not as near of kin to them as the Swedes, Geats, and Norwegians, who spoke an almost identical tongue. The place of honour given to Angul as one of the two sources of the Danish race probably points back to a time when Danish bards and genealogists were conscious that their nation contained an Anglian element.

Again, we have seen that the cult of Ing and Nerthus spread into the heart of Sweden. This cult can have passed from the isle of the ocean mentioned by Tacitus to old Uppsala only through the intermediate Danes, who still at this time held the whole of what is now the south coast of Sweden; and friendly relations and inter-marriage rather than incessant warfare would make it easy for the Ingaevonian worship to spread among the Danes, till we find in *Beowulf* an Anglian poet bestowing upon them the title of "friends of Ing[1]." The Angles came to regard the Danes as peculiarly the worshippers of Ing, for at last an English poet says "Ing was first seen among the east Danish folk[2]."

The silence of our authorities is also strong evidence that the Danish settlement of Anglian lands was a quiet and peaceable one. Had there been a protracted struggle between Angle and Dane, heroic defences of old halls against overmastering odds, these things would probably have passed into legend and song. But we hear nothing of such contests. On the contrary, every reference to the Danes in old English verse

---

[1] Hrothgar is twice called protector or prince of the Friends of Ing, *eodor Ingwina* (1044), *frea Ingwina* (1320). His more usual title is *frea* (*eodor*) *Scildinga*. It would be interesting to know whether an English poet of the seventh century regarded *Ingwine* and *Scildingas* as synonyms, or if the names are felt to refer to two sections of a mixed people, over whom the Danish king rules. Cf. Sarrazin in *Engl. Stud.* XLII, 3, 11, etc.

[2]
> *Ing wæs ærest mid East Denum*
> *gesewen secgun, oþ he siðða est* [*eft* Grein, Kluge]
> *ofer wæg gewat; wæn æfter ran;*
> *ðus Heardingas ðone hæle nemdun.*
>
> *Runic Poem* (67–70).

We must not however forget that Tacitus does not count the Nerthus-tribes as Ingaevones, but as Suevi.

is couched in the most friendly and respectful tone : a tone which would be inconceivable if the English settlers had sailed from the old Angle land leaving behind them burning home-steads, slaughtered friends, and triumphant Danes[1].

And this gradual settlement of the Danes amid the gradually departing Anglian tribes would explain why old English poetry is interested in the Danes: their kings, their foes, and above all their great Hall. It is not, as we might too hastily assume from *Beowulf,* that the English were normally more concerned with the doings of Scandinavian kings than with those of their own heroes; for *Beowulf* is exceptional in the interest shown in the warfare of Swedes and Geats. Putting together all the references we can find in English to heroic stories, we find no particular interest in these matters[2]. Geats and Swedes and the Swedish king Ongendtheow are just mentioned in *Widsith*. But on the other hand in *Widsith* we hear of four different Danish kings: Alewih, Sigehere, Hrothwulf and Hrothgar; whilst the fight at Heorot must have been very well known, for the names of the hostile chiefs, Froda and Ingeld, are to be met with often enough in England[3]. Alcuin the Northumbrian, writing to a bishop of Lindisfarne, quotes Ingeld as the typical hero of song[4]. That the English should have long felt an interest in the fate of Heorot is, after all, natural, when we remember that the ground on which it stood had perhaps been theirs, and may have been an Anglian stronghold or sacred place. Bold theorists have even

---

[1] The argument is stated very well by Müllenhoff, *Beovulf*, 88. But the case is even stronger than Müllenhoff saw; for the lines in *Widsith* do not point to any conflict between Offa and Alewih the Dane. It is merely stated that Alewih, though the bravest of men, did not surpass Offa (see note to l. 37). The name of Alewih was remembered in Mercia, and comes into the pedigree of Offa II. See also Weiland, p. 40; otherwise Binz in *P.B.B.* xx, 169.

[2] The name *Hygelac* is met not infrequently in northern England.

[3] See Binz in *P.B.B.* xx, 173–4.

[4] *Verba dei legantur in sacerdotali convivio; ibi decet lectorem audiri, non citharistam, sermones patrum, non carmina gentilium. Quid Hinieldus cum Christo?* The king of Heaven must not be mentioned with pagan kings who are now lamenting in Hell. The passage is quoted by Oskar Jänicke in his *Zeugnisse und Excurse zur deutschen Heldensage* (*Z.f.d.A.* xv, 314), on the authority of a MS of which he does not give particulars. The reference to Ingeld does not occur in the received text (*Letter to Speratus*, ed. Froben, 1, 1, 77). It will be found however in P. Jaffé's *Monumenta Alcuiniana* (*Bibliotheca Rer. Germ.* VI), Berlin, 1873, p. 357 ; *Epistolæ*, 81.

identified the town where Hrothgar built Heorot[1] with the sacred place of the Nerthus-cult: and the holy grove with its dread lake in Tacitus may remind us of the mere, overshadowed by trees, in *Beowulf.*

The onslaught at Heorot.

Hroþwulf and Hroðgar...
forheowan æt Heorote Heaðo-Beardna þrym.

The chief value of the references to Heorot in *Widsith* lies in their correcting the impressions which we get from *Beowulf.* Heorot is not thought of by our poet as the place where Beowulf fights with monsters, but as the scene of a struggle between Danes and Heathobards.

This struggle is not forgotten in *Beowulf,* but it is pushed into the background, and appears as a mere ornament to decorate the speech of the hero, and show his foresight. Beowulf, on his return home, tells his king how the old feud between Dane and Heathobard has for the moment been settled, and how Freawaru, the daughter of Hrothgar, has been given in marriage to Ingeld, the son of the Heathobard chief Froda, who had fallen in the feud. But the peace, Beowulf thinks, will not be lasting. Some survivor of the fight will urge on the younger man to revenge, showing him a young Dane wearing his father's sword:

Canst thou, my lord, tell the sword, the dear iron, which thy father carried to the fight, when he bore helm for the last time, where the Danes slew him and had the victory?...And now here the son of one of those slayers paces the hall, proud of his arms, boasts of the slaughter and wears the precious sword which thou by right shouldst wield.

Nothing could better show the disproportion of *Beowulf,* which "puts the irrelevances in the centre and the serious things on the outer edges[2]," than this passing allusion to the story of Ingeld. For in this conflict between plighted troth

---

[1] See Much in *P.B.B.* xvii, 196–8, Mogk in *Pauls Grdr.*(2) iii, 367, Kock in *Historisk Tidskrift* (Stockholm) 1895, 162–3, identifying Leithra with the Nerthus-temple; and an article by Sarrazin, *Die Hirsch-Halle,* in *Anglia,* xix, 368–91; also his *Neue Beowulfstudien* and *Der Grendelsee* in *Engl. Stud.* xlii, 6–13, identifying both Leithra and the Nerthus-temple with Heorot.

[2] Ker, *Dark Ages,* 253.

and the duty of revenge we have a situation which the old heroic poets loved, and would not have sold for a wilderness of dragons.

Perhaps the speech of the old warrior in *Beowulf* is taken, with little or no modification, from an Ingeld lay[1]. In any case, this egging on is evidently an essential, perhaps the essential part of the story, for it reappears in the Danish song, as paraphrased by Saxo Grammaticus. His version however is distorted. Frotho, the ancient foe of the Danes, has become a Danish king[2], slain by the Saxons. Yet the speech of the *eald œscwiga* survived these changes, and has provided Saxo with material for eighty sapphic stanzas.

> Ut quid, Ingelle, vicio sepultus
> Vindicem patris remoraris ausum?
> Num pii cladem genitoris equo
> Pectore duces?......
>
> Re magis nulla cuperem beari
> Si tui, Frotho, juguli nocentes
> Debitas tanti sceleris viderem
> Pendere penas[3].

Needless to say the old warrior's egging on is successful. Ingellus is stirred, and successfully avenges his father. Saxo is correct, in so far as he preserves the tradition of a Danish victory. For *Widsith* shows us that in the original story the Danes were victorious; but both *Widsith* and *Beowulf* show that in this story Ingeld was the leader, not of the victorious Danes, but of their defeated foemen[4]. Probably

---

[1] Müllenhoff, *Beovulf*, 43; Möller, *V.E.* 105.

[2] Hence the degradation of Frothi in later Scandinavian tradition, where he becomes a slayer of his kin (*Saga of Rolf Kraki*, *Gróttasǫngr*). This is because Frothi, having been taken into the line of Danish kings, could be regarded as having a feud with the family of Halfdan only by the supposition of domestic strife. Cf. Neckel, *Studien über Fróði* in *Z.f.d.A.* xlviii, 182, and Heusler, *Zur Skiöldungendichtung* in *Z.f.d.A.* xlvii, 57.

[3] Ed. Holder, pp. 205-13. For a parallel between the *wicinga cynn* of *Widsith* and the viking life as outlined in the song translated by Saxo, cf. Neckel in *Z.f.d.A.* xlviii, 183 *etc.*

[4] Koegel has argued that Saxo, in representing the attacking party as Danes, is true to the original version. He thinks that in this original story Hrothgar and his people were Angles of the islands, defending their homes, still with success, against the forward pressing Danes (*Heaðo-beardan*). Later, in the 7th or 8th century, when the fact that of old the Angles dwelt on the islands of the Cattegatt had been forgotten, it was assumed that a king ruling there must necessarily have been a Dane, and the story recast accordingly (*Ltg.* i, 1, 157). Not only is there much to be said against this interpretation, but also the grounds upon which it rests are quite unsound, for

Ingeld[1] was slain in this struggle, and certainly the *eald æscwiga* fell, fighting to the last. In Scandinavian story the death of this old warrior, Starkath, was remembered, though not in connection with Ingeld's revenge. According to one version his severed head bit the earth when it met the ground: in another story "the trunk fought on when the head was gone[2]."

The Lords of Heorot.

Hroþwulf and Hroðgar heoldon lengest
sibbe ætsomne suhtorfædran.

It was possible for Saxo to transform the foes of the Danes, Frotho and his son Ingellus, into Danish kings without deposing their adversaries Rolf and Roe (Hrothwulf and Hrothgar) from their true place as Danish monarchs. For he has divorced the story of Ingellus' revenge entirely from that of Hrothgar and his kin, which he gives in a quite different part of his book.

This Danish story of Hrothgar and Hrothwulf, though it preserves the kinship exactly as in the old English tradition, represents differently the parts played by the members of the Danish house towards each other. It is preserved not only in Saxo, but also in the *Saga of Rolf Kraki*, which was written down from tradition some two centuries after Saxo's time. Haldanus as Saxo calls him, Halfdan as he is in the *Saga*, leaves two sons Roe (Hroarr) and Helgo (Helgi). Roe rules Denmark and founds Roskild, but Helgo becomes a mighty sea-king—he is, in fact, that Helgi Hundingsbane who is the hero of the Eddic *Helgi* lays. In time Roe is slain—his slayer in Saxo is called Hodbroddus, in which name we may perhaps see

(1) we have seen that even in the 9th century the fact that the Angles had once held the islands of the Cattegatt was *not* forgotten, and (2) it is nowhere explicitly stated in *Beowulf* or *Widsith* that Hrothgar did rule these islands. We simply infer it from the fact that he and his people are called *Scyldingas, Dene*. There are in fact no geographical data in *Beowulf* sufficient to enable us to identify Hrothgar as a Dane: we only know that he is one because the poet tells us so. Had Hrothgar been an Angle in the original story, there is, then, nothing to have prevented him from having been localized in England, as, in spite of much more serious difficulties, Offa was.

[1] Sarrazin has suggested a connection between our Ingeld and another Ingellus of Saxo (Book II, ed. Holder, p. 56). See *Engl. Stud.* XXIII, 233. There seems very little in favour of this.

Saxo VIII (ed. Holder, p. 274); *Helga kviþa Hundingsbana*, II, 19. See also Bugge, *H.D.* 157.

a survival of the Heathobeardan, the foes of Hrothgar in *Widsith*[1]. But Helgo avenges his brother, and in course of time is succeeded on the throne of Denmark by his son Roluo (Hrolfr Kraki).

In *Beowulf* the same four Danish chiefs meet us. The "high" Healfdene has sons Heorogar (not paralleled in Saxo), Hrothgar and Halga the good[2]. But Hrothgar is not, as in Danish tradition, slain in war, and avenged by Halga: on the contrary, he outlives Halga, and we find him both in *Beowulf* and *Widsith* with a nephew Hrothulf, who is evidently Halga's son.

For a very long[3] time did Hrothwulf and Hrothgar keep the peace together.

These words, in *Widsith*, seem to imply that at length the bond between Hrothwulf and Hrothgar *was* broken: and that it was we gather also from the hints in *Beowulf*, where we see Hrothulf always overshadowing Hrothgar's sons and nephew,— those younger cousins who should stand nearer to the throne than he.

In *Beowulf* it is to be noted that, although Halga is clearly the younger brother, his orphan son Hrothulf is represented as older than Hrethric and Hrothmund, the sons of king Hrothgar. For Hrothulf has won his place of honour, and is allowed to sit side by side with the king; "where the two good ones sat, uncle and nephew: *as yet* was there peace between them, and each was true to the other[4]." Hrothgar's sons on the other hand have to sit with the juniors, the *giogoth*[5]. About Heoroweard, the son of the elder brother Heorogar who had reigned before Hrothgar, little is said expressly in *Beowulf*: but it is evident that he too has been overshadowed.

Everywhere we see, hanging in the background, like a black thunder cloud, the rivalry which is to arise between the too-

[1] See Bugge, *H.D.* 153–8, 181; Boer in *P.B.B.* xxii, 377–8; Sarrazin in *Engl. Stud.* xxiii, 233–5; xxviii, 411; Chadwick, 300. The conjecture that the Hothbrodd of Saxo and of the *Helgi* lays is a personification of the *Heathobeardan* was made independently by Bugge, Boer and Sarrazin. It seems exceedingly probable, in view of the way in which kingly and tribal names interchange. Cf. *Ostrogotha, Hocing, Hunding, Scylding.*
[2] Enumerated in order of age, as is proved by ll. 465–9.
[3] Literally "for the longest time," *lengest.* See note to l. 45.
[4] 1163–5.
[5] 1188–91.

mighty Hrothulf and his young cousins. Equally with the poet
of *Widsith*, the poet of *Beowulf* cannot mention Hrothulf and
Hrothgar together without foreboding evil:

> Hrothgar and Hrothulf. Heorot was filled full of friends : *at that time*
> the mighty Scylding folk in no wise worked treachery[1].

But the impending evils are alluded to most clearly in the
"tragic irony" with which the *Beowulf* poet makes Hrothgar's
queen refer to Hrothulf and his future bearing toward her sons.
Addressing Hrothgar, she says:

> I know that my gracious Hrothulf will support the young princes
> in honour, if thou, friend of the Scyldings, shouldst leave the world sooner
> than he. I ween that he will well requite our children, if he remembers
> all which we two have done for his pleasure and honour, being yet a
> child.
> Then turned she to the bench where her children were, Hrethric
> and Hrothmund[2].

The story has been lost: but fitting together one obscure
allusion in Saxo, which he himself reproduced without understanding[3], with a name in an old genealogy, we find, almost
beyond doubt, that Hrothulf not only deposed but also slew this
young Hrethric.

It is in contrast with this tragic background that the poet
of *Beowulf* emphasizes the generous confidence towards each
other of Beowulf and his kinsman, king Hygelac. After
Beowulf, like a good thane, has presented to his lord the
spoils he has just won, the poet moralizes, "So should a
kinsman do: and not weave a net of malice for another with
secret craft: nor prepare death for his comrade in arms." Such
comment seems harsh, and the allusion to treachery uncalled
for, until we notice *what* that present is which Beowulf has just
given to his lord. It is a war-panoply, which of old belonged
to Hrothgar's brother, King Heorogar, but which has *not* been
given to Heoroweard, Heorogar's son. No: the armour has
been given to Beowulf the stranger, and Heoroweard has been
deprived of his father's weapons. Small wonder if later he is

---

[1] 1017–19.　　　　　　　[2] 1180–9.

[3] Saxo, ɪɪ (ed. Holder, p. 62). Roluo is referred to as *Qui natum Bøki Røricum
stravit avari* : the reign of Roricus is placed by Saxo after that of Roluo (Books
ɪɪɪ and ɪv) : Saxo does not connect him with Røricus son of Bøkus. In *Lang-
feðgatal* we have *Hrærekr Hnauggvanbaugi* son of Ingiald, and *Hrærekr
Slaungvanbaugi* son of Halfdan. See Langebek ɪ, 5.

contemptuously thrust aside by Hrothulf. But Heoroweard had his revenge. Saxo and the *Saga of Rolf Kraki* tell us how Hiarwarus (Hjǫrvarðr) treacherously plotted against Roluo (Hrolfr). Saxo did not know who Hiarwarus was, or what was the ground of his quarrel with Roluo: but he tells how, by night, after a banquet, he and his men rose upon Roluo and his warriors, and how Roluo's loyal men fell around him, fighting in the burning hall.

We cannot rightly understand *Beowulf* unless we realise the background against which the hero is depicted. The poet meant Beowulf to stand out in contrast to the masters of Heorot, a house of heroes second to none in all northern story, but tainted by incest and the murder of kin almost beyond the measure of the lords of Thebes or the house of Pelops. So he depicts in his hero loyalty, duty, subordination of his own fortunes to those of his chief.

Widsith shows us that it was this terrible and tragic tale which the old poets associated with the name of the hall Heorot, rather than that figure of Beowulf the monster-queller which the later poet has chosen to paint in the foreground[1].

Offa of Angel.

Offa weold Ongle.

The essential part of the tale of Offa is the story of his duel, while yet a boy, at Fifeldor: the river Eider[2]. In *Beowulf* we find another story connected with Offa's name: that of his

[1] See especially a short but most valuable note by Sarrazin in *Englische Studien*, xxiv, 144–6: *Rolf Krake und sein vetter im Beowulfsliede*; and Axel Olrik, *Danmarks Heltedigtning*, 1903, pp. 11–27. Amidst so much that is conjecture, the identification of Healfdene, Hrothgar, Halga, and Hrothulf with Halfdan, Hroar, Helgi, and Hrolf may be accepted as certain. Three out of four of the names correspond exactly, and the fourth approximately: the relationships correspond, and half-a-dozen subsidiary marks of identification are forthcoming. Conjectures, however ingenious, which overlook this are simply in the air (e.g. the article on Hrothulf by Wilbur C. Abbott in *M.L.N.* xix, 122–5, 1905, cf. conclusive answer by Klaeber, *M.L.N.* xx, 9, 1905).

It seems almost equally incontestable that the Røricus and Hiarwarus of Saxo are the Hrethric and Heoroweard of *Beowulf*, and that the *Beowulf* poet foreshadows the quarrel between Hrothulf and his kin. To my mind the assertion made twice in *Beowulf* and once in *Widsith* that 'as yet' or 'for a very long time' or 'at that time' there was peace within the family implies necessarily that at last the peace was broken. For a contrary view see Clark, 100.

[2] See note, l. 43.

queen Thryth[1], and her fierceness which none but he could tame. Whether this story belonged from the first to Offa of Angel we cannot say ; later, it became attached to the name of Offa the Second, the historic tyrant-king of Mercia, who, if pedigrees are to be trusted, was descended in the twelfth generation from the legendary Offa of Angel. But the investigation of the Thryth story may be left to the student of *Beowulf*[2]: we have no evidence that it was known to *Widsith*.

In *Beowulf* Offa is mentioned as famous in war, as one who held his land with wisdom ; but the story of his fight at Fifeldor is not directly referred to.

It is another sign of the close connection between English and Danish saga that for the details of this story we must turn to two Danish historians of the end of the twelfth century, Sweyn Aageson and Saxo Grammaticus. The following is a summary of Saxo's story, which is the fuller and better of the two.

Wermundus, the son of Vigletus, king of Denmark, after a long and prosperous reign begat in his old age his only son Uffo, who grew up tall beyond the measure of his age, but dull, stupid, and speechless, so that all men despised him. His father wedded him to the daughter of Frowinus, the illustrious governor of Schleswig, for from Frowinus and his sons Keto and Wigo he hoped that Uffo would receive help in ruling the kingdom after his death. But Frowinus was slain by Athislus, king of Sweden, and Keto and Wigo brought disgrace upon themselves and their country by avenging their father in a combat of two against one. Meantime Wermundus had grown old and blind, and the king of Saxony laid claim to Denmark on the ground that its king was no longer fit to rule his realm : if he would not abdicate, let the quarrel be decided by their sons in single combat. Wermundus, sighing deeply, answered the Saxon envoys that it was not just to reproach him with his age, for he had not shirked battle in his youth : and that, as to his blindness, that deserved pity rather than insult. He would accept the challenge himself. The ambassadors replied that their king would not consent to the disgraceful mockery of fighting with a blind man, and that it would be better that the matter should be settled by the sons of each. The Danes knew not what to answer : but Uffo, who by chance was present, asked leave to speak, and "suddenly from dumb became capable of speech." Wermundus asked who it was who had thus craved permission to speak, and was told by his retainers that it was his son. He replied that it was enough to be insulted by foreigners, without the taunts of his own household. But when they

---

[1] For the form of the name see J. M. Hart in *M.L.N.* xviii, 118 ; but cf. Klaeber in *Anglia*, xxviii, 448–452 ; Holthausen in *Z.f.d.Ph.* xxxvii, 118.

[2] A detailed study of both stories by Miss E. Rickert will be found in *Mod. Philol.* ii, 29–76, 321–376.

insisted that it *was* Uffo, "Let him speak," he said, "whoever he be."
Then Uffo said, "In vain does the king of Saxony covet the land of
Denmark, which trusts to its true king and its brave nobles : neither is
a son wanting to the king nor a successor to the kingdom." So saying he
offered to fight not only the Saxon prince but, at the same time, any
champion the prince might choose from his nation : hoping in this way to
wipe out the disgrace left upon his country by the murder of Athislus,
perpetrated by Keto and Wigo.

The Saxon envoys jeered, accepted the offer, and withdrew. The
Danes were astonished, and Wermundus praised the valour of the speaker.
He could not believe him to be really Uffo, but he said he would rather
yield up the kingdom to him, whoever he might be, than to the proud foe.
But, when all assured him that it was his son, he asked him to draw near,
and passing his hands over him, recognised his son by the size of his limbs
and by his features....

But when arms were brought, no coat of mail could be found large
enough to fit Uffo, who split the rings by the breadth of his chest : even
his father's was too small. Wermundus accordingly ordered it to be cleft
down the left side and fastened with a clasp, thinking it of small moment
if the side protected by the shield lay open to the sword.

Several swords were offered to Uffo, but there was none so well
tempered that he did not shatter into fragments upon first wielding it.
Now the king had a sword of exceeding sharpness, called Skrep, which
could cut, at one blow, through any obstacle whatever. This sword he
had buried deep, despairing of his son's improvement, and wishing to deny
the use of the sword to others. When he was now asked whether he had
a sword worthy of Uffo's strength, he replied that he had, if he could
recognise the appearance of the place, and find the sword of old committed
by him to the earth. He then commanded his attendants to lead him out
into the open country, and, enquiring the landmarks from them, found the
place, drew forth his sword, and gave it to his son. The sword was frail
from age, and Uffo refrained from testing it ; for Wermundus told him
that if he broke it there was no other left strong enough for him.

So they sought the place of combat, an island in the river Eider[1] ;
Uffo alone ; the son of the Saxon king accompanied by a famous champion.
Crowds lined either bank ; Wermundus stationed himself at the end of a
bridge, meaning to throw himself into the river should his son be slain.
Uffo parried the blows of his assailants with his shield, but from distrust
of his sword he hesitated to strike, till he discovered from which of the
two he had most to fear, so that him at least he might reach with the one
blow. Wermundus, attributing this hesitation to helplessness, drew
himself gradually to the edge of the bridge. Meantime Uffo first urged
the prince not to let himself be surpassed by his low-born comrade, and
then, to test the courage of the champion, called upon him not to keep in
the rear of his lord, but to repay the confidence which had been placed in
him. Then, when the champion was driven by shame to come to closer
quarters, Uffo clove him asunder with one stroke. Restored by the sound
of the blow, Wermundus cried that he had heard his son's sword, and
asked where it had fallen. And when his attendants told him that the
blow had not pierced any one part but the man's whole structure, he drew
back from the edge of the bridge, desiring now life as keenly as he had

---

[1] This place is referred to again by Saxo in a later book (xII ; ed. Holder, 402)
*ubi Wermundi filium Vffonem cum duobus Saxonice gentis lectissimis manum
duelli nomine conseruisse proditum est.* The site can be identified with that of
the modern Rendsburg (Müllenhoff, *Beovulf,* 79).

before longed for death. Uffo then urged the prince to avenge his retainer, and, having brought him to close quarters by these appeals, he smote him through with the back of his sword, fearing that the edge was too weak for his strength. Then Wermundus exclaimed that he had heard a second time the sound of his sword Skrep, and, when the judges announced that his son had slain both his foes, burst into tears of joy.

So Uffo ruled over both Saxony and Denmark: by many he is called Olaf and surnamed 'the Gentle' on account of the modesty of his spirit. His further deeds have been lost, though, after such a beginning, we may well believe them to have been glorious[1].

Such is the outline of the story which Saxo tells at considerable length in his elaborate and artificial Latin. Very similar in its main outlines, though not so well told, is the version given in the scanty chronicle of Saxo's predecessor, Sweyn Aageson[2]. In Sweyn, while we miss much that is most picturesque in Saxo's tale, we get a few additional details of value. Thus Saxo does not seem to have made up his mind as to the reason of Uffo's dumbness and incapacity. Saxo's Uffo, after his reply to the envoys, is questioned by Wermundus, "why he had taken care to cover his sweet eloquence by the most studied dissimulation and had borne to pass so great a period of his age without speech," and merely makes answer that he had been content to live under the defence of his father, and had had no use for his voice until he had observed the wisdom of his own land hard pressed by the quick speech of foreigners. To which Wermundus replies that his son has made a just judgement in all matters. Yet Uffo's explanation seems somewhat inadequate. It is Sweyn Aageson who tells us that Uffo had been rendered dumb by the shame brought upon his country by two men having combined to avenge their father upon a single foe: obviously an allusion to the matter of Keto and Wigo, concerning which we hear at length in Saxo. This detail, supplied by Sweyn, explains in its turn a detail given

---

[1] Saxo, ɪᴠ, xxxiv–vi (ed. Holder, 106–115).

[2] Langebek, ɪ, 45–47. The story is also given, very briefly, in the *Annales Ryenses* :

"*Wermundus Blinde.* Hic vir bellicosus erat. Hujus tempore Keto, & Wiggo, filii Frowini Præfecti Sleswicensis, occiderunt Athislum Regem Sveciæ, in ultionem patris sui. Huic successit Uffo Starke filius ejus.

Uffo Starke. Iste a septimo ætatis anno usqve ad trigesimum noluit loqvi, qvousqve in loco, qvi adhuc *Kunengikamp* dicitur, super Eydoram cum filio Regis Teutonicorum & meliore pugile totius Teutoniæ solus certans, ambos occidit & sic conditione utriusqve gentis, Teutonia Danis jam qvarto tributaria facta est." *Annales Ryenses.* In Langebek, ɪ, 152, under the name of *Chronicon Erici Regis.*

only by Saxo : that Uffo's reason for demanding two opponents *is that he may wipe off the disgrace left upon his country* by the shameful act of Keto and Wigo; a disgrace of which, had we Saxo's story only, we should have supposed that he had hitherto taken no heed. It is evident that in the poem which formed the common source of both accounts this deed of shame was intimately connected with Uffo's victory, the significance of which lay, not, as it apparently does in *Widsith*, merely in the saving of the land from foreign aggression and the extending of its borders, but rather in the wiping off, by a deed of prowess, of the shame left by a dastardly murder.

In Sweyn, Wermundus, when he has felt over the mighty limbs of Uffo to satisfy himself that it is of a truth his son, exclaims "Such I remember was I myself in the flower of my youth!" Finally in Sweyn Uffo enters the lists girt with his father's sword, but holding another in his hand. When the worthless sword breaks asunder the German foes exult, and the Danes quake with fear; but Uffo suddenly draws his second sword and fells his adversary. From this it has been argued that the immediate source of Sweyn was not identical with that of Saxo; for Saxo, it is said, and with reason, would not have knowingly slurred over a situation like this[1].

It is, then, from a comparison of the historians that we must reconstruct the Danish lay. We see that, as in the old English battle poems, the speeches of the combatants played an important part. Uffo's words to his two foes, the prince and the champion, are recorded at length in both accounts.

About the same time that these Danish ecclesiastics were compiling their histories of Denmark out of old traditions and war poems, an unknown monk of St Alban's[2], in the hope of glorifying his monastery by commemorating its founder Offa II, and his namesake and ancestor Offa I, was committing to writing the traditions of the two Offas, as current in his day[3].

---

[1] Olrik, *Sakses Oldhistorie*, II, 182.

[2] Miss Rickert has shown that there is every possibility of the author having been abbot John de Cella (1195–1214). See *Mod. Philol.* II, 29 (1904). The author was not, as is often asserted, Matthew Paris.

[3] *Solent autem de isto Offa multa narrari...ut dicunt*, etc. in MS Cotton

The English story is substantially the same as the Danish: it is however located in England: all recollection of the continental Angel has vanished. Warmundus is a king of the Western Angles, ruling at Warwick. Offa, his only son, is blind till his seventh, dumb till his thirtieth year. A certain Riganus claims to be recognised heir in Offa's place, and, when Warmundus refuses his consent, raises an army. In answer to prayer Offa receives the gift of speech, harangues the council, leads his army against the foe, joins battle, dashes with his men across the river, and in the midst of the combat slays the two sons of the usurper, fighting one against two. Then follows the romantic story of Offa's queen: not the tale referred to in *Beowulf,* which in the *Vitae Duorum Offarum* is transferred to Offa II, but a version of the widely spread motive of the fugitive princess who is wedded to a great king, of the intercepted letters, of the consequent attempted slaughter of the queen and her children, and of the final reconciliation—in fact the *Man of Law's Tale*[1]. Offa is instructed by a hermit to build a monastery as a thank offering for his recovery of wife and children, but he omits to perform his vow, as do all his house after him till the days of Offa II, to whose life the monkish biographer then passes. The history of Offa II is a combination of historic fact with details repeated from the legend of Offa I, and does not concern us here.

The relationship of the *Vita Offae I* to the Danish histories was a subject often discussed during the 18th and early 19th centuries. Early students necessarily ignored the reference in *Widsith,* which was not published till 1826; and therefore, though they are sometimes useful in points of detail, their conclusions are valueless[2]. We now know that, five or six

Julius D vII, supposed by Miss Rickert to be an earlier draft by the compiler of the *Vitae*; *omnium fere conprouincialium assercio* in the *Vita Offae I.*

These *Vitae* were published with Wats' edition of Matthew Paris, London, 1640. They have since only been reprinted in extracts.

[1] See the *Originals and Analogues of Chaucer's Canterbury Tales* (Chaucer Soc.) pp. 1–84 (where part of the *Vita Offae I* is reproduced), 221–250, 365–414.

[2] Bibliographies of the Offa legend will be found, by Suchier, in *P.B.B.* IV, 500, and by Miss Rickert in *Mod. Philol.* II, 29. P. E. Müller's discussion of the subject in his edition of Saxo (Copenhagen, 1858, Part II, *Not. Ub.* 137), as it was made without reference to *Widsith,* must be ranked with the earlier criticisms. An interesting Celtic parallel has been pointed out by G. H. Gerould: *Offa and Labhraidh Maen,* in *M.L.N.* xvII, 201 *etc.* (1902).

centuries before either Saxo or the monk of St Albans was writing, the story of the duel on the island of the Eider was being told of Offa, king of Angel. The allusions in *Widsith* are not detailed enough to enable us to reconstruct fully this most ancient version : but we can see that it was nearer to the story, as later preserved in Denmark, than to that preserved by the monk of St Albans. The quarrel was with an alien and not with a domestic foe ; the fight took place by the Eider ; it was a duel, and not a pitched battle ; *Widsith* shows us that in all these points the Danish version is the original one. It is natural that this Danish account should make Offa into a Danish prince : the fact that he defended his frontiers on the river Eider necessitated this, at a date when the Eider had come to be the frontier between the Danes and the German races of the south. Naturally, too, the foe has come to be identified in Danish story with these Germans: Saxo calls them Saxons, Sweyn *Alamanni*. From *Widsith* we learn that the contending parties were really the Angles and Myrgings, who seem to have been neighbours of the Angles on the south. There can be little doubt that so much of the story as is common to English and Danish tradition goes back to an early Anglian lay, brought over to England by the Angles, but surviving also in the neighbourhood of the ancient Angel, and incorporated by the Danes into their national stock of stories, just as they incorporated into their kingdom the ancient Angèl and the remnants of its people.

That the English life of Offa and the Danish story of Uffo were not derived the one from the other, but were independent traditions from the same original, had been perceived by one historian[1] even before the discovery of *Widsith*, which has rendered it certain. More recently Müllenhoff[2], it is true, has argued that the story had no continuous life in Denmark, but was reintroduced there from England ; but his arguments, on examination, have fallen to the ground[3]. All the evidence

---

[1] Dahlmann, *Forschungen*, I, 234, 235.
[2] *Beovulf*, 80 etc.
[3] See the criticisms of Müllenhoff's view by Chadwick (125-6) and by Olrik in the *Ark. f. nord. Filologi* VIII (N. F. IV) 368-75 : *Er Uffesagnet invandret fra England ? Bemærkninger til Müllenhoff's 'Beovulf.'*

indicates that Saxo's story goes back to a Danish lay, which, in its turn, was founded upon a tribal lay of the continental Angel. Many of Saxo's proper names such as Uffo[1], Frowinus, Skrep[2], and, above all, the localization of the fight on the Eider, point to the story having had its original home not in England but in the old home of the Angles in Schleswig. It is indeed impossible that Saxo could have known of the localization on the Eider, if, as Müllenhoff supposed, he drew from a tradition which had travelled to England in the sixth century and back to Denmark perhaps in the tenth. On the contrary, the tradition Saxo used must have handed down the fame of Offa of Angel continuously in the near neighbourhood of those lands where Offa had fought and ruled.

Yet we must not suppose that the tale as known to *Widsith* was in all respects that which Saxo has preserved for us. We cannot exactly gauge what has been the loss and the gain of the centuries intervening between *Widsith* and Saxo. We may safely suppose, though the scanty allusions of *Widsith* do not tell us so, that the sluggish youth of the hero was an original feature of the story. The fact that this trait is preserved in the twelfth century English and Danish versions alike, proves that it must have occurred in the common original of both; and we know from *Beowulf*[3] that the sluggish hero who proves in the end a good champion was as well known a character in Old English as he was in Middle English story. It is puzzling, however, to find that, in *Widsith*, Offa wins his honours while still a youth (*cniht wesende*) whilst the later versions, both English and Danish, agree in making the period of torpor last till his thirtieth year[4].

---

[1] Chadwick (126–7).

[2] Koegel, *Ltg.*, I, i, 162–3. "The name of the sword *skrep* is not Danish, and not Norse as Uhland thought (Schriften, VII, 215) but Anglian. If any further proof were needed that the ultimate source of Saxo's story is an Anglian poem, composed by the countrymen of Offa, and dating at the latest from the beginning of the sixth century, it would be afforded by this word. For *skrep* is the same as the West Frisian *schrep*, the Low German *schrap*, firm, steadfast (Doornkaat Koolmann, 3. 145 a). The name bears upon the story, for Skrep is the only sword which is sufficiently firm and steadfast to endure Offa's test."

[3] l. 2187. For Miss Rickert's interesting suggestion that we should retain the MS reading *geomor* in *Beowulf* as a reference to Offa's heaviness, see *Mod. Philol.* II, 54–58.   [4] See note to l. 39.

What gives its dignity to the Danish story is the connection, which Saxo himself only partly understood, between Uffo's combat and the deed of shame wrought by Keto and Wigo. By this connection the interest of the story centres no longer in any single person, but in the honour of Uffo's people[1]. One would like to think that this was a feature of the original Anglian story. We cannot be sure that it was: yet it may well have been, for Freawine and his son Wig were known to English tradition. We find them in the West Saxon pedigree among the ancestors of Cerdic[2]. And we shall find that *Widsith* seems to show some trace of a knowledge of their story.

Perhaps, finally, we should not be wrong in attributing to the ultimate Anglian source that quality of straightforward narrative in virtue of which Saxo's story of Uffo stands out from most of his history. Koegel[3] has claimed for this episode an 'epic breadth,' such as we find in Old English, but not in Old Scandinavian heroic verse. Every reader of Saxo must feel the difference between the manner in which this story is told and the lyrical treatment which is given, for example, to the story of the death of Rolf Kraki, where we know that Saxo was following a Scandinavian lay. But it may be dangerous to argue too much from this difference of treatment.

Eadgils.

The story of the slaying of Athislus, king of Sweden, as told by Saxo, is briefly this. He invaded Schleswig, defeated Frowinus, the governor, and slew him in single combat. Upon his making a second attack, Wermundus, assisted by Keto and Wigo, the sons of Frowinus, drove him back: but Athislus escaped with his life, although he bore the brunt both of the attack and of the retreat. Keto and Wigo journeyed to Sweden, and, finding Athislus alone, challenged him to combat; but he, pitying their youth, offered to pay the money compensation for their father's death. Keto refused the offer, and

---

[1] Olrik, *Sakses Oldhistorie*, II, 185.

[2] Olrik thinks the episodes were originally distinct, "Oprindelig har de to begivenheder næppe hørt sammen" (184); but the reasons he gives are not conclusive. For Freawine see Grimm, trans. Stallybrass, I, 211.

[3] *Ltg.* I, 1, 159.

attacked Athislus, bidding his brother stand aside, "for the men of old time held it unjust and scandalous for two men to fight against one, and counted such a victory as a disgrace." Athislus for some time held back, bidding the two youths come on together; till the vigour of Keto's attack compelled him to put forth his full strength, and he struck him to his knees. Then Wigo "made affection conquer shame" and interfered to save his brother: and together they slew Athislus.

Now we have much information, half legendary, half historic[1], about the kings of Sweden, dating from the days, three centuries earlier than Saxo, when Thiotholf the scald made his *Ynglingatal* for king Rognvald Higher-than-the-Hills. But we know of one Swedish king alone named Athils, the son of Ottar (the Eadgils, son of Ohthere, of *Beowulf*), who gained the kingdom by the rout of Ali (Onela)[2] and whose dealings with Rolf Kraki (Hrothulf) were such a favourite subject of Scandinavian story[3].

But this Athislus-Eadgils cannot be the Athislus who was slain by Keto and Wigo: for our authorities are agreed that he died, not in fight, but whilst celebrating a ceremony:

King Athils was at a sacrifice of the goddesses, and rode his horse through the hall of the goddesses : the horse tripped under him, and fell, and threw the king ; and his head smote a stone so that the skull broke, and the brains lay on the stones, and that was his death. He died at Uppsala, and there was laid in mound, and the Swedes called him a mighty king[4].

Since there is no other Swedish king of the name, Saxo must be wrong in supposing the king Athislus who was slain by Wigo to have been a Swede. But in that case he is most probably identical with Eadgils, lord of the Myrgings, in *Widsith*. For the Myrgings, we gather from *Widsith*, were probably also called *Swœfe*[5], and, in view of the frequent

---

[1] Chronologically the *Ynglingatal* is remarkably consistent. Cf. Heusler, *Zeitrechnung im Beowulfepos* in Herrig's *Archiv*, cxxiv, 9.

[2] *Beowulf* 2392 etc. *Ynglingasaga* in *Heimskringla*, ɪ, 29. Sn. *Edda*, Skáld. 41 (44), udg. Jónsson p. 108.

[3] *Hrolfs Kraka saga*, especially cap. 28 etc. ; *Heimskringla*, Sn. *Edda*, as above ; Saxo ɪɪ (ed. Holder, pp. 54–5).

[4] *Heimskringla* ɪ, 29. Saxo has a different account. Athislus brought on his own death through celebrating, with immoderate drinking, the funeral of his enemy Roluo (Book ɪɪɪ ; ed. Holder, p. 75).

[5] See note to l. 44.

mediæval confusion of Sweden and Swabia, a king of the Swæfe is most likely of all men to have been made into a king of Sweden. Besides, no other Athils-Eadgils is, so far as I know, forthcoming to contest this place with Eadgils the Myrging[1]. But if Old English tradition represented the Eadgils slain by Wig as a Myrging, and Offa as defending his country against an attack of the Myrgings, it becomes highly probable that the two stories were even more closely connected than we find them in Saxo. Eadgils the Myrging slays Freawine, an Anglian chief: Ket and Wig avenge their father: Offa repels the avenging Myrgings and restores the honour of the Angles by his duel at Fifeldor.

This story is probably based upon events which actually happened in the later half of the fourth century of our era[2].

Much further back than this we can hardly trace English history. Wermund's father is Wihtlæg in the O.E. genealogies, Vigletus in Saxo: these may be identical, and point to some hero of history or legend. Beyond Wihtlæg we have only Woden in the English genealogy. Saxo makes Vigletus slay Hamlet, and wed Hamlet's wife; but we have no evidence that this Jutish saga was known in England.

---

[1] That the Athislus of Saxo (Book ɪᴠ) is identical with the Eadgils of *Widsith* seems of recent years to have occurred independently to at least three scholars: Sarrazin in *Engl. Stud.* xxɪɪɪ, 234; Chadwick (135); Weyhe in *Engl. Stud.* xxxɪx, 37. Sarrazin and Chadwick both point out how easy and how frequent is the confusion of Swedes and Swabians. But the identification of the Athislus of Saxo with the Eadgils of *Widsith*, and of the Swedes of Saxo with the *Swæfe* of *Widsith*, was first proposed at least sixty years ago (by P. A. Munch, *Det norske Folks Historie*, 1851, ɪ, 1, 244).

[2] For this date Chadwick (p. 136) relies largely upon *Widsith*, which represents Eadgils as a contemporary of Ermanaric (died *c*. 375). But *Widsith* equally represents him as a contemporary of Alboin (died *c*. 573) and on this ground Eadgils used to be placed with equal confidence in the sixth century. In fact, no chronological arguments can be safely drawn from *Widsith*. However, as Chadwick points out, if we reckon the generations back from the earliest figures which we can date in the Mercian and West Saxon pedigrees, allowing thirty years for a generation, we should have to put the birth of Wig *c*. 350, and that of Offa *c*. 360. This would agree excellently with the story in Saxo. The West Saxon pedigree is not reliable, but the Mercian probably is, and similar results have been drawn from it by Müllenhoff, (*Beovulf*, 85–6.)

The tale of Wade.

Wada [weold] Hælsingum.

Perhaps Wade was originally a sea-giant, dreaded and honoured by the coast tribes of the North Sea and the Baltic[1]. That he retained something of this character in these regions till the thirteenth century is proved by the references to him in the *Thidreks saga*, where the giant Vathe is the offspring of King Villcinus and of a sea-wife. The *saga* has, however, little to tell concerning him; he owes his place in the story to his being the father of the more interesting Weland: a connection which is no doubt late. On one occasion "a kind of heathen Christopher" he *wades* over the swollen sound with his son upon his shoulder[2]. Vathe is finally overwhelmed in an avalanche[3]. Perhaps we may see in this a survival of some legend of the storm-divinity.

We meet with Wade again in a High-German disguise in the poem of *Kudrun*, almost contemporary with the *Thidreks saga*. Here he has been brought into subjection to the laws of chivalry, and becomes the type of the faithful retainer, but his old aquatic habits peep forth. To him the ways of the sea[4] and the tales of the sea[5] are known : and when the angel tells Kudrun that her deliverers are at hand, it is Wade who steers the fleet which brings them :

> dir kumet in ditze lant
> Wate von den Stürmen ; der hât an sîner hant
> ein starkez stiurruoder[6].

In England the memory of Wade lived longer than that of any of the old heroes of song, Weland only excepted. The references to him by the two greatest writers of the Middle English period have kept his name from being ever quite

---

[1] Müllenhoff in *Z. f. d. A.* vi, 62; Symons in *Pauls Grd.* (2) iii, 718–9. It is not necessary, with Müllenhoff, to assume a Frisian or Frankish origin for Wade ; evidence would rather lead to our placing both him and his people on the Baltic, very near the old Anglian home. See note to *Hælsingas*, l. 22, and cf. Golther, 176.

[2] cap. 58.   [3] cap. 60.
[4] Stanza 836.   [5] 1128.   [6] 1183.

forgotten. In Chaucer's *Troilus* a "tale of Wade" helps to while away an evening, when Pandare entertains Criseyde[1]:

> And after souper gonnen they to ryse
> At ese wel, with hertes fresshe and glade,
> And wel was him that coulde best devyse
> To lyken hir, or that hir laughen made.
> He song ; she pleyde ; he tolde tale of Wade.

Elsewhere Chaucer refers to Wade's boat[2].

In Mallory's *Morte d'Arthur* the damsel Linet says to Sir Gareth of Orkney:

> For were thou as wight as ever was Wade, or Launcelot, Tristram, or the good knight Sir Lamorake, thou shalt not pass a pass here, that is called the pass perilous[3].

References in less famous works are fairly frequent. *Sir Bevis of Hamton* classes Wade amongst the few champions of romance who have slain their dragons[4]. We shall probably be right if we regard this dragon episode[5] as a later development of his story.

In the alliterative *Morte Arthure* the " wery wafulle wedowe " warns King Arthur that it is useless for him to attack the giant :

> Ware thow wyghttere thane Wade or Wawayne owthire,
> Thow wynnys no wyrchipe, I warne the before[6].

Even in 1598, when Speght edited Chaucer, the name of Wade's boat was remembered :

> Concerning Wade and his bote called Guingelot, as also his strange exploits in the same, because the matter is long and fabulous, I passe it over[7].

Speght has been denounced by Tyrwhitt[8], and by Sir

---

[1] Bk iii, l. 614, ed. Skeat. For further notes on Wade, see Grimm, *Kl. Schr.* viii, 502, Kemble, *Saxons*, i, 419–20. The suggestion made by Kemble in his footnote is quite untenable.

[2] *Marchantes Tale*, 180 (T. 9298).

[3] Book vii, cap. ix.

[4]
> Sire Launcelet de Lake,
> He faugt wiþ a fur drake,
> And Wade dede also.
>
> Sir Beues of Hamtoun, ed. Kölbing, *E.E.T.S.* 2603–5.

[5] Cf. Binz in *P.B.B.* xx, 197 ; Panzer *H.G.* 289.

[6] Ed. Brock, *E.E.T.S.* 1865. Another reference to the romance of Wade will be found quoted in Warton's *History of English Poetry*, 1774, vol. i, p. 120.

[7] *The Workes of Chaucer*, 1598. *Annotations.*

[8] Tyrwhitt's *Canterbury Tales*, W. Pickering, 1830, iv, 248.

Walter Scott, for having " to the great prejudice of posterity[1] " given us only this tantalizing reference. But probably he knew little of the story. He wrote more than a century after the latest of the references given above, and it is unlikely that, except locally, any tale of Wade was remembered, in the year 1600. To the antiquary Leland, much earlier, the name Wade had no meaning. Leland notes that at Mulgrave, near Whitby, are "certen stones communely caullid Waddes Grave, whom the people there say to have bene a Gigant[2]." Camden also, a contemporary of Speght, visited Wade's grave, but the name does not seem to have awakened in him any recollection of old tradition. He connects the eleven foot high giant with the historic Northumbrian chief named Wade[3]. Finally, Sir Francis Kynaston, in his commentary upon *Troilus* (c. 1635), professed to give an account of Wade, which shows that he could find nothing to add to what Speght had condescended to state :

Tale of Wade, &c. Chaucer means a ridiculous romance, as if he had told a story of Robin Hood, for in his time there was a foolish fabulous Legend of one Wade & his boate Guingelot, wherein he did many strange things & had many wonderfull adventures; not much unlike that man and his boate in our time, who layed a wager, that he never going out of his boate, & without any other helpe but himselfe, he would in a certaine number of dayes go by land & by water from Abington to London, & in his passage would go over the top of a square Steepel by the way, which thing he performed & wonne his wager[4].

It is evident, then, that by the early seventeenth century the tale of Wade was forgotten.

Locally, Wade's name was remembered much later. At Mulgrave the grave of the giant Wade was shown, almost down to our days. Also, says an antiquary of the late eighteenth century :

The common people...shew...a huge bone which they affirm to be one of the ribs of Bell Wade's cow ; believing her, as well as her owner, to

---

[1] *Lay of the Last Minstrel,* note 2 E. Compare Scott's introduction to *Sir Tristrem,* 1804, p. lxi (1806, p. lviii).

[2] Leland's *Itinerary,* second edit., Hearne, 1745, I, 60.

[3] *Hic in colle inter duo saxa solida septem plus minus pedes alta tumulatur, quae cùm vndecem pedibus distarent illum gigantea fuisse mole non dubitant affirmare. Britannia,* Londini, 1594, p. 555. See Gough's Camden for further notices of Wade, especially " Wades gap."

[4] This commentary has never been published. The extract above is taken from *The Loves of Troilus and Creseid, written by Chaucer ; with a commentary, by Sir Francis Kinaston: never before published* [edited by F. G. Waldron] 1796. Only the first part was issued.

have been of an enormous size. But to me this appears a mere fiction; for the bone now preserved there has doubtless belonged to some fish, probably a whale; though such a suggestion is by no means agreeable to its present possessors[1].

The name of "Wade's causey" was also given to a disused Roman road

which leads from it [the village of Dunsley, on the sea coast] many miles over these vast moors and morasses toward York. This extraordinary road, at present disused, is called by the country-people Wade's causey, concerning which they relate a ridiculous traditional story of Wade's wife, and her cow. The fabulous story is, that Wade had a cow, which his wife was obliged to milk at a great distance, on these moors; for her better convenience he made this causeway, and she helped him by bringing great quantities of stones in her apron; but the strings breaking once with the weight, as well they might, a huge heap (about twenty cartload) is shown that dropped from her[2].

Such is the last echo, on the Yorkshire coast, of the tales of the dread sea giant which the conquerors had brought with them across the North Sea thirteen centuries before.

The name Wade was frequently borne in Old English times by historic chiefs[3]. We cannot therefore feel sure that the many places associated with the name[4] all point to a localization of stories of the mythical hero. It is particularly tempting to assume this, however, when we find the name associated with mills and bridges[5].

Of the lost *Tale of Wade* six lines were discovered by Dr Montague R. James in a Latin sermon on Humility, of the early thirteenth century. As emended and explained by Prof. Gollancz, they run:

Ita quod dicere possunt cum Wade:
Summe sende ylues
and summe sende nadderes:
summe sende nikeres
the bi den watere wunien.
Nister man nenne
bute Ildebrand onne[6].

The allusion to nickers dwelling by the water seems

---

[1] *The History of Whitby*, by Lionel Charlton, York, 1779, p. 40.

[2] *The history and antiquities of Scarborough and the vicinity*, by Thomas Hinderwell, second edit., York, 1811, p. 19.

[3] About a dozen *Wades* are recorded in Searle's *Onomasticon*.

[4] For a list of these see Binz in *P.B.B.* xx, 198.

[5] For instances of these see Francesque Michel, *Wade, Lettre sur une tradition angloise du moyen âge*, Paris et Londres, 1837. For German examples of Wade in place names, *Watanbrunno*, etc., see Müllenhoff in *Z.f.d.A.* vi, 65.

[6] See *Academy*, 1241, Feb. 1896, p. 137; *Athenæum*, 3565, Feb. 1896, p. 254.

appropriate to the tale of Wade. But this reading is conjectural, and the lines still leave us in the dark as to Wade
and his boat Guingelot.

Perhaps more help is to be got from the story of Gado,
told us by Walter Map[1].

Gado was the son of the king of the Vandals; but, from love of
adventure, left his home when a boy. A mighty hunter, versed in all
knowledge, he wandered through the world redressing wrongs, and at last
he came to the court of King Offa, the builder of the Welsh dyke. Offa,
to his sorrow, wedded the daughter of the Roman emperor; his covetous
Roman guests, returning home, urged the emperor to make Offa tributary,
and were deterred from attacking him only by fear of his friend Gado.
However, when Gado was called off, to right wrongs in the furthest Indies,
and had been dismissed by Offa with rich gifts, the Romans, with a mighty
army, attacked Offa unawares. But Gado, having righted things in India,
was returning to his native land: when against his wish, his ship was
carried to England, near Colchester. There Offa had come to meet the
Romans, who had just landed, and who had refused his terms of peace.
After greeting Offa, Gado, clothed in his wonted glorious vestments, and
accompanied by a hundred chosen knights (for he always led with him at
least a hundred), went to the Roman quarters to act as mediator, but was
repulsed. So Gado arrayed the English forces, placing Offa with the main
body in the market place of the town, the king's nephew Suanus with a
chosen five hundred at one exposed gate, and himself, with his hundred,
at the next.

Fearing Gado, the Romans concentrated all their attacks upon Suanus,
who, at the third assault, had to appeal to Gado for help. But Gado
refused, and Suanus was preparing to sell his life dearly, when Gado
commanded him to draw back. He obeyed: the enemy rushed in, and
were met by Offa in the market place, whilst their retreat was cut off by
Gado from behind. Thus caught, the Romans were mowed down, till
quarter was offered to the survivors, who returned to Rome with their
dead.

Map has rationalized the story, and has toned down, without
obliterating, its supernatural features. The boat which enables
Gado to go to the uttermost Indies, to accomplish his adventure
there, and to return in time to thwart the emperor, a boat which
carries him magically to the spot where there is work for him to
do, can be no other than Guingelot. Gado's wisdom, and his white
hair[2] (characteristics which are also preserved in *Kudrun*), are
probably derived from the original figure of the dreaded old

---

[1] *De nugis curialium*, ed. Wright, *Camden Soc.*, 1850, II, 17. The parallel
has been pointed out by Miss Rickert in *Mod. Philol.* II (1905), and by Brandl
in *Herrigs Archiv*, cxx, 6, and *Pauls Grdr.*(2) II, 1, 1085.

[2] Compare *Omnem enim habere sapientiam aiebant, linguas quorumlibet
loquebatur regnorum, et frequenti felicitate successuum totius vitæ videbatur
obedientiam obtinere, tanquam optioni suæ parerent animantia omnium motabilium,
et haberent intelligentiam*, with the thrice repeated formula *Wate der vil wise* ;
respersum canis quasi semicanum with *swie gris er dô wære*.

man of the sea. In other points the coincidence between the Anglo-Latin and the High German story may be accidental. The glorious clothing of Gado and his companions astonishes the emperor and his knights; we are reminded of the magnificence of Wate's companions at the Irish court; when Gado takes over the command from king Offa and directs all the fighting around the town gates, we are reminded of the similar commanding part assumed by Wate at the end of the Kudrun story.

That Gado should be the son of a Vandal king carries us back to the flourishing days of the Old English heroic story, when the Vandal name was clearly remembered; this feature would hardly have been invented later. It was probably the exigencies of alliteration that originally caused a Vandal king to be chosen for Wade's father, just as in the *Thidreks saga* he is made the son of king Villcinus.

Putting together, then, the accounts of Wate and Vathe, of Wade and of Gado, we find these common characteristics, which we may assume belonged to their ancient prototype, Wada of the Hælsingas:

(1)   Power over the sea.

(2)   Extraordinary strength—often typified by superhuman stature.

(3)   The use of these powers to help those whom Wade favours. Not that he is necessarily gracious or benevolent. Originally he was perhaps the reverse[1]. But probably he grew out of the figure, not of a historic chief, but of a supernatural power, who had no story all his own, and who interested mortal men only when he interfered in their concerns. Hence he is essentially a helper in time of need: and we may be fairly confident that already in the oldest lays he possessed this character.

Hagena and Heoden.

Hagena [weold] Holmrygum and Heoden Glommum.

In these words we have a reference to one of the greatest

---

[1] This sinister character he keeps in the *Thidreks saga*; cf. *Hann var illr viðrskiptis, oc firir þa sæc var hann opockasæll.* Wate, too, has something of this grim nature.

of the old tales: a tale so popular that allusions to it are to be found everywhere, and that four complete, although late, versions have come down to us.

The best of these is the Icelandic version as given by Snorri[1], in explanation of the allusions of the poets:

A battle is called the blast or shower of the Hjathningar [O.E. Heodeningas], and arms the fire or wands of the Hjathningar, and there is a tale as to this.

The king named Hogni [O.E. Hagena] had a daughter named Hild; the king named Hethin [O. E. Heoden] son of Hjarrandi [O. E. Heorrenda] carried her off by force. At that time Hogni was gone to a meeting of chieftains, but when he heard that his kingdom had been raided, and his daughter carried off, he went with his company in search of Hethin, and learnt that he had gone North, coasting the land. And when king Hogni reached Norway he learned that Hethin had sailed West, over the sea. Then Hogni sailed after him to the Orkneys; and when he came to the island called Hoy, Hethin was there, with his company.

Then Hild went to meet her father and offered him a necklace[2] as a peace offering, on behalf of Hethin. But on the other hand she said that Hethin was ready to fight, and Hogni need expect no forbearance from him. Hogni made answer sternly to his daughter: but she, returning to Hethin, told him that Hogni would have no peace, and bade him prepare himself for battle. And so they did on both sides; they went up on to the island, and drew up their companies.

Then Hethin called to Hogni, his father-in-law, and offered him peace, and much gold in atonement. But Hogni made answer, "Too late dost thou proffer peace, seeing that I have now drawn *Dainsleif*, which the dwarfs smithied: and it must be the death of a man every time it is drawn, nor does it ever fail in its stroke, nor may a scratch from it be healed." Then said Hethin: "There thou dost boast of thy sword, but not of the victory: I call that good which is true to its lord."

Then they began the battle, which is called *Hjathningavíg*; and they fought all the day, and in the evening the kings went to their ships. But Hild went by night to the corpses, and awoke the dead by magic. And the next day the kings went to the battlefield and fought, and so did all those who fell the day before.

In such wise the battle continued, day after day; so that all those who fell[3], and all the weapons and shields which lay on the battlefield, were turned into stone. And when it dawned, all the dead men stood up and fought, and all the weapons were sound: and it is told in songs that the Hjathningar shall so abide till Doomsday. And of this tale Bragi the poet wrought in the song of Ragnar Lodbrok.

This is the same song of Bragi which is our oldest Norse authority for the tale of Ermanaric[4]. We must not, however, argue that the Hild story was known to Bragi in the ninth century exactly as Snorri tells it in the thirteenth. The references in the *Háttalykill* of Rognvald, earl of the Orkneys,

---

[1] Sn. *Edda*, udg. Jónsson, *Skáldskaparmál*, 47 (50).
[2] Reading, with Jónsson, *men at sætt*. But cf. Panzer, *H.G.* 160.
[3] Cf. Panzer, *H.G.* 160 (footnote 2).   [4] See above, pp. 19-20.

which are much nearer to Snorri's time than Bragi's references,
show a version of the story not quite consistent with Snorri's,
and in the *Sǫrlatháttr*[1] the tale is told again with many
additional details, not all of them to be attributed to the
fourteenth century compiler.

But, however they may differ in detail, all these Norse
versions bear a common stamp[2]. In them all the essential
feature is the tragic fight between father-in-law and son-in-law,
following a vain attempt at reconciliation. How Hethin gained
the love of Hild we are not told[3].

But at the same time that Snorri was writing his " poets'
manual " in Iceland, the story was being made the theme of epic
song in Austria. In this southern version the essential part of
the tale is the wooing of Hild : the battle between father- and
son-in-law, which follows, ends in a reconciliation. Two striking
features of the High German epic are the griesly old warrior
Wate [Wade], the irresistible servant and protector of Hetel
[the M. H. G. equivalent of Hethin or Heoden], and the sweet
song of Hôrant, by means of which the love of Hild is won.

This southern version is represented to us by *Kudrun*, a
High German poem founded upon Low German tradition. After
the story of the youthful adventures of Hagen—a later development of the tale—we are told how Hagen rules in Ireland, and
hangs all the messengers sent to beg for his daughter's hand :
conduct which nevertheless does not check the crowd of wooers.

The wise men of King Hetel of the Hegelings counsel him to wed.
Hetel consults his vassal Hôrant as to his suit for Hild : only by the help
of Wate, Hôrant says, can the lady be won. Wate is summoned : and it
is decided that he and Hôrant, with other champions, shall sail in disguise to Ireland, and carry off the bride. They are to feign themselves

---

[1] *Fornaldar Sǫgur*, ed. Rafn, I, 389–407, §§ 5–8. It is to be noted that this
version makes Hogni and Hethin foster brethren. Hethin is left in charge of
Hogni's land : an enchanted drink causes him to break his trust, murder Hogni's
wife, and carry off his daughter.

[2] The versions and allusions were compiled by P. E. Müller in his edition of
Saxo, *Notæ uberiores* (vol. II, pp. 158–61), and more fully by Prof. Piper in
his edition of *Kudrun* (*Anhang zur Einleitung*, 60–135). This collection does
not however include the *Háttalykill*, an extract from which will be found in
Panzer, *H.G.* 171.

[3] It must be remembered, however, that Snorri tells the story in order to
illustrate a particular phrase. He *may* have known more of the earlier part of
the story than he thought it worth while to tell.

merchants, or else exiles outlawed by Hetel; but with armed men concealed in the hold. Both disguises are combined (the poet is apparently harmonizing two dissimilar traditions[1]); the magnificent merchants are invited to Hagen's court. Wate excites first terror by his grim appearance, then admiration by his skill in swordsmanship. Equally admired is Hôrant's morning song, which shames into silence the birds singing in the bushes[2]. Hild is charmed by it; she cannot rest till Hôrant comes to sing to her in her chamber. So Hôrant sings a song of Amilé: the like of which was never known by Christian man before or since, unless he heard it upon the wild waves.

Then he throws off his disguise and woos for his lord. "Noble maid, my lord has in his court twelve who sing far beyond me: and all so sweet as is their song, yet my lord sings best of all."

The maiden is won, and consents to flee with the wooers. So Wate announces to Hagen that the ban has been removed, and he and his companions have been summoned home. He asks the king to do them one last favour by visiting their ships with his daughter and his wife. The wish is granted; Hild is cunningly separated from her father. Then the armed men spring up: anchors are weighed, sails hoisted and the adventurers return to Hetel's land; whilst Hagen, whose ships are unready, is for the moment unable to pursue.

Wate and his companions, so soon as they land, send news of their success to Hetel, who hastens to meet his bride: but Hagen soon arrives in pursuit, and a battle takes place upon the shore. Hagen wounds Hetel, but is himself wounded and hard pressed by Wate: at last Hetel, at the request of Hild, parts the combatants. Wate, skilled in leechcraft, heals the wounded, and Hagen returns to Ireland, satisfied that his daughter is worthily wedded.

The subsequent story of Kudrun, daughter of Hild and Hetel, does not concern us; in many respects it is a duplicate of the story of the wooing of Hild.

A third version of the story is given by Saxo Grammaticus. The inferiority of the bombastic Latin of Saxo, that "very curious Northman," to the perfect Icelandic prose of Snorri, has caused less attention to be given to Saxo's story than it deserves. Chronologically it is the earliest of the versions, and it has fine features of its own.

Hithinus, prince of a Norwegian tribe, loved Hilda, a maiden of excellent renown, daughter of Höginus, a chieftain of the Jutes. "For before they had met face to face, the fame of each had fired the other. But when they had an opportunity of beholding each other, neither was able to look away, so constant was the love which held their eyes[3]." Höginus betrothed his daughter to Hithinus, and the two chieftains became sworn brethren: but Hithinus was falsely accused of having betrayed Höginus' daughter. Höginus believed the report and they thrice met in combat. First Höginus attacked Hithinus in a pitched battle, but was repulsed: a second time they fought singly, and Hithinus fell,

---

[1] Panzer, *H.G.* 222. [2] Cf. *Kudrun*, st. 389.
[3] Ed. Holder, v, xlviii; pp. 159–60.

grievously wounded; but pitying his beauty and youth his foe spared his life (for of old it was held shameful to slay a stripling). So Hithinus was carried back to his ship by his men. After seven years they met again on the island of Hithinsö, and wounded each other mortally. "It is said that Hilda burned with such love for her husband that by night she raised up, through spells, the spirits of the slain, to renew the combat."

It seems probable that Saxo is here harmonizing two distinct accounts. For whilst it is quite intelligible that the sorceress Hild, as depicted by Snorri or Bragi, with her valkyrie-like love of slaughter, should renew the combat from day to day, it is not clear why Saxo's Hilda should do so, from love for Hithinus. Again, according to Saxo, it was slanderers who caused the breach between the chiefs: Hithinus is not represented as having forcibly seized his wife, yet Saxo uses a phrase *patre filiam pertinacius reposcente* which shows that he knew a version in which Hithinus carried off Hilda by force. It is even possible that Saxo, after the manner of rationalizing compilers of all ages, is harmonizing his two sources by introducing the same incident twice in different forms; and that in the second and third combats we have traces of two versions, in one of which the combatants depart alive, reconciled, whilst in the other the battle is renewed everlastingly[1]. But it may well be doubted whether any of Saxo's sources had other than a tragic ending.

Which, if any, of these divergent versions preserves the original tale, as it was sung in the halls of Germanic chiefs six centuries before Snorri or Saxo wrote? Almost all students have agreed that the eternal fight of the Heodenings, as told in the Norse versions, is the essential part of the myth[2]: that

---

[1] Axel Olrik has attempted to disentangle the two versions used by Saxo. The eternal battle he thinks is peculiar to the Norse version: the loves of Hithinus and Hilda, the slanderous tongues, and the localization of the last fatal battle at Hiddensö, peculiar to the Danish tradition. See *Sakses Old-historie*, II, 191–6.

[2] On few points has so much unanimity been shown: "Ihre im wesent-lichen ursprünglichste Gestalt......bietet Snorri......Der ewige Kampf, das endlose *Hjaðningavig* ist offenbar der eigentliche Kern des alten Mythus." Symons in *Pauls Grdr.* (2) III, 711; cf. 718, "Wate gehört der Sage nicht ursprünglich an." "In uralter Zeit von den das Meer berührenden fränkischen Stämmen ausgebildet ist sie...nach dem Norden gewandert und dort wie so vieles andere in ihrem alten Zusammenhange erhalten geblieben." Koegel, *Ltg.* I. 1, 170. "Der *Hiaðningavig* aber bildet den eigentlichen Kern der Sage." Martin's *Kudrun* (2) XLIV, XLVII. "The oldest form of the story is to be found in the later Edda." Robertson, *History of German Literature* (1902), p. 72.

the features which distinguish the High German epic, such as the help given by Wate[1], or the sweet song of Hôrant[2], had originally no connection with the story.

This unanimity is the more extraordinary in view of the fact that the Old English allusions to the story, certainly the oldest by many centuries, seem to incline rather to the German than to the Norse version. For it is probably not by a mere coincidence that in *Widsith* Wada is mentioned in the line following that devoted to Hagena and Heoden[3]. The reference in *Deor* is unfortunately obscure, but two things are clear: firstly that Heorrenda was known to the Old English poets as a mighty singer, just as Hôrant later was in Germany: secondly that this Heorrenda was connected with the Heodenings. So much we can certainly draw from Deor's words:

"—of myself will I say it : of old I was the poet of the Heodenings, dear to my lord, and Deor was my name. For many a year had I a good service and a gracious lord : till now Heorrenda, the man cunning in song, received the land-right, which of old the lord of earls gave to me."

These references seem to show that Wada and Heorrenda had their part in the Anglian lay, just as they had in the Middle High German epic. That, in spite of these references, critics should have insisted that Snorri's well-told little tale preserved the original version, is a remarkable testimony to the power of style.

Breaking away from this tradition, Friedrich Panzer[4] saw the germ of the story not in the eternal battle, but in those parts which previous critics had regarded as excrescences: in the loves of Hild and Heoden, in the supernatural help given to the lover by Wade, in the magic song of Heorrenda. Panzer believed the story to be of the same origin as the widely spread fairy tale, known to most in the collections of Grimm and Asbiornsen, but of which as many as seventy-two variants have been collected, sometimes from sources as remote as the Swahili tales of Bishop Steere. In this tale a boy, generally a king's

[1] Symons, p. 713.   [2] Symons, p. 714.
[3] Of course it *may* be a coincidence: but the chances are against such a coincidence occurring, and we have no right to assume that it did.
[4] *Hilde-Gudrun*, 1901.

son, falls into the power of a supernatural being—the Eisenhans, Iron John, of Grimm's story, a wild man who dwells at the bottom of a lake. From him the boy parts at length, having acquired magic gifts, generally including that of hair of gold. In rough disguise, and with head covered, he enters the service of a king, generally as a gardener; gains the love of the king's daughter, who alone discovers his golden hair; and at last weds her. Thanks to the help of Iron John he repeatedly saves the king from disaster in war, riding off unknown, and returning to his humble disguise. But the king is determined to know who the strange knight is, and he or his men intercept and wound the hero. The king recognises from the wound that the despised lover of his daughter is the same as the strange knight, and all ends well.

Theories which derive ancient epics from modern fairy tales ought to be received with caution. To collect a number of stories in which the same motive occurs; to argue that they are, in virtue of this motive, all descended from one original; to reconstruct this original, selecting an episode here and a figure there, till the reconstructed original assumes a likeness, more or less remote, to some ancient epic or romance, to conclude therefore that this epic is to be regarded as a literary elaboration of the original fairy tale—all this is a process in which the individual feeling of the investigator counts for so much that, though he may convince himself, he can hardly hope to convince others. Panzer has argued his case with extraordinary conviction, erudition and plausibility, but he has made few converts to his theory.

It is unlikely that the fairy tale—of the age and origin of which we must necessarily remain quite uncertain—is the source of all the numerous mediæval romances (many of them bearing only a most remote resemblance) which Panzer would derive from it. Certain features recur so repeatedly in all popular story that a collection of seventy-two fairy tales on the one hand, and half-a-dozen romances on the other, may easily between them show many common features, without its following that all the romances are drawn from the prototype of the fairy tale.

Perhaps the strongest evidence against the identification of the story with the fairy tale lies in the fact that the fairy tale ends in a reconciliation. Now all the evidence of Northern story points to a tragic ending: there is nothing to show that the story in Old English was not tragic; whilst the oldest German reference is to "the battle betwixt Hagen and Wate, *where Hild's father lay dead*[1]." We can understand why in the later Middle High German epic the fierce old version was toned down; but that so many different versions should have agreed in turning an original reconciliation into a tragedy would be almost incredible.

But a new light has been thrown by Panzer upon many features of the story—the daemonic helper, the magic song of Heorrenda: these will never again be so hastily dismissed as later additions to the tale.

Above all, the old English allusions receive from Panzer's study their due place in the history of the development of the story. There was something paradoxical in the view which accepted Snorri's thirteenth century tale as the original version, whilst condemning as secondary Old English references which could hardly by any possibility be put later than the eighth century, and were probably much older. Yet earlier critics had, in spite of *Widsith*, excluded Wade from the original tale. He was a mythical figure, a water giant, and had no place in the warfare of Heoden and Hagena. It is just because he is a water giant, Panzer urges, that he so obviously belongs to the story. He is an essential part of the tale, the supernatural, daemonic figure who helps the hero at his need ; a figure which agrees admirably with that of the English Wade. Hence the help given to students by Panzer's monograph can hardly be exaggerated, even though his view of the origin of the story has not in its entirety met with any general acceptance[2].

Whilst believing that Panzer has shown Wada to be a much older figure in the story than has generally been admitted,

---

[1]
> *von einen volcwige hôre wir sagen*
> *der ûf Wulpinwerde gescach,*
> *dâr Hilden vater tôt lach,*
> *inzwischen Hagenen unde Waten.*

Lamprecht's *Alexander*, herausg. Kinzel, Halle, 1885, 1830 (1321). Compare note, p. 459.

[2] So far as I know, Panzer's view that the Goldener-myth is the origin of the Hild and Heoden story has not been endorsed by any critic. It has been

we need not therefore identify him with "Iron-John": for the helping and protecting spirit is a figure common enough in all folk-lore, not belonging necessarily to this one particular story[1].

In all probability then, features of the Old Anglian lay were the wooing of the heroine by the magic song of Heorrenda: the help given to the hero by the terrible Wada: and the fall of Hagena, if not of both Hagena and Heoden. But we cannot reconstruct the story in detail with any degree of certainty.

Critics have been influenced by the interest they have felt in the vernacular versions of Snorri or of the *Kudrun* poet. Yet the charm of these, great as it is, is not the same as that of the old poetry. It is when we turn to Saxo's version that we are reminded of the great fragments which have come down to us from the seventh and eighth centuries. The situations are those of the heroic age. The tragedy of strife between kinsfolk and sworn brethren, as we find it in Saxo, was probably the theme of the old poet of Heoden, as it was that of the poets of the lays of *Finnesburh*, of *Ingeld*, of *Hildebrand*, and, in a smaller measure, of *Waldere*.

In *Widsith* the story is localized among the Hælsingas, the Island-Rugians, and the Glommas. The last we cannot identify with any certainty; the two former tribes almost certainly dwelt, in the fourth century, on the islands and peninsulas of what is now the Baltic coast of Germany[2]. It should be noted that in Saxo the last fight takes place in the Baltic upon the island of Hiddensö, off the coast of Rügen. That Saxo's original was localized among the Hælsingas and the Glommas is

examined by Much (in *Herrigs Archiv für das Studium der Neueren Sprachen*, CVIII, 1902, 395–416); E. Martin (in the *Deutsche Litteraturzeitung*, XXII, 1901, 2327–30); B. Symons (in the *Litteraturblatt f. germ. u. roman. Philol.* XXIII, 1902, 321–8); Ehrismann (*Z.f.d.Ph.* XXXVII, 515), and by an anonymous critic (in the *Athenaeum*, No. 3849 ; 1901, II, 152–3). All these critics express dissent, Much and Ehrismann in a reasoned statement of considerable length. But it is admitted that Panzer's study has thrown a new light upon the poem. "Damit sind auch nach meinem Urteil einige Sagenzüge erst ins rechte Licht gerückt," *Much*, 397 ; "Auch in dem zweiten Teile hätte...noch vieles hervorgehoben werden können, dem ich entweder unbedenklich oder doch bedingt zustimmen kann," *Symons*. Symons instances the treatment of Heorrenda and the discussion of his original relation to Heoden.

[1] Cf. Ehrismann in *Z.f.d.Ph.* XXXVII, 521.
[2] See notes to ll. 21, 22.

rendered probable by the fact that the Helsingi, and a roving captain Glomerus[1], are used by Saxo to fill up the intervals of the Hild story in a strange, inconsequential way, as if he knew that they had a place in the tale, but did not remember what it was[2].

Hence, although it has been usual to regard the Hild story as belonging to the North Sea[3], its earliest home would seem to have been among the islands of the Baltic. From these islands its passage to the adjoining Angles was easy, and they must have brought it with them to England. The evidence that it was known to the Franks in the sixth century[4] is insufficient[5]; and the theory that it spread to the Franks from Anglian settlements in the Netherlands[6] depends upon the very uncertain evidence for such settlements. The Old English allusions are by far the earliest reliable documents which we have for the Hild story: and as such their importance has hardly, in the past, been fully recognised.

Evidence points to the story having died out early in England. The earliest charters frequently show the signature of an Abbot Hagona; he and the Abbess Hild of Whitby both belong to the seventh century. After this date place-names founded upon the Hild story are found surviving, but men and women[7] bearing the name Hagana or Hild do not meet us till we find the name Hagana reappearing (owing probably to Danish and Norman immigration) after the conquest. Wade alone retains his popularity: but, it would seem, quite independently of the Hild story.

---

[1] This has been noted by Panzer (*H.G.* 180).

[2] By the *Helsingi* Saxo of course understands the inhabitants of Helsingaland in Sweden. To justify a connection between *Glomerus* and the *Glommas* many instances could be quoted for the interchange of the names of chiefs and peoples. This occurs principally in names ending in *ing* (cf. note to *Hundingum*, 1. 23) but we have also *Hoðbroddr* and *Heaðobeardan* (cf. Bugge, *H.D.* 153, and above, p. 82).

If the Glommas are to be located near the river Glommen (see note to l. 21) we have a confirmation of the conjecture of Dr Lawrence that Heoden was a Geat (*Mod. Philol.* IX, 36, *etc.*).

[3] Cf. Koegel, *Ltg.* I, 1, 169; Binz in *P.B.B.* XX, 192; Symons in *Pauls Grdr.*(2) III, 714.

[4] Panzer, *H.G.* 438.   [5] Much in *Herrigs Archiv*, CVIII, 415.

[6] *H.G.* 440.

[7] See Binz in *P.B.B.* XX, 192–6.

Breca of the Brondings.

Breoca weold Brondingum.

The Breoca, prince of the Brondings, who is mentioned in our
catalogue of kings, is known to us from *Beowulf* (499—606)
where Unferth taunts Beowulf with his unsuccessful swimming
match with Breca, the son of Beanstan[1]. Beowulf asserts that he
was the better swimmer, and he silences his opponent by personal
abuse; but his explanation, that he could have swum faster
than his rival, but did not choose to do so, seems insufficient.
And Beowulf nowhere says that Breca was defeated or humiliated.
The poet has not made the swimming match very clear. The
heroes are apparently swimming northward. Breca after seven
nights reaches the land of the Heathoræmas (in the neighbourhood of the modern Christiania). Beowulf swims side by side
with Breca for five nights, till the flood drives them asunder.
He is attacked by the sea monsters, slays them [on the sixth
night] and sees in the morning before him the sea-nesses of the
land of the Finns. This is hardly intelligible if we suppose
Beowulf to have started from his home among the Geatas. The
story seems most naturally to belong to the ancient Angel, from
which both the land of the Finns (Lapps) and of the Heathoræmas would alike lie in the vague regions of the distant North.

The mention of Breca in *Widsith* justifies us in believing
that Breca had a history of his own as a swimmer, even though
the *Beowulf* poet has introduced him only as a foil to his own
hero[2]. Breca's name, and that of his folk, point distinctly to
some sea story. *Brecan* is used in Old English in the sense

---

[1] For Beanstan see Krüger in *P.B.B.* ix, 573, Bugge in *Z.f.d.Ph.* iv, 198,
Bugge in *P.B.B.* xii, 55; Zupitza in *D.L.Z.* vi, 489-90.

Müllenhoff would connect with O.N. *bauni*, another reference to the sea and
to sea monsters. (*Z.f.d.A.*, vii, 421; *Beovulf*, 2.) The word *bauni* has been
questioned (by J. M. Hart in *M.L.N.* xviii, 118). It will however be found
in Haldorsen's *Islandske Lexikon*, Copenhagen, 1814: "*bauni*, hundefisk" (a
dog fish). I owe this reference to Mr S. Blöndal, of the Royal Library,
Copenhagen.

[2] It certainly does not justify us, with Koegel (*Ltg.* i, 1, 109), in assuming that
there was an old lay of Beowulf and Breca, used by the poet of *Beowulf*. For,
since in *Widsith* heroes of the same cycle are, as far as possible, grouped
together, the absence of Beowulf or Beowa here would be difficult to explain,
the more so since (as has been observed by Möller, *V.E.* 22) the alliteration is so
convenient.

of ploughing the sea[1]: *breki*[2] signifies a breaker in Old Norse poetry; *brandr* in Old Norse means the prow of a ship, whilst *branding, branting* has for many centuries been in use among the sailors of the North Sea to signify "a place where the sea dashes on the rocks[3]."

We cannot, then, dismiss as irrelevant or accidental this fact that both prince and people bear a name which is reminiscent of the sea[4]. But, on the other hand, the context, both in *Widsith* and *Beowulf*, shows that Breca of the Brondings is regarded *there* as the real prince of a real people, not as a mythological abstraction of the breakers conquered by Beowulf[5]. The swimming contest is a favourite episode in Germanic story, and Brecca is as concrete an antagonist as was Olaf Tryggvason, when he dived under water with Kjartan, till "Kjartan thought he had never come in so tight a place before."

In the tale of Breca and his Brondings we have clearly some tale of power over the sea; exactly what it is difficult to say. It is going too far to see in the story of Beowulf and Breca a myth of the Gulf Stream flowing North, and overcoming the colder polar stream[6]: for we have no reason to think that this phenomenon had been observed so early[7].

---

[1] "brecan ofer bæþweg," *Elene*, 244, *Andreas*, 223, 513, is used of a boat being dashed over the waves. See *Andreas u. Elene*, herausg. v. J. Grimm, Cassel, 1840, pp. 109, 147.

[2] The two words come together in the Edda, *fellr brattr breke brøndum hǽre* (*Regensmál*, 17). "The steep billow surges high above the prows" (Symons u. Gering, I, 314).

[3] Compare Dutch *branding*, Danish *brænding*, breakers, surge. The use of *brandung* in the same sense in High German is comparatively recent. See Kluge, *Seemannssprache*, p. 141. There seems no reason (with Chadwick, 269) to connect the *Brandings* with the *Brond* of the Northumbrian pedigree.

[4] This, and the absence of any geographical data with which we can connect their names, make it highly probable that the Brondings are a poetical fiction. Heyne-Schücking (314) seeks to locate them in Mecklenburg and Pomerania, and Thorpe (*Cod. Ex.* 514) in Brännö in the Cattegatt: but there is no satisfactory evidence for either theory. This makes their case different, for example, from that of the *Hælsingas* of l. 22. Yet it might be argued that they were a real tribe or family, that the name *Brondingas* meant originally "men of the sword" like *Helmingas* "helm-men," and perhaps originally *Scyldingas*, "shield-men" (Chadwick, 284), and that they subsequently came to be connected with the hero of a sea story through a false etymology.

[5] Cf. Panzer, *Beowulf*, 271; Lawrence in the *Pub. of the Mod. Lang. Association of America*, XXIV, 262, 269.

[6] Möller, *V.E.* 22 (note); cf. Brandl in *Pauls Grdr.*(2) II, 1, 992.

[7] Heinzel in *A.f.d.A.* XVI, 266–7.

For a reference to a possible development of the swimming match story in the Icelandic sagas, see Bugge in *P.B.B.* XII, 51–5.

Theodoric the Frank.

Þeodric weold Froncum.

The Theodric mentioned as ruling over the Franks is to be identified with Theodoric I, the son of Chlodowech (Clovis), who ruled over the Salian Franks from 511 to 534, the conqueror of the Thuringians, and, through his son Theodebert, of Hygelac the Geat. And Theodric, no less than Hygelac, has his place in heroic song.

The *poeta Saxo* who wrote *De gestis Caroli magni* toward the end of the ninth century makes mention of popular songs in praise of Theodric:

> Est quoque iam notum, vulgaria carmina magnis
>   Laudibus eius avos et proavos celebrant,
> Pippinos, Carolos, Hludowicos et *Theodricos*
>   Et Carlomannos Hlothariosque canunt[1].

About a century later we have a note concerning Theodoric I: *Hugo-Theodoricus iste dicitur, id est Francus, quia olim omnes Franci Hugones vocabantur, a suo quodam duce Hugone*[2]. Another two hundred years and we reach the early thirteenth century, the great age of German epic poetry, to which period belongs the earliest portion of the Middle High German poem of Hug-Dietrich and Wolf-Dietrich[3].

This story is a romantic one: the relation to the historic events of the sixth century is slight, and became still slighter as the tale was overlaid, in the days of the decline of the High German epic, with wild tales of adventure among paynim kings. In the name Dietrich, and in the fact that the story turns upon the suspicion of illegitimate birth, upon the jealousy of brothers, and the loyalty and disloyalty of retainers, we can see the last traces of traditions of the historic Merovingian kings, Theodoric and Theodebert.

We must be careful not to read the Middle High German story into *Widsith*, which chronologically stands much nearer

---

[1] *De gestis, etc.* v. 117, in Pertz (fol.), *SS.* I, p. 268.

[2] *Quedlinburg Chronicle*, in Pertz (fol.), *SS.* III, p. 31; see Schröder in *Z.f.d.A.* XLI, 24 etc.

[3] See Müllenhoff, *Die Austrasische Dietrichssage*, in *Z.f.d.A.* VI, 435–59, and the chapter *Teoderico e Teodeberto* in the *Origini* of Pio Rajna.

to the days of the historic Theodoric, than to the German epic of the thirteenth century. We have seen that we are not justified in assuming that the Theodric and Seafola who are mentioned in l. 115, as retainers of Eormanric, are the same as Wolf-Dietrich and the traitor Sabene[1]. The Theodric mentioned in l. 24 is undoubtedly Theodoric the Frank, and therefore ultimately to be identified with the hero of the *Wolf-Dietrich* story : but the stories to which he owes his mention in *Widsith* are probably not those known to us (in their later form) through the Middle High German epic of *Wolf-Dietrich*, but rather the much earlier traditions, at least half historical, of Theodoric's conquest of the Thuringians.

This event made so strong an impression upon the tribes of North Germany as to form a landmark in their annals. Thus the continental Saxons, according to a lost work of Einhard, quoted by Adam of Bremen, dated their origin from the period *quo Theodericus, rex Francorum, contra Hirminfridum, ducem Thuringorum, generum suum, dimicans, terram eorum crudeliter ferro vastavit et igne*[2]. The Saxons according to this story helped Theodoric, and received in return settlements in the old Thuringian land. In the fragment known as the *de Suevorum origine*[3], the same story is told of the " Suevi "; and the whole legend of Theodoric's Thuringian war, as it was current in the second half of the tenth century, is given by Widukind[4].

This story is quite dissimilar from the legends later associated with the names of Hug-Dietrich and Wolf-Dietrich, but for one remarkable point of likeness. The true hero of the Middle High German epic is neither Hug-Dietrich nor Wolf-Dietrich, but the faithful retainer Berhtunc von Meran : to him is opposed the faithless Sabene. Similarly Widukind's story

---

[1] See above, pp. 41–4.

[2] *Adam of Bremen*, i, 4 in Pertz (fol.) *SS.* vii, 285 (1846). The same account occurs, almost word for word, though without mention of its being taken from Einhard, in the ninth century *Translatio S. Alexandri*. Pertz (fol.) *SS.* ii, 674–5 (1829).

[3] Published, with commentary, by Müllenhoff in the *Z.f.d.A.* xvii, 1874, pp. 57–71.

[4] i, 9–13, in Pertz (fol.) *SS.* iii, 420–424. The version given below is a paraphrase and summary of Widukind's story, which is told at too great length to be given literally.

contrasts the figures of the true and the false servant. Theodoric owes his success, Irminfrid his defeat and death, each to
the counsel of his trusted servant.

Huga, king of the Franks, died, leaving no heir save Amalberga, wedded
to Irminfrid, king of the Thuringians. The Franks anointed king Huga's
bastard son Thiadric, and he at once sent a message to Irminfrid offering
peace and friendship. Irminfrid would have accepted Thiadric's proffer,
had not his wife, claiming that she was heir to the throne, persuaded the
king's counsellor Iring *acer ingenio, acutus consilio, facilis ad suadendum
quae vellet,* to advise war.

So, against the will of his chief nobles, Irminfrid replied that Thiadric
was by birth his bondsman, and that he would not yield to him. "Rather
would I give thee my head," replied the messenger, "than hear such
words, knowing that they must be washed out by the blood of many
Franks and Thuringians."

So Thiadric and Irminfrid met ; and the battle lasted three days :
Irminfrid was at last beaten off, though with such loss to Thiadric that
retreat was advised. But, by the words of one counsellor, *servus satis
ingeniosus, cujus consilium expertus est saepius probum, eique propterea
quadam familiaritate conjunctus,* Thiadric was urged to press his beaten
foe, which he did, summoning the Saxons to his aid. [The story of how
the Saxons helped the Franks does not concern us : in the end Irminfrid
and his Thuringians were utterly routed.] Iring, sent by Irminfrid to beg
for mercy, was persuaded by Thiadric to turn traitor : to lure his master
into the presence of the Frankish king, and then to slay him, in the
moment of making his obeisance. But the promised reward did not
follow. "Hateful to all men for having slain thy lord," cried Thiadric,
"depart from us : we will have neither part nor lot in thy wickedness."
"Justly am I hateful to all men," Iring replied, "having yielded to thy
wiles : but I will purge my sin and avenge my lord." With his still
unsheathed sword he smote Thiadric, and, having placed the dead body
of his master above that of the Frankish king, so that he might conquer
even in death, he cleared a *way* for himself, and departed. If any faith is
to be placed in this story, Widukind says, the reader must judge, but the
Milky way to this day is known by Iring's name[1].

The details of this story are, of course, fabulous : but it
reflects accurately the character of Theodoric, as he is depicted
by Gregory of Tours[2], as well as the fact that Irminfrid was
slain, after his surrender, apparently through the treachery of
Theodoric.

Now both the treacherous Iring and the nameless faithful
counsellor seem to belong to the class of retainer known in Old

---

[1] In the *Quedlinburg Annals* another version of the story is given, in which
Iring is apparently the faithful companion of Irminfrid. See Pertz (fol.)
SS. III, 32. In the *de Suevorum origine* Irminfrid escapes to the court of
Attila. A version similar to these must lie behind the mention in the
Nibelungen Lied of the two heroes Iring and Irnfrit at Etzel's court. As to the
origin of the *Quedlinburg* version, see *Z.f.d.A.* XLI, 24.

[2] *Hist. Franc.* III, 7, 8.

English society as *thyle* : the professional orator and counsellor[1]. It is therefore remarkable, as Müllenhoff noted long ago[2], that in our list *Thyle* of the Rondings is coupled with Theodric of the Franks. *Thyle* as a proper name is in any case strange enough : can we interpret it as referring to the faithful counsellor of the Thuringian war ?

It is difficult to track this story in England. Here personal names help us but little. The name Theodric is inconclusive, for Englishmen bearing it were probably named after the Gothic rather than the Frankish king[3] : the faithful servant is anonymous : no argument can be drawn from the rarity of the name Iring in England, for a man would hardly name his son from the villain of the story: the scene of the tale is in Thuringia, so we should not expect to find it localised in English place names. It seems clear that, in the name *Iringaes uueg*, applied to the Milky way[4], we have not necessarily a reminiscence of the traitor but rather of an ancient mythological figure whose relation to his namesake in the Thuringian story, and in the *Nibelungen Lied*, is a difficult problem[5], lying outside the scope of this study.

The Lombards.

Tacitus describes the Longobardi as a small but excessively warlike nation[6], successfully maintaining their independence against overwhelming odds. This character they retain throughout the ages, so that the sentence of Tacitus would form an

[1] For the functions of the *thyle*, cf. Müllenhoff, *D.A.* v, 288–9, and Kaufmann in Sievers' *Philologische Studien*, Halle, 1896, pp. 159–162. Kaufmann would make Widsith a *thyle*, by reason of his relation to queen Ealhhild, and his extraordinary knowledge of princes and peoples. For an Irish parallel to the *thyle* see Deutschbein in the *Germ. Rom. Monatsschrift*, i, 114.

[2] *Z.f.d.A.* xi, 280–1.

[3] If indeed we are justified in assuming that they were named after either. For, as saints' names are often given to children at the present day, without any thought of the patron saint, so a child may have been named Theodric without thought of any hero : perhaps because he had two uncles, Theodred and Godric, and his father wished to compliment both at once.

[4] *Epinal Gloss.*, ed. Sweet, *E.E.T.S.* (1883), p. 28.

[5] See Grimm, *Mythology*, tr. Stallybrass, i, 234–5 ; 358–362 ; Symons in *Pauls Grdr.* (₁) ii, 1, 32 ; Koegel, *Ltg.* i, 1, 124–129 ; Grimm, *Heldensage*, 401 ; Koegel in *P.B.B.* xvi, 504.

[6] *Germania*, xl.

appropriate motto for the narrative of their national historian, Paul the Deacon. It is this picture of a valiant little nation, in the midst of overbearing neighbours, which gives its lasting interest to their story, from the traditional days of the fight of Agio and Ibor, and their scanty array[1], against the Vandals, to those of their historic victories over the Herul and the Gepid[2].

Traces of the early Lombard home on the lower Elbe probably remain in the mediaeval Bardengau and Bardowyk[3]. It is here too, between the Angles on the North, and the main Suevic confederation on the South, that all the early authorities, Strabo[4], Tacitus[5] and Ptolemy[6], seem to agree in placing them.

But they must have left this home at some period prior to A.D. 165, when we find them on the Roman border. Their departure would leave the Anglian and Suevic folk immediate neighbours, and there was probably some trouble before boundaries could be readjusted. Finally, as we know from *Widsith*, the matter was settled by the victorious sword of Offa:

> heoldon forð siþþan
> Engle and Swæfe, swa hit Offa geslog.

Like their neighbours, the Angles and Saxons, the Lombards were less civilized than those East Germanic peoples with whom the Romans were more familiar. At the beginning of their career, a Roman historian, who had seen them at close quarters, characterizes them as 'savage beyond the measure of even German ferocity[7],' whilst six centuries later Gregory the Great, whatever fallacies he might cherish as to the angelic nature of their far-off Anglian kinsmen, could only describe his Lombard neighbours as 'unspeakable[8].'

The persistency of these national characteristics is the more

---

[1] Paulus, I, 7.   [2] Procopius (*Bell. Gott.* ii, 14 ; iii, 34).

[3] Cf. Hodgkin's *Italy*, v, 100 ; Von Stoltzenberg-Luttmersen, *Die Spuren der Longobarden*, Hannover, 1889.

[4] vii, 290 : μέγιστον μὲν οὖν τὸ τῶν Σοήβων ἔθνος· διήκει γὰρ ἀπὸ τοῦ Ῥήνου μέχρι τοῦ Ἄλβιος · μέρος δέ τι αὐτῶν καὶ πέραν τοῦ Ἄλβιος νέμεται καθάπερ Ἑρμόνδοροι καὶ Λαγκόβαρδοι. Strabonis *Geographica*, rec. Meineke, Lipsiæ (Teubner), 1852, p. 399.

[5] *Germania*, XXXIX, XL.   [6] II, 11, 8.

[7] Vellejus, II, 106 (ed. Ellis).

[8] See Gregorii I, Papæ, *Registrum epistolarum*, ed. P. Ewald and L. M. Hartmann, in *M.G.H.* (Ep. VII, 23 ; v, 38 ; App. II.)

noteworthy as the Lombards, though frequently mentioned in the first century of our era, disappear altogether in the middle of the second, and do not emerge again till the sixth, when they achieve a number of victories culminating in the conquest of Italy. As our poem reflects the historic events of the fourth and fifth centuries, precisely the period when the Lombard nation was out of the sight of Roman chroniclers, its references to Lombard kings need peculiar care, and are of peculiar importance.

Sceafa.

Sceafa [weold] Longbeardum.

No name of any such Lombard king Sceaf is known to the historians[1]; but it is with this same king Sceaf[2] that the pedigree of the West-Saxon kings began, until a monkish annalist, by the discovery that Sceaf was a son born to Noe in the ark, enabled us to trace back to Adam the genealogy of king George V.

This reference to king Sheaf ruling the Lombards means, then, that our poet knew of Lombard lays dealing with Sheaf[3], or, if this is saying too much, at least that some allusion founded upon such traditions had reached him[4].

Sceaf is then, apparently, the mythical civilizer whom more than one of the tribes dwelling near the north sea coast regarded as their founder, and the parent of their royal race: the divine foundling who introduces, amid a hitherto barbarous people, the tillage of the earth[5], and with it the settled rule of a king. The fine story of Sceaf is, by a fortunate chance, preserved to us, by two Anglo-Latin historians, respectively of the tenth and twelfth centuries, Ethelwerd and William of Malmesbury. Taking their account in connection with the Prologue of *Beowulf*, we find the story to have been this.

---

[1] Cf. Hodgkin's *Italy*, v, 176.

[2] *Sceaf* stands to *Sceafa* as *Scyld* to *Sceldwa* or *Hreðel* to *Hreðla*. See note to l. 32.

[3] Koegel, *Ltg.* i, 1, 104.

[4] Cf. Müllenhoff, *Beovulf*, 10; Grimm, *Mythologie*, 1835, 219.

[5] 'So lässt sich nicht verkennen dass hier ein mythus von dem anfang und der einführung der altdeutschen cultur vorliegt'—Müllenhoff in *Z.f.d.A.* vii, 413.

He was driven, as a small boy, in a swift boat without any oarsman to the Island of Scandza[1], and found, by the folk of that land, sleeping, with his head upon a sheaf of corn, surrounded by weapons. These folk, marvelling, fed and reared the unknown child, till, in his manhood, he came to rule over the ancient land of the Angles in Sleswig. When he died, full of years, his people placed him, as he had commanded them, in a boat filled with weapons and treasures, and let the sea bear him away, alone, as it had borne him to them[2].

The mention of the sheaf of corn, and the connection of Sceaf with the old Anglian home in Sleswig, we owe to William of Malmesbury alone. The account of the funeral rites is found only in the Prologue to *Beowulf*[3].

But here, at once, we are faced with a difficulty. In *Beowulf* the hero is called not *Sceaf,* but *Scyld Scefing* " Shield with the Sheaf," and is identified with " Shield," the ancestor-king of the Danes.

It has been argued that in this *Beowulf* is true to the original form of the story : that " Shield with the Sheaf" was misunderstood as " Shield son of Sheaf " ; that a new ancestor-king, Sheaf, was thus placed at the head of the genealogy ; and that the story (which must of necessity be told of the earliest ancestor) was then transferred from Shield to his supposed father Sheaf.

---

[1] Not Angeln or Sleswig, as sometimes stated on the high authority of Kemble (*Beowulf,* ii, *Appendix to Preface,* iii) and Grimm (*Mythologie,* 1835, 218). The point is of some importance.

[2] Sceldius [fuit filius] Sceaf. Iste, ut ferunt, in quandam insulam Germaniæ Scandzam, de qua Jordanes, historiographus Gothorum, loquitur, appulsus navi sine remige, puerulus, posito ad caput frumenti manipulo, dormiens, ideoque Sceaf nuncupatus, ab hominibus regionis illius pro miraculo exceptus et sedulo nutritus : adulta ætate regnavit in oppido quod tunc Slaswic, nunc vero Haithebi appellatur. Est autem regio illa Anglia vetus dicta....

William of Malmesbury, *De Gestis Regum Anglorum,* Lib. ii, § 116, vol. i, p. 121, ed. Stubbs, 1887.

Ipse *Scef* cum uno dromone advectus est in insula Oceani, quæ dicitur *Scani,* armis circundatus, eratque valde recens puer, & ab incolis illius terræ ignotus ; attamen ab eis suscipitur, & ut familiarem diligenti animo eum custodierunt, & post in regem eligunt.

Ethelwerdus, iii, 3 in Savile's *Rerum Anglicarum Scriptores post Bedam,* Francofurti, 1601, p. 842.

[3] See discussion of Scyld in Olrik's *Danmarks Heltedigtning,* 1903, pp. 223-277 : *Skjold.*

This view, which was originally suggested by Leo[1], has of more recent years become the accepted one; and the theory that Scyld is the true hero of the story has been endorsed by Möller[2], Sarrazin[3], Binz[4], Sievers[5], Olrik[6], Symons[7], Mogk[8], Koch[9], Chadwick[10], Lawrence[11], Gering[12], Heyne-Schücking[13], and Henry Bradley[14]. On the other hand, the older view, that Sceaf is the original subject of the rudderless boat tale, and that this story is, in the Prologue to *Beowulf*, erroneously applied to the hero Scyld, has been supported among others by Grimm[15], Kemble[16], Ettmüller[17], Müllenhoff[18], ten Brink[19], Koegel[20], Heinzel[21], Henning[22]; and there is more to be said for it than has of late been generally admitted.

For Sceaf as an ancient king is vouched for

(1)   by this passage in the catalogue of kings in *Widsith*.

(2)   by the West-Saxon genealogy in the *Chronicle*. It is true that the name does not occur in the oldest MS (the Parker MS of the late 9th century) and that the three MSS in which it does occur are all of the 11th century. But the name of Sceaf has simply fallen out of the Parker MS by a scribe's blunder, together with a group of other names; and the *agreement* of the other three MSS, though each individually is late, carries us back to the archetype of all three, which is also the original of the Parker MS itself. We can be certain, then, that Sceaf was recognized as standing at the head of the West

---

[1] *Ueber Béówulf*, Halle, 1839, p. 24.   Grundtvig at an earlier date had expressed the belief that the story originally belonged to Skjold (*Danne-Virke*, II, 218), but Leo was the first to explain how Sceaf could have supplanted Scyld.
[2] *V.E.* 43.
[3] *Engl. Stud.* XVI, 73–80 (Review of Müllenhoff's *Beovulf*); cf. *Anglia*, XIX, 383; XXVIII, 410–13. Since writing the above, I notice that Sarrazin quite recently gave the weight of his authority to the support of Sceaf (*Engl. Stud.* XLI, 10).
[4] *P.B.B.* XX, 147–150.   [5] *S.B. Sächs. Akad.* 1895, 176.
[6] *Helte-Digtning*, 223–277.   [7] *Pauls Grdr.*(2) III, 645.
[8] *Pauls Grdr.*(2) III, 320.
[9] *Ynglingar*, in *Historisk Tidskrift*, 1895, 164.   [10] 282.
[11] *Pub. of the Mod. Lang. Association of America*, XXIV, 1909, p. 259.
[12] 100.   [13] 320.   [14] *Encyclopædia Britannica, sub voce* Beowulf.
[15] *Mythology*, trans. Stallybrass, 1880, I, 170.
[16] *Beowulf*, II, *Postscript to Preface* v.   [17] *Beowulf*, 1840, p. 6.
[18] *Z.f.d.A.* VII, 412–14; *Beovulf*, 10–12.
[19] *Pauls Grdr.*(1) II, 1, 532; *Beowulf*, 195.
[20] *Ltg.* I, 1, 105; *Z.f.d.A.* XXXVII, 274.   [21] *A.f.d.A.* XVI, 267–8.
[22] *Z.f.d.A.* XLI, 156–169. Golther (209) and Meyer (193) also give a tacit support to Sceaf, by telling the story of him, not of Scyld.

Saxon pedigree in an official list which was drawn up, certainly before the end of the ninth century, and probably in the middle of that century[1]. We have, of course, no allusion in this list to the "mysterious boat" story: but the fact that Sceaf is an ancestor of Scyld and stands at the head of the pedigree, proves that at this date the story must have been told of him, rather than of Scyld.

(3) We have the evidence of Ethelwerd for the Sceaf story in the tenth century and

(4) of William of Malmesbury in the twelfth. Late as William is, the character of the additional details which he gives shows them to be genuine folk lore, not a mere amplification of Ethelwerd's story; and he is a historian who avowedly drew very largely from popular songs[2].

The only evidence on the other side is that already mentioned of the prologue to *Beowulf*, where the story told of Sceaf by Ethelwerd and William is attributed to Scyld.

That Scyld was an early king of the Danes we know from Saxo: another account makes him *primus inhabitator Germanie*: but nowhere save in *Beowulf* is the story of the boat told of him. It is quite conceivable that the author of the prologue to *Beowulf* has transferred to Scyld, whom he knew as ancestor of the Danish house, a story which belongs of right to Sceaf, the ancestor of the West-Saxon house. This would be quite in accordance with that blending of English and Danish tradition which we seem to be able to trace elsewhere in *Beowulf*.

Either theory is possible, and if we had only Ethelwerd and William on the one hand, and the prologue to *Beowulf* on the other, it would be difficult to decide. But the mention of Sceaf at the head of the pedigree in the *Chronicle* and still more this mention in *Widsith* render very difficult the position

---

[1] I hope later to give a critical text of the West Saxon pedigree, with a fuller discussion of the *Sceaf-Scyld* problem.

[2] Cf. *Gesta Regum Anglorum*, II, §§ 138, 148, 188 (ed. Stubbs, vol. I, pp. 155, 165, 230). Macaulay, in his *Introduction* to the *Lays of Ancient Rome*, instances William as a typical example of the historian who draws upon popular song: Freeman (*Historical Essays, First Series*) has shown the same. A further piece of evidence tending to show that William is recording genuine tradition has been pointed out by Chadwick (278).

of those who suppose him to be a late creation, a figure formed from a misunderstanding of the epithet *Scefing* applied to the hero Scyld.

Till more evidence appears, it would seem that we are justified in following in the steps of Kemble and Grimm : in accepting the story of William of Malmesbury as a true piece of folk lore, and in accepting Sheaf as the hero of the story, as the primitive king alike of Lombard and English tradition.

Ægelmund.

No mention of either Shield or Sheaf is to be found in the Lombard historian, Paul the Deacon, though he, like William of Malmesbury, has drawn liberally enough upon the songs of his people, either directly, or through an intermediate Latin document, the *Origo gentis Langobardorum* of the end of the seventh century. In one case indeed the *Origo* and, following it, Paul, have given the old story in such detail that students have thought that they could trace the alliteration of the old Teutonic verse under the Latin paraphrase[1]. This story, telling how the Long-beards came by their name, is the one which has been put back into stirring English verse by Kingsley, as Wulf's song in *Hypatia*.

After the death of their two dukes Agio and Ibor (the victors in this battle with the Vandals) the Lombards, we are told by the *Origo* and by Paul, were governed by kings, of whom Agelmund, the son of Agio, was the first. An Ægelmund is mentioned in our poem, together with a hero who bears the name of another Lombard king, Eadwine (i.e. Audoin, the father of Alboin).

> ...Hliþe and Incgenþeow
> Eadwine sohte ic and Elsan, Ægelmund and Hungar,
> and þa wloncan gedryht Wiþ-Myrginga.

It is usually assumed that we have here a series of Lombard kings, who have been attracted into the circle of Ermanaric, among whose champions they are numbered. Hlithe has

---

[1] Koegel, *Ltg.* I, 1, 107–8. Bruckner, *Die Sprache der Langobarden (Q.F.)*, 1895, pp. 19, 20.

generally been identified with Leth or Lethuc, an early Lombard king[1]: but we have seen above that the linking of Hlithe with Incgentheow makes it almost certain that he is rather a hero of the wars of Goth and Hun[2]. The evidence which has led to Elsa being declared a Lombard chief is ludicrously inadequate[3]: Hungar, if we can identify him at all, is a Goth[3]. The explanation of the *Wiþ-Myrgingas* as neighbours of the Myrgings, i.e. Lombards, depends upon the assumption, which itself is groundless, that in our poem Myrgings and Lombards are regarded as allies[4].

We are left then with two names alone, *Eadwine* and *Ægelmund*, to support the theory that a group of Lombard kings and heroes has deliberately been incorporated into the company of the retainers of Eormanric.

That the Lombard dynasty was connected by the Old English poets with Gothic story is possible enough. A similar connection is said to be found in Hungarian legend[5]. We have seen, too, how in our poem Ealhhild, the wife of Eormanric, is spoken of as daughter of Eadwine[6], who is apparently the Lombard king. But this hardly supports the theory that the Eadwine mentioned among the household of Eormanric is identical with the Lombard. For if Widsith escorts Ealhhild, daughter of the Lombard king Eadwine, to the court of Eormanric the Goth, then the Eadwine whom he meets there as one among the Gothic king's retainers can hardly be the Lombard.

It is quite possible then, but it seems to me unlikely, that the poet meant to include Lombard champions among the host of Eormanric, waging battle with the people of Attila.

I should be much rather inclined to surmise that the two lines containing the names *Eadwine, Elsa, Ægelmund, Hungar* and *Wiþ-Myrgingas* are a random interpolation, the work of the same unintelligent person who inserted the Biblical and Oriental names among the list of peoples[7]. *Eadwine* is mere repetition, like the repetition of *Creacas, Finnas* and *Casere*;

---

[1] See note to l. 116. [2] See above, p. 47. [3] See note to l. 117.
[4] See note to l. 118. [5] See Matthaei in *Z.f.d.A.* xlvi, 3 *etc.*
[6] See above, pp. 23–24. [7] See above, pp. 7–8.

Elsa may very possibly, like *Hwala*[1], come from the widely
known genealogy of the West-Saxon kings; *Wiþ-Myrgingas*
looks like a mechanical repetition of *wiþ Myrgingum* in l.
42, which the interpolator perhaps took to be one name. He had
a particular weakness for scattering the Myrging name over
the page, cf. ll. 84–5: *mid Myrgingum...ongend Myrgingum.*

But what most of all points to these five names being an
interpolation, is that they interrupt the series of heroes of the
wars of Goth and Hun. When we eliminate the interpolation,
the list runs, as it should: Hlithe, Incgentheow, Wulfhere,
Wyrmhere, and then the reference to the fight in the Vistula
Wood.

If these lines are an interpolation, it is not clear how the
interpolator got the name of Ægelmund. In this form the
name is hardly known in England. It may be a last echo of
the story of the Lombard hero: if it be we cannot judge how
much of his legend was still remembered.

Paul[2] tells us how Agelmund saved from the water a child,
whose father was unknown, and caused him to be carefully
brought up: and how this child, named Lamissio[3] by the king,
grew in time to be a great champion.

This story is generally supposed to be a reflection of the
Sceaf myth[4], but the likeness is not sufficiently strong to
enable us to speak with certainty.

Ælfwine and Eadwine.

Swylce ic wæs on Eatule mid Ælfwine...
...bearn Eadwines.

The identification of Hlithe and Elsa with Lombard kings
and chiefs is then improbable: but as to Eadwine and his
son Ælfwine there is no doubt that they are the Audoin and
Alboin under whom the Lombard people emerge again into

---

[1] See note to l. 14.   [2] I, 15.

[3] *Laiamicho* in the *Origo*: which however knows nothing about the marvellous origin of the hero, but makes him *ex genere Gugingus*, like his (foster-)
father.

[4] See Leo, *Beovulf*, p. 31; Leo connected the stories of Sceaf, Lamissio, and
the Knight of the Swan; cf. also Müllenhoff, *Beovulf*, 10 and (to the contrary)
Koegel, *Ltg.* I, 1, 106.

the light of history[1]. Not but what the stories of these two chiefs, as given by Paul, show clear traces of the Germanic poet at work : for Paul, writing after the Lombard overthrow, is separated by more than two centuries from Alboin's invasion of Italy: probably the poet of *Widsith* stands nearer to that event than does the historian of the Lombards. Thus the greatest of all Germanic tales is woven in Paul's history round the figures of Audoin and his son Alboin. The story, which reminds us of the twenty-fourth *Iliad* by its bringing into conflict the two strongest motives of the primitive warrior, the duty of hospitality, and the duty of revenge, tells how Alboin won a battle over the Gepidae and slew in single combat Thurismod, the son of their king Thurisind. Yet Audoin, according to the Lombard custom, would not give his son the rank of companion at his table, because he had not received weapons from the king of some other people[2].

When Alboin heard this reply of his father, he took with him forty youths only, and betook himself to his old foe Thurisind, king of the Gepidae, and told him why he had come. Thurisind received him gently, invited him to the feast and placed him at his right hand, where Thurismod, his dead son, had been wont to sit. And, whilst they feasted, Thurisind, beholding his son's seat, and calling to mind his death, and seeing his slayer seated in his room, sighed deeply; nor could he forbear but that his grief burst forth, and he said " Lovely to me is that seat, but he who sits in it is hard enough to look upon." Then the king's second son, moved by his father's speech, began to revile the Lombards, comparing them, because they wore white cross-garters, to white-shinned mares[3]. Then a Lombard replied, " Go to Asfeld: and there canst thou well find how hard those whom thou namest mares can kick : where the bones of thy brother lie scattered like those of a hack in the midst of the fields." The Gepidae were unable to bear this, and, moved to mighty wrath, pressed to avenge these open insults : the Lombards, on their side, ready to fight, placed their hands upon their hilts. Then the king, leaping from the table, threw himself between them and restrained his men : threatening to punish first him who first began the fight. It was no victory pleasing to God, he said, when a man in his own house destroyed his guest. So at last the quarrel was stayed, and they finished the banquet with revelry. Thurisind, taking the arms of his son Thurismod, gave them to Alboin, and sent him back in peace, safe to his father's land[4].

[1] The names correspond exactly, and the mention of Italy makes the identification certain.

[2] Similarly Beowulf, even after he has slain Grendel, still sits with the giogoð, and with Hrothgar's two young sons.—*Beowulf*, 1189-91.

[3] The point of *Fetilæ sunt equæ quas similatis* is not clear. Waitz supposes *Fetilæ = fœtulæ*. Sievers (*P.B.B.* xvi, 363-5) and Koegel (*Ltg.* i, 1, 118) connect it with O.H.G. *fizzil*, dappled. But is this sufficiently offensive ?

[4] i, 24.

What element of truth this story of Alboin may contain, we can never know: the events in the background are historical and certain enough. The great battle between Lombards and Gepidae probably took place in 554. In 565 Audoin died, and Alboin became king: he annihilated his ancient guests in a second great battle in 567: and on Easter Monday, 568, he set out from the highlands of Noricum, which had long been the Lombard home, to conquer Italy.

But the Lombards had always been a scanty people, and had lost heavily in the terrible battle in which Alboin had struck down Thurismod[1]. Not merely 'Widsith,' but all the masterless men in Germany, would seem to have joined Alboin's ranks. Two hundred years later, the descendants of Gepidae and Bulgarians, Sarmatians and Suevi could still be distinguished in Italy[2]. Some thirty thousand Saxons, with their wives and children, joined the invaders.

Wasted as Italy had been by pestilence and famine, it could make no adequate resistance to this motley host, and, with the exception of the great coast towns, Ravenna, Rome, and Naples, the whole country was soon in the hands of the conquerors: not, however, before Alboin had been murdered: according to the Lombard story by his wife, a Gepid princess, in vengeance for the wrongs which he had inflicted upon her race.

Perhaps Alboin, like Attila, possessed exceptional powers of holding together jarring nationalities: certainly his death, like that of the Hun, was followed by dissensions among his host. The Saxons were given the choice of adopting Lombard laws and customs, or leaving the country: and they chose to go[3]. Most of them were slaughtered in their attempt to regain their old homes. But many of Alboin's host, disappointed, in the anarchy which followed his death, of their share in the plunder,

---

[1] Jordanes refers to the battle as one of the three bloodiest of recent times, *cecideruntque ex utraque parte amplius LX milia.* Jordanes, *Romana*, ed. Mommsen, p. 52.

[2] *Certum est autem, tunc Alboin multos secum ex diversis, quas vel alii reges vel ipse ceperat, gentibus ad Italiam adduxisse. Unde usque hodie eorum in quibus habitant vicos Gepidos, Vulgares, Sarmatas, Pannonios, Suavos, Noricos sive aliis huiuscemodi nominibus appellamus.* Paulus, *Hist. Lang.* II, 26.

[3] Gregory of Tours, *Hist. Franc.* IV, 42; V, 15. Paulus, *Hist. Lang.* II, 6; III, 5-7. Hodgkin's *Italy*, V, 189.

may have returned to their northern tribesmen with tales of the treasures of Welsh land, and of the great deeds of its conqueror.

So a very few years after Alboin's death his name may have been a household word in North Germany : while at the same time the distance of the scene of his exploits would make him seem, to the wild North Sea tribesmen, a half-mythical hero ; since for popular poetry ' a distance of a thousand miles is as good as one of a thousand years[1].' Before the end of the sixth century the names of Ælfwine, Eormanric and Ætla may well have been thrown together as they are in our poem : nor are we necessarily compelled to regard the reference to Alboin as an interpolation differing very widely in date from the matter of which the bulk of our poem is made up.

That, two centuries later, Alboin was remembered among High and Low Germans alike we know on the authority of Paul the Deacon. " His generosity and his glory, his valour and his success in war, are celebrated in the songs of Bavarians and Saxons, and other people of kindred speech[2]."

It is a pleasing accident that our catalogue of heroes, as it includes Eastgota, the first, should also include Ælfwine, the last, the wildest and the most romantic of the German conquerors of Rome.

---

[1] *On peut dire que le respect que l'on a pour les héros augmente à mesure qu'ils s'éloignent de nous. L'éloignement des pays répare, en quelque sorte, la trop grande proximité des temps, car le peuple ne met guère de différence entre ce qui est, si j'ose ainsi parler, à mille ans de lui, et ce qui en est à mille lieues.* Racine, *Preface to Bajazet.*

[2] *Alboin vero ita præclarum longe lateque nomen percrebuit, ut hactenus etiam tam aput Baioariorum gentem quamque et Saxonum, sed et alios eiusdem linguæ homines, eius liberalitas et gloria, bellorumque felicitas et virtus in eorum car-minibus celebretur.* Paulus, *Hist. Lang.* I, 27.

CHAPTER IV.

WIDSITH AND THE CRITICS.

THE views which scholars have held about *Widsith* have mainly been based upon a literary study of its style and heroic legend. Before going on to examine the geography, grammar and metre of the poem, we may see what measure of agreement has been arrived at upon grounds of style and legend. We can then decide whether or not these conclusions are confirmed by a study of metrical and grammatical details.

Natural divisions of the poem.

There is, at any rate, a *prima facie* case for the theory that *Widsith* is compounded from several sources. If, as is likely enough, several metrical catalogues existed in early times, enumerating kings and tribes, they would be likely to coalesce. And it cannot be denied that the poem, as we have it, falls into certain well-defined sections :

(*a*) First, we have an introduction of nine lines, characterizing Widsith, and introducing the poem proper : " Widsith the far-travelled Myrging, who, with Ealhhild, sought the home of Ermanaric, spake and said "—

(*A*) Then follows a catalogue of kings and tribes, two kings and two tribes being generally mentioned in each line :

Ætla weold Hunum, Eormanric Gotum.

The Traveller's personality is here kept quite in the background. The list, it is true, begins "I have heard of many kings ruling over the nations " : but *ic gefrægn* is an epic formula with little meaning. Widsith is not said to have himself visited either the kings or their folk. After seventeen lines in which the names of kings and princes are crowded together, we get, in more detail, allusions to the stories of Offa of Angel, of Hrothwulf, Hrothgar and Ingeld.

(*B*) Then the Traveller gives the list of the tribes which he himself has visited. For the most part these are grouped three in a line:

Mid Wenlum ic wæs, and mid Wærnum, and mid Wicingum.

It is among these names that the evidently late passage of Biblical and Oriental lore occurs. The chiefs alluded to in section (*B*) are few, and they are mentioned, in some detail, with words of praise. Particular honour is done to the lady Ealhhild. Her praise the poet has sung through many a land.

(*C*) "Thence I fared through the land of the Goths, and visited the champions of Ermanaric." A catalogue of these Gothic champions follows: two, Wudga and Hama, are selected for special honour.

(*b*) Finally come nine lines of epilogue. "In such wise do gleemen wander from land to land." This passage, like the introductory lines, is not supposed to be spoken by Widsith, but is the moralization of the poet.

Without prejudice to the question of unity of authorship, we will call A, B, C, respectively the "Catalogue of kings," the "Lay of Ealhhild"—for it is to her praise that this portion of the poem leads up—and "The Champions of Ermanaric."

Early Criticism : Müllenhoff, Möller, Ten Brink.

Yet, in spite of the ease with which it may be divided up, our poem, with the exception of the one passage in which the names of the Biblical folk occur, bears upon it the impress, if not of one mind, at any rate of one race and of one period.

We have seen that this suspicious passage was rejected quite early: by Kemble in 1833, and, with the addition of another two lines, by Leo in 1838. Six years later (1844) came Müllenhoff's study of the poem in the *Nordalbingische Studien.* Müllenhoff tried to distinguish a number of early interpolations, such, for instance, as the passages dealing with Offa, Hrothgar and Hrothwulf[1]. He did not, however, make any detailed dissection of the poem into its presumed component parts.

In his subsequent study, fifteen years later, in the *Zeitschrift für deutsches Alterthum*, he abandoned any such dissection as hopeless. He rejected the lines already rejected by Kemble and Leo, together with some others, twenty-one in all[2], which he regarded as the work of one and the same interpolator. "I cannot distinguish," he wrote, "earlier and later additions in this poem. It appears to me to have undergone interpolation from one hand only. But let no one think that, by rejecting these additions, he can restore exactly the original poem. In its essence it is certainly the oldest which Anglo-Saxon literature possesses. But when was it first written down? And has no word been distorted, deranged, or lost[3]?"

Müllenhoff, then, allowed fully for the different corruptions which might have crept in between the seventh century and the eleventh. He also recognized, what could scarcely have escaped the observation of a much less able critic, that the poem fell into three main divisions: the catalogue of kings; the catalogue of tribes and chiefs whom Widsith had known; and the Ermanaric catalogue[4]. But Müllenhoff at this date seems to have regarded all these as merely sections of one poem, the work of one mind[5].

Close on a quarter of a century later, in his *Beovulf*, he

---

[1] *Nordalb. St.* I, 162. Compare also " Wenn nun aber Burgunden genannt werden und ihr König jetzt Günther Gûdhhere genannt wird, so konnte das wieder nicht derselbe Sänger thun der früher ihnen Gifica gab " (p. 165).

[2] 14–17, 75–87, 131–134.   [3] *Z.f.d.A.* XI, 294.

[4] Müllenhoff in 1859 divided thus :

1–9. Introduction.

10–49. First section, with 10–13 introduction [rejecting 14–17].

50–108. Second section, with 50–56 introduction [rejecting 75–87, thus bringing the passage in praise of Ælfwine nearer to that in praise of his sister Ealhhild].

109–130. Third section.

131–143. Conclusion [rejecting 131–134].

He adhered to this division in his later work, but added 45–49 to the list of supposed interpolations.

[5] Cf. *Z.f.d.A.* XI, 285, where unity of authorship is assumed. Some years earlier (1848) Müllenhoff seems to have held the theory, later advanced by Möller, that the Ermanaric-catalogue differed in date from the rest of the poem. In the *Z.f.d.A.* VI, 458 he attributes it to the eighth century.

expressed his agreement with the theory which recognized in these three sections three originally unconnected poems. But with regard to details he was still cautious. " The work of each of these poets can be separated from that of the two others, but not from that of the man who bound the three lays into one." All three poems, he thought, bore the stamp of the same age, or at least fell within a century of each other : the period was the later sixth and the earlier seventh century : the first section, the catalogue of kings, was the oldest[1].

In regarding the three lays as the work of distinct authors, Müllenhoff was following in the steps of Hermann Möller, who, in his *Altenglische Volksepos* (1883), had attempted to define the work of the different poets with that exactitude which Müllenhoff regarded as beyond the power of the critic.

Broadly speaking, Möller divided the poem as Müllenhoff had done in 1859 ; he distinguished a prologue (ll. 1–9) followed by (I.) the catalogue of kings (10–49), in which he supposed the more detailed passage in praise of Offa and Hrothgar to be a later addition ; (II.) the Ealhhild lay (50–81, 90–108); (III.) the catalogue of Ermanaric's champions (88–90, 110–134); and finally the epilogue (135–143). A number of minor alterations were made in the poem by Möller, in order to force it into those four line stanzas in which he believed the Old English lays to have been originally composed. But the gist of Möller's criticism lay in the fact that, whilst accepting Müllenhoff's division of the poem into three, he confidently attributed each of these three sections to a different author and a different period.

One further essential alteration he made. Four persons are specially praised in the Ealhhild lay for their generosity : Guthhere the Burgundian, Ælfwine son of Eadwine the Lombard, Eormanric the Goth, whose splendid gift to the poet is specially mentioned. This gift, as we know, Widsith, on his return home, presented to Eadgils, his lord, from whom he held his fief. Then, in conclusion, we have the praise of the generosity of Ealhhild, daughter of Eadwine.

---

[1] *Beovulf*, 1883 (published posthumously, 1889), p. 92.

But Möller would not allow a place to Eormanric in the Ealhhild lay. That Eormanric should have bestowed a ring upon our poet was, he argued, chronologically impossible, whilst a gift from Ælfwine need not have been fictitious. Secondly, Ælfwine is praised in the poem as the most generous of princes. So it must have been he who gave our singer his most precious gift. Finally, as Möller read the poem, Eadgils was the husband of Ealhhild, and consequently brother-in-law of Ælfwine. "The singer after his return would have presented to his lord the gift of an allied and related prince, not of any other."

This last argument is certainly unsound. Teutonic custom allowed the passing on of a gift from one great chief to another, without postulating any friendship between them. Besides, we have seen that the supposed relationship between Ælfwine and Eadgils is an entirely baseless assumption[1]. The first argument is without weight to those of us who hold the whole of Widsith's travels for an epic fiction. The second argument, that our poet graduated his scale of praise exactly in accordance with the supposed generosity of the chiefs, can hardly be maintained seriously. Eormanric, "more cunning than all in guile, more generous in gift[2]," could not be praised as enthusiastically as Ælfwine, though he might be represented as giving Widsith an even more magnificent gift.

Yet on these grounds Möller, by transferring certain lines from one section of the poem to the other, excluded the name of Eormanric from the Ealhhild lay, and made Ælfwine the donor of the precious armlet[3].

Möller's dissection of the poem commanded in general, as we have seen, the assent of Müllenhoff. It was also followed, in its main details, by Ten Brink. Individual lines, which Möller had cast out, because they interfered with his arrangement of the poem in strophes, were indeed readmitted by Ten Brink, who owed no allegiance to this metrical theory. And in one point particularly Ten Brink greatly improved upon Möller's scheme. He recognized the close relationship which

---

[1] See above, p. 21 *etc.*   [2] See above, p. 34.   [3] *V.E.* 3, 9.

exists between the second and third sections of the poem, as divided by Möller; the Ealhhild lay and the Ermanaric catalogue. So close a connection could only be accounted for, he thought, by their having been early fused into one poem: lines had been transferred from the one to the other, and the two poems had become so wound together that it was difficult to separate them with any certainty[1]; and they had been so combined, he held, since the latter half of the seventh century[2].

Ten Brink followed Möller in regarding the Offa episode as a later addition to the catalogue of kings, but one made, perhaps, whilst the Angles were still on the continent[3].

One may doubt whether it is possible for any critic, however brilliant, to trace the minute history of a poem so far back into heathen times. But it should be noted that, in Ten Brink's opinion, the compiler who, perhaps in the eighth century, put our poem together in its present form, had before him only two songs: on the one hand the catalogue of kings together with the Offa and Hrothgar episodes, and on the other hand the contaminated lay of Ealhhild-Eormanric. Both of these, whatever their ultimate origin, Ten Brink believed to have been complete poems for some generations.

In Ten Brink's view Ealhhild was the wife of Eadgils: her relation to Eormanric was negligible: she had on one occasion visited his court. Hence he naturally regarded the Ealhhild and the Eormanric episodes as distinct in origin, although very early brought together. Now we have seen that the balance of probability is strongly in favour of Ealhhild being, not the wife of Eadgils, but, as suggested by Heinzel[4], another form of Sonhild or Swanhild, the luckless wife of Ermanaric. But, if Ealhhild is to be identified with Swanhild, who has no existence in story apart from Ermanaric, it is absurd to continue to speak of an Ealhhild lay and an Eormanric lay as distinct. The second and third sections of the poem *must* be one lay. And here comes in the importance of Ten Brink's

---

[1] P. 540.   [2] P. 544.   [3] P. 539.
[4] *W.S.B.* cxiv, 514–16. See above, p. 22 *etc.* It is not necessary for the argument that Ealhhild should be Swanhild, but only that she should be wife of Eormanric. And so much, at least, seems fairly certain.

conviction, that the Ealhhild lay and the Eormanric lay are not distinguishable in metre and style. His adherence to the old view that Ealhhild is Eadgils' wife forced him to regard these two sections as originally distinct lays. When, in spite of this presupposition, he recognizes their remarkable likeness[1], we have evidence of the greatest value: for it is that of an able critic given, not in support of, but in opposition to, his preconceived theories. In order to make the phenomena of the poem fit these theories, and to build up a distinction between the Ealhhild and Eormanric lays, Ten Brink had to transfer lines from the one section to the other.

At least then from line 50 to line 130 the poem would seem to be a fairly consistent whole. It may be compounded of various elements, and it is probable enough that reminiscences of a dozen different lays lie behind it. But everything has been so fused and absorbed that it is impossible for us to distinguish the different strata, or to subdivide the poem further[2]. We cannot follow Ten Brink in venturing back into the remote past, and showing how the seventh century poet put the *Ealhhild-Eormanric* lay together; we have not evidence enough to do so[3]. All we can do is to mark as doubtful any lines like the 'Biblical' passage, which seem to indicate a date later than that of the bulk of the poem.

But are we justified in following Ten Brink in maintaining a distinction between this Ealhhild-Eormanric lay on the one hand, and the preceding catalogue of kings (ll. 10–49) on the other?

Here, I think, a further examination entirely bears out Ten Brink's theory. There is a clear break in the continuity of the poem at l. 50[4]. *Swa*, in view of what has preceded, makes no sense. And the passage which precedes is of a different character from that which follows.

The catalogue of kings is an impersonal list: the Ealhhild-Eormanric lay is a personal narrative. They have no organic

---

[1] *Pauls Grdr.*(₁) II, 540–541. Compare for example ll. 68, 69, with ll. 113, 114.

[2] Always, of course, excepting the late "Biblical" interpolation.

[3] For an opinion to the contrary see Schütte, *Oldsagn*, 47.

[4] See note to that line, and cf. Möller, *V.E.* 34.

connection; to print them as separate poems would not involve the change of a single word. And there are serious discrepancies between them.

Whereas the *scóp* of the Ealhhild-Eormanric lay owns for his lord Eadgils, prince of the Myrgings, the poet of the catalogue of kings mentions with pride the victory of Offa over the Myrgings at Fifeldor. Old Germanic literature is chivalrously ready to applaud valour, on whichever side displayed : but the exultant reference to Offa's victory cannot have been intended to have been put into the mouth of Widsith, who is represented as belonging to the defeated foemen.

In the catalogue of kings Gifica rules the Burgundians, Meaca the Myrgings, Sceafa the Lombards. In the Ealhhild-Eormanric portion Guthhere rules the Burgundians, Eadgils the Myrgings, Eadwine and Ælfwine the Lombards. The Ælfwine passage has been thought by many critics to be a later interpolation. Granting that it is, the contrast is still sufficiently striking between the at least half-historical figures of Eadgils and Guthhere and the apparently quite mythical figures of Gifica, Meaca, Sceafa.

It may be said that there is here an intentional distinction. The first list enumerates mythical kings of old time of whom the poet has but heard ; the other enumerates those semi-historical figures who were nearer his own day, whom his Widsith has actually seen[1]. But on this hypothesis it would be difficult to account for the inclusion of Ætla and Eormanric in both lists.

Again, in the first list the Burgundians are apparently thought of in their old eastern seat by the Goths; in the second, under Guthhere, they must have been on the Rhine. Sceafa in the first list assumes (perhaps) the old Lombard home by the sea; Ælfwine in the second list rules the Lombards in Italy. The reference to the Rugians in the first list

---

[1] Cf. Heinzel, *A.f.d.A.* x, 232. Heinzel, reviewing Möller's work, refuses to accept his view of three lays welded together. He admits two lays only : roughly the catalogue of kings and the champions of Ermanaric. The lay of Ealhhild he divides between the two. But the effect of this division of the Ealhhild lay is to separate the praise of Ælfwine from that of his sister Ealhhild. It is much easier to take the whole of the "Ealhhild lay" with the "champions of Ermanaric."

assumes that they are a seafaring folk : in the second list they
are mentioned together with the Romans ; a reminiscence, it
may be, of the days when they ruled in Italy together with the
Ostrogoths.   The variance in these two last instances is however too hypothetical to have more than a slight subsidiary
value.

Only one of these discrepancies is in itself very convincing :
but taken together, in the bulk, they seem to indicate a
difference[1], both in age and character, such as that which Ten
Brink postulated, between the catalogue of kings and the
Ealhhild-Eormanric lay.

Further, the phenomena of the poem justify the distinction
which Ten Brink made between the catalogue of kings proper,
and the lines celebrating Offa and Hrothgar, which he regarded
as later excrescences upon that list.   For in the catalogue
proper one king only is allotted to each tribe : Sigehere ruled
the Danes.   When we find a second Danish king Alewih, and
a third and fourth Hrothgar and Hrothwulf, it is manifest that
they interfere with the scheme of the original list, and probable
that they are additions to that list made by a later hand[2].

Merits of the older criticism.

The view expressed above that the poem falls into two
divisions, the catalogue of kings, and the Eormanric-Ealhhild
lay, is not inconsistent with the views of the earlier critics,
Müllenhoff, Möller, and Ten Brink.   Indeed, it develops out of
these views inevitably, so soon as we abandon the unjustifiable
assumption of these older critics that Ealhhild is the wife
of Eadgils.

In recent years a reaction against the school of Müllenhoff
has set in.   So far as this reaction is a protest against the too

---

[1] Cf. Schütte, *Oldsagn*, 47 ; for arguments to the contrary, Heinzel as above.
[2] Mention should perhaps be made of the view, originally suggested by
Ettmüller(₂), 211, that *Widsith* is an episode, a fragment from some longer epic.
This was also held by Wright (*Biog. Brit.* 1842, I, 4), Thorpe (*Cod. Ex.* 512–3)
and Klipstein (II, 422).   None of them produced any arguments in favour of
this theory : yet they were right in feeling that *Widsith* is no isolated phenomenon, but one fragment which has been saved from a great body of story
which has been lost.

great certainty sometimes claimed by that school for its results, it is justified. But, on the whole, a comparison of the methods and results of Müllenhoff and his contemporaries with those of some of their critics is in favour of the earlier school. The results of the older students of *Widsith*, up to and including Ten Brink, represent a consistent evolution, resulting from many years of patient study and interchange of ideas. No man's work breaks violently away from that of his predecessor. The views of Kemble, Leo, Müllenhoff in 1844, Müllenhoff again in 1859, Rieger, Möller, Müllenhoff a third time as published in 1889, and Ten Brink all develop quite naturally the one out of the other.

Certainly, in their later stages, these views become somewhat complicated. But it is no true objection to the theories of Müllenhoff, Möller and Ten Brink to say that they are "complicated." Of course they are, *ex hypothesi*. These critics believed that the old English poems had had a complicated past; and who will deny that much lies between the defeat of Chochilaicus and MS *Cotton Vitellius* A. xv? A complicated theory of how *Widsith* might have arisen may not be convincing in every detail. But if it shows us the way in which the poem might have grown up, it is surely better than a theory of artificial simplicity which does not correspond to the complicated and sometimes even contradictory traces of date and origin which our poem bears.

Recent Criticism of Widsith.

The study on the style and interpretation of *Widsith* recently published by Dr W. W. Lawrence[1] is characterized by this distrust of the methods of the older school.

The elaborate patchwork theory of Ten Brink, who distinguishes in the piece four separate lays, not including introductory and connecting material, has never been adequately criticised and refuted, although the general weakness of his method is apparently coming more and more to be recognized[2]....

It is not so difficult for an unprejudiced person to admit that some such additions as Müllenhoff describes may have crept into *Widsith*, however unlikely he may think it that Müllenhoff succeeded in defining their limits with certainty[3].

[1] In *Mod. Philol.* IV, 1907, pp. 329 *etc.*
[2] P. 332. [3] P. 342.

But Müllenhoff did not claim to have defined these limits with certainty. On the contrary, he frequently declared that this cannot be done. Müllenhoff, like other critics of the "dissecting school," was often very definite in his theories: but the willingness which he showed to reconsider these theories acquits him of any charge of undue dogmatism. It is not sufficiently realized that this definiteness of theory is the only alternative to a vagueness and confused thinking which must ensue, if we argue about interpolations without defining to ourselves their exact scope. It is therefore the duty of a critic who believes a poem or play to be the work of several hands, to form a hard and definite theory, consistent with the facts that he has noted. The law of chance is against his theory being right in every detail. But a critic who is quite clear in his own mind as to exactly what he is trying to prove may often prove his general theory, even though we are in doubt as to many of the details. If he confines himself to generalities he will prove nothing.

For example, Möller thought he detected traces of a strophic system in the Old English epic, and he accordingly published a *Beowulf*, arranged in four-line strophes. He cannot have hoped that his reconstruction reproduced exactly the original *Beowulf*. Yet his *method* was right enough, for the only way of testing his theory was to attempt such reconstruction, and to see how it worked out. Most critics will agree that it works out badly; that it involves too much violation of the text. But Möller did a service by demonstrating how much violation of our existing text is necessary in order to force *Beowulf* into strophic form.

Rejecting the theories of the origin of the poem evolved by Müllenhoff, Möller, and Ten Brink, Dr Lawrence gives a study of *Widsith* of which the general principles are indicated by the following extracts :

If *Widsith* is inferior in poetic quality to other pieces of lyric character in Anglo-Saxon, it is by no means wholly lacking in this respect. The passage describing the singer's relations with his lord Eadgils and with queen Ealhhild (ll. 88 ff.) serves to indicate what the general tone of the poem in an earlier form may have been. For, as will be seen, closer study shows that it has been much overlaid and defaced by the addition of inferior material, like a Gothic building rudely modernized with bricks and mortar[1]....

We shall surely not err in looking to this thread of story for the earlier material at the basis of the poem, rather than to the lists of names, etc. which precede. Instances of expanding a tale by the interpolation of inferior matter are common enough, but to enliven cataloguing by the composition of epic verse dealing with different material, and telling a separate story, is, so far as I am aware, unheard of. It seems reasonable, then, to regard much of this ethnological tediousness as a later addition to the main theme, having crowded out earlier portions of the poem, so that the real narrative of Widsith's adventures is preserved in a fragmentary condition only[2]....

One would like to believe that the references to Guðhere (ll. 64–67) and to Ælfwine (ll. 70–74) formed originally a part of the same story as ll. 88 ff., as they are similar to it in style and metre, and unlike the material in which they are imbedded. It is almost impossible to resist the conclusion that there is here preserved some of the good old piece which formed the nucleus of the present poem, much mutilated and interpolated, indeed, but still showing its presence, wherever it remains, by its superiority to the matter which surrounds it[3].

But is not this open to the very objection which Dr Lawrence brings against the school of Müllenhoff: that of "dependence upon subjective and *a priori* conceptions of Anglo-Saxon style"? Who is to decide what is inferior matter, and what better material? And why should the better be necessarily old, the inferior new?

Müllenhoff and his school did sometimes, it is true, reject a passage for no other reason than that it appeared to them inferior, and therefore, they argued, was later. But, generally, their criticism depended upon a number of discrepancies, found in the course of a minute study of details of ethnology, heroic lore, dialect, and metre. In so far as it depended upon these things it was more reliable than the criticism which threatens to replace it, which is based, to a much greater degree, upon the personal impression of the critic.

Why should the superiority in style or interest of the passages dealing with the generosity of Guthhere, Ælfwine, Eormanric, Eadgils, and Ealhhild prove these passages to constitute parts of the original poem?

And does such superiority exist? True, a modern reader will find these parts more interesting than those which are crowded with names. But this is because he does not know

---

[1] P. 330.   [2] P. 340.   [3] P. 343.

the stories, and therefore the poet's allusions awake no echo in his mind. Working on this principle, a modern Bentley might eject much " inferior matter " from the text of Milton :

> Nymphs of *Diana's* train, and *Naiades*
> With fruits and flowers from *Amalthea's* horn,
> And Ladies of th' *Hesperides*, that seem'd
> Fairer than feign'd of old, or fabl'd since
> Of Fairy Damsels met in Forest wide
> By Knights of *Logres*, or of *Lyones*,
> *Lancelot* or *Pelleas*, or *Pellenore*.

Mid Rugum ic wæs and mid Glommum is a statement which, to a modern reader, may be devoid of interest. But there was a time when the naming of Rugians and Glommas in the same breath would have sufficed to call up one of the most glorious of the old tales. It is our misfortune that many of the lines no longer give up their secrets to us ; it is our fault if we therefore condemn them. And our poem shows no little art in the way names are grouped so as to recall the old stories, and the monotony of the lists is varied by occasional rhyme or transposition :

> Þeodric weold Froncum, Þyle Rondingum,
> Breoca Brondingum, Billing Wernum.
> Oswine weold Eowum and Ytum Gefwulf,
> Fin Folcwalding Fresna cynne.
> Sigehere lengest Sæ-Denum weold,
> Hnæf Hocingum, Helm Wulfingum,
> Wald Woingum, Wod Þyringum,—

I cannot call verse like this 'inferior'—the poet seems to me to have accomplished a difficult task extraordinarily well. Still less can these lists of names be condemned as ' late.' On the contrary, it is in virtue of the proper names, and of these only, that so many critics have pronounced *Widsith* the earliest of all English poems. For these names of kings and tribes show an extraordinary knowledge of the old stories; *Maldon*, on the other hand, shows us how the old commonplaces were applied to a new generation of heroes, and how descriptions of the bestowal of rings *might* have been written during the latest period of the Old English epic.

Indeed, Dr Lawrence admits that some of the interpolated passages " may have existed previously, and may be as old as the narrative portion, or even older." But, if this is so, we are

driven back to the old theory of the contamination of two or
more lays. I cannot see how the poem can be compared to
"a Gothic building rudely modernized with bricks and mortar"
if the bricks and mortar form a building which is in some cases
as old as or even older than the Gothic building itself. It is
the great merit of the clearly defined theories of Möller and
Ten Brink that, by their very dogmatism, they saved the critic
from the danger of self-contradiction[1].

How contradictory recent criticism of the poem has proved,
when compared with the criticism of the school of Müllenhoff,
is shown by the fact that Professor Brandl singles out as the
oldest element in the poem just those lists of names which
Dr Lawrence regards as the modern bricks and mortar[2].

The poem, Professor Brandl thinks, may have been put into
its present form in the eighth century. It was constructed out
of three old mnemonic catalogues, which can be distinguished
by their style from the story of Widsith the wanderer, in which
they are framed.

We have seen that there is reason for thinking that the
catalogue of kings is such a mnemonic list, and that it betrays
its origin by certain inconsistencies when compared with the
rest of the poem. In fact, as Ten Brink said, ll. 18–34 are
"uralte *versus memoriales.*"

But that the two other catalogues, of peoples and of
Eormanric's champions, are to be distinguished from each
other, and from the narrative in which each is imbedded, is not
so clear. No doubt there is a difference in style between the
narrative and the lists. How Widsith sang in the hall of
Eadgils is told in the manner which the Old English poets
love : in lines following the one upon the other, with sense
variously drawn out. On the other hand, the names of the
tribes and champions he visited are enumerated in the most
rapid way. But are we justified in assuming that the verse of
an Old English bard was always of one pattern, and that the

---

[1] Whilst dissenting from Dr Lawrence's results, I wish to express my keen
appreciation of his most useful essay. No one before Dr Lawrence seems to
have sufficiently appreciated the importance of Heinzel's work on the subject.
[2] *Pauls Grdr.* ($_2$) II, 1, 966–69.

same man could not be terse in writing a catalogue, diffuse in singing a chieftain's praise ? If not, then arguments drawn from dissimilarity of style cannot rank with arguments based upon differences of tradition and outlook, such as we have seen separate the catalogue of kings from the rest of the poem.

Excluding this catalogue of kings (18–49) and, of course, the later interpolations, the poem seems homogeneous enough. It is of course quite possible that Professor Brandl is right, and that between our poem, and the mass of lays of the Eormanric and other cycles which lie behind it, there may intervene some heroic catalogues of champions or of peoples[1]. But I do not think this has been demonstrated. It is not clear that the same poet who depicted the figure of Widsith the traveller could not have drawn up these lists for himself from the lays which he knew.

However widely they may differ as to what are the old and what the more modern parts of the poem, Professor Brandl and Dr Lawrence agree in regarding the story of Widsith as ficti- tious. Mr Chadwick, in his recent study of the poem[2], returns to the old point of view of Guest and Haigh, Kemble and Conybeare :

> Any hypothesis which would represent the minstrel as a fictitious character is open to the objection that, in that case, he would hardly have been associated with so obscure a person as Eadgils, prince of the Myrgingas, a family not mentioned except in this poem[3]. On the whole, then, the hypothesis that the kernel of the poem is really the work of an unknown fourth century minstrel, who did visit the court of Eormenric, seems to involve fewer difficulties than any other. In that case, of course, such passages as ll. 82 ff. must be regarded as merely the last stage in a process of accretion which had been going on for some three centuries.

[1] Mnemonic verses similar to those of *Widsith* occur, as has been noted, in Icelandic : and it is important to note that they occur in connection with the same cycle of the struggle between Goths and Huns. It might plausibly be argued that there existed in the late fifth or early sixth century a poem in which this great fight was made the occasion of an "heroic muster roll" similar to that which in later times was attached to the story of the battle of Bravalla : that from this ancient poem much of the tradition of *Widsith*, of the *Hervarar Saga* and of the "Lay of Hloth and Angantyr" is derived, and that faint echoes of it are to be found in the *Elene* and in Saxo.

[2] In the *Cambridge History of Literature*, I, 36.

[3] Whatever might be the force of this argument if any considerable propor- tion of O.E. heroic poetry were extant, it can hardly count for much considering how few fragments have survived.

With this view I cannot agree. It is not merely that almost every allusion which we can date—and there are many—shows it to be a chronological impossibility that the poem, as we have it, should record the real travels of a real scop[1]. This difficulty might perhaps be evaded by a sufficiently thoroughgoing application of the interpolation-theory. But the visit to Ermanaric, in which Mr Chadwick himself finds the original kernel of Widsith's wanderings, is depicted in an atmosphere not of history, but of heroic legend.

The Ermanaric of history ruled a mighty empire: only at the very end of his long reign did the Huns appear, and he slew himself before the contest between his people and the Huns reached its climax. But in heroic story it is the chief business of Ermanaric and his men to fight against the hosts of Attila, who as a matter of history is younger by two generations. And it is this heroic fiction which we see reflected in *Widsith*. A real visitor to the court of Ermanaric would probably have had nothing to say about the Huns, since their ravages belong only to the last episode in Ermanaric's life. Had he mentioned them, he could not have represented the Goths as fighting them in the Vistula wood, which they had left some generations earlier[2]; neither would he have represented the Huns as "the people of Attila." Neither could he have met in his visit to the land of the Goths the champions whom he names. Even when we have condemned as interpolations and excluded the names of Ægelmund and Eadwine, or even Theodric or Freotheric, our list is still an impossible one. It includes Eastgota and his son Unwen, who had been dead for generations when the Huns appeared; it includes Wudga, probably the foe, not of the Huns, but of the Sarmatians. The mention of the Harlung brethren points to the legendary Ermanaric, the slayer of his kin, rather than to the conqueror-tyrant of history. The most important person in the poem is Ealhhild, and if she be Eormanric's murdered wife, she belongs to legend and not to history. Reject all these things as interpolations, and what have we left?

Again, the evidence that the catalogue of kings is older

---

[1] See above, p. 5.   [2] See below, p. 163.

than the story of Widsith's wanderings seems conclusive. Yet the catalogue of kings can hardly be older than the sixth century, since it includes the name of the Frankish Theodoric ; to say nothing of other chiefs, like Attila, who are much later than the period of Ermanaric.

Most of these facts have long been known : they were so well known to Ten Brink and Müllenhoff that these critics often assumed them to be known to their readers also, and thought it unnecessary to instance them : a reticence which has given an undue appearance of dogmatism to their statements.

These difficulties seem to me insuperable. Yet they are only one portion of those that have to be faced, if we are to believe that the kernel of our poem actually dates back to the fourth century. But Mr Chadwick regards this date as involving fewer difficulties than the objection that, if the minstrel were a fictitious character, he would not have been associated with so obscure a person as Eadgils. Yet he has himself shown how baseless this objection is. For if, as is exceedingly probable, and as Mr Chadwick himself holds[1], Eadgils is the Athislus of Saxo's Fourth Book, then he can have been by no means an obscure person, to have been remembered, eight centuries after his death, in popular tradition, as a king " of notable fame and vigour ": *vir fama studioque conspicuus*[2].

During the closing weeks of last year a study of *Widsith* was published by Professor Siebs[3]. Whilst Chadwick regards the Eormanric passages as essential, and the reference to Ælfwine as later accretion, Siebs sees the kernel of the poem in the lines on Ælfwine, and regards the four passages in which Eormanric is referred to as four separate additions.

Siebs strikes out as an interpolation ll. 88, 89 :

> And ic wæs mid Eormanrice ealle þrage,
> Þær me Gotena cyning gode dohte,

together with the preceding passage. The name of Ælfwine is,

---

[1] See above, pp. 92–94, and Chadwick (135).
[2] Saxo, IV (ed. Holder, p. 107).
[3] *Festschrift Viëtor*, Marburg, 1910, pp. 296–309.

by this means, brought into immediate contact with the episode describing the gift of the *beag*[1]. This, according to Siebs, is the nucleus of *Widsith* : a short poem telling how (not Eormanric, who has thus been cancelled, but) Ælfwine gave the minstrel a gift, how Widsith gave it on his return home to his lord Eadgils, and how Ealhhild, sister of Ælfwine, gave him a second gift.

What I do not understand is *why* such a poem as Siebs constructs, in praise of Ælfwine and his sister, should have been afterwards interpolated and altered in the way he assumes. I can understand an interpolator being supposed to add additional episodes to an epic, additional names to a list, in order to make them, as he conceives, more complete. But I do not understand why, finding a poem in praise of the generosity of Ælfwine, whose glory was, as Siebs rightly urges, so widely known, our interpolator should have deliberately altered it, so as to make it celebrate the generosity of Eormanric, who, though always reputed munificent, was certainly also regarded in England, at this date, as a treacherous tyrant: *wraþ wærloga, grim cyning*[2].

It has been urged by one of the greatest of Homeric critics that, though a scholar may suspect certain passages to be interpolated, he can hardly expect to convince others unless he can show a reason *why* they were interpolated[3]. Siebs has still to show *why* an Ælfwine lay such as he postulates should have been altered into an Eormanric lay.

---

[1] In this Siebs follows Möller.

[2] Siebs suggests that ll. 88, 89 may have been added to make a transition to the *innweorud Earmanrices* (l. 111). But ll. 110–130, on his own theory, were themselves added after ll. 88, 89. For they were, he thinks, added later than the Introduction (1–9) (p. 307); and the Introduction is, he thinks, later than ll. 88, 89, and is based upon a misunderstanding of them (pp. 298, 300–301). How then can ll. 88, 89 have been added to make a transition to the *innweorud Earmanrices* (l. 111, *etc.*)?

Siebs' theory entirely depends upon his being able to *prove* ll. 88, 89 spurious. Yet in order to account for the Introduction, he is compelled to admit them to have been present in the poem at a very early stage. This admission naturally renders any proof of spuriousness exceedingly difficult.

[3] "Denn die Annahme einer Interpolation kann erst dann als erwiesen betrachtet werden, wenn eine Veranlassung, die sie hervorrief, überzeugend dargethan ist; ohne diesen Nachweis bleibt sie ein subjectives Meinen, welches vielleicht nicht widerlegt werden, aber auch auf keine Beachtung Anspruch machen kann." Kirchoff, *Composition der Odyssee*, 1869, p. 77. With this Ten Brink, *Beowulf*, p. 3, may well be compared.

And the objection that a passage cannot be dismissed by simply declaring it to be an interpolation might also be raised against Siebs' treatment of the Introduction (ll. 1–9). Most scholars will agree that Siebs is justified in regarding this as a later addition: but they will hardly agree that he is therefore justified in dismissing forthwith what we are told in the Introduction regarding Widsith's journey to Eormanric in the company of Ealhhild. The Introduction seems to belong to the flourishing period of Old English poetry, and its allusions are good evidence that, *at the time it was added,* Widsith's wanderings were connected rather with Eormanric than with Ælfwine [1].

In face of these difficulties very heavy evidence should be brought forward, if it is to be proved that all the Eormanric passages are later additions to an original Ælfwine lay. What is needed is that a series of discrepancies between the Eormanric and the Ælfwine passages in syntax or metre or dialect or heroic legend or geography, should be demonstrated, similar to those upon which Müllenhoff and Ten Brink founded their theories. But no such evidence has yet been produced.

The process postulated by Siebs has, then, no likelihood on *a priori* grounds, and is supported by no positive evidence Finally, it leads to rather incredible results. For, Siebs argues, if the starting point of the poem was a song in praise of Alboin, this gives a date too late to allow of a continental outlook: Eadgils and his Myrgings must, he concludes, have dwelt in England: they are perhaps identical with the Mercians, or at any rate with the Mercian royal house.

Now there is a good deal of evidence which tends to place the Myrgings on the continent [2], but Siebs rejects this, on the ground that some of the proposed identifications are not philologically exact. Yet, in the case of remote names which are based upon epic tradition, some degree of corruption may fairly be expected, and page upon page of precedent for such corruption might be, in fact has been, collected [3].

But I do not understand how, having rejected identifications

---

[1] See below, p. 151.

[2] See above, *Eadgils* (pp. 92–94), and below, *the Myrgings* (p. 159); and cf. notes on *Fifeldor* (l. 43) and *Swæfe* (l. 44).

[3] See above, p. 23: below, p. 160: and cf. Heusler in *Z.f.d.A.* LII, 97.

such as those of the Myrging land with Maurungani, and Fifeldor
with the Eider, where corruption is easily intelligible, Professor
Siebs can approve, even tentatively, of an identification of the
Myrgings with the Mercians. For this is just one of those
cases where a phonetic discrepancy *is* difficult to account for.
The word *Mierce* must have been familiar to every eighth-
century Englishman. Why should this familiar word be altered
to the unintelligible *Mierging, Myrging*?

But let this pass. To balance the abundant external
evidence favouring a continental home for the Myrgings, Siebs
produces none whatsoever tending to support the explanation
" Mercians." But on the other hand there is heavy evidence
against it. We are told " Meaca ruled the Myrgings " (l. 23).
Now we possess the genealogy of the Mercian royal house back
to Woden, but there is no Meaca there. And what of Eadgils
himself? This Mercian genealogy goes back to the tenth
generation before Penda. Is it likely that there could have
been, as Siebs thinks possible, an Eadgils, king of Mercia,
only a decade or so before the birth of Penda, that his fame
could have lasted in poetry into the eighth century or later,
and yet no trace of him remain either in the genealogies or
chronicle-entries? And how can the Myrgings, if they are a
people dwelling in England, be spoken of either as identical
with, or neighbours of, the *Swæfe* (i.e. Suevi)? And how can
Offa, king of Angel, ancestor of the Mercian house (in whose
figure in *Widsith* Prof. Siebs thinks there may even be
reminiscences of the historic Offa II, king of Mercia), be said
to have marked off the borders of his kingdom *wiþ Myrgingum*,
if this means ' against the Mercians '—his own people?

Recent scholarship has been rather too ready to dismiss the
conclusions of earlier students without sufficiently examining
the facts from which those conclusions were drawn. In this, as
in some other things, it hardly compares favourably with the
school of Müllenhoff, Möller and Ten Brink.

For each of these critics based his work upon a careful
study of his predecessors' investigations, and a general acceptance of their results. Ten Brink's theory represents in its main

outline the gradual evolution of opinion : only its details are the hazardous guesses of a single scholar. The view which I have expressed above as to the structure of *Widsith* is little more than an adaptation of Ten Brink's in its main outline, allowing for the discoveries which have been made since his time, and for certain publications issued shortly before he wrote but which he appears to have overlooked. I regret that for this opinion I cannot claim the support of many recent critics, to whom every student of Old English is so much indebted: but I have been pleased to find that it is the view of Dr Axel Olrik. The poem has, Dr Olrik thinks, with reason been regarded as the oldest poem of the German race, yet more rightly it may be regarded as a concretion of several pieces of old poetry : the first of these is the " Catalogue of Kings " to which the lines on Offa and the lines on Hrothgar were subsequently added[1].

Indications of Date.

In endeavouring to date *Widsith*, two extreme courses are open to the critic. He may refuse to take into consideration the possibility of interpolation, and so insist upon judging the poem exactly as he finds it. In this case he will clearly have to date it somewhat late.

This, we have seen, was the view of K. Maurer :

> I cannot persuade myself that a poem which collects in the baldest way the names of heroes and people, and withal goes so far as to mingle in the most motley style with the figures of Germanic history and saga Israelites and Syrians, Hebrews, Indians and Egyptians, Medes, Persians and Idumaeans, Saracens and Seres, Alexander the Great, the Emperor of the East, and a second emperor...can really date, as Müllenhoff assumes, from the seventh century[2].

Maurer accordingly suggested the age of the Vikings or the beginning of the ninth century as more in accordance with the phenomena of the poem. A similar view had previously been taken by E. Jessen[3], who dismissed the poem as a mere

---

[1] *Helte-Digtning*, 11. I cannot say whether Dr Olrik would agree with my other contention that it is not possible to divide *Widsith* further into component lays, but only to mark off certain later interpolations.
[2] *Z.f.d.Ph.* ii, 447 (1870).
Undersøgelser til nordisk oldhistorie, København, 1862, p. 51.

promiscuous collection of some monk or priest, and very similar was the opinion subsequently expressed by F. Rönning[1] and by A. Erdmann[2].

But none of these students had devoted any special attention to the poem. They are concerned with maintaining theories of different kinds against which *Widsith* might be quoted as evidence, and they proceed accordingly to disqualify that evidence by judging *Widsith* on the merits of its most doubtful passage. It is a case of abusing the plaintiff's attorney. Naturally, a scholar who is seeking to rewrite history, and in spite of Tacitus, Bede, Nennius and king Alfred, to make the Angles an inland tribe, finds *Widsith* one of the first impediments which he must clear out of his way[3]. Our confidence in *Widsith* should be strengthened when we find that, the more paradoxical a critic's views are, the more anxious he is to attribute a late date to the poem.

But if some critics have refused to allow for interpolations, others have surely pressed the theory of interpolations too far. They have started with the assumption that the poem, or at any rate the original kernel of it, is the work of a contemporary of Ermanaric, and have then dismissed as interpolated every passage which would not harmonize with this date. This, as we have seen, is the view of most English critics : of Conybeare, Kemble, Guest, Haigh, Stopford Brooke, Earle, Garnett and Chadwick[4]. The objection to this theory is that it compels us to dismiss as interpolations almost all the historical data (and they are many) which the poem affords[5].

The extreme dates attributed to *Widsith* are, then, nearly five hundred years apart. Yet it would seem possible to arrive at some approximately accurate results, upon which the majority of critics are agreed. "A mean there is between these extremes, if so be that we can find it out."

---

[1] *Beovulfs-Kvadet: En literær-historisk undersøgelse*, København, 1883. *Widsiδ...er sikkert et temmelig sent forfattet "register"* (p. 3 ; note 2) : *forfattet vi véd ikke når* (p. 104).

[2] *Heimat der Angeln*, p. 50.

[3] See Appendix, Note E, On the original homes of the Angli and Varini.

[4] See above, p. 4, and cf. Lawrence in *Mod. Phil.* IV, 355–6.

[5] See above, p. 142.

Some criterion is wanted by which we can judge of inter-polations. Perhaps we may accept the principle that, *in investigating the date of the poem,* we have no right to reject a passage as interpolated on the sole ground that it does not agree with our view of the date; for to do this is to argue in a circle. On this principle, we ought not to dismiss a passage like that relating to Ælfwine, if in spirit, metre, and style it is exactly in harmony with the rest of the poem; but we should be quite justified in refusing to admit any argument as to date which is based on ll. 75–88. These lines are full of Biblical names, whilst elsewhere we meet with no Biblical names whatever in the poem. Some of them cannot be scanned, whilst elsewhere the poem is metrically accurate. The whole spirit and atmosphere is different. We must then either reject the lines altogether, or isolate them as suspect.

Every reader must be struck by the knowledge of conti-nental conditions displayed by the poet; he knows the most ancient figures of Gothic tradition, Eastgota and Unwen, and, to judge from the way in which he introduces their names, he expects his audience to be intimate with their story. Traits such as the coupling together of Rugians and Romans seem reminiscent of the early sixth century. The mention of the Goths fighting in the Vistula wood is a reminiscence of an earlier period still[1]. The poet's interest seems to centre in continental Angel.

Hence so many critics have argued that the poem was *composed* before the conquest of Britain. This however by no means follows. Even if Widsith's visit to the Gothic court does witness to a time when that court set the fashion in minstrelsy to Western Europe (and we have seen that the evidence for this Gothic preeminence in song is insufficient[2]) this would not prove that *Widsith* must have been composed at that time[3].

In a Mercian hall, in the opening years of the seventh century, some of the older men would have been of continental

---

[1] See also notes to ll. 121–122.
[2] See above, p. 13.
[3] Bojunga (*P.B.B.* xvi, 548) puts *die älteren bestandteile des Widsið* in a time when the Gothic court was still preeminent.

birth, and many more would be the sons of those who had been
born in Angel. The songs sung in the hall would still be the
old continental lays, the traditions would be those of the sixth
century or earlier, of Goth and Hun. This is all that the data
of *Widsith* demand.

Putting aside the criticisms which would date the kernel
of our poem in the fourth century, and those which will not
allow it to antedate the ninth, we find a considerable measure
of agreement on the part of the more moderate critics. *Widsith*
is the oldest English poem (Müllenhoff[1], Gummere[2]), which is
equivalent to saying the oldest poem of any Germanic people
(Olrik[3]); it reflects the traditions of the time of the migrations
(Jiriczek[4]); traditions which the Angles must have brought
with them to England (Leo[5], Wülcker[6], Panzer[7]); belongs in its
essential part mainly to the seventh century (Symons[8], Möller[9],
Müllenhoff[10], Ten Brink[11]); incorporating in the catalogue of
kings an earlier poem belonging to the close of the period of the
migrations, the sixth century (Olrik[12], Möller[13], Müllenhoff[14],
Ten Brink[15]).

These students have based their results upon a study of the
heroic traditions of the poem, including geography only in so
far as that is necessarily involved by the heroic traditions.

We may, then, perhaps outline these as the results which
follow from a study of the heroic lore of *Widsith*:

We have an exceedingly early poem, belonging probably to
the seventh century, but reflecting the traditions of the fifth

---

[1] *Z.f.d.A.* xi, 294.　　　　　　　　　[2] *M.L.N.* iv, 418.
[3] *den gotiske folkestammes ældste digtning. Helte-digtning*, 11.
[4] Jiriczek (₁) 110 ; (₂) 101.　　　　　[5] *Sprachproben*, 76.
[6] *Grundriss*, 329.　　　　　　　　　[7] *H.G.* 436.
[8] *Pauls Grdr.* (₂) iii, 621.
[9] *V.E.* 18, where Möller puts " das eigentliche Widsith-lied " after A.D. 580.
[10] *Beovulf*, 93.
[11] *Pauls Grdr.* (₁) ii.　Ten Brink puts the contamination of the Eormanric-
Ealhhild lay, which constitutes the main poem, in the late seventh century (544),
though he thinks the constituent parts earlier (541).
[12] *forfattet omkring folkevandringstidens slutning. Helte-digtning*, 11.
[13] *V.E.* 18 : *aus der mitte oder dem anfang des sechsten jahrhunderts.*
[14] *Beovulf*, 92, 93.　　　　　　　　[15] *Pauls Grdr.* (₁) ii, 1, 538.

and sixth, and incorporating one piece of verse, the Catalogue of Kings, which seems older than *Widsith* proper.

Widsith has been interpolated: and though it would be too ambitious to hope that we can define exactly the limits of the interpolations, it may be well to make a list of the passages open to suspicion, upon which argument should therefore not be based, without remembering that they are probably later accretion. In this schedule of suspected passages we must place the Biblical interpolation, with the other lines condemned by Müllenhoff (ll. 14–17, 75–87, 131–134)[1], and the not dissimilar lines which occur in the list of the champions of Eormanric[2] (ll. 117–118).

In view of the way in which the other secular poems of the Exeter book have been "edited," and of the very similar prologue and epilogue with which the *Wanderer* is furnished, we are bound to regard the prologue and epilogue of *Widsith* with some suspicion[3]. But I do not think we are therefore justified in dismissing as worthless what we are there told. Granting the prologue to be a later addition, its metre and style show it to belong to the best period of old English versification. It tells us things about the Traveller which could not have been gathered merely from the extant poem as we have it. It seems reasonable to conclude that, even if the Prologue is a later accretion, its author was using traditions of which we now have no other record[4].

The lines on Ælfwine form a problem which has met us more than once. In date there is a considerable period between Alboin and the other heroes of the poem[5], but, as pointed out above[6], we cannot put these lines aside on this score *alone*. If a more minute examination of grammar and metre shows this passage to have peculiarities which are also common to the other suspected lines, but which are not shared by the unsuspected passages, then we must regard it also as interpolated.

---

[1] See above, p. 8.
[2] See above, p. 122.   These lines were rejected by Möller.
[3] So Möller, *etc.*
[4] See above, pp. 28, 145.
[5] Müllenhoff (*Nordalb. Stud.* I, 149) suggested that this passage was perhaps an interpolation.
[6] p. 149.

Otherwise we must regard it as original: meantime it is doubtful.

We have then:

The *Catalogue of Kings*: 17 ll.
With lines on Offa, Hrothgar, Hrothwulf and Ingeld: 15 ll.
Widsith proper: 65 ll.
Possible later interpolations: 46 ll.

} 97 ll.

These results as to date and interpolations are, of course, provisional, and must be checked by any other information which we can procure.

In the first place we may be able to control them by a systematic survey of the geography of the poem. This will involve a certain amount of repetition, as we have already had to consider geographical points necessarily involved in the study of heroic legend. But it is worth while to see what results we can draw from a comparison of *all* the geographical data of *Widsith*.

Secondly, we may be able to check these results by a study of the grammar, dialect and metre. Here especially we may hope for some additional light, for in these matters more progress has been made since the days of Müllenhoff than in the investigation of the ancient geography of the coast tribes.

CHAPTER V.

THE GEOGRAPHY OF *WIDSITH.*

HOWEVER wide his wanderings, no poet could know equally well the national sagas of all the Germanic tribes, and we shall find that the stories known to *Widsith* are those belonging particularly to two of the five great divisions of the Germanic race, as it existed in the early centuries of our era.

But in any attempt to classify, into their groups and sub-groups, the tribes and heroes of *Widsith,* we are met at the outset by the difficulty of an unsettled terminology. The result is that this chapter cannot be written as simply as might have been wished.

Linguistic Classifications.

In trying to realize these ethnographical divisions of ancient Germany, scholars have had to rely chiefly upon linguistic evidence, and this evidence only gives up its secrets very gradually. More and more accurate results are obtained, but even the final result is only an approximation to the truth.

Hence the old classification—Scandinavian, Low German, High German—has been superseded by that of Scandinavian or North Germanic, West Germánic (embracing both Low and High German) and East Germanic (embracing Gothic and the other kindred tongues).

Yet even this perhaps does not represent ultimate truth. The so-called "Northern" and "Eastern" families are possibly more intimately interrelated. Even if the purely linguistic evidence is not strong enough to establish this connection—and many scholars have held that it is—there remains the

significant fact that the same tribal names, Rugian and
Vandal, East Goth and West Goth, occur in both the
Northern and the Eastern family, but not in the West. One
of the minor difficulties of *Widsith* is to decide when the
reference is to the "Northern" and when to the "Eastern"
people of the same name.

Nor must we forget that the apparent homogeneity of the
West Germanic group may be deceptive. It has been argued
that the West Germanic peculiarities are a development of the
early centuries of the Christian era. Barred by the Roman
legions from spreading, as their fellows in Northern and Eastern
Germany might do, a number of distinct German tribes were
pressed together between the Elbe and the Rhine. During
these years, it is urged, peculiarities were developed which
have overlaid and concealed earlier dialectal differences. We
group these tribes together as West Germanic, but it may well
be that the difference between the so-called Anglo-Frisian stock
of the North-Sea coast and the inland tribes is ancient and
deep-lying[1].

In dealing with *Widsith* it is of particular importance to
keep in mind this distinction between the "Anglo-Frisian"
tribes of the coast, and the inland *Deutsch,* or Germans proper.

But, owing to peculiarities developed in the High German
dialects of the South, this *Deutsch* or German speech was itself
soon cloven into two great sections, the so-called High and
Low German. Now English students have generally, in prac-
tice, applied the term "Low German" to *all* those West
Germanic dialects which did not undergo the High German
sound changes: whilst the Germans have kept in mind that,
obvious and striking as are the distinctions which differentiate
the High German from the other West Germanic dialects, yet
those more obscure differences which separate the Anglo-Frisian
from the German proper are more ancient and fundamental.
"Low German" therefore, in the terminology of English
scholars, generally includes English and Frisian, whilst *Niederdeutsch* in the terminology of German scholars excludes them.

---

[1] See Bremer in *Pauls Grdr.* (2) iii, 809 ; Bremer in *I.F.*, iv, 8–31; Siebs in
Pauls Grdr. (2) i, 1154.

I propose to use " Low German " as excluding the Anglo-Frisian dialects. For to do otherwise is to overlook the early difference between the coast tribes and the Germans of the inland plains ; a difference which is demonstrable philologically, and which is important to the student of the geography and heroic tradition of *Widsith.*

We have then East Germanic, North Germanic, and three divisions of West Germanic : Anglo-Frisian, Low German and High German.

The Roman classification, and its relation to the linguistic divisions.

To harmonize the linguistic classification with that of the Roman writers is not easy. Tacitus' famous threefold division of the Germans cannot be reconciled with modern philological classifications unless we suppose that, knowing little of either the North or the East, he left these regions out of his consideration, and intended his[1] classification of the Germans into Ingaevones, Herminones and Istaevones to point only to the three great sections of the Western folk. On this theory the Ingaevones[2] [Ingyaeones[3]] who dwell *proximi Oceano* are what philologists call the " Anglo-Frisians" : the North-Sea folk. The Istaevones[2] [Istraeones[3]] are defined by Pliny as *proximi Rheno,* they are therefore the predecessors of the group of peoples later known as the Franks. The Herminones[2] [Hermiones[3]] stretch further inland : they are *medii*[2] or *mediterranei*[3], and so coincide with that great stock which subsequently, spreading further south, became the High German people. That Tacitus should have left the Eastern and Northern tribes out of account seems strange. Pliny mentions the East Germanic group by name. Owing to the prominent part which the Gothic tribe has played in history, and to the accident that their language, alone of the East Germanic tongues, has been preserved, *we* think of the Goths

---

[1] The classification was, of course, derived by Tacitus from the tribes of the lower Rhine, and represents their point of view. Cf. Olrik in *Folk-Lore,* XIX, 398.

[2] *Germania,* II.   [3] Pliny, *Nat. Hist.* IV, 14 (28), ed. C. Mayhoff.

as the typical East Germanic people[1]. But Pliny applies to the Eastern group the name Vandili[2]: a name which subsequently came to be restricted to one particular tribe of the group, the conquerors of Africa[3]. For the North Germans no satisfactory collective name has ever been found. They are the dwellers in the "island" of "Scandia" or "Thule," and classical writers pass, hastily and with a shudder, to more congenial topics.

This classification may be expressed in tabular form. Bu a table is too dogmatic: it compels us to draw hard and fast lines between groups of dialects when these dialects, in point of fact, probably shaded imperceptibly into one another. When we speak of Anglo-Frisian we must not imagine one homogeneous speech with definite boundaries, but a number of dialects grouped together in virtue of common characteristics. And these dialects had also other connections: the Anglian speech had affinities with the neighbouring Scandinavian, the Frisian is stated to have had similar affinities with the neighbouring Low German[4].

---

[1] Already in the sixth century the general name of the "Gothic races" has come to be applied to the East Germans: Γοτθικὰ ἔθνη πολλὰ μὲν καὶ ἄλλα πρότερόν τε ἦν καὶ τανῦν ἐστι, τὰ δὲ δὴ πάντων μέγιστά τε καὶ ἀξιολογώτατα Γότθοι τέ εἰσι καὶ Βανδίλοι καὶ Οὐισίγοτθοι καὶ Γήπαιδες...φωνή τε αὐτοῖς ἐστι μία, Γοτθικὴ λεγομένη, καί μοι δοκοῦν ἐξ ἑνὸς μὲν εἶναι ἅπαντες τὸ παλαιὸν ἔθνους. Procopius, *Bell. Vand.* I, 2.

[2] Tacitus refers to this group-name without explaining it.

[3] The interpretation of Tacitus' nomenclature in the terms of modern philology is, of course, highly conjectural. But it has the advantage of enabling us to attach a meaning to Tacitus' classification, which otherwise would be unintelligible to us, and it is convenient. Hence it has been widely, and sometimes too dogmatically, accepted.

On the other hand, a recent English critic is perhaps unduly sceptical. "The whole scheme indeed seems to me to be based on a fundamental error. The sound-changes which differentiated the Scandinavian, Anglo-Frisian, and German groups of languages from one another appear to have operated in the fifth, sixth, and seventh centuries. On the other hand the ethnic groups called Istaeuones, Inguaeones and Hermiones, seem to have been obscure and probably antiquated in the first century." (Chadwick, 223.) Now this criticism would be quite just if levelled against any attempt to equate the classification of Tacitus with that of the philologists of half a century ago. Their classification often did rest upon changes of the fifth, sixth and seventh centuries. But the classification now in use is founded upon those much older linguistic differences which have only gradually been revealed, because they were overlaid and concealed by the drastic sound-changes of the later centuries. It may well be that some of these older linguistic differences go back to the time to which the classification of Tacitus refers. See Bremer in *I.F.*, IV, 8–31.

[4] See Morsbach, *Beiblatt* to Anglia, VII, 323–332; Siebs in *Pauls Grdr.*(₂) I, 1154–7 ; Bremer in *I.F.* IV, 8, *etc.*

With this caution we may classify the Germanic dialects thus :

I. East Germanic. Latin and Greek writers use Gothic or Vandalic to cover the whole of this group.

II. North Germanic or Scandinavian.

III. West Germanic.

A. Anglo-Frisian (perhaps corresponding to an earlier Ingaevonian group of tribes).

B. Deutsch or German in narrower sense.

Low German proper (*Niederdeutsch*), perhaps corresponding to earlier Istaevonian (Frankish) group.

High German (*Hochdeutsch*), perhaps corresponding to earlier Herminonian group.

These two classes being free from the High German peculiarities are often inaccurately grouped together as "Low German."

Later Movements.

The terms 'East' and 'West' have reference, of course, to the original positions of these groups. By the sixth century the Eastern people had migrated, and were South and West of the Western people. One of the extraordinary things about *Widsith* is that its author's geographical lore seems often to date back to a period before these migrations.

The East Germans—Goths, Gepidae, Burgundians and Vandals—battered down the Roman Empire and divided the fragments among themselves; but they perished in the process, and their widely scattered tribes were soon absorbed in the Romanized populations among whom they settled ; they were defeated piecemeal by later conquerors, and have left no modern representatives. A Gothic remnant maintained themselves throughout the Middle Ages on the mountainous southern coast of the Crimea—a little nation of a few thousand souls, subject to a Tartar prince. At the end of the sixteenth century they disappear from history[1], and with them the East Germanic races end. The North Germans, on the other hand, in spite of their plundering viking raids at a later period, have mostly

---

[1] Gislenii Busbequii, *Epistolæ*, Parisiis, 1589, pp. 135-7. Cf. *Life and Letters of Ghiselin de Busbecq* by Forster and Daniell, 1881, pp. 355-9.

remained in Gothland, Sweden and Norway—their ancient seats. Of the West Germans, the sea tribes, who once held the coast from the Zuider Zee to the Baltic, have paid the penalty of their piracy. Angles and Jutes conquered Britain, and Danes occupied their ancient continental homes. The Lombards—if indeed they are to be classed with this group— left the lower Elbe, and were lost amid the Italians, while the Saxons, besides helping in the settlement of England, first conquered and then absorbed various inland tribes dwelling in the modern Hanover and Westphalia. The continental or "Old" Saxons therefore ceased to be purely Anglo-Frisian in blood or speech, and have rather to be counted as "Low German." So that the "Anglo-Frisian" speech is now represented only by a few hundred thousand Frisian-speaking folk in the north of Holland and in the islands of the North Sea, and by English-speaking people in other parts of the world. The Istaevones, if we equate them with the Franks, became the ancestors of the Dutch, of the Flemings and of the Germans of the Lower Rhine : these "Low Frankish" together with the "Low Saxon" dialects constitute the "Low German" proper. The Herminones of Roman times included the Hermunduri, Marcomanni and Suevi : great nations which, with some changes both of boundaries and name, are represented by High German peoples—Thuringians, Bavarians, Swabians.

But though it may be possible to trace some measure of continuity in the different classifications of the Germanic people from the days of Tacitus onwards, it is better not to follow certain German scholars in speaking of an *Ingaevonian* dialect when we mean *Anglo-Frisian*. That the two terms corresponded is, after all, but a theory ; that they corresponded *exactly* is unlikely.

Although the many peculiarities common to Old English and Frisian point to intimate intercourse between Angles and Frisians in the early centuries of our era, this does not in the least preclude intercourse, on the other side, between Angles and Danes. This communication has left its mark in certain phonetic peculiarities which Anglian possesses in common with the Scandinavian tongues. Anglian bards, we have seen, were interested in the fight at the Danish Heorot, as well as in the fight at the Frisian Finnesburg. The Baltic, like the North Sea, would unite rather than separate seafaring nations.

It is quite likely, then, that the Ingaevonians may have included not only "Anglo-Frisian" but also Scandinavian tribes[1]: and, however this may be, the intercommunication between the most northern of the Anglo-Frisians and the most southern of the Scandinavians is obvious. Evidence of it meets us everywhere in *Widsith*.

The Traveller and his people—The Myrgings.

More than once in our poem mention is made of the Myrgings, a tribe to which, it would seem, Widsith himself belongs. Unfortunately the text is not clear. *Hine from Myrgingum œþele onwocon* cannot be construed; but, whatever be the correct reading, some connection between the *scóp* and the Myrgings is indicated. In a latter passage, too, Widsith speaks of the prince of the Myrgings, Eadgils, as his liege-lord.

Who these Myrgings were it is not easy to say. We should gather that, on the north, their boundaries touched those of the Angles, for a frontier dispute was settled by Offa with the sword at Fifeldor—i.e. the river Eider, which is still the boundary between Schleswig and Holstein[2]. Again the word *Swœfe* seems to be used as synonymous with *Myrgingas*. We should conclude then, from the poem, that the Myrgings dwelt south of the Eider, and that they were members of the wide-spread Suevic stock.

From other sources little help is to be got. A *Mauringa* is mentioned by Paul the Deacon[3] as having been visited by the Lombards early in their travels, whilst the "Geographer of Ravenna[4]," who is supposed to follow an original composed

---

[1] For the evidence see Schütte, *A.f.d.A.* xxviii, 9–10; Kossinna in *I.F.* vii, 308–11; Chadwick, 209, *etc.*, 295–6.

[2] See note to l. 43.

[3] *Igitur Langobardi tandem in Mauringam pervenientes...egressi itaque Langobardi de Mauringa applicuerunt in Golanda.* Paulus I, 13 in *Script. Rer. Lang.* ed. Waitz, in *M.G.H.*, 1878.

[4] *Ravennatis anonymi cosmographia*, ed. Pinder and Parthey, Berolini, 1860, pp. 27, 28 (§ I, 11).

in the sixth century, twice mentions *Maurungani*: *gani* is, I suppose, miswritten for *gaui* (cf. Goth. *gawi*, "country").

The attempt of Müllenhoff[1] to make the Myrging name coincide linguistically with *Mauringa, Maurungani* was hardly successful: we should expect an O.E. form *Miering*, not *Mierging*. In the most elaborate recent study of early German geography the identification has therefore been abandoned altogether[2], whilst those who have adhered to it have had to admit that the names do not linguistically quite correspond, and that corruption of some kind has crept in[3].

It is perhaps permissible to point out that *g*, especially in the neighbourhood of a *u*, is a difficult sound to be certain about, and that a somewhat similar intrusive *g*, which at one time seemed as inexplicable as the *g* of *Myrging*, has since been shown to be in accordance with phonetic laws[4]. But let it be granted that the *g* of *Myrging* is "unphonetic." It does not therefore follow that the identification of the two words is "impossible on philological grounds[5]." It is true that in dealing with the native words of a language, the presumption is that such words will only change in accordance with phonetic law. But this does not apply to legendary and foreign geographical names which, as they pass from mouth to mouth, often undergo transformations which are the result, not of phonetic law, but of mere error[6]. Are we to account phonetically for every letter in such a change as *Stafford* for *Oxford*, through an intermediate *Asquesufforch*, in Berners' Froissart?

[1] *Z.f.d.A.* xi, 279–80. See also Möller *V.E.* 28, 29 and *A.f.d.A.* xxii, 152. Möller would connect the Myrgings with the Μαρουίγγοι of Ptolemy [ii, 11, 22] and the Marsigni [for *Marvigni] of Tacitus.

[2] Much in *P.B.B.* xvii, 192–4. Attempts to account for the name etymologically will be found there, and in *A.f.d.A.* xvi, 24 (by Kossinna). Cf. Hirt in *P.B.B.* xxi, 148.

[3] Thus Heinzel suggests that the *g* may be due to a popular etymology connecting the name with *mirige* "merry"; see *Ostgotische Heldensage*, in *W.S.B.* cxix, 3, p. 25, 1889.

[4] By Sophus Bugge in *P.B.B.* xiii, 504 "*Germanisch ug aus uw.*" The *g* or *ug* seems generally, though not always, to have developed out of an earlier *uw*. Cf. O.E. *geoguð*: Gothic *junda*; O.E. *sygel*: Goth. *sauil*; O.E. *nigon*: O.H.G. *niwan*; O.E. *sugu*: O.E. *sū*. See A. Noreen, *Abriss der urgermanischen Lautlehre*, Strassburg, 1894; Kluge, *Vorgeschichte der altgerm. Dialekte*, in *Pauls Grdr.*(2) i, 380; Möller in *A.f.d.A.* xxii, 152 (footnote).

[5] Lawrence in *Mod. Philol.* iv, 362, following Heinzel, *Ostgot. Heldensage*, 25, and followed by Holthausen, ii, 166.

[6] See Heusler in *Z.f.d.A.* lii, 97, etc. *Heldennamen in mehrfacher Lautgestalt.*

It does not appear that Paul himself was certain where *Mauringa* was: in his account of the early Lombard wanderings he blindly followed older authorities, and was obviously puzzled by the names of tribes and places which he reproduced[1]. Of the "Geographer's" two references, the one is vague, and the other corrupt[2]. It seems clear, however, that this *Maurungani* is a district bordering on the Elbe, and apparently extending indefinitely in an eastward direction over those lands which the Germanic tribes had vacated when they broke into the Roman Empire[3]. Northward it borders on the Danish country (*Dania*). It therefore includes Holstein, together with an uncertain amount of what is now Eastern Germany. Here too, east and north of the Elbe, it seems best to place Paul's *Mauringa*; and certainly it is here that we must place the Myrgings, south of the Eider, in the modern Holstein.

Both phonetically and geographically *Myrging* sufficiently coincides with *Maurungani* to make the identification highly probable. But it would not be safe to base argument upon it.

Geographical classification of the names in Widsith.

An attempt to classify geographically the tribes, localities and heroes mentioned in the undoubted portions of *Widsith* gives this result.

EAST GERMANIC.

Tribes and Places: [HRETH-]GOTAN, BURGENDAS[4], GEFTHAS, WISTLA-WUDU.

Heroes: *Eormanric, Becca, Gifica, Guthhere*[4], *Herelingas, (Emerca* and

---

[1] Most of the names come from the *Origo gentis Langobardorum*: *Mauringa* however is not found there.

[2] See Appendix B, *Maurungani and the Geographer of Ravenna*.

[3] Zeuss (472) and Schmidt (*Zur Geschichte der Langobarden*, 1885, p. 47) identify Mauringa with [Maurungani] which they place east of the Elbe. Bluhme (*Die Gens Langobardorum und ihre Herkunft*, Bonn, 1868, p. 23) placed Mauringa to the west, but on quite insufficient grounds. Müllenhoff, who so read the poem that Eadgils, prince of the Myrgings, was the husband of Ealhhild, made the Myrgings extend towards the old Lombard home in Pannonia, in order to supply a motive for the match: which would, he thought, have been unreasonable had the Myrgings not extended beyond Holstein. See *Z.f.d.A.* xi, 279; *Beovulf*, 99; *Nordalb. Stud.* i, 140, *etc.*

[4] Geographically, the Burgundians are, when we first meet them, indisputably East Germanic. Evidence for the character of the Old Burgundian speech is scanty, but is generally considered to confirm its East Germanic

Fridla), East-Gota, Unwen, Sifeca, Hlithe, Incgentheow, Wyrmhere, Rumstan, Gislhere, Freotheric, Wudga, Hama.

*** Probably we should include WULFINGAS : *Helm* ; also *Theodric, Seafola, Heathoric.*

The following are spoken of as Gothic champions, and may therefore be classed here, though we have no information outside our poem for so placing them : *Hethca, Secca, Wulfhere, Rædhere, Rondhere, Withergield.*

NORTH GERMANIC.

Tribes and Places : DENE, SÆ-DENE, SUTH-DENE, SWEON, GEATAS, WENLAS, HEATHOREAMAS, HEOROT.

Heroes : *Sigehere, Alewih, Hrothwulf, Hrothgar, Ongendtheow.*
*** Perhaps we should include THROWENDAS.

ANGLO-FRISIAN.

Tribes and Places : WÆRNAS, EOWAN, YTE, FRESNA CYNN (FRYSAN), HOCINGAS, SYCGAN, ENGLE (ONGEL), SEAXE, FIFELDOR.

Heroes : *Billing, Oswine, Gefwulf, Finn, Folcwalda, Hnæf, Sæferth, Offa, Beadeca.*

*** Probably we should include WOINGAS, WROSNAS : *Wald, Holen.*

LOW GERMAN.

Tribes : FRONCAN, HETWARE.
Heroes : *Theodric, Hun.*
*** Probably we should include THYRINGAS : *Wod.*

HIGH GERMAN.

Tribes : ? ÆNENAS, ? THYRINGAS. (Both very unlikely.)
Heroes : ? *Wod.* (Very unlikely.)

The following tribes and heroes cannot be classified exactly, but it is clear that they are all maritime, and are to be localized somewhere on or near the Baltic :

Tribes : HOLMRYGE, GLOMMAS, HÆLSINGAS, YMBRE, LONGBEARDAN (l. 32), WICINGA CYNN, HEATHOBEARDAN.

Heroes : *Hagena, Heoden, Wada, Sceafthere, Sceafa, Ingeld.*

*** Near the Baltic we must also place the BRONDINGAS, HUNDINGAS, MYRGINGAS, SWÆFE : *Breoca, Mearchealf, Mearca, Witta, Eadgils* ; perhaps WULFINGAS : *Helm* ; the HEREFARAN and *Hringweald* on either the North Sea or the Baltic.

---

character. Hempel (*Linguistic and Ethnografic status of the Burgundians : Trans. Am. Philol. Assoc.* xxxix, 1909, pp. 105–119) argues for Anglo-Frisian and Norse affinities. But this theory rests upon the interpretation of certain runic inscriptions the reading of which is exceedingly doubtful, and which in any case cannot be proved to be Burgundian.

The non-Germanic people mentioned in the undoubted parts of *Widsith* all belong to the Mark :

Tribes : HUNAS, CREACAS, FINNAS, WINEDAS, RUMWALAS.

Heroes : *Ætla, Casere, Cœlic.*

The following are quite uncertain :

Tribes : BANINGAS, RONDINGAS, GEFFLEGAS, SWEORDWERAS, HRONAS, DEANAS, FRUMTINGAS.

Heroes : *Thyle, Scilling, Ealhhild* daughter of *Eadwine* (unless the reference to *Ælfwine* son of *Eadwine* be genuine, in which case it is probable that Ealhhild is regarded as a Lombard princess, sister of Ælfwine).

The following names occur in the suspected passages only :

Tribes and Places : "EASTAN OF ONGLE," EATUL, SERCINGAS, SERINGAS, WALA RICE, SCOTTAS, PEOHTAS, SCRIDE-FINNAS, LIDWICINGAS, LEONAS, HÆTHNAS, HÆRETHAS, ISRAHELAS, EXSYRINGAS, EBREAS, INDEAS, EGYPTAS, MOIDAS, PERSAS, MOFDINGAS, ONGEND-MYRGINGAS (?), WITH-MYRGINGAS (?), AMOTHINGAS, EAST-THYRINGAS, EOLAS, ISTE, IDUMINGAS.

Heroes : *Widsith, Hwala, Alexandreas, Ælfwine* son of *Eadwine, Elsa, Ægelmund, Hungar.*

In these lists we notice that

(1) a wide knowledge is shown of Gothic story. But this is legendary, as is all the knowledge our poet shows of East-Germanic tribes : it sometimes reflects a state of things which had passed away even in the fourth century. Thus the localization in the Vistula-wood of the struggle between Goth and Hun is unhistoric ; in Ermanaric's day the Goths were dwelling on the plains near the Black Sea, and it was on these plains, between the Sea of Azov and the Danube, that the struggle took place. The term *Hrœdas*, applied to the Goths, is apparently legendary, not historic[1]. The grouping of Burgundians and Goths together is legendary geography[2].

(2) Of the North Germanic tribes there is most knowledge of those bordering on the Baltic, and especially of the Danes.

(3) Full information is shown of the Anglo-Frisian tribes and heroes, and also

---

[1] See Appendix H.

[2] See note to l. 19. Schütte (*Oldsagn*, 46) finds a similar archaism in the grouping of Gepidae and Wends, which he thinks points to "Gepidernes gamle Bopæle ved Østersøen." But this is not conclusive : for the Wends moved southward also, and still bordered on the Gepidae after these latter had settled in Dacia. It is clear from Jordanes, v (33, 34), that the two tribes were still immediate neighbours in the sixth century.

(4) of a large number of tribes which we cannot place exactly, but which clearly dwelt upon the coast, in some cases perhaps of the North Sea, but more generally of the Baltic.

(5) Of Low German tribes and heroes there is little cognizance. Of the many Frankish heroes Theodoric (the son of Clovis) alone is mentioned: and we happen to know that Theodoric's victories were famed not only among his own people, but also among the coast-tribes. The other Low German peoples mentioned, the Hetware, and probably the Thyringas, were immediate neighbours of these coast tribes.

(6) Of High German tribes and heroes there seems to be no knowledge whatever. For the identification of the Ænenas with a Bavarian family is more than doubtful, and the Thyringas are apparently the Low German Thoringi. The absence of any mention of such mighty nations as the Bavarians and Alamanni is remarkable. The word *Swœfe* occurs three times, but in each case the tribe referred to is grouped with peoples dwelling on the Baltic, and it seems that the North Suavi, not the great Southern people, are meant.

(7) Out of thirty-one tribes and places which we can identify all but two are connected with either the North Sea or the Baltic: and these two exceptions are not far remote.

The deductions seem obvious. The geography is not that of a traveller going from Angel to the Black Sea in the days of Ermanaric. Neither is it that of one going from Angel to Italy in the days of Alboin. Such a traveller must have passed through the lands of the Alamanni and Bavarians: *Swœfe* would have meant to him not the Baltic folk but the mighty Southern tribe: he must have met with the Heruli, Sciri, Turcilingi, Slavs, Avars, not one of which tribes is mentioned. Of the races specially recorded by Paul as having accompanied Alboin's Lombards into Italy—the Gepidae, Bulgarians, Sarmatians, Pannonians, Suavi and Noricans—two only are known to *Widsith*.

Further, the names occurring in the unsuspected portions of *Widsith* are systematic: they are not the casual accretion of successive interpolators. The only non-Germanic names are those of the border-peoples, which must have been known to the most stay-at-home German. And even of Germanic tribes those only are mentioned which might have come within the view of one whose outlook was confined to the North Sea and the Baltic—a tribesman situated *be sœm tweonum.*

We have such a survey of Germanic geography and legend as might have been made by a gleeman who drew his lore from the traditions of the ancient Angel. From this point of view everything drops into its right place : the knowledge shown of the Anglo-Frisian tribes and of their legends, of their immediate neighbours, and the more or less complete ignorance of everything else, with the one exception of Gothic saga, become at once intelligible.

I do not mean that the geography of the poem shows that it was made before the Angles came to England : but that it was made not long after, whilst the traditions of the continental home were still fresh. How different the English outlook ultimately became is shown in the geography of Germany added by Alfred to the *Orosius*[1].

When we turn to the suspected passages we find a casual collection of names, most of them non-Germanic. Many of these names, Ælfwine, Ægelmund, Hwala, may represent genuine tradition : but taking them in the mass, they are a jumble such as might have been made by some half-learned and quite stupid person[2]. The phrase *eastan of Ongle* seems definitely to point to an English origin[3].

An examination of the geography of *Widsith* confirms us, then, in the belief that *Widsith* cannot have any autobiographical basis, but that it represents an exceedingly early form of traditional lore, and that certain portions, which can be defined with some accuracy, are likely to be later interpolations. The ease with which the passages containing the suspected names can be disentangled, leaving nothing which does not bear the stamp of great age, is remarkable.

---

[1] See Appendix L.

[2] Brandl supposes them the work of a cleric who had read Alfred's Orosius (*Pauls Grdr.* ii, 1, 966–7. See Appendix L).

[3] See note to l. 8.

CHAPTER VI.

LANGUAGE AND METRE OF *WIDSITH*.

Dialect.

Widsith, like almost all Old English poetry, is written in the normal Late West Saxon literary speech. But certain words, chiefly proper names, show that the poem has been transliterated from a non-W.S. dialect. Such are *Breoca, Eatul, Earmanric, Heaðo-, Seafola, Wald, freoðu-, geofum, meodu-, scæceð, sprēcan*[1]. Some of these forms, like *Wald,* though commoner in Anglian, are not unknown in W.S.: but most are quite impossible in a pure W.S. dialect. Equally significant is the odd form *Creacum,* where we should expect *Crecum.* For, if the scribe had been transliterating from an Anglian original, he would have often had to change Angl. *ē* to W.S. *ēa:* and he might easily have done this once too often, and have wrongly written *Creacum* for *Crecum,* just as he would rightly have written *eac* for *ec*[2].

The dialect points, then, to a non-W.S., and probably Anglian, origin for our poem: and this confirms what we should expect from the place allotted to Offa, the greatest of all Anglian heroes.

The language has been too much altered for it to give much indication of date, except where a change involves a difference in the number of syllables: in which cases the

---

[1] *Headen* and *wiolena* rest upon conjectural emendation, and should therefore hardly be counted: it is also conjecture that *Eowan* stands for *Eawan.* Brandl quotes *Deanum* as non-W.S.: but we cannot be certain what the original form of this word was.

[2] Pointed out by Holthausen, II, 165.

metre sometimes preserves the earlier form, or more often betrays what the earlier form must have been.

Syntactical Usages.

Attempts to determine the date of O.E. poems by observing the usage of the demonstrative, *se, seo, þæt,* and of the weak adjective, were made by Lichtenheld in 1872[1]. Lichtenheld examined the usage of *Beowulf, Genesis, Andreas, Maldon* and the poems in the *Anglo-Saxon Chronicle.* He showed that, taking *Beowulf* as a specimen of the earliest O.E. poetry, *Genesis* and *Andreas* as intermediate, *Maldon* and the *Chronicle*-poems as late, there is a progressive alteration in usage:

(1) *se, seo, þæt* becomes more and more common[2]. This is largely due to the fact that:

(2) in the older poems the weak adjective + noun occurs frequently where we should now use the definite article: *wisa fengel,* "the wise prince"; whilst *se wisa fengel* is used only when a demonstrative is needed, "that wise prince."

(3) Later, however, *se, seo, þæt* comes to be used in the common and vague sense in which the definite article is used in Modern English, so that we get with increasing frequency the usage, definite article + weak adjective + noun[3]; whilst the usage, weak adjective + noun, decreases[4].

(4) The use of the instrumental, and particularly of the instrumental of the weak adjective + noun, becomes more and more rare[5].

Lichtenheld also investigated (5) the use of the weak adjective without noun (*se wisa* "the wise one"). His figures here[6] showed no very marked tendency either to an increased or decreased use. These cases need careful examination and discrimination, which, so far as space allowed, was given to them by Lichtenheld[7].

Lichtenheld's tests have since been applied to all the longer O.E. poems by A. J. Barnouw[8].

---

[1] *Z.f.d.A.* xvi, 325, *etc.*
[2] P. 332.   [3] Pp. 335, 357-69.   [4] Pp. 334, 375.
[5] Pp. 326-7.   [6] P. 331.   [7] P. 352.
[8] *Textkritische Untersuchungen,* 1902.

That the use of the article becomes commoner as time goes on in O.E. poetry is indisputable : how far we are justified in using the statistics of Lichtenheld and Barnouw as criteria of *exact* date is more open to dispute[1].

Now Brandl[2] notes in *Widsith* three examples of the use of the weak adjective + noun (without the definite article). Against this he alleges three instances of the use of the definite article + weak adjective + noun, and accordingly pronounces, so far as judgement is possible on such limited figures, for the eighth century, and the period before Cynewulf.

But, as a matter of fact, only one of the three alleged instances of the late usage, def. art. + weak adj. + noun, is correct. The other two are examples not of the def. art. + weak adj. + noun but of the def. art. + weak adj., a usage which needs scrutiny and which, on the whole, may be an indication rather of early than of late date[3]. These two examples are *gesiþa þa selestan* (l. 110), *gesiþa þa sæmestan* (l. 125). Now here the article is fully justified, according to the oldest usage, and according to what appears to have been the original force of *se*, and of the weak adjective. Both Lichtenheld (p. 343) and Barnouw (pp. 42–43) speak expressly with regard to this use of the article *with the superlative*. *Widsith* here conforms to the usage of *Beowulf*, where, as Barnouw points out, *selest* is employed for inanimate things, *se selesta* for persons : *husa selest*, but *magoþegna þone selestan*. We certainly cannot regard it as in any sense a late usage. We have here, then, in *Widsith*, not three examples of early against three of late usage, but three of early against one of late usage.

Widsith is too brief a poem to afford a satisfactory basis for argument from statistics; on the other hand, its brevity will permit of our applying *all* Lichtenheld's tests, and considering all the *circumstances* under which the article is or is not used. Such full examination is necessary, if we are to use the tests with any degree of safety[3].

---

[1] See Sarrazin in *Engl. Stud.* xxxviii, 145 *etc.*
[2] *Pauls Grdr.*(2) ii, 1, 968.
[3] Foster, *Judith*, 1892, p. 54 (*Q.u.F.* lxxi).

I. Use of *se, seo, þæt.*

Se, seo, þæt is used six times in *Widsith* (ll. 36, 110, 118, 125, 127, 131): four times in undoubted, twice in suspected passages. This is a very small percentage. We must of course allow for the fact that 47 lines are filled only with lists of names, and that in them we should hardly expect to find either articles or adjectives. These lines should, no doubt, be dismissed from the reckoning; but we are still left with six instances in 96 lines, or one in every 16. The article is found in *Beowulf* once in every 11 lines, more frequently in *Genesis*, once in seven lines in the *Andreas*, about as often in the *Chronicle* poems, once in four lines in *Maldon*[1]. So far, then, as restraint in its use is a test of antiquity, *Widsith* is more archaic than *Beowulf*, as *Beowulf* is more archaic than *Andreas* and *Andreas* than *Maldon*.

When we examine the individual instances we find that in five cases out of six the use of *se, seo, þæt* is justifiable : with superlatives, *þa selestan, þa sæmestan* ; with distinct demonstrative effect, *of þam heape* "from that company of which I was speaking," *þara monna modgast* "bravest of those men just mentioned," *on þære feringe* "in my travels of which I have been telling." Only in one instance *þa wloncan gedriht* "the proud company" have we the late, rather meaningless use of *se* as the definite article. And this instance occurs in a passage which we have already concluded, on grounds quite other than those of grammar, to be probably a late interpolation.

II. Weak Adjective + Noun.

Of this early usage we get one instance in the suspected lines (*forman siþe*), two in the undoubted passages (*wundnan golde, sciran reorde*). Excluding, as before, lines containing proper names only, we have three examples in 96 lines, or, if we prefer to take the undoubted passages only, two in 64 : as it happens, precisely the same proportion : a proportion greater than the 80 instances in *Beowulf,* and much greater than the 25 in *Genesis,* seven in *Andreas,* none in the *Chronicle,* two in *Maldon*[2].

---

[1] These are Lichtenheld's figures : *Z.f.d.A.* xvi, 332, 334.
[2] Again I give Lichtenheld's figures : *Z.f.d.A.* xvi, 334.

Here again, then, *Widsith* shows a usage more archaic than that of *Beowulf,* and much more archaic than that of the other poems.

III.   Definite Article + Weak Adjective + Noun.

This usage, we have seen, occurs only once in *Widsith,* and then in a passage which, on the ground of legend, looks like an interpolation. The usage occurs 13 times in *Beowulf*[1], 60 times in *Genesis,* 12 times in the *Chronicle*-poems (a proportion equal to 200 in *Beowulf*). If we take *Widsith* as a whole, this would place it between *Beowulf* and *Genesis.* But if we are allowed to take the undoubted passages separately, we find them entirely free from this late usage.

IV.   Weak Instrumental.

This occurs three times in the 96 lines, twice in the 64 undoubted lines : an equal proportion, and one larger than we get elsewhere in O.E. poetry. Here again, then, we have an argument making for very early date.

V.   Definite Article + Adjective : *þa selestan, þa sœmestan.*

This has been dealt with already. It is a usage from which chronological argument cannot be drawn ; it is admittedly consistent with very early date.

I doubt whether we are justified in attaching very great importance to figures so limited[2]. But, *if we are to draw inferences,* then there is no doubt that the usage of the definite article and of the weak adjective in *Widsith* points, not to the eighth century and the time before Cynewulf, but rather to the time before *Beowulf,* i.e. to the seventh century. Brandl's statement to the contrary rests upon one of those slips from which the work of the best scholars can never be absolutely free.

[1] Lichtenheld says 21 times (*Z.f.d.A.* xvi, 335). But eight of these are really examples of def. art. + weak adj. (with noun in apposition), *se goda, mæg Higelaces,* not 'the good kinsman of Hygelac' but 'the good one, the kinsman of Hygelac.' There remain 13 undoubted examples.
[2] Cf. Sarrazin in *Engl. Stud.* xxxviii, 146 *etc.*

Metrical Tests.

One of the most important contributions to the study of O.E. made in recent years was the essay in which Morsbach strove to prove that certain sound-changes, and especially the loss of *u* after a long stem syllable, took place in England at the end of the seventh century: that the metre of *Beowulf* shows that the shortened form only was used, and that we must therefore date *Beowulf* after 700[1].

But the ground upon which this whole theory is built is rendered infirm by the scantiness of the evidence. Two facts stand out clearly: that in the Franks-casket inscription, dating apparently from the end of the seventh century, the *u* is found surviving (*flodu* for *flod*); that in charters dating from 692 or 693 the *u* is already lost[2]. The inference certainly is that the *u* was lost at the end of the seventh century. But we cannot be certain: *flodu* on the casket *may* be a deliberate archaism[3], it may be due to analogy, it may be a local peculiarity.

Morsbach's test has been applied by Carl Richter[4] to the whole body of Old English poetry, with a thoroughness accompanied by an absence of dogmatism deserving of the highest praise. Richter dates *Widsith*[5] after *Beowulf*, but before Cynewulf: but in this he seems to have been largely influenced by Brandl's argument as to the article[6]. A consideration in detail of the instances noted by Richter will, I think, show that, even granting the accuracy of Morsbach's data, and granting that their application to *Beowulf* proves that poem to be later than 700, no similar result can be drawn from their application to *Widsith*.

45[a]. *Hroþwulf and Hroðgar.* "The substitution of **Hroð-garu* would," says Richter, "make an impossible half line." Even if this were so, it would not be quite conclusive against a seventh century date. For, as Morsbach admits, the *u* in

---

[1] *Zur Datierung des Beowulfepos* in the *Nachrichten der k. Gesell. d. Wissenschaften zu Göttingen*, 1906, pp. 251–72.

[2] *in silua quae dicitur* uuidmundes felt. Kemble, *C.D.S.* I, 40.

[3] Chadwick in the *Trans. of the Cambridge Philological Society*, IV, ii, 116, 156.

[4] *Chronologische Studien*, 1910.　　　[5] P. 92.　　　[6] See above, p. 170.

compound words was probably lost before the *u* in mono-syllables. The form *Hroðgar*, then, is conceivable in the seventh century. But I do not think that *Hroðgaru* is unmetrical here. On the contrary we should have a line of a rare, but recognized type: Sievers "Expanded D, 9th sub-class[1]." The scheme is ⊥ × × | ⊥ ⊰ ×, and Sievers quotes seven examples of it from *Beowulf*. For, *Hroþwulf* being a proper name, the second element may count either as secondary accent or as a dip[2]. All that can be demanded is that such a type, to compensate for its extra weight, should have double alliteration. That condition being complied with there is no further objection to be made. The earliest recorded half-line of Germanic poetry is of this type[3], complicated by an unaccented syllable as "prelude":

<blockquote>Ek Hlewagastiz Holtingaz.</blockquote>

The substitution of the early form **Hroðgaru* leaves us here, therefore, with a satisfactory line.

This is hardly the case with Richter's second instance: 117[b], *Ægelmund and Hungar*. If we substitute **Hungaru* here we certainly have an overweighted line, and one which it would be difficult to parallel[4]. For, coming as it does in the second half of the line, the extra weight cannot be carried off by any double alliteration.

72[a]. *leohteste hond*. Substituting **hondu* we should have an uncommon line, but one which, as Richter admits, is not unparalleled. It would be[5] Expanded A*, subtype a. This type usually has double alliteration: *leohteste *hondu* would have but one parallel in *Beowulf*, *Wiglaf wæs haten* (2602)[5].

---

[1] See *P.B.B.* x, 304. Cf. *Beowulf* (ll. 712, 1790, 2462; 1426, 1440, 612, 232). Some of these verses, and the one under consideration, might perhaps rather be regarded as expanded A types.

[2] Dagegen haben die zweiten Glieder von Eigennamen (wie *Bēowŭlf*, *Hẏgelăc*), nur einen schwächeren Nebenton, der nach Belieben des Dichters zur Bildung eines besonderen Gliedes verwandt oder ignoriert werden kann. Sievers, *Metrik* in *Pauls Grdr.*(2) II, 2, p. 30.

[3] The dropping of the final unaccented syllables, which was completed about the year 700, must have diminished the tendency towards the "expanded" type of verse. Types which after 700 are rare *may* have been common when, with a larger number of unaccented syllables in the language, there was more oppor-tunity for their use.

[4] For *wundor is to secganne* (*Beowulf*, 1724) *etc.* cf. Sievers *P.B.B.* x, 255.

[5] Also called expanded E, subtype 8: Sievers, *P.B.B.* x, 310.

There is also the test of post-consonantal *h* before vowels. This also is supposed to have been lost about 700. If *Widsith* dates from the seventh century we should then have to read *and Wal*[*h*]*a rices* × | ⌣́ × | ⌣́ × instead of *and Wala rices* × ⌣ × | ⌣́ × : an A line with prelude instead of a C line with resolution. This would indeed give a less usual type of line, though one not unparalleled : there are only four instances of the one in the second half lines of *Beowulf* against 76 of the other[1].

To sum up: there can then, I think, be no dispute that verse 45[a] gives us a satisfactory line, when we restore the seventh century form. As to the other three, there might be two opinions. *But they all occur in those passages of the poem which, on other grounds, we have marked as doubtful.* If therefore we grant these lines to be clumsy or impossible in a seventh century form, we do not prove a post-seventh century date for *Widsith*. We merely have a confirmation of the doubts which, on quite other grounds, Kemble, Müllenhoff and Möller have entertained as to the originality of these very passages.

Finally, there are certain usages in which the earliest poems fluctuate. For example, though few poems use early forms exclusively, we can get some estimate of age from the proportion of instances where the metre demands the Anglian mutated form *frega* or the later contracted form *frea*. *frea Myrginga* (*Widsith*, l. 96), according to Richter, is an example of the later form: to me it appears to be ambiguous; we could quite well scan *fre*[*g*]*a Myrginga*, like *dohtor Hroþgares*[2], a type of which there are ten examples in *Beowulf*[3]: so that we can draw no argument from this line. In the only other case where a word of this type appears, *þeah þe ic hy anihst*, we must read *anihst* in its earlier trisyllabic form *anehist* (× ╱ ×) if we are to make the line scan at all. The proportions for early as against late usage in this respect are then in *Widsith* 1 : 0, compared with 36 : 48 in *Beowulf*, 44 : 32 in *Genesis A*, 13 : 5 in *Daniel A*[4].

As to the treatment of syllabic liquids and nasals, we have in *Widsith*, on Richter's reckoning, two examples of the earlier

[1] *P.B.B.* x, 234, 244.
[3] Sievers in *P.B.B.* x, 233, 255.
[2] Cf. however Richter, 11.
[4] Richter, 79.

against two of the later usage. The proportions of early to
late are in *Beowulf* 35 : 42, in *Genesis A* 17 : 73, in *Daniel A*
3 : 21[1].

These instances occur in the undoubted passages of *Widsith*.

It may be unwise to argue upon such limited evidence :
but if we are going to argue, the evidence again points to
Widsith being older than *Beowulf, Genesis A, Daniel A*—the
three poems regarded by Richter as the earliest.

Sentence Structure and Verse Form.

But there is another striking characteristic of *Widsith*,
which, fortunately, it has not been in the power of the scribe
to obliterate : the poet's habit of terminating his sentences at
the end of the line, with the result that the poem seems to
fall into irregular strophes of anything up to six lines in length.
Only three times does the full stop come at the half line, and
in each case in a passage which, on quite other grounds, has
been marked as interpolated. The exact number of stops in
the undoubted lines might be anything from twenty-four to
thirty-five : *but they all come at the end of the line.*

Now this is a most unusual feature in Old English verse,
where the stop occurs almost as often at the end of the half
line as at the end of the line. In two groups of poems only
do we find consistent and unbroken " end stopping "[2]. It occurs
in the long Riddle (No. XLI), in the Hymn (Grein-Wülcker,
II, 2, 244), in the poems on the Day of Judgement and on the
death of Edward the Confessor, in the metrical version of the
Psalms almost without exception, and in the Kentish version
of Psalm LI. But these are all monkish effusions, written
under the influence of the ecclesiastical Latin : and we have
only to turn to the *de die Judicii*[3], or the riddle of Aldhelm,
de Creatura, to see that the Old English poet is imitating the
structure of the Latin text he is translating, precisely as in the

---

[1] Richter, 76.

[2] Poems less than twenty lines in length are too short for purposes of
comparison, yet some confirmation of the argument below might be derived
from poems like *Cædmon's Hymn* or the *Leiden Riddle.*

[3] Bede, v, 634, in Migne, 1846.

Anglo-Saxon version of the Psalms the strophes correspond to the verses of the Latin original. But there is another class of poems to which this explanation does not apply: for if, on the one hand, we find this "end stopping" in the monkish poetry, we find it on the other hand in the most purely Germanic of all the Old English poems: in the *Charms*, in the *Rune Song*[1], in *Deor*, and here in *Widsith*. This is not due to accident: for the tendency to strophic form is emphasized in *Deor* by the refrain, and occasionally in *Widsith* and the *Charms* by the repetition of certain words. Besides, the contrast is too striking to be accidental. For, whilst the proportion of end-stopped to mid-stopped lines is in *Beowulf* 385 : 282, in *Genesis A* 259 : 255, in the *Elene* 105 : 138, in the *Andreas* 221 : 112, it is in the *Rune Song* 29 : 0, in *Deor* 10 : 0, in the *Charms* 32 : 1 (or rather 0[2]), in *Widsith* (undoubted portions) 29 : 0. To what, then, are we to attribute this remarkable difference?

That the earliest poetry of the Germanic tribes was lyric and strophic is admitted. I believe the strophic character of *Widsith* and of the *Charms* to be due to a survival of the influence of this earlier Germanic tradition, precisely as the strophic character of the monkish verse is due to the influence of example, though in that case of an alien one. Of this earliest lyric poetry we have several records in the historians[3]: the fullest is the description of the Gothic lays sung in the hall of Attila[4]. We are told how two minstrels came before Attila, singing songs they had made of his victories and glory

---

[1] Contrast with the *Rune Song* the enjambment of the Cynewulfian rune-passages.

[2] As some impartial criterion of what constitutes a full-stop is necessary, I follow the punctuation of Grein-Wülcker, where l. 28 of the second *Charm* is printed *hal westu. Helpe þin drihten.* Yet a comma or colon would perhaps be better.

I only count the three longer charms. If the shorter ones had been included my point would have been unduly exaggerated, since, of course, a number of short poems would tend to show a high percentage of "end stopped" sentences.

[3] Jordanes, c. 41, c. 49. Cf. also Sievers, *Metrik* in *Pauls Grdr.*(2) II, 2, 5.

[4] Priscus (in Möller, *Frag. Hist. Græc.* 1851, IV, 92). That the minstrelsy and indeed all the civilization of Attila's court was Gothic seems certain. Cf. Socin, *Schriftsprache u. Dialekte*, 1888, p. 8; Schütte, *Oldsagn*, p. 82.

in war, and how the company were moved, even to tears. The introduction of two singers together seems to postulate either a choral lay or the singing of alternate stanzas; the poem too is encomiastic, not narrative. In both respects the minstrelsy differs from that of Hrothgar's poet, telling in Heorot the story of Finnesburh. Now, when Widsith sings before his lord, it is with a second minstrel: the two together sing one song (for the company say they had never heard, not better songs, but a better song); the song too is not a narrative, but a song of praise, the composition of the singers themselves. The coincidence may, of course, be accidental, and encomiastic and narrative poetry flourished, we know, side by side; the names in *Widsith* are themselves evidence for the existence of many narrative lays. Yet it is worth noting that the singing before Widsith's lord reminds us rather of the hall of Attila than of Hrothgar[1].

And it can hardly be accident that four poems, the subject-matter of which carries us back to the most primitive period, should agree in the retention of a primitive form. They may have been modernized and interpolated: we know that the *Rune Song*[2] and the *Charms* have been largely rewritten: but all four seem to have their roots in an age more primitive than that which rejoiced in the rhetorical interlaced periods of the *Beowulf* or *Genesis*: an age when the tendency, inherited from the strophic poetry, to make the sentence end with the line, was still strong.

And here, as elsewhere, we find a distinction between the parts of *Widsith*: the Introduction, which on other grounds we have thought to be later, shows the enjambment familiar in *Beowulf*: whilst in ll. 17 etc. which, on other grounds, we have found to be exceedingly early, we have, not merely "end stopping," but definite and regular strophic form[3].

---

[1] For the importance of *Widsith* as illustrating the duties and position of the *scóp*, see Anderson, *passim*, and Köhler in *Germania*, xv, 37 *etc*.

[2] Cf. R. M. Meyer in *P.B.B.* xxxii, 76.   [3] Cf. Neckel, pp. 1–21.

CHAPTER VII.

SUMMARY AND CONCLUSION.

THE passages in *Widsith* which show traces of being later additions, and which were on that account rejected by the earlier critics, have been enumerated at the end of Chapter IV. A survey of the geography of the poem[1] has emphasized the contrast between the stamp of definite locality borne by the undoubted portions, and the chaos of names found in the doubtful passages. A study of the grammar of the poem[2] has shown that such examples of late usage as we do find occur in just those passages which the earlier critics, on grounds quite other than those of metre or language, had suspected of being later additions[3]. The poem as a whole, and still more the undoubted portions, taken by themselves, we find to be more primitive in grammar and metre than the poems usually regarded as the oldest in English literature, such as *Beowulf* and *Genesis A*[4]. Above all, the habit of always concluding the sentence with the line, never with the half line, dissociates these undoubted portions of the poem from Old English epic poetry, and connects them with a small group of poems which, in subject matter, all seem to go back to a more primitive period than that of the courtly or learned epic, as we know it[5].

Reason has been shown for believing that these undoubted portions of the poem fall into two sections[6], originally distinct, the Catalogue of Kings, and the lay of Ealhhild and Eormanric

---

[1] Chap. v.   [2] Chap. vi.   [3] pp. 169, 173.
[4] pp. 170, 174.   [5] pp. 175-6.   [6] pp. 133-5.

which we may regard as the essential *Widsith*. *Widsith*, alike
on grounds of legend[1] and of geography[2], cannot be the work
of a contemporary of Eadgils and Ealhhild who really visited
the court of Eormanric. The Catalogue of Kings is older
than *Widsith* proper[3], yet on account of the names it contains
it can hardly be earlier than the middle of the sixth century,
and may be considerably later. *Widsith* seems to belong to
a period later than this, but earlier than *Beowulf* or *Genesis*:
that is to the seventh century.

This too is the date which has already been approved by
those who have studied the poem chiefly from the point of
view of heroic legend[4] and of geography[5]: it has been widely
accepted, but not universally, because the view has hitherto
been entertained that the language and metre of *Widsith*
pointed rather to the eighth than to the seventh century.
This view has been shown to rest partly upon a miscount,
partly upon a failure to differentiate from the rest of the poem
those parts which (on grounds not grammatical or metrical)
had been already suspected of being later interpolations.

It has still to be shown that interpolation and amalgamation
of the kind postulated are inherently probable. For, as has been
urged above, it is not enough to show that certain passages are
inconsistent with others, in order to dismiss one or other as an
interpolation. A *reason* which can have prompted such interpolation should be forthcoming[6]. We only escape from one
difficulty into another, if we explain an inconsistent text by
assuming an irrational interpolator.

Now, if a poem existed telling of the journey of a Myrging
minstrel to Eormanric, and enumerating the tribes and heroes
he had met, and if, as is most probable, a mnemonic catalogue
of tribes and heroes existed of the kind we find so often in
kindred literatures[7], the tendency to amalgamation would be
strong. If these poems did not contain the name of Ælfwine,
then, when Ælfwine passed from history to the same plane

---

[1] p. 142.   [2] pp. 163–5.   [3] pp. 134–5, 150, 176.
[4] e.g. Symons. See above, p. 150.   [5] e.g. Much, 65.
[6] See above, pp. 6, 144.   [7] See above, p. 6.

of heroic poetry as Eormanric, the temptation to add some lines mentioning the generosity of Ælfwine would also be strong. An introduction binding the somewhat inconsistent Catalogue of Kings[1] with *Widsith* proper[2] and explaining who Widsith, Ealhhild and Eormanric were, would become necessary, more particularly when the Eormanric cycle was beginning to be less generally familiar.

Again, our poem owes its preservation, where so much has been lost, to the fact that it interested a monkish scribe, probably because of its encyclopædic geographical information. But the world of this scribe was very different from that of the tribal bard who first devised the lay. Could a man of ancient days have been really travelled, he would ask, if he did not know of Alexander, had not seen Medes and Persians and Hebrews? Hence interpolations, which are but a necessary corollary of the new civilization which had been superimposed upon the old Germanic life. There may have been a more definite motive: the scribe may have wished to bring up the number of tribes to 72, the supposed number of the nations of the earth[3]: or the poem may have been transmitted to him as an imperfect one, and he may have been filling the gaps as best he could. The latter hypothesis seems the more probable one: for there are incoherencies in the poem which may well be the result of something having been lost.

Such a development seems then to be likely enough on *a priori* grounds: whether the evidence produced in its favour has been sufficient the reader must judge. The strength of such evidence varies, of course, in the different cases: the

---

[1] It would be difficult to say how far the parallels between the Catalogue of Kings (ll. 18, 20, 21, 44) and *Widsith* proper (57, 76, 69, 61) are the cause, and how far the result, of amalgamation. The collocation of Huns and Goths is part of the common Germanic tradition, found also in the *Elene*, and in Icelandic; its repetition need not therefore be due to imitation; l. 76, on the other hand, is probably the conscious imitation of an interpolator.

[2] The statement that the Myrging Widsith started from Angel is strange (see note to l. 8). It may point to some details of the legend, or some lines of the poem which have been subsequently lost. If not, it looks like a conscious attempt to harmonize the Anglian patriotism of ll. 38–44 with the Myrging patriotism of ll. 93–96. Ll. 84–85 may be an interpolation having the same object, (See note to l. 85.)

[3] R. Michel in *P.B.B.* xv, 377 *etc.*: cf. Bojunga in *P.B.B.* xvi, 545 *etc.*; Brandl in *Pauls Grdr.*(2) II, 1, 967.

spuriousness of the "Biblical" passage rests upon grounds of outlook, geography, and metre which seem to me over-whelming : the spuriousness of the Ælfwine passage rests upon one chronological and one grammatical detail, neither of which appears to me quite conclusive.

But much more important than these controversies as to the structure of *Widsith* are the conclusions we can draw from the poem regarding the ancient poetry of our race.

The place of Widsith in the history of Germanic poetry.

In attempting to estimate the value of the Old English heroic poetry, allowance is too often not made for the frag-mentary way in which that poetry has been handed down to us. We have not, as we have in Homer, that which the con-sidered judgement of the race thought most worthy to survive in its national poetry. The story of *Beowulf* is preserved, not because it was better or more popular than other stories, but because it happened to get written down (by no means a criterion of merit, in an age when there was little sympathy between the monk and the minstrel); because this copy hap-pened to get transcribed before it was destroyed ; because, in the Middle Ages, it happened that nobody was sufficiently energetic to cut up the *Beowulf* MS in order to bind more intelligible books ; because at the dissolution of the monasteries it happened not to be used for packing paper ; because it happened not to blaze up in the great Cottonian fire. It must not then be taken for granted, without examination, that *Beo-wulf* is a fair specimen of the old heroic poetry, still less that it is the best specimen.

A comparison with the extant fragments of the older heroic verse, with later poetry like *Maldon*, and with those poems in which biblical stories are told in the old epic style, shows us that in style at least *Beowulf* is a noble representative of its class. But is it so in plot ?

Monstrous and childish elements, belonging to the youth of a nation, are often found surviving sporadically in the poetry of a more mature age : the Cyclops and the No-Man story, for example, have kept their place in the most polished of all epics. Now, if the story told by Odysseus in the hall of Alcinous were all that remained to us of Homer, we should be in much the same position in judging the Greek epic as we are when we try to judge of the Old English heroic poetry from *Beowulf*. We should be puzzled by the obvious incongruity between the childish story, and the epic dignity with which that childish story is treated. And, just as we might have been helped to a truer perception of a lost Homer by the briefest summary of the fight in the hall of Odysseus, or by even such a travesty of the xxivth book of the Iliad as Tzetzes has left us, so we can to some extent reconstruct the matter of the Old German lays from Paul the Deacon or from Widukind, from the *Elder Edda* and the sagas.

Herein consists the real value of *Widsith* : it shows us what was the stock-in-trade of the old Anglian bard : and if *Widsith* be of composite origin, this only makes the evidence more representative. Read in a sympathetic mood, by anyone who has taken the trouble to acquaint himself with such of the old stories as time has left to us, *Widsith* demonstrates the dignity of the Old English narrative poetry, and of the common Germanic narrative poetry of which the Old English was but a section. The conquerors of Europe were not primarily interested in inarticulate water-demons or fire-drakes. The stories told in their lays were amongst " the best tales sorrow ever wrought." And we know from *Beowulf* that the style was not unworthy of such matter.

We find in *Widsith* no allusion to Beowulf: no reference to fights with giants or dragons : Wada, the only clearly supernatural character mentioned, has been rationalized as the chief of a historic tribe[1]. The supernatural had a place in Old English heroic verse : but, as in the Greek epic, this place was a subordinate one. If we pass once more hastily in review these old Germanic tales, we shall see that what chiefly

---

[1] For evidence that the *Hælsingas* are historic see note to l. 22. Breca may have been originally mythical: but he is grouped with historic kings. See above, p. 111.

interested the poet was character : the behaviour of his hero
or heroine under the stress of conflicting passions. The story
of Eormanric tells how, stirred by an evil counsellor, a great and
aged king was moved to take a wild revenge upon his young
bride, and how vengeance befell him ; the tale of Hagena and
Heoden tells how mischief was wrought between a young chief
and the father of his betrothed, so that no reconciliation could
be made ; similar, in its main outline, is the story of Sigehere
(Sigar, Hagbard and Signy), save that here, if Saxo has told
the tale aright, the poet was interested rather in the lovers
than in the father; in the story of Ingeld and Hrothgar we
have the same tale once more, but again with a difference, for
here it is the mischief-maker himself who attracts the poet's
interest, the *eald æsc-wiga* whose loyalty to the old time is
such that he cannot allow the ancient grudge to be forgotten.
The story of Guthhere was one of retainers falling around their
lord ; in the lay of Hnæf and Finn the retainers at last take
quarter, and heartburnings and new sorrows ensue; in the
tale of Hrothgar and Hrothulf a noble chief usurps the throne,
not without injustice and perhaps treachery to the sons of his
benefactor, and in the end falls himself by treachery. Occasionally, though rarely, the tragedy is relieved. In the story
of Wermund and Offa, the grief of the old king, whose heir is
unworthy to follow him, is turned into joy when, in the
moment of peril, that heir proves himself worthy. In the
greatest of all the stories, that of Ælfwine at the court of
the Gepid king, the ties of hospitality overcome the passion for
revenge.

Of course we cannot be certain that in every one of these
cases the name conveyed to the Anglian minstrel in the
seventh century just that meaning which has been here indicated : we cannot say, for example, how much story had as yet
collected round the name of Ælfwine. But the general
deduction to be drawn from these names is not open to doubt.
It is that the old poets had the right tragic feeling, the sane
and just outlook. The situations are those which we find later
in the Icelandic sagas; in *Othello* and *Romeo and Juliet*, in
Henry IV and *Macbeth*.

The place of Heroic Poetry in the Dark Ages.

And, apart from questions of poetic form and literary history, the fragmentary records of the old heroic poetry have their value in helping us to estimate the meaning of the "Dark Ages." With certain notable exceptions the events of Western Europe during these ages are told by contemporaries only in dry annals or very meagre histories, which chronicle the facts, mostly bloody and often disgusting, but leave us in the dark as to the motives of the men who did the deeds. Sometimes the history of Western Europe seems to be only one monotonous sordid tale of lust and bloodshed. Yet this is an illusion. The acts of fratricide and treachery which caused an upheaval are just the things which find their way into the brief annals; the daily life, the long years of faithful devotion of the retainer to his lord, are taken for granted. Yet without such faithful devotion the retention of the throne during many centuries in the hands of one family, Amal, Balt, Merowing, Iceling, would not have been possible. We obviously need some corrective to the annalists.

The motives of the leading figures in the history of these ages can seldom be accurately measured : it is still more difficult to estimate the feelings of the rank and file. But the fragments of the old heroic poetry show us at least what kind of men these retainers, the "swæse gesithas," *wished* to be. The story of England in the days of Ethelred the Unready, as told by chroniclers and homilists, is a sorry record of defeat. We are ready to exclaim with Falstaff "Is there no virtue extant?" till the poem of Maldon makes us feel ashamed of the estimate we have formed of tenth century England. Or to take a rather earlier and perhaps healthier period. The eighth century, to judge from the *Anglo-Saxon Chronicle*, seems a welter of internecine strife, treachery and cruelty ; yet the men among whom the song of *Beowulf* was loved, however given to deep drinking and hard fighting, were not, in the main, treacherous and cruel. It is the fallacy of the brief, unexplained annal. Stated in bare annalistic form, the deeds of

Shakespeare's noblest men, of Brutus, Hamlet, or Othello, would appear as the acts of a gang of gaol-birds. Had we more of the old lays, whether English, Gothic, Old Saxon or Frankish, this impression of cruelty would probably be softened; we should find that deeds of murder and treachery did not meet with approval when songs were sung and talk was free in the mead hall, after the day's hunting.

Only too often we hear in the annals of the guardian uncle or retainer who supplants his young king. What Gothic singers had to say about such things we learn from Cassiodorus' allusion to the song of Gensimund. Gensimund, a valiant chief, though not by birth an Amal, was adopted into the royal house. After the king's death the throne was offered to him, but he refused it, remaining faithful to the young princes, so that he is famed in song and will never be forgotten so long as the Gothic name lasts[1].

Of Beowulf almost exactly the same is told us. He was received by his king, and treated no whit worse than the king's own sons[2]. When the old king and his sons were dead, the last widowed queen offered the kingdom to Beowulf: "she trusted not to her son that he could hold the throne against foreign foes, now his father was dead. But none the more could the helpless folk in any wise prevail upon the prince [Beowulf] that he should be lord over Heardred and accept the kingdom : but he supported him amid the folk with friendly counsel, love and honour, till he grew older and ruled over the Weder-Geatas[3]."

---

[1] Heinzel (*Hervararsaga* in *W.S.B.* cxiv, 497) suggests that the faithful Gizur of that saga is a survival of Gensimund. Müllenhoff (*Z.f.d.A.* xii, 254) sees in Gensimund the historic forerunner of the Hildebrand of later story. Müllenhoff (as subsequently Scherer) assumes that Gensimund has a place in Gothic history, as the guardian of the father and uncle of Theodoric the Great. He would thus come very near to the Master Hildebrand of High German tradition. But the insertion of Gensimund into Gothic history at this point is a mere conjecture of R. Köpke (*Die Anfänge des Königthums bei den Gothen*, Berlin, 1859, p. 141) to which further currency was given by Dahn's apparently independent hypothesis (*Könige der Germanen*, Bd ii, München, 1861, pp. 60–61). The difficulties of this chronology are shown by Hodgkin (*Italy*, iii, 9). We have no sufficient grounds for making Gensimund an historic figure, though he may well have been such. W. Scherer (Review of Heyne's *Beóvulf* in the *Zeitschrift für die österreichischen Gymnasien*, xx, 1869, p. 95) seems to have been the first to draw attention to the remarkable parallel between Gensimund and Beowulf.

[2] 2435, *etc.*   [3] 2370, *etc.*

Nowhere do we find the judgement of the mead-hall expressed better than in the change undergone by the story of the treachery of the Frankish Theodoric. The Theodoric of history lured his old foe Irminfrid of Thuringia into his power, with promises of safe conduct and with rich gifts. Then, as they were talking one day on the walls of Zülpich, Irminfrid was pushed over, and killed. Who actually did the deed was never known: Theodoric was suspected of having instigated it[1].

But poetry did not allow Theodoric to enjoy the fruits of his treachery. In the place of the unknown assassin was substituted a demi-god : that Iring who had left his mark across the heavens in what we call the Milky Way. We wonder what that figure is doing in the character of traitor: till, when Theodoric disclaims the crime, Iring rises to the height of his daemonic power, slays the perfidious king, humiliates him even in death; and then making his *way* through the midst of the royal retinue, vanishes.

"The greater part," said Sir Thomas Browne, "must be content to be as though they had not been ; to be found in the register of God, not in the record of man. Diuturnity is a dream and folly of expectation." Yet in the old heroic poetry we get a glimpse of the thoughts of those men whose unrecorded lives and deaths have done more towards the building up of Europe than have the intrigues and quarrels of their lords. This should render sacred not only every recorded line of the old poems, but every paraphrase and every allusion.

---

[1] *Sed quis eum exinde deiecerit ignoramus ; multi tamen adserunt Theudorici in hoc dolum manifestissime patuisse.* Gregorii *Hist. Franc.* p. 116.

TEXT OF WIDSITH, WITH NOTES.

A very accurate facsimile of the *Exeter Book* was made for the British Museum, and checked by Sir Frederic Madden in Feb. 1832 (Add. MS. 9067). It was upon this facsimile that Kemble based his text, but only after comparison with the transcript of the *Exeter Book* which had been already made by Thorpe, who, however, did not publish till 1842. Mr Anscombe's theory (*Anglia*, xxxiv, 526-7) that Thorpe derived his text from Kemble is disproved by Kemble's express statement, and by the fact that Thorpe's text is much the more correct of the two.

Later editors based their texts on Kemble and Thorpe, either directly or at second hand, till Schipper again collated the *Exeter Book* in 1870-1, and published his results in 1874. Wülcker again collated the MS. for his *Kleinere Dichtungen* (1879 ; 1882). The text in his edition of Grein's *Bibliothek* (1883) is even more accurate, and may be the result of a second collation. Möller, who published in the same year, and all subsequent editors, based their texts upon this.

Some details as to the relations of the different editions of *Widsith* to one another, and of the British Museum facsimile to the MS. at Exeter, are given by the present editor in *Anglia*, xxxv, 393-400.

I have twice examined the MS. and noted the marks of length, and one or two other details not recorded by Wülcker : but there is nothing of importance to be added to his collation of the MS.

A collation of the seven chief texts of *Widsith* was appended by Wülcker to his text of the poem, issued in 1883. In a volume specially devoted to *Widsith* it seemed right to go somewhat more into detail. The first and second editions of Kemble have accordingly been distinguished (K_1 and K_2). They differ considerably, Kemble having incorporated into his second edition many important emendations. As Leo founded his text upon Kemble's second edition, with a general acknowledgement only, credit for Kemble's elucidations of the text has sometimes been given to later editors. By collating the edition of Ettmüller published in 1839, and Lappenberg's commentary of the same year, the important part played by both these scholars in the interpretation of the text of *Widsith* is made more clear.

The texts given by Ebeling, Schaldemose, Klipstein, Möller, and Kluge in his *Lesebuch* have also been consulted. The text of Ebeling is exceedingly bad; he follows Ettmüller[1] but with many misprints and many wanton alterations, whilst Klipstein derives direct from Thorpe (*Cod.-Ex.*). Schaldemose gives the MS. readings, recording the conjectures of Kemble, Leo, Ettmüller in his footnotes. He generally adopts these conjectures in his translation. Corruptions have, however, crept into his text (e.g. ll. 33, 93, 98, 118). Accordingly the readings of Ebeling, Klipstein and Schaldemose have not usually been recorded. Nor have

Möller's transpositions been noted, as they can be clearly understood only by consulting his complete text. The texts of Holthausen and Sedgefield, which appeared whilst this edition was in the press, have also been compared.

A number of the readings of the earlier editors are due to the elementary condition of Old English studies in their time: such for example as that of Ettmüller and Schaldemose in l. 134 *þenden he here* [for *her*] *leofað* "so lang er Heerfahrt liebet": "mens Feide han elsker." Whilst fully recognising how excellently the earlier editors did their work, I have not felt compelled to carry respect for them so far as always to record these, and similar obvious blunders, which they could not have made had they possessed the apparatus of dictionaries and grammars which we now have. Neither have readings been recorded which are misprints or oversights. The earlier editors, Kemble, Leo, Ettmüller, attempted to normalize the text, writing or suggesting *on* for *an* (3rd pers. plu.), *i* for *ie*, *h* for *g*, *est* for *ast*, *eo* for *ea*, *æ* for *ē*. In most cases it seemed unnecessary to record again wanton alterations of this kind, as they will be found in the apparatus criticus of Grein-Wülcker. In the few cases where my collation did not agree with that of Wülcker, I have verified the reading.

WIDSIÐ MAÐOLADe, wordhord onleac,
se þe [monna] mæst mægþa ofer eorþan,
folca geondferde: oft he [on] flette geþah
mynelicne maþþum. Him from Myrgingum

Widsith spake, unlocked his store of words, he who of all men had wandered through most tribes and peoples throughout the earth: oft in hall had he received the lovely treasure. His race sprang from the

1. *Widsið.* A proper name, that of the supposed traveller: not, as the earlier editors, before Thorpe (1842), take it: "the long journey" spoken of by him "who wandered through most tribes." Wülcker (*Kl. D.* 164) also supported this rendering: but in his *Grundriss* (328) he regards *Widsið* as a proper name. The name is recorded as having been borne in historic times (*Uidsith, Liber Vitae,* 179). Cf. Koegel, *Ltg.* I, 1, 138.

2. *se þe monna mæst mægþa ofer eorþan.* The MS. reads *se þe mæst mærþa ofer eorþan*; so K₁: K₂ conjectured *se þe mæst fandode mægþa ofer eorþan*: Leo, Ettmüller (₁) and Schaldemose adopted *fandode* but kept *mærþa,* which they rendered "das was gerühmt wird über die Erde," "Mannruhm" etc.: *mæst gemunde mærða,* Ettmüller (₂) and Rieger: *mæst mette mærða,* Thorpe (*Cod. Ex.*): *mæst mægða mette,* Thorpe (*Beowulf*).

se þe monna mæst mægþa... is Grein's reading; it was at once endorsed by Müllenhoff (*Z.f.d.A.* XI, 275) and later by Grein, Gr.-Wülcker, Holt. and Sedg. Kluge, however, retains *mærþa,* being probably influenced by the parallel passage in *Beowulf* (2645)

  forðan he manna mæst mærða gefremede.
For the construction, cf. also *Judith* (181)
  þe us monna mæst morðra gefremede
  sarra sorga.

on flette. on supplied by Grein, followed by all later editors.

4. *mynelicne.* ἅπαξ λεγόμενον. Not "memorable" as Thorpe (*Cod. Ex.*) following Ettmüller's "Erinnerungs Kleinod": but "lovely," "pleasant," cf. Icel. *munlegr,* "pleasant," O.S. *munilika magað,* "a lovely maiden."

5. *Him from Myrgingum æðelo onwocon.* The MS. has *hine from Myrgingum æþele onwocon,* concerning which Conybeare remarked "it may imply that the nobles of his own country had encouraged him to travel, as appears to have

5 æþelo ónwocon.   He mid Ealhhilde,
   fælre freoþuwebban,   forman siþe
   Hreðcyninges   ham gesohte
   eastan of Ongle,   Eormanrices,

Myrgings : it was with the gracious lady Ealhhild that he first, from
Angel in the East, sought the home of the Gothic king Eormanric, fell and
faithless....

been the case with Gunnlaug. See *Gunnlaug Sag.* p. 96." [The reference is to
the Copenhagen edition of 1775. But the passage probably does not bear the
interpretation put upon it. Yet the travels of the poets Gunnlaug and Widsith
offer an interesting parallel.] Kemble, Leo, Ettmüller and Thorpe also keep
the MS. reading. This, however, is impossible, for *onwacan* is intransitive.
Thorpe (*Cod. Ex.*, notes) suggested, though he did not read, *him* : "from him
among the Myrgings nobles sprung," comparing *Beowulf*, 112, and the mention
of *cnosl* below. Klipstein follows Thorpe's conjecture, which is possible, but
not likely, for *cnosle* in l. 52 probably means kindred, not offspring. *Him from
Myrgingum æðelu onwocon* is Grein's reading, and has been followed by later
editors (*æþelo*, Rieger, Grein-Wülcker, Kluge, Holt., Sedg.).
    5. *Ealhhilde.* See Introduction, pp. 21–28.
    6. *fælre freoþuwebban.* *Fæle* in this connection is a hackneyed epithet : *fæle
friðowebba* (*Elene*, 88) : *fæle freoðoscealc* (*Gen.*, 2301, 2497), *fæle freoðuweard*
(*Guthlac*, 144), cf. Möller, *V.E.* 32–3 ; Grimm, *Andreas u. Elene*, 143–5 ;
Lawrence in *Mod. Philol.* IV, 350–1.
    Freoþuwebbe was rendered " Fridensweberin " by Leo ; so Ettmüller, Thorpe,
etc. But it must not be supposed that Ealhhild goes to the court of Eormanric
to negociate peace. The idea conveyed by *freoþuwebbe* is rather that of
domestic peace than of diplomatic service ; cf. Lawrence in *Mod. Philol.*
IV, 350.
    forman siþe. Gummere(1) translates "once." But it probably means more
than this. In *Beowulf* (716) where *forma sið* occurs in a similar context,
it is emphatic enough :

           Ne wæs þæt forma sið
        þat he Hroþgares ham gesohte.
So Gummere(2), "first."
    7. *Hreðcyninges.* See Appendix, Note H : *The term Hrædas applied to the
Goths.* Holt. regards as a common noun : glorious king, "Ruhmkönig."
But cf. *Frescyning* (*Beowulf*, 2503).
    8. *Ongle.* The old home of the Angles, the *Angulus* of Bede, the *Angel* of
King Alfred. Now, in the second century, the Goths were dwelling on the
banks of the lower Vistula, due east of Angel. By the third century they had
left their old home, and were soon on the shores of the Black Sea, whilst by the
sixth century they were mainly in the south and west of Europe. Critics,
reading *eastan of Ongle* as a statement that the Goths dwelt east of Angel
(Grimm, *Heldensage*, 18, 19 ; Leo, 76 ; Boer, *Ermanarich und Dietrich*, p. 12 ;
cf. Weiland, 15 ; Gummere in *M.L.N.* IV, 210), have seen in this a proof of the
early date of the poem (Müllenhoff, *D.A.* II, 99 ; Klipstein, II, 422 ; Möller,
V.E. 32 ; Weiland, 15 ; Koegel, *Ltg.* I, 1, 179). The words, however, cannot
mean this : "The home to the east of Angel" would be *ham be eastan Ongle*.
    In the course of a controversy with Sarrazin, Sievers examined elaborately
the syntax of the O.E. adverbs of place with verbs of motion (*P.B.B.* XII, 168,
etc. ; also, less important, XI, 361 ; cf. Erdmann, 48). In *Pauls Grdr.* (1) I, 408,
he shows the bearing of this upon *Widsith*. *Eastan of Ongle* means "from the
east, from Angel," and was apparently written by a resident in England,
referring to the old Anglian home in the east. It therefore tends to prove the
later date of, at any rate, this introduction. But the whole thing is puzzling.
Why should a Myrging bard start from Angel? See Introduction, p. 165, 179, *note.*

wraþes wærlogan.　Ongon þa worn sprecan :
10 "Fela ic monna gefrægn　　mægþum wealdan ;
　sceal þeod[n]a gehwylc　　þeawum lifgan,
　eorl æfter oþrum　　eðle rædan,
　se þe his þeodenstol　　geþeon wile !
85 a　‖Þara wæs [H]wala　　hwile selast
15 *ond* Alexandreas　　ealra ricost

He began then to speak many words :
"Of many men have I heard, ruling over the nations.　Every chieftain must live virtuously (one lord after another, ruling his land), he who desires his throne to flourish.
Of these was Hwala for a time the best, and Alexandreas most mighty

9.　*wraþes wærlogan.*　The same expression is in the *Andreas* (613) applied to the Devil.　Thorpe assumed a gap : "Here some lines are evidently wanting, although there is no hiatus in the ms., as the words *wraþes wærlogan* cannot apply to Eormanric, the object of the poet's praise."　But this assumption is groundless.　See Introduction, pp. 34–36.

worn.　Many words ; cf. *Beowulf* (530).

11.　*þeodna.*　ms. *þeoda*, so K($_1$).　*þeodna*, the conjecture of K($_2$), was adopted by Leo, and has been accepted by all later edd., except Thorpe (*Cod. Ex.*) and Ettmüller($_2$).

12.　*eorl æfter oþrum.*　See Leo (87).　Möller (*V.E.*) followed by Ten Brink (539) transposed verses 11, 12, to the great improvement of the sense.

14.　*Hwala.*　ms. *Wala*, followed by K($_1$)($_2$), Leo, Schaldemose.　Thorpe and Rieger attribute to Kemble the emendation *Hwala* : but it seems to have been made by Ettmüller($_1$).　It is clearly right, and has been adopted by all later edd.　Hwala, son of Beowi (Bedwi) son of Sceaf, is found in the West Saxon pedigree in three mss. of the Chronicle (Cotton Tiberius A vi, B i, B iv : see entry for year 855, death of Æþelwulf).

That Kemble should have overlooked so obvious a correction here is strange, for whilst editing *Widsith* he was also working at the O.E. genealogies, and had pointed out that *Wala* in the later versions of these genealogies should be read *Hwala* : "Wir werden hernach sehen dass die Lesart Hwala allein die richtige ist, wenn wir die herrschende Alliteration in diesen Listen betrachten."

See Kemble, *Ueber die Stammtafel der Westsachsen*, München, 1836, pp. 11–13, 26.

15.　*ond Alexandreas.*　Obviously Alexander the Great : though Grein would read *ond* as a preposition, "among the Alexandrians," and Haigh, in his vain attempt to make all the heroes of *Widsith* contemporary, interpreted the name as a reference to one of the sixth century Alexanders mentioned by Procopius.　Holt. suggests *Alexandros.*

Müllenhoff, followed by Rieger, condemned ll. 14–17, on the ground that they interrupted the sequence, for after the mention of Ermanaric in l. 8 we should expect the catalogue to begin among the Goths and their neighbours : he therefore supposed 14–17 interpolated by the same hand as ll. 75–87 ; they "show the same combination of national tradition [Hwala] with idle monastic learning" [Alexandreas, Alexander the Great, with the name assimilated to that of the saint Andreas].　Other edd. (e.g. Ebeling) condemn only l. 15 (Alexandreas).　The fact that the scribe of the *Exeter Book*, or perhaps an earlier transcriber, did not know who Hwala was, and misspelt his name, shows that Hwala had been forgotten, and is therefore against the theory that line 14 is a late, monastic, interpolation.　Nor need the reference to Alexander be the result of monastic learning.　That the Alexander story was well known throughout western Europe is proved by king Alfred's reference to Nectanebus

16 monna cynnes   *ond* he mæst geþah,
þara þe ic ofer foldan   gefrægen hæbbe.
Ætla weold Hunum,.   Eormanric Gotum,
Becca Baningum,   Burgendum Gifica.

of all the race of men, and flourished most of those of whom I have heard
tell throughout the world....

(Orosius, ed. Sweet, 1883, *E.E.T.S.* p. 126), by the Macedonian descent attributed to the Franks (Otfrid, *Evang.* I, 1, 87–91) or Saxons (Widukind, I, 2),
and by the Old English translation of Alexander's letter to Aristotle. The
mediæval Alexander saga has its root in popular traditions going back to the
third century of the Christian era (see *Notice des Manuscrits contenant l'histoire
fabuleuse d'Alexandre le Grand* par J. Berger de Xivrey, in the *Notices et
Extraits des Manuscrits de la Bib. du Roi*, Paris, t. XIII, 1838, p. 178: Spiegel
Die Alexandersage, Leipzig, 1851, p. 2). Alexander may therefore well have
been known by name among German tribes at a very early date. According to
Jordanes Ermanaric and Alexander had been coupled together: *Hermanaricus
...quem merito nonnulli Alexandro Magno comparavere maiores* (ed. Mommsen,
XXIII). So, though ll. 14–17 are *probably* later, we cannot be certain.

18. *Ætla.* Kluge has pointed out that this form of the name corresponds to
the O.N. *Atli*, as against the M.H.G. *Etzel*, O.H.G. *Ezzilo* (by i-umlaut from
Attilo). The English and Norse forms come from a syncopated **Atlo*, presumably the Low German form about 500 A.D. See *Engl. Stud.* XXI (1895),
447. But the form *Etla* also is found in England.

Hunum....Gotum. A rough approximation to geographical order can be
traced throughout this catalogue: ll. 18, 19 deal with the tribes and chiefs
of Eastern Germany. Ostrogoths and Huns were not only neighbours, but
closely associated in story both as allies and as foes. Hence they are again
coupled below (l. 57) and twice in the *Elene*: *Huna leode ond Hreðgotan*, 20;
Huna ond Hreða here, 58. So in the Icelandic *Lay of Hloth and Angantyr*:

> *Ár kvóðo Humla Húnom ráða,
> Gitzor Gautom, Gotom Angantý...*

where *Gautom* is very possibly a miswriting for *Grytingom*—the Greutungi, a
Gothic tribe. See *C.P.B.* I, 349.

19. *Becca.* The Bikki of Northern story. See Introduction, pp. 19, 20, 33.
Mentioned again, l. 115, as one of Eormanric's retainers. The facts that he
is here spoken of as prince of an independent tribe, that in Saxo he is son of
a Livonian king, and that the *Atlakviþa* mentions the "warriors of Bikki"
Bikka greppa (see *C.P.B.* I, 57, Symons u. Gering, I, 426–7), seem to indicate
that in the original story Becca was the prince of a tributary race, not a
Gothic servant of Ermanaric.

Baningum. Müllenhoff (*Z.f.d.A.* XI, 276–7) suggests that this is a fictitious
name "the sons of the slayers," φονείδαι—a fit tribe for the faithless Becca to
rule. This would necessitate *ǎ*: but on metrical grounds it is better to read *ā*.
The name means then, presumably, "the righteous, hospitable" (Icel. *beinn*,
see Much, 126), a name which might have been assumed by a real people.
This interpretation seems preferable to the "Beininge" of Holthausen [of
course *beinn* may be connected with O.E. *bān*, Germ. *bein*, through the meaning
"the straight (i.e. shin-) bones"]. The probability that the Banings were a
real people is increased by an apparent reference to them in the *Origo gentis
Langobardorum* where the land of the Bains is linked with that of the
Burgundians, just as here Banings and Burgundians are classed together.
But this does not enable us to identify the Banings with any known tribe.
Schütte (*Oldsagn*, 61, 106) suggests the Sarmatians. But evidence to prove
this is lacking. The Sarmatians had, Schütte points out, a king Beuka
(Jordanes, LIV).

Burgendum. Originally an East Germanic tribe, and, in the second and

20 Casere weold Creacum   *ond* Cælic Finnum,

third centuries, neighbours of the Goths. See Ptolemy, ii, 11, 8–10 (where they are mentioned as dwelling north of the Lygii: i.e. in the modern Posen) and perhaps iii, 5, 8 (where if the Burgundians are to be identified with the Φρουγου[ν]δίωνες they must have extended east of the Vistula). From Jordanes (xvii) it is clear that Goths, Gepidae and Burgundians were neighbours about the middle of the third century, when Fastida was encouraged by his victory over the Burgundians to attack the Goths under Ostrogotha. (*Nam Burgundzones pene usque ad internicionem delevit.*) After this the Burgundians moved west, and by the end of the third century were threatening Gaul. (*Cum omnes barbaræ nationes excidium universæ Galliæ minarentur, neque solum Burgundiones et Alemanni, sed et Heruli et Chæbones in has provincias irruissent—* Mamertinus, *Panegyr.* i, 5; 289–290 A.D.) For the later history of the Burgundians see Introduction, p. 63. This mention of the Burgundians along with the Eastern folk seems accordingly a reminiscence of a state of things which had passed away before the fourth century (see H. Derichsweiler, *Geschichte der Burgunden*, 1863; Bremer in *Pauls Grdr.* (₂) iii, 824), and hence an indication of a very early date for at least this section of the poem. We cannot be quite certain of this, however, for a portion of the Burgundian nation may have remained in the East. Burgundians are reckoned by Sidonius Apollinaris among the host of Attila invading Gaul in 451 (*Carm.* vii, 322), and it has been supposed that these were "a portion of the tribe who had lingered in their old homes by the Vistula" (Hodgkin's *Italy*, ii, 107). Whether there were any Burgundians by the Vistula so late as this may be doubted. Attila's Burgundians may well have been a portion of the Rhenish people, which may have been incorporated by the victorious Huns, after the Burgundian defeat in 437. The main body of the Burgundian survivors was, of course, in the opposite camp (Jordanes, ed. Mommsen, xxxvi).

Gifica. See Introduction, p. 64.

20. *Casere.* The emperor of the East. The Kaiser's name was so current in early Germanic times, that, at last, as the son of Woden, he comes to stand at the head of the East Anglian genealogy. (See Florence of Worcester, ed. Thorpe, i, 249.) He occupies this position in that genealogy as given in MS. C.C.C.C. 183, and in MS. Cotton Vespasian B 6, where we should read *caser*, not (as Sweet, *Oldest English Texts*, 171) *care*. The word *casere* may well have been borrowed very early : possibly through Anglian mercenaries in Roman pay (cf. Hoops, *Waldbäume*, 569). For *Casere* see also note in *M.L.R.* iv, 1909, p. 508.

Creacum. The Greeks. Paul (*P.B.B.* i, 197) has argued that the *C*, which is always found in this word both in the East and West Germanic dialects, and which was only driven out later by the influence of the Latin *Graecus*, is due to the fact that the last stage of the Germanic sound shifting was not completed when the word was borrowed from the Latin, and that hence the voiced stop became voiceless along with the other similar sounds. This would make the word a very early loan indeed. A more probable theory is that of Kossinna (*Weinholdfestschrift*, Strassburg, 1896, p. 40) and Kluge (*Pauls Grdr.* (₁) i, 325) who suppose that, at the time the word was borrowed, the voiced stop *g* had not come again into use at the beginning of words, and that thus the voiceless stop *k* was substituted, as the nearest approximation.

For the spelling *Creacum* for *Crecum*, here and in l. 76, cf. Holthausen, 165. See also Introduction, p. 166.

Cælic. Heinzel (*Hervararsaga* in *W.S.B.* cxiv (1886) p. 507) suggests that this is a corrupt form of *Kalew*. It is certainly the case, as Heinzel points out, that stranger corruptions are found in the Anglo-Saxon and Old Norse genealogies. The MS. has *Cęlic* (= *Cælic*).

21. *Hagena.* See Introduction, p. 100, etc.

Holm-Rygum. An emendation of Grimm (*G.D.S.* 469 ; following a suggestion of Lappenberg, 175) for the MS. *Holmrycum.* Grimm's conjecture is certain (cf. l. 69) : it has been followed by later editors. Ettm., Thorpe, Ebeling, Klipstein, and Grein, however, follow Leo, *Holmricum*, or MS. *Holmrycum.*

21 Hagena Holm-Rygum *ond* Heoden Glommum.

The Rugian name, like the Gothic, is found both in Scandinavia and in Eastern Germany (*Pauls Grdr.* (₂) III, 818; Much in *P.B.B.* XVII, 184). The Scandinavian Rygir, Holmrygir (Island-Rugians) dwelt in Rogaland, on the banks of the southernmost islands and fiords of Norway. But not even the Norwegian versions place Hogni in Norway. Saxo puts him in Jutland, and Snorri imagined him as dwelling well to the south of Norway. The Holmryge are therefore more probably the Rugii of Tacitus, a people dwelling on the Baltic coast not far from the Goths (*protinus deinde ab Oceano Rugii ; Germania,* XLIII). That these were also known as "Island-Rugians" is clear from Jordanes, according to whom the Goths, on leaving Scanzia, reach the mainland *unde mox promoventes ad sedes Ulmerugorum, qui tunc Oceani ripas insidebant, castra metati sunt, eosque commisso proelio propriis sedibus pepulerunt, eorumque vicinos Vandalos iam tunc subiugantes suis aplicavere victoriis* (ed. Mommsen, IV). The Island-Rugians must have dwelt on the islands and peninsulas at the mouth of the Vistula (Müllenhoff in Mommsen's Jordanes) and perhaps also of the Oder (Zeuss, 484), whence the modern Rügen. It is to be noted that, according to Saxo, the last fight of Höginus and Hithinus took place on the island of Hiddensöe (*Hythini insula*) off the coast of Rügen.

Later the Rugians moved south, and in the fifth century occupied the present Austria. The story of Hagena and Heoden, essentially one of sea roving, could accordingly no longer be associated with them. Hence the confusion of the later versions : *Kudrun* places Hagen in Ireland: the *Sǫrla þáttr* and Saxo in Denmark.

That *Widsith* still connects the story with a tribe which, by the fifth century, had ceased to be maritime, is another proof of early date: but the possibility that the reference is to the Norwegian Holmrygir must not be left quite out of sight. Compare Koegel, *Ltg.* I, 1, 169 ; Müllenhoff in *Z.f.d.A.* XXX, 230 ; *Pauls Grdr.* (₂) III, 826–7 ; Panzer, *H.G.* 436–7. Boer (*Z.f.d.Ph.* XXXVIII, 47) would make the Danish islands the original home of the " Island-Rugians." But there is no evidence for this. Bugge (*H.D.* 314–5) sees a connection between the Holmryge and the *Rogheimr* of *Helga kviða Hjǫrvarðssonar,* 43. This again seems unlikely.

Heoden. MS. *Henden.* The emendation *Heoden* (which is certainly right, although Schaldemose, Ettmüller(₁), Thorpe, Ebeling, Klipstein, and Grein retained the MS. reading) was suggested by J. Grimm (*Z.f.d.A.* II, 2 ; cf. *G.D.S.* 470). Möller suggests an intermediate *Headen* : so, independently, Anscombe in *Anglia,* XXXIV, 527 : in view of ll. 70, 111, it is quite likely that *Heoden* was written *Headen* : and *ea* would then easily be miswritten *en*.

Glommas. Lappenberg (175), Müllenhoff, *Nordalb. Stud.* I, 151, Grimm, *G.D.S.* 752, Thorpe, Grein (*Sprachschatz*), and Holt. suggest a connection with Norway (the river Glommen). It is in favour of this conjecture that Saxo places Hithinus in Norway, as apparently does the catalogue of the battle of Bravalla (*Hythin gracilis,* in Saxo, VIII, p. 258). See also Introduction, p. 109, *note.*

Conybeare would make the Glommas " a Sorabic tribe," his evidence being apparently Ditmar v. Walbeck, who speaks of " *provintiam quam nos Teutonice Deleminci vocamus, Sclavi autem Glomaci appellant* " (Thietmari *Chronicon,* I, 3, recog. F. Kurze, Hannoveræ, 1889). Glomazi is the modern Lommatzsch near Dresden. The ancient province coincides approximately with the later Erzgebirgischer Kreis of the electorate of Saxony. For the exact limits, cf. Kurze's note to Ditmar, and Böttger's *Diocesan- u. Gaugrenzen Norddeutschlands,* IV, 224, *etc.* That there is any connection between Glomazi and the Glommas is, however, in the highest degree unlikely. Still more so is the suggestion of Koegel (*Ltg.* I, 1, 169) that, as Heoden's folk, the Glommas should be sought near the mouth of the Schelde. This is an application to *Widsith* of features belonging to a much later version of the story.

The only evidence then, though that is insufficient, points to Norway as the home of the Glommas.

C.   13

22 Witta weold Swæfum,　　Wada Hælsingum,

22. *Witta* occurs in the genealogy of Hengest as given by Bede, *H.E.* I, 15; and following Bede, by the Laud ms. of the *A. S. Chronicle*: *Hengest and Horsa, þæt wæron Wihtgilses suna. Wihtgils wæs Witting, Witta Wecting, Wecta Wodning.* The same genealogy is also given in the *Historia Brittonum*, § 31, cf. Grimm, *D.M.* Anhang, IV, V. A not very probable conjecture by Fahlbeck as to the origin of this genealogy will be found in *A.T.f.S.* VIII, 48. The name Witta is found associated with that of Watte (? = Wade) in a tradition of Northern Schleswig, recorded by Müllenhoff. Vitte and Vatte are two dwarfs dwelling in neighbouring hills : a farmer passing one hill at night is told to "greet Vitte, Vatte is dead." See Müllenhoff, *Sagen, Märchen und Lieder der Herzogthümer Schleswig-Holstein u. Lauenburg* (1848), No. 400, p. 242. In England the name is found in *Wittanham* in Berkshire (see Binz in *P.B.B.* XX, 221).

Swæfum. Swabians, Suevi. The name is used, broadly, to cover a large number of tribes in central Germany : *Nunc de Suevis dicendum est, quorum non una ut Chattorum Tenctcrorumve gens ; majorem enim Germaniæ partem obtinent propriis adhuc nationibus nominibusque discreti quamquam in commune Suevi vocentur.* (*Germania*, XXXVIII.) Schwabsted in Schleswig, compared with the South German Schwaben, perhaps bears witness to this wide diffusion. But Tacitus probably exaggerates the extent of the Suevic name, making it cover the Angles, and many tribes of Eastern and Northern Germany who were very probably not of Suevic stock. That the Suevi extended as far as the coast is probable from a passage in the *Agricola* (XXVIII) where some shipwrecked men fall first into the hands of the Suevi, then of the Frisii (*primum a Suevis, mox a Frisiis intercepti*) ; see Chadwick (203). Amongst this large family of Suevic tribes there was, however, one tribe to which the name peculiarly belonged: the Suebi of Cæsar, dwelling on the Main. These, after many wanderings, mingled with the Alamanni, themselves Suevi in the broader sense of the word, and to this mingled stock the name Swabian has in later times been specially applied. See Bremer in *Pauls Grdr.*(₂) III, 918–38. The name had therefore two significations, one broader, the other more particular. Below, where the *Swæfe* are linked with the Angles (ll. 44, 61), the reference is apparently to the northernmost section of the great people, dwelling near the modern Schwabsted (Much, 28, 102): and here the context favours a similar explanation. Whereas in l. 44 the Swæfe are apparently synonymous with the Myrgings, it should be noted that here the two peoples are clearly distinguished.

Wada, see Introduction, p. 95, *etc.*

Hælsingum. Müllenhoff (*Z.f.d.A.* VI, 65 ; cf. XI, 278) regards this as a feigned name, connected with *hals*, the neck, or prow of a ship (*flota fami-heals, Beowulf*, 218) chosen as appropriate to the people of a hero, like Wada, connected with the sea. More probably the Hælsingas are a real people, whose colonists have left their name in many places on the Baltic coast : Helsingör (Elsinore) in Zealand ; Helsingborg on the adjacent coast of Sweden ; Helsingland, a province of Sweden ; Helsingfors, on the opposite coast of Finland. In spite of this wide diffusion, there is considerable agreement among philologists in placing the original home of the Hælsingas on the Χάλουσος ποταμός of Ptolemy, but great disagreement in identifying this with any modern river. Zeuss (150), Seelmann, who argues the question at length (43), Weiland (27) and Chadwick (204) suggest the Trave; Möller (*V.E.* 28) the Eider or Halerau ; Müllenhoff (*Nordalb. Stud.* I, 115) the Eider ; Much (*P.B.B.* XVII, 186) the Warnow. Cf. also Möller, *A.f.d.A.* XXII, 155.

In any of these cases the Hælsingas would be neighbours of the Angles, and probably of "Anglo-Frisian" stock. (Kögel, *Ltg.* I, 1, 155–6.) If, as is probable (cf. Panzer, *H.G.* 436), the Middle High German *Wate von den Stürmen* means Wade "of Stormarn" this would be a strong argument for placing Wade's people, the Hælsingas, in that district, i.e. on the Trave. In any case Wade and his people are to be put on the Baltic coast : and with this the reference in the *Thidreks saga* agrees (c. 57, *Vaðe rise er a Siolande*).

²³ Meaca Myrgingum,   Mearchealf Hundingum.
Þeodric weold Froncum,   Þyle Rondingum,

23. *Meaca.* Müllenhoff (*Nordalb. Stud.* i, 152) followed by Rieger, conjectured *Meara*, the eponymous form from which Myrging might be supposed to be derived. He abandoned the conjecture (*Z.f.d.A.* xi, 277) but returned to it (*Beovulf*, 99). In *Z.f.d.A.* xi, 277 Müllenhoff would connect Meaca with O.E. *gemaca*, Icel. *maki*, companion, and would interpret Mearchealf as "colleague." He apparently regarded the two as forming a heroic pair, the Theseus and Pirithous of early German story.

Mearchealf. Ettmüller (₁) suggested *Mearcvulf* (notes, p. 15) but returned to *Mearcealf* in his second edition. *Mearcvulf* was also suggested in a note by Rieger, who however retained *Mearchealf* in his text, following Müllenhoff's explanation (see *Meaca*, above). If we read *Mearcwulf* we must interpret as the Marculf of *Salomo and Saturn*. Sophus Bugge (*H.D.* 171) has independently made the same suggestion as Ettmüller, pointing out, what is at any rate an odd coincidence, that Marculf is spelt *Marcholfus* by Notker. Marculf's son and successor in Middle English verse is Hendyng. It would be rash to argue any connection between this name and the *Hundingas* whom Mearchealf rules (cf. Binz, *P.B.B.* xx, 222).

Hundingum. King Hunding is mentioned in the prose introduction to the song of Helgi Hundingsbani, *Hundingr het rikr konungr, viþ hann er Hundland kent* (Symons, *Edda*, i, 272). Tribal and kingly names tend to interchange: cf. *Hocing*, below, and *Scylding*. The Hundings are apparently to be placed on the south coast of the Baltic   See Müllenhoff in *Nordalb. Stud.* i, 153, *Z.f.d.A.* xi, 278, xxiii, 128, 170; Jiriczek, 292; Bugge, *H.D.* 91, 169–70; *P.B.B.* xxxix, 479. Hund may be either from *hund* "dog," or *hund* "hundred"; in the former case we may compare the *cynocephali* of Paulus (i, 11), see also Anscombe in *Eriu*, iv, 87; for the latter compare Tacitus' mention of the hundred pagi of the Semnones (*Germania*, xxxix). For another interpretation, see Chadwick, 299–300.

24. *Þeodric.* See Introduction, p. 112. Möller (*V.E.* 18) supposes Theodric to be an interpolation from some poem dealing with the victory won by Theodric over Hygelac. There is little to be said in favour of this conjecture, which seems to spring from the very common habit of exaggerating the importance of those remnants of the old epics which happen to have come down to us. The rout of Hygelac was only one of Theodric's victories, less important and less personal than many others.

Froncum. If the name of the Franks means the "spearmen," as argued by Kluge (*Etymol. Wörterbuch*) and, with some doubt, by Erdmann (*Die Angeln*, 80), then we might take the "Rondingas" as an epic fiction echoing the name. "Theodric ruled the Spearmen: Thyle (his retainer) the Shieldmen."

But it seems unlikely that the Franks derived their name from the *franca*, for two reasons. (1) As has been frequently noted, the root *frank*=spear is not found in continental German, but only in English and Scandinavian dialects. (2) Equal attention has not been given to the argument that the *franca* was used certainly as much, possibly more, by other nations. The characteristic Frankish weapon was the hurling axe, frequently referred to by Procopius (see Keller, M. L., *Anglo-Saxon Weapon Names*, Heidelberg, 1906, pp. 18–31, 133–4). According to Agathias (ii, 5) the Franks used a peculiar barbed spear, the *ango* (cf. our angle) similar to the "cruelly hooked boar spear" which in *Beowulf* is used to attack sea-monsters. Agathias gives a detailed description of the *ango*: it was a species of harpoon, and could not be withdrawn from a wound. Some good illustrations of these weapons, recovered from the graves of Ripuarian Franks, will be found in *Archæologia*, xxxvi, 78–84 (cf. also xxxv, 48–54). There seems to be no connection between the *ango* and the O.E. *franca*, which was a gentlemanly weapon:

> he let his francan wadan
> þurh ðæs hysses hals.

25 Breoca Brondingu*m*, Billing Wernum.

According to Procopius, the Franks in A.D. 539 were remarkable for *not* carrying spears: ἱππέας μὲν ὀλίγους τινὰς ἀμφὶ τὸν ἡγούμενον ἔχοντες, οἳ δὴ καὶ μόνοι δόρατα ἔφερον. οἱ λοιποὶ δὲ πεζοὶ ἅπαντες οὔτε τόξα οὔτε δόρατα ἔχοντες, ἀλλὰ ξίφος τε καὶ ἀσπίδα φέρων ἕκαστος καὶ πέλεκυν ἕνα. (*Bell. Gott.* II, 25.) It is very doubtful, therefore, if the word Frank conveyed the idea of "spearman." The rival etymology " the Freemen " suggested by Grimm, *G.D.S.* 512, *etc.* is also open to grave doubt: it has been supported by Bremer in *Pauls Grdr.*(₂) III, 878. (But cf. *P.B.B.* xxv, 223, *etc.*)

þyle. See Introduction, p. 115.

Rondingum. Perhaps an epic fiction, the " shield men " (a name appropriate to the retainers of Thyle, Theodric's follower) as Müllenhoff suggested. No historic tribe of this name is known : it certainly means "men with shields," cf. Icel. *hyrningr*, one carrying horns. (See Much in *P.B.B.* xvii, 120 ; Binz in *P.B.B.* xx, 148 ; Müllenhoff in *Z.f.d.A.* xi, 281 ; Chadwick, 284.) Leo (77), Conybeare (12), Lappenberg (178) and Brandl (*Pauls Grdr.* 966) suppose the Rondings to be a real people, and their name to be preserved in the Reudigni of Tacitus : a somewhat unlikely conjecture. For these Reudigni see Much in *P.B.B.* xvii, 192.

25. *Breoca Brondingum.* Breca also in *Beowulf* rules over the Brondings. See Introduction, p. 110.

Billing. This name is best known in connection with the famous house which ruled in Saxony during the latter part of the tenth and ·the whole of the eleventh century. See Prutz, *Staatengeschichte des Abendlandes im Mittelalter*, 1885, i, 189, 400 ; E. Steindorff, *De ducatus qui Billingorum dicitur, origine*, Berolini, 1863 ; E. Wintzer, *De Billungorum intra Saxoniam ducatu*, Bonnœ, 1869. The name is of frequent occurrence in England, Lappenberg's statement (*Geschichte*, i, 214) notwithstanding, and has left its mark in names like Billingborough, Billinge, Billingham, Billinghay, Billingshurst, Billingsgate, Billington. Of the original Billing nothing is known, but we may assume, from his connection here with the Werne or Wærnas, and the subsequent appearance of the name in England and Saxony, that he was essentially a hero of the coast tribes. See also Grimm, *D.M.* (219: trans. Stallybrass, i, 373–4) : Kemble, *Saxons*, i, 458 (Appendix A). For name (*bill*, sword) cf. *Ronding* above. Billing's daughter is the beloved of Odin : *Hávamál*, 96.

Wernum. The Varini of Tacitus, a people closely connected with the Angles, and belonging to the group of Nerthus-worshipping tribes. We gather from the order of Tacitus' enumeration that the Varini probably dwelt North of the Angles, and their name may perhaps be preserved in *Warnæs* (i.e. Warna næs, *promontorium Varinorum*, now corrupted to Warnitz, a promontory in the N.E. of Sundewitt). See Müllenhoff in *Nordalb. Stud.* i, 129. Procopius, in the middle of the sixth century, makes the Οὔαρνοι spread as far as the Rhine, which separates them from the Franks : διήκουσι δὲ ἄχρι τε ἐς ὠκεανὸν τὸν ἀρκτῷον καὶ ποταμὸν Ῥῆνον ὅσπερ αὐτούς τε διορίζει καὶ Φράγγους. (*Bell. Gott.* iv, 20, 1833; a strange story follows of a war between the Angles of Brittia and the Warni.) Another reference (ii, 15) marks the Warni as dwelling more where we should expect them : south of the Danes. The Varini can hardly have occupied these wide stretches of country continuously, as Hodgkin (*Italy*, iii, 355) seems to suppose. They must have been scattered, and settled in isolated groups. Hence the difficulty of localizing the *Werini* of the *Lex*, and the *Guarni* addressed by Theodoric. (See Appendix E : *The original home of the Angli and Varini.*) That a contingent also accompanied the Angles to England appears likely from the names *Wernanbroc*, *Wernanford*, *Wærnanhyll*, *Wernanwyl*. (See Seelmann, *Die Ortsnamenendung -leben* in the *J.d.N.f.n.S.* xii, 1886, p. 23 : for other place names, many very doubtful, see Haigh (113) ; certainly not *Warwick* as suggested by Müller, *Lex Salica*, 123 ; corrected by Müllenhoff, *Nordalb. Stud.* i, 133. See also Zeuss, 360 ; Müllenhoff, *D.A.* iv, 465 ; Much in *P.B.B.* xvii, 204 ; Bremer in *Pauls Grdr.*(₂) iii, 851.)

26 Oswine weold Eowum   *ond* Ytum Gefwulf,
  Fin Folcwalding   Fresna cynne.
  Sigehere lengest   Sæ-Denum weold,
  Hnæf Hocingum,   Helm Wulfingu*m*,

26. *Oswine.* Unknown, unless he is to be identified with the Oslaf mentioned in the Finnesburh episode in *Beowulf.* See Much in *Herrigs Archiv*, cviii, 407 and cf. Grimm, *G.D.S.* 472, and Müllenhoff in *Z.f.d.A.* xi, 281.

Eowum. Allowing for the interchange of *eo* and *ea* (*Beowa* and *Beawa*, *Z.f.d.A.* vii, 411) and assuming a weak nominative *Eawan*, we have the Aviones of Tacitus (see Müllenhoff, *Nordalb. Stud.* i, 156; Grimm, *G.D.S.* 472; Koegel, *Ltg.* i, 1, 155). The Aviones belong to the group of Nerthus-worshipping people. Much (*P.B.B.* xvii, 195) would locate them on the islands of the Cattegat, interpreting the name as "Islanders." Bremer (*Z.f.d.Ph.* xxv, 129) suggested that the name was preserved in the traditions of the North Frisian islands, as recorded by Hansen. In the muster of warriors in the Sylt story we have "De Uuwen kam fan Uasten," the Uuwen came from the east; and Bremer derived Uuwen from a primitive *Auwaniz*, whence *Aviones, Eawan*: see C. P. Hansen, *Uald Söld'ring Tialen*, 1858, p. 22, and, dissenting from Bremer's suggestion, Möller in *A.f.d.A.* xxii, 158. Subsequently Much (₂ 101, and in *Hoops Reallexikon*, i, 146), whilst adhering to the explanation of *Eowan, Aviones* as "Islanders," would place them in the North Frisian islands of the North Sea rather than in the Baltic.

It has also been proposed to connect the Eowan with Oeland (called Eowland in Alfred's Orosius, ed. Sweet, p. 20). But this would take us into quite another part of the Baltic. We need an identification of the Eowan which leaves them neighbours of the Wærnas and of the Yte. This is supplied by the connection with the Aviones, but not by the connection with Eowland.

Ytum. See Appendix, Note D: *The Jutes. Gefwulf* is unknown.

27. *Fin Folcwalding.* See Introduction, p. 67.

Fresna cynne. See Introduction, p. 67, and compare Zeuss, 136 *etc.*; Grimm, *G.D.S.* 668-81; Erdmann, 83-86; Siebs in *Pauls Grdr.* (₂) i, 1153; Bremer in *Pauls Grdr.* (₂) iii, 844-849. Cf. also note to l. 68 below.

For the structure of the two lines, 26, 27, see Neckel, pp. 5, 6, 47, 480.

28. *Sigehere.* Undoubtedly identical with the O.N. *Sigarr* (Heinzel in *A.f.d.A.* xvi, 272). Saxo, Bk vii, tells how Sygarus, king of Denmark, caused Hagbarthus, the lover of his daughter Sygne, to be slain, and how Sygne shared her lover's death (ed. Holder, pp. 230-237). The story is a particularly fine one. It must have been popular throughout the Scandinavian countries: references to it are frequent, especially in the form of place names (Heinzel). The tale is also extant in a Danish ballad, of which there are many versions. See *Danmarks Gamle Folkeviser, udgivne af Svend Grundtvig.* Kjøbenhavn, 1853 *etc.* i, 1, 258-317. But in England it seems to have been little known, and the name *Sigehere* is rare. (Binz in *P.B.B.* xx, 169; cf. Müllenhoff, *Beovulf*, 52.)

lengest. Sygarus is styled *senilis* by Saxo (ed. Holder, 237). I understand *lengest* here, and in l. 45, below, to mean "for a very long time." Cf. the use of *swi∂ost* for "very greatly" in Alfred's Boethius (p. 37, ed. Sedgefield, 1899).

29. *Hnæf Hocingum.* Strictly Hnæf is himself the son of Hoc: but the family name is extended to his people, just as in *Beowulf* the Danes are called *Scyldingas*, from the ancestor of their kings. Hocing is perhaps found for the hero Hoc, the father of Hnæf, in the genealogy of Hildegard the wife of Charles the Great, whose grandfather and greatgrandfather bore the names of Nebi [? = Hnæf] and Huochingus (see Müllenhoff in *Z.f.d.A.* xi, 282). Hildegard was of Alamannic race, and we have therefore in the juxtaposition of these two names an indication that the story was known in High Germany in the seventh century. The names of the heroes of this cycle are found fairly frequently in England, but more particularly that of Hoc (see Binz in *P.B.B.* xx, 179-186).

30 Wald Woingum,   Wod þyringu*m*,

For the use of *Hocing* both as a family name, and as equivalent to that of the ancestor Hoc, cf. *Vǫlsungr*, which is applied not only to members of the family, but also to the eponymous ancestor, who, in *Beowulf*, is called, more correctly, *Wæls*.

Helm. Perhaps the imaginary name of a typical king: cf. the common expression *helm Scyldinga, Scylfinga.* But it is no mere fiction of our poet, for that there was a hero *Helm*, though his story has been lost, is likely from the mention of a *Helmes treow* (*Cart. Sax.* ed. Birch, III, 1213) whilst a *Helmes welle* is mentioned several times in Domesday Book. The Helming family —presumably that of which Helm was the eponymous ancestor—is referred to in *Beowulf* (620), and place names derived from *Helming* are fairly common in England (see Haigh, 63 ; Binz in *P.B.B.* xx, 177–8). Continental parallels are not so easy to find : but there seems reason to suppose, with Ettmüller (₁) 17, some connection with the *Helmschrot* or *Helmschart* of German story (*Dietrichs Flucht* passim). At any rate *Helmschrot, Helmschart* and *Helmnot* all belong to the Wülfinge (cf. Matthaei in *Z.f.d.A.* xlvi, 55–6).

Wulfingum. The name occurs in *Beowulf.* Ecgtheow having incurred a blood feud *mid Wilfingum*, Hrothgar pays the fine and sends *ofer wæteres hrycg ealde madmas.* The phrase seems to imply a sea-journey of some distance. As the Wülfinge, the faithful retainers of Dietrich von Bern, play an important part in the High German versions of Gothic legend, it is likely that the original *Wylfingas* should be thought of as neighbours of the Goths, dwelling on the Baltic coast. See Müllenhoff, *Beovulf*, 14, 90 ; *Z.f.d.A.* xi, 282 ; xxxiii, 170 ; Jiriczek (₂), 292. That the Wylfingas of the O.E. heroic verse are the same as the Wülfinge of the *Heldenbuch* is the more likely because in both cases members of the family form their names by compounds in *heaðo-* ; e.g. *Heaðolaf, Hadubrant* (Binz in *P.B.B.* xx, 216) ; see also the preceding note on *Helm.* Traces of the name are to be found in England : *Wolfinges læw, Wylfingaford.* The *Ylfingar* occur in Scandinavian poetry : Helgi Hundingsbane is called "the son of the Wolfings" *Ylfinga nið.* Cf. Bugge, *H.D.* 84–87 ; 164–166 ; 313–314 ; see also Symons in *P.B.B.* iv, 176 ; and, for some further notes on the Wolfings, and on Helm, Sarrazin in *Engl. Stud.* xxiii, 228 : Heinzel, *Hervararsaga* in *W.S.B.* cxiv, 510.

30. *Wald.* Wald is regarded by Müllenhoff as an epic fiction, the typical name of a tyrant (*Z.f.d.A.* xi, 283).

Woingum. In *Nordalb. Stud.* i, 158, Müllenhoff suggested a connection between the *Woingas* [primitive form **Wanh-*] and the island of Wangeroge, and the district Wangerland, the older Wangia or Wanga. (See the *Chronicon Moissiacense* and the *Vita S. Willehadi* in Pertz (fol.) *SS.* ii, 257 and 383.) They would therefore be the inhabitants of the coast of East Friesland and Oldenburg. In his later commentary (*Z.f.d.A.* xi, 283) Müllenhoff proposed to take the name of the Woingas as an epic fiction, as well as that of their king: a typical name for an evil people, from *woh* "crooked," "evil." This last explanation seems less satisfactory. Müllenhoff's further development of it (*Z.f.d.A.* xxiii, 124), in which he attempts to connect Wald and his Woings with the family of the tyrant Siggeir of the *Vǫlsunga Saga*, wants evidence to support it.

Wod. Here again Müllenhoff suggests that the name is fictitious and chosen with reference to the Thuringians, over whom Wod (i.e. mad) rules: (there was a popular etymology which connected Thuringian with *thor* " fool "). But see Grimm, *G.D.S.* 597.

For the Wod of Germanic mythology (O.N. *Óðr*, the husband of Freyja, *Hyndloljóð*, *Vǫlospá*), see Golther, 283 *etc.* We cannot say whether Wod of the Thuringians has any connection with him.

þyringum. The *þyringas* may be the Thoringi of Gregory of Tours (*Hist. Franc.* ii, 9) who dwelt in the present Zeeland and North Brabant, in the neighbourhood of Dordrecht, at the mouths of the Rhine and Maas. These Möller (*V.E.* 16) identifies with the *Turii* or *Sturii* who are mentioned by Pliny as occupying the same territory. (*Nat. Hist.* iv, cap. 15 [29].) These Thuringians

31 Sæferð Sycgum,   Sweom Ongendþeow,

were apparently a Frankish people, who were subsequently pressed South and East by the Saxons and Frisians. It was Hermann Müller (*Der Lex Salica u. der Lex Angliorum et Werinorum Alter u. Heimat*, Würzburg, 1840, p. 122 etc.) who first pointed out the existence of these Thoringi, and the necessity of distinguishing them from the Thuringians proper; cf. Waitz, *Das alte Recht der Salischen Franken*, Kiel 1846 ; Grimm, *G.D.S.* 601; Möller (*A.f.d.A.* xxii, 152) ; Erdmann (28). As we are dealing here with North Sea peoples and heroes, it is probably these Rhenish Thuringians who are meant (cf. Müllenhoff in *Nordalb. Stud.* i, 159). It is possible, however, that here as in Alfred's Orosius (ed. Sweet, 1883, p. 16) þ*yringas* means the main stock of the Thuringians, identical with the Hermun-Duri of classical times, whose name is in the fifth century replaced by that of Thuringian : (the Thuringians, however, cover a wider area, from the Harz mountains to the Danube). The Thuringian kingdom was overthrown by Theodoric, king of the Franks (cf. l. 24) in 531–6. See Zeuss (353 etc.) ; Bremer in *Pauls Grdr.* (₂) iii, 938 etc.; Grimm, *G.D.S.* 596–607 ; Seelmann (*Nordthüringen*) in the *J.d.V.f.n.S.* 1886, 12.

31.   *Sæferð*. Identical with the *Sigeferð*, *Secgena leod* of *Fin.* l. 42. For the confusion of *Sæ* and *Sige*, cf. *Sæberht*, king of the East Saxons, who appears as *Saberchtus* or *Saeberchtus* in the text of Bede, but as *Sigberchtus* (at any rate in certain mss.) in the Chronological Summary (cf. Möller, *V.E.* 87). The name *Sigeferð* is common in England, and so, to a less degree, is *Sæferð* (Binz in *P.B.B.* xx, 184–5). It has been argued by Uhland that this Sigeferth or Sæferth is to be identified with Sigfried (Sigurd) the Volsung (*Germania*, ii, 357–63 ; *Schriften*, viii, 497). This view has been more recently supported by Golther (*Germania*, xxxiii, 474–5) and apparently for a time by Müllenhoff (see the next note). It seems exceedingly improbable, though it is difficult to speak with certainty, in the absence of sufficient evidence as to the Sigfried story in England.

Sycgum. Koegel (*Ltg.* i, 1, 164) and Möller (*V.E.* 86) connect the *Secgan* with the Saxons " for Secga like Sahso signifies swordsman " (Koegel). *Secgan* and *Seaxan* would then be related as *secg*, "sword" (*Beowulf*, 684) and *seax* "knife," from Prim. Germ. *sag-*, *sahs-* (cf. Lat. *secare*). These *Secgan* Möller supposes to have dwelt between the Elbe and the Eider, and to be identical with the tribe who colonized Essex. The evidence for this, however, is not convincing, and turns chiefly upon the occurrence of the names *Gesecg* and *Antsecg* in the Essex genealogy, together with *Seaxnete*, the son of Woden, with whom the genealogy begins. (See genealogies in Florence of Worcester, ed. Thorpe for English Historical Society, 1848, i, 250 ; and Henry of Huntingdon, *Historiæ Anglorum*, ii, § 19, ed. Arnold, Rolls Series, p. 49.) Müllenhoff (*Nordalb. Stud.* i, 164) had drawn attention to Gesecg and Antsecg: he suggested an identification of the Secgan with the Reudigni of Tacitus. All this is exceedingly hypothetical, but it seems likely, from the context in which they are mentioned here, in l. 62, and in the Finnesburh fragment, that the Secgan were a coast tribe. Uhland, having identified Sigeferth with Sigfried, had to identify the Secgan with his people, deriving the name from Sigi, who in the *Vǫlsunga Saga* stands at the head of the family [precisely as the Danes are called Scyldings because Scyld is the first of their royal house]. This identification was rejected by Müllenhoff in 1859 (*Z.f.d.A.* xi, 283) but accepted by him in 1877 (*Z.f.d.A.* xxiii, 117–124), although with a full recognition of the etymological difficulty of bringing Secgan and Sigi together (155–7). Finally, however, Müllenhoff recognized this identification as unlikely (*Beovulf*, 97) whilst at the same time rejecting Möller's explanation.

Lappenberg (177) suggests a connection with the Σιγούλωνες (recorded by Ptolemy in the Cimbric Chersonese, next to the Saxons). Geographically this is satisfactory, but linguistically the gap is too great, as corresponding to *Secgan* we should expect *Sagiones*.

For *Secgum* : *Sycgum*, see Möller, *V.E.* 153–4.

Sweom. The Swedes. The name however at this date embraces only a small section of the inhabitants of modern Sweden, which was held by Finns in the

32 Sceafthere Ymbrum,   Sceafa Longbeardum,

North, Norwegians in the West, Geatas and Danes in the South.   See note to p. 72.   Möller (*V.E.* 15) considers that the name of the Swedes is substituted here for that of some other tribe beginning with S—*Sweordwerum, Sweardum,* or *Seaxum*—on the ground that the transition from tribes at the mouth of the Elbe to the Swedes is too sudden.   But it does not follow, because the names in *Widsith* are usually grouped geographically, that they must always be so.

Ongendþeow.   The king of Sweden, frequently mentioned in *Beowulf* (2476, *etc.* : 2923, *etc.*).   The name *Ongenþeow* is unknown in England in historical times, nor is any tradition of him retained, beyond the references in *Beowulf* and in *Widsith.*   A reminiscence of the name is to be found in the fact that the son of Offa I, called *Angelþeow* in the *Chronicle,* is called *Ongen* in the *Historia Brittonum* (in *M.G.H.* p. 203).   Möller (*V.E.* 19) regards the name here as an interpolation—but the reasons brought forward are insufficient.   Ettmüller (1) (2) and Grein read *Ongenþeow,* to bring the name into line with the forms used in *Beowulf.*

For the story of Ongenthew, which is clearly in great part historic, see H. Weyhe, *König Ongentheows Fall,* in *Engl. Stud.* xxxix, 14–39 ; Gering, 115, *note,* 118 ; Bugge in *P.B.B.* xii, 16.

32.   *Sceafthere.*   Possibly, like *Helm, Scild,* or *Æsc,* a typical name for a war-king (Müllenhoff in *Z.f.d.A.* xi, 283 ; cf. also vii, 414).

Ymbrum.   Perhaps the inhabitants of the island Fehmarn and the adjoining coast.   Fehmarn is repeatedly called *Ymbria, Imbra* in Danish chronicles and documents (see Langebek, *passim*), as also by Adam of Bremen (Pertz (fol.), *SS.* vii, 373, where compare the note).   This suggestion was originally made by Lappenberg (p. 177), and has been again made independently by Siebs (*Eng. Fr. Sprache,* 17).   It is the best explanation of the name.

But Thorpe (*Cod. Ex.* 516) and, apparently independently, Müllenhoff (*Nordalb. Stud.* i, 159 ; cf. also *Z.f.d.A.* xi, 283) would connect the Ymbre with the district of Ammerland, west of the Weser, known in the 11th century as *Ammeri* or *Ambria* (see Staphorst, *Historia Ecclesiæ Hamburgensis Diplomatica,* Hamburg, 1723, i, 425, and i, 603, where in a charter of ? 1199 we have *comes Elimer Ambriæ* ; see also Ledebur, *Die fünf Münsterschen Gaue und die sieben Seelande Frieslands,* Berlin, 1836, especially map at end : and H. Böttger, *Diöcesan u. Gaugrenzen Norddeutschlands,* Halle, 1875–6, ii, 161).   Perhaps, also, the name is preserved in Amrum, one of the North Frisian islands.   Cf. also Ettmüller (1) 18 ; Much, 101.

It may be that in these two names *Ambria, Amrum* we have traces of fragments of the famous tribe of the Ambrones, for whom see Lappenberg, i, 101–2 ; Zeuss, 147–150 ; Müllenhoff, *D.A.* ii, 114, 118, *Beovulf,* 95.   The Ambrones are mentioned by Plutarch as taking part in the expedition of the Cimbri and Teutones (ed. Reiske, Lipsiæ, 1775, ii, 830, Life of Marius, Τεύτονες δὲ καὶ Ἄμβρωνες ἐφαίνοντο πλήθει τ' ἄπειροι καὶ δυσπρόσωποι τὰ εἴδη).   They seem, in fact, to have early got a bad name, and the word *Ambrones,* as is clear from the many instances quoted by Müllenhoff, is often used simply as a synonym for robbers.

There is some evidence, though far from conclusive, that a section of the Ambrones took part in the colonization of England.   Siebs (*Eng. Fries. Sp.* 15, 16) sees many traces of their name in ancient Wessex (Worcestershire and Wiltshire) : and the close connection which many students have seen between the North Frisian dialect of Amrum and Old English might also be urged in support (cf. Möller in *A.f.d.A.* xxii, 157).   The heavy evidence for a settlement of Ambrones in England is that the *Historia Brittonum,* describing the baptism of the Deirans (more correctly the Bernicians, as Ten Brink has pointed out, referring to Bede, *H.E.* ii, 14), calls them Ambrones : *et per quadraginta dies non cessavit baptizare omne genus Ambronum,* where a 13th century ms. (Corp. Christ. Camb. 139) records the gloss *id est Ald-Saxonum.*   See Nennius, ed. Stevenson, *Eng. Hist. Soc.* 1838, § 63 ; Möller, *V.E.* 89 ; Ten Brink, *Beowulf,* 198–9.

33 Hún Hætwerum   *ond* Holen Wrosnum.

Perhaps, however, the use of the term in the *Historia Brittonum* is not ethnographical at all, but expresses the previous unregenerate state of the converts : the gloss may then be the conjecture of some scribe who did not understand this; or, as Chadwick suggests (56), *Ambronum* may be an error for *Umbronum*, men of the Humber. (Cf. also Latham's *Germania*, 1851, cviii.)

Müllenhoff's connection of the Ymbre with Ambria has been generally followed (e.g. by Rieger in *Z.f.d.A.* xi, 202–4), but Lappenberg's identification with Imbria is far more satisfactory. Whether there is a connection between any or all of the names Ambria, Amrum, Imbria and the classical Ambrones cannot be decided with certainty, but such connection is very probable. The differences of vowel would presumably be due to ablaut (Much in *Hoops Reallexikon*, 77).

Sceafa. Binz, following Möller, would read here *Scyld*, or *Scefing* (*P.B.B.* xx, 148). He continues ''Sceafa ist übrigens auch wegen der schwachen form sehr verdächtig.'' But strong and weak forms of the proper noun interchange not infrequently. Thus we have *Sceldwea, Sceldwa* in the Parker ms. of the *Chronicle* (*sub anno* 855), in Asser, and in Florence of Worcester, as against *Scyld* in *Beowulf*, Ethelwerd, *etc.*: *Geat* in the Parker and most mss. of the *Chronicle* against *Geata* in ms. Cot. Tib. A. 6, in Asser, and in the text of Florence of Worcester (i, p. 71, ed. Thorpe, 1848), who, however, writes *Geat* elsewhere : *Beowan ham* in the charter of 931 (Birch, *Cart. Sax.* ii, 677, Kemble, *C. D.* ii, 353) as against *Beaw* in the Parker ms. : *Hreðles* [ms. *Hrædles, Beowulf*, 1485] as against *Hreðlan* [ms. *Hrædlan*, 454]: *Hors* in the *Historia Brittonum*, § 31, against the more usual *Horsa*. Some O.H.G. parallels will be found in *Z.f.d.A.* xii, 260. There seems then no reason for doubting the identity of *Sceaf* and *Sceafa*, or for regarding *Sceafa* as a shortened form of a compound name with two elements (parallel to *Cuþa* for *Cuþwine*) as suggested by Chadwick (282).

See also Koegel in *Z.f.d.A.* xxxvii, 270 : Müllenhoff in *Z.f.d.A.* vii, 410 : Heusler in *A.f.d.A.* xxx, 31.

Longbeardum. The context in which the Lombards are here mentioned seems to point to their ancient home between the Baltic and the Elbe.

The connection between the *Longbeardan* and the *Heaþobeardan* is doubtful. See below, l. 49.

33. *Hun.* The name of this chief is to be found in *Beowulf*, if we construe ll. 1143–4 with Bugge (*P.B.B.* xii, 33), Holder, Ten Brink and Gering "when Hun thrust (or placed) in his bosom Lafing, best of swords." But the difficulties of this interpretation were demonstrated by Imelmann in the *D.L.Z.* (xxx, 999 : April, 1909). Chadwick (52) had drawn attention to the hero Hunleifus in the *Skioldunga saga*. R. Huchon, in a review of Chadwick in the *Revue Germanique* (iii, 626), pointed out that, on the evidence discovered by Chadwick, *Hunlafing* in *Beowulf* must be the name of a man. This was confirmed by Imelmann's discovery of Hunlapus (see Appendix, K). It may be therefore taken as demonstrated that the name in *Beowulf* is *Hunlafing*, not *Hun.* Possibly the name of a hero *Hun* is preserved in the Frisian *Hûnesgâ* (Müllenhoff in *Nordalb. Stud.* i, 160, Rieger in *Z.f.d.A.* xi, 188). The name *Hunn* occurs in the list of sea-kings in the *Thulor* (*C.P.B.* ii, 422). There does not appear to be any connection between Hun of the Hætwere and the king and champion named Hun in Saxo. The name is not connected with the racial name, being found as an element in personal names before the arrival of the Huns in Europe. (Müllenhoff in *Z.f.d.A.* xi, 284.)

Hætwerum. Leo first detected the Hætwere in this passage: Kemble had read *Hun-hæt Werum.* The ms. may be read equally well either way. Grundtvig (*Dannevirke*, 1817, ii, 285) had identified the Hetware of *Beowulf* with the classical Hatuarii : an identification which has been universally accepted. See Grimm, *D.M.* xxii; Zeuss, 100 ; *Z.f.d.A.* vi, 437 ; Müllenhoff, *Beovulf*, 17, 18, 94 ; Bremer in *Pauls Grdr.* (₂) iii, 894.

The Hatuarii were a Frankish people dwelling on the Rhine, near its mouth.

Hringweald wæs haten   Herefarena cyning.

35 Offa weold Ongle,   Alewih Denum :

Offa ruled Angel, Alewih the Danes : he was boldest of all these men,

Zeuss would identify them with the Batavi of Tacitus, who were a branch of the Chatti (*Germ.* xxix), but apparently the Hatuarii dwelt between the Rhine and the Zuider Zee, whilst the Batavi dwelt south of them. They are first mentioned as having submitted to Tiberius with other tribes of the lower Rhine (Vellejus, ii, 105 ; *subacti Canninefates, Attuarii, Bructeri*). Subsequently they spread somewhat higher up the Rhine, in the neighbourhood of Cleves, where they were attacked by Hygelac in the sixth century, and overthrew him. (*Beowulf*, 2363, 2916 ; Gregory of Tours, *Hist. Franc.* iii, 3.) This district appears to be designated by the O.N. *Hunaland* ; and Sigfrid, who in the *Nibelungen Lied* is connected with it, is called *inn hunski* in the *Edda* (cf. Kaufmann in *Z.f.d.Ph.* xl, 283–4). There may possibly be some connection between these terms and the traditional king Hun of the Hætware.

Holen. Müllenhoff (*Nordalb. Stud.* i, 160) interpreted "elder-tree," comparing for the naming of a hero from a tree the hero Assi in Lombard story [cf. O.E. *Æsc*]: and for the sacredness of the elder comparing Grimm, *D.M.* 374 (trans. Stallybrass, ii, 651). Later he interprets it as a fictitious hero's name, "Holm-oak," emphasizing the idea of immemorial age (*Z.f.d.A.* xi, 284) and compares O.H.G. *hulis* (modern *hulst*) used as a proper name. Neither of these explanations is satisfactory, as the elder (Germ. *holunder*) is surely quite distinct from the holly (O.E. *holen*) ; and it seems unlikely that O.E. *holen* can mean "holm-oak."

Bugge (*P.B.B.* xii, 78) would identify Holen with the *Holdinus rex Rutenorum* who is mentioned by Geoffrey of Monmouth as one of Arthur's barons (x. 6 : x. 9). But this seems far-fetched.

Wrosnum. Müllenhoff (*Nordalb. Stud.* i, 161) compares the Rosogavi whose inhabitants were rooted out by Charles the Great in 804. *Et deinde misit imperator scaras suas in Wimodia et in Hostingabi et in Rosogavi, ut illam gentem foras patriam transduceret.* *Chronicon Moissiacense*, in Pertz (fol.) SS. i, 307. See also Böttger, *Gaugrenzen Norddeutschlands*, 1875–6, ii, 144.

The people seem to have been coast tribes, dwelling between the Weser and the Elbe, but nearer the latter. They would be close neighbours, if Müllenhoff's conjectures are right, to the Woingas and the Ymbras, and not far removed from the old home of the Lombards (Bardengau) or from Ymbria (Fehmarn). The identification is therefore plausible, in view of the context.

Lappenberg's attempt (p. 176) to identify the Wrosnas with the Scandinavian tribe who gave their name to Russia is, of course, chronologically and phonetically impossible ; cf. Ettmüller (₁) 19.

34. *Hringweald, Herefarena cyning.* Possibly, as Müllenhoff supposes (*Z.f.d.A.* xi, 284), "epic fictions" ; typical names for a treasure-giving king and his conquering people.

Herefaran simply means the warriors or pirates. Müllenhoff (*Nordalb. Stud.* i, 161) compares *Lindesfaran* : a band of sea-rovers who gave their name to Lindisfarne. Möller (*V.E.* 90, 91) builds an elaborate theory on these similar names, connecting the Lindesfaran or Herefaran, their king Hringweald, and their Holy Island off the coast of Northumberland, with Heligoland, and the neighbouring island of Sylt, where traditions of a king Ring remain.

35. *Offa.* See Introduction. Müllenhoff (*Nordalb. Stud.* i, 162) regards these lines (35–49) as interpolated, although at an exceedingly early date. They do not suit the context, and the praise of Offa, the foe of the Myrgingas, does not suit a Myrging minstrel. Müllenhoff's other reason is that the historic Offa lived in the sixth century, and therefore too late to have appeared as a hero of song in the original *Widsith*. This last argument is certainly wrong (see Müllenhoff, *Beovulf*, 85, 86). Later (*Z.f.d.A.* xi, 294) Müllenhoff does not try to distinguish this passage, in date, from the bulk of the poem.

Ongle. Kemble suggested *Onglum* ; wrongly. Cf. l. 8.

se wæs þara manna   modgast ealra;
nohwæþre he ofer Offan,   eorlscype fremede;
ac Offa geslog   ærest monna
    cniht wesende   cynerica mæst;
40 nænig efeneald him   eorlscipe maran
    on orette   ane sweorde:

yet did he not in his deeds of valour surpass Offa. But Offa gained, first
of men, by arms the greatest of kingdoms whilst yet a boy; no one of his
age [did] greater deeds of valour in battle with his single sword; he drew

Alewih. Unknown. Thorpe (*Cod. Ex.* 517) followed by Müllenhoff (*Nordalb.
Stud.* I, 162) identified with the Olo, king of Denmark, frequently mentioned by
Saxo (Books VII, VIII). But the names do not correspond phonetically, and
Müllenhoff subsequently gave up this explanation, suggesting another in his
Beovulf, 53. The name occurs in England in the Mercian pedigree (*A.S.
Chronicle*, Parker MS. *sub anno* 716) *Alweo Eawing*, a nephew of the great
Penda. Binz supposes the fact of a descendant of Offa having been named
Alweo to point to the survival of a tradition in which the two kings were
connected. Elsewhere the name occurs rarely in England and always north of
the Thames, on Anglian soil (*P.B.B.* xx, 169). The name is also fairly common
in continental Germany; see instances in Förstemann, 54, 76; *Alawig,
Alahwih.* The O.N. form is *Ǫlvér* (Kluge, *Engl. Stud.* XXI, 447).

37. *nohwæþre he ofer Offan eorlscype fremede.* It has generally been assumed
that this means "Alewih could not exercise dominion over Offa" and that
it points to a struggle between the two kings. (Müllenhoff, *Nordalb. Stud.*
I, 162; *Beovulf*, 74; Möller, *V.E.* 30.) *Eorlscype* = (1) deed of valour, (2)
dominion, authority. The latter sense, however, is the rarer, and the phrase
fremman or *æfnan eorlscype* seems always to mean "to perform deeds of
valour"; e.g. in *Beowulf*, 2622, where it cannot mean to exercise dominion, as
Wiglaf is not a prince. *Ofer* may be [to rule] "over" as in *rice ofer heofonstolas*
"mighty over the thrones of heaven" (*Genesis*, 8) or "than," as *Ioseph was
gleawra ofer hi ealle* (*Orosius*, 34, 1). The rendering given above (which is the
one adopted by Koegel, *Ltg.* I, 1, 159) is therefore the more probable, though
both are grammatically possible. Bosworth-Toller gives both renderings, the
one under *onorettan*, the other under *eorlscype*. For *ofer* cf. F. Wullen in
Anglia, XXXIV, esp. p. 448.
The allusion does not therefore necessarily point to any contest between
Danes and Angles.

38. *geslog* "gained by striking," as in the Brunanburg poem *ealdorlangne
tir geslogon æt sæcce*: so in *Beowulf* (459) *gesloh* means "settled by blows."
Cf. Müllenhoff, *Beovulf*, 74. Not "he smote the greatest of kingdoms," viz.
Denmark, as taken by Möller (*V.E.* 31).

39. *cniht wesende...nænig efeneald.* But in both English and Danish story
Offa had reached the age of thirty before his combat. *Mutus autem et verba
humana non proferens usque ad annum ætatis suæ tricesimum*; *De Offa primo in
Matthaei Paris Historia*, ed. Wats, 1640. *Qvi usqve ad tricesimum ætatis suæ
annum fandi possibilitatem cohibuit*, Sweyn in Langebek, I, 45; and cf. the
extract from the *Annales Ryenses* quoted on p. 87 (footnote).
Müllenhoff (*Sagen, Märchen u. Lieder der Herzogthümer Schleswig-Holstein
u. Lauenburg*, p. 4) supposed that "thirty" was a blunder for "thirteen":
Chadwick (129) more plausibly suggests that such a phrase as *þritig missera*
may have been misunderstood as thirty years. But the extraordinary thing
is that the Danish and the English traditions should later agree in a common
error.

41. *on orette.* Thorpe (*Cod. Ex.* and *Beowulf*), Grein and Bosworth-Toller
suggest that this should be read as one word *onorettan*, to accomplish, a word

<blockquote>

42 merce gemærde   wið Myrgingum
bi Fifeldore: heoldon forð siþþan
Engle *ond* Swæfe,   swa hit Offa geslog.

</blockquote>

the boundary against the Myrgingas at Fifeldor.   Engle and Swæfe held it afterwards as Offa struck it out.

which, if we adopt the reading of Dietrich, Grein (₁) and Grein-Wülcker, is also found in *Exod.* 312–3 : *Judisc feða an onorette uncuð gelad,* "alone the folk of Judah accomplished the strange path."
Although the editors have always read the ms. *on orette*, this might rather be read as one word : but little importance can be attached to the spacing of the ms. Kemble adopted *on orette*, which his punctuation shows that he took as an adverbial phrase "in battle" going with *gemærde.* Ettmüller (₁) (₂) suggested *æfnde on orette,* "accomplished in battle": so Ebeling, Klipstein, Sedg.; Leo, Grein (Sprachschatz), Rieger, Gr.-Wülcker and Kluge also have *on orette,* though Leo, Grein and Rieger certainly regarded *orette* as a verb (and connected with *georettan, orrettan* ; which however means "to confound"). I follow Kemble in the interpretation of *on orette,* and, with Rieger, make the pause after *sweorde.*

oret is from **or-hat,* a calling out, challenging: cf. O.H.G. *urheiz.*

ane sweorde. "Einzig mit dem schwerte, d. h. wohl durch zweikampf," Müllenhoff, *Beovulf,* 74. So Koegel, "allein mit dem Schwerte stellte er die Grenze fest," *Ltg.* I, 1, 159. "With single sword he spread his borders, against the Myrgings marked the bound," Gummere in *M.L.N.* IV, 420.

42. *merce.* *mearce* K (₂), Ettmüller (₁) (₂) ; *mærce,* Leo.

gemærde. Fixed (not as Thorpe or Gummere take it "enlarged," "spread" from *mára* but) from *gemǽre* boundary. Cf. *lehtes singal tido gelimplicum gimaerende,* translating *lucis diurna tempora, successibus diterminans—Rituale Ecclesiæ Dunelmensis,* 1840, p. 164.

43. *Fifeldor.* The combat, according to Saxo, took place on an island of the river Eider (ed. Holder, IV, 115 ; XII, 402). The Eider is the *Egidora, Ægidora* in the Frankish annalists of the 9th century (see Pertz (fol.) *SS.* I, Einhardi *Annales,* 808, 811, 815, 828 ; *Annales Fuldenses,* 815, 857, 873) ; *Ægisdyr* in the Old Norse (*Jomsvikinga Saga,* 8, 9). O.N. *Ægir* signifies both the sea and the sea divinity, who was remembered in England till modern times : he is the "monster Agar" of Lyly's Gallathea, and "eager" is still used for the sea wave or bore of rivers. The O.E. is *Egor (Eagor),* which is synonymous and interchangeable with *Fifel*: eagorstream (sea), *Andreas,* 441 ; *egorstream,* Boethius, *Metra,* XX, 118 ; *egor-here* (deluge), *Genesis,* 1402, 1537, alternate with *fifel-stream,* Boethius, *Metra,* XXVI, 26 ; *fifelwæg, Elene,* 237. *Egordor* and *Fifeldor* alike mean the mouth where the river opens on the dread sea. This interchange of synonyms in a place name, although it is certainly rare, can be paralleled from the same passages in the *Jomsvikinga Saga* where the Eider is mentioned : the mouth of the Schlei being first called "mouth" and then "door" (*millom Ægisdura ok Slesmynna,* cap. 8 ; *Haraldr konúngr fer til Ægisdyra, en Hákon jarl fer til Slesdöra,* cap. 9 ; *Fornmanna Sögur,* XI (1828), pp. 28, 31. See Seelmann, *Die Bewohner Dänemarks vor dem Eindringen der Dänen,* in the *J.d.V.f.n.S.* XII, 1886 ; and Bugge, *H.D.* 131–2).

Lastly, in the Chronicle of Dietmar, the Eider is called *Wieglesdor,* which is best explained as a corruption of *Fiflesdor* (Thietmari *Chronicon,* recog. F. Kurze, Hannoveræ, 1889, III, 6 (4), p. 51).

There would therefore, even apart from Saxo, be no difficulty in identifying Fifeldor with the Eider : and, since Saxo definitely places Offa's combat on that river, it seems carrying scepticism far to doubt the certainty of the identification, as is done by Erdmann (p. 48), Holthausen and Siebs.

See also Grimm, *D.M.* 1835, 147, 197 ; Leo, 79. Rieger in *Germania,* III, 173 would connect Egidora, Fifeldor, with the Germanic idea of hell.

44. *Swæfe.* How do the Swæfe come in? The contending parties are the

45 Hroþwulf *ond* Hroðgar   heoldon lengest
85 b   sibbe ‖ætsomne   suhtorfædran,
siþþan hy forwræcon   Wicinga cynn
ond Ingeldes   ord forbigdan,
forheowan æt Heorote   Heaðo-Beardna þrym.

For a very long time did Hrothwulf and Hrothgar keep the peace together, uncle and nephew, after they had driven away the race of the Vikings and humbled the array of Ingeld, hewed down at Heorot the host of the Heathobards.

Angles and the Myrgingas. Therefore we must either (1) suppose that the Myrgingas and Swæfe are here the same people, the Myrgingas counting as one branch of the wide-spread Suevic stock. (Müllenhoff, *Beovulf*, 99-103 ; Möller, *V.E.* 26.) Möller points to the name Schwabsted on the Trene, in Schleswig, as a proof that the Suevic family extended to the borders of the Angles; also the grouping of *Engle* and *Swæfe* together in l. 60 supports the idea that these races were neighbours. The fact that in ll. 23, 24 the Swæfe are differentiated from the Myrgingas does not render this explanation impossible ; we have seen that the term *Swæfe* from the time of Cæsar and Tacitus has a broader and a narrower signification. Or we may (2) take *Swæfe* as a section of the Suevic tribe, isolated and settled around Schwabsted. Offa perhaps rules both the Angles and this small tribe of Swabians : they are bracketed together and opposed to the Myrgingas. This, certainly less plausible theory, is supported by Koegel (*Ltg.* i, 160) and Seelmann (p. 57). (3) Rejecting altogether the usual interpretation of *Myrgingas* as "people of Maurungani," Much (*P.B.B.* xvii, 193) would regard the name as synonymous with Saxon, and would accordingly substitute *Seaxan* here for *Swæfe*. This view derives some little support from Saxo Grammaticus, who makes the opponents of Offa Saxons, but the conjecture is an improbable one.

Of the three theories (1) seems to present us with the fewest difficulties.

45. *Hroþwulf, Hroðgar, Ingeld.* See Introduction, pp. 79-84.

lengest. See note to l. 28, above.

47. *Wicinga cynn.* Siebs (p. 304), like Maurer earlier, regards this phrase as indicating a late date. *Wiking* certainly in O.E. comes to mean a Scandinavian pirate : but there is abundant evidence that, so far from being a Scandinavian loan word, it existed in the West Germanic languages before the Viking era. See Müllenhoff, *Beovulf*, 95, *etc.* ; Bugge, *Studier over de nordiske Gude- og Heltesagns oprindelse*, i, 1881, pp. 5, 542 ; Much in *P.B.B.* xvii, 201, *etc.* ; Sweet, *History of English Sounds*, p. 90. The original meaning seems to have been "warrior," but the word came early to be connected with the sea : cf. *sæwicingas, Exodus*, 333.

49. *Heaðo-Bearda.* It has been frequently argued that the true name of the Langobardi was *Bardi*, and that hence the *Heaðobeardan* are identical with the Lombards, the epithet being varied precisely as we get sometimes *Dene*, sometimes *Gár-Dene*, or *Hring-Dene*. (So Ettmüller (₁) 20 ; Heyne's *Beowulf*; Wülcker, *Kl. Dicht.* 121 ; Bremer in *Pauls Grdr.* (₂) iii, 949.) In support of this has been urged (1) the use of *Bardi* for *Langobardi*, in Paul the Deacon and other writers in touch with Lombard tradition. But this use of *Bardi* for *Langobardi* is almost limited to Latin *verse*. It is first found in the epitaph on Droctulf, who was a contemporary of Alboin : an epitaph obviously written by a Roman, not a Lombard (see *SS. Rerum Langobardicarum* in *M.G.H.*, Hannoveræ, 1878, p. 102). The form *Bardi* is used in several epitaphs written in much later times by Paul the Deacon and others (see *id.* p. 22, on Arichis, apparently by Paul ; p. 23 on Paul himself

    Eximio dudum Bardorum stemmate gentis ;

the epitaph on Queen Ansa, attributed to Paul ; other epitaphs, 235, 238, 429). It has not, I think, been noted that *Langobardi* is a word *quod versu dicere non*

50 Swa ic geondferde fela   fremdra londa

In such wise I fared through many strange lands throughout this wide

est, and which had to be mutilated before it could be got into a hexameter. The use of *Bardi* for *Langobardi* in verse proves, then, nothing at all. The only early instances I can find of *Bardus* for *Langobardus* in prose are *cohors Bardica* in the late 9th century Erchemperti *Historia Langobardorum Beneventanorum* (*SS. Rer. Lango.* 262), and *Bardan þone beorh* for the Apennines in Alfred's Orosius (cf. Icel. *Munbard*, and *Mons Bardonis* in Otho of Frisingen).

Again, it has been pointed out (2) that men of Bardengau and Bardewik on the Elbe are repeatedly called *Bardi* in the *Chronica Sclavorum* of Helmold : but, granting that these men of Bardewik were a remnant of the old Lombard stock, it seems perilous to argue, from the form of their name in the 12th century, as to the form of the Lombard name, and consequent Lombard affinities, in the sixth century. Moreover, it does not seem clear how the Bardi remaining behind in Bardowyk could have been neighbours and foes of the Danes : still less could the main body of the Lombards, who since A.D. 168 were on the borders of the Roman Empire, by the Danube. If then we are to equate the Heathobeardan and the Lombards, we must adopt the suggestion of Bugge (*H.D.* 159–163) that a body of the Lombards was left behind on the Baltic coast. But there is nothing to show that this was the case. Any evidence leading us to identify the Heathobeardan and the Langobardi is therefore entirely wanting, though of course the two nations may have been originally connected (cf. Binz in *P.B.B.* xx, 174 ; Möller, *V.E.* 29). Müllenhoff (*Beovulf*, 29, 32, followed by Much in *P.B.B.* xvii, 201 ; Heinzel, *A.f.d.A.* xvi, 271) suggested that the Heathobeardan are rather to be identified with the Heruli (for whom see note to l. 87). Certainly the name *wicing* is most appropriate to the Heruli, who were essentially sea-robbers : and they are the only people whom we know to have had a blood feud with the Danes in the early ages. They were expelled from their territory by the Danes, according to Jordanes. But, as the Heruli are first heard of ravaging the Roman Empire in the second half of the third century, it has been thought that their expulsion from their homes by the Danes probably dates about A.D. 250 (Bremer in *Pauls Grdr.* (₂) iii, 834) ; whilst the wars of Danes and Heathobeardan can be dated with some certainty about A.D. 500. Yet since the Heruli who are met with in the Roman historians about the end of the fifth and the early sixth century are still heathen, they had probably only recently arrived from the North (Zeuss, 479), and it may have been these sixth century Heruli, rather than the pirates of the third century, whose influx into the Empire was due to their having been displaced by the Danes. This would agree well with the chronology of *Beowulf*.

It seems probable that the Heathobeardan are personified in the hero Hothbrodd (see Introduction, pp. 81–2) and since he is localized by the *Helgi* lays on the south shore of the Baltic, and since this suits the data of *Beowulf* and of *Widsith* well, we may perhaps regard this as the seat of the Heathobeardan. More than this cannot be said, and evidence for identification with any historic tribe, Langobardi or Heruli, is insufficient, though early kinship with the Langobardi is probable enough.

See also Olrik, *Heltedigtning*, 21, 22 ; Sarrazin in *Engl. Stud.* xlii, 11.

d of *Heaðobeardna* added in ms. over line : cf. the spelling in *Beowulf*, 2037, 2067 ; *Heaðabearna, Heaðobearna.*

50. *Swa.* As the preceding passage has had nothing to do with the poet's travels we must either (1) refer *swa* to what follows : I went through many strange lands in such wise that...etc. (with Müllenhoff, *Z.f.d.A.* xi, 285) or (2) we must suppose that the logic of the passage has been destroyed by omission or interpolation (with Möller, *V.E.* 34 ; Langhans *Ueber den Ursprung der Nordfriesen*, Wien, 1877). Langhans regards the whole of ll. 10–49 as an interpolation and would thus connect *swa* directly with the opening lines : "In such wise (i.e. accompanying the lady Ealhhild)." In this Langhans may be right : but when he argues that 18–49 are drawn from *Beowulf*, and from those parts of *Beowulf*

geond ginne grund ;   godes *ond* yfles
þær ic cunnade   cnosle bidæled,
freomægum feor,   folgade wide.
Forþon ic mæg singan   *ond* secgan spell,
55 mænan fore mengo   in meoduhealle,
hu me cynegode   cystum dohten.
Ic wæs mid Hunum   *ond* mid Hreð-Gotum
mid Sweom *ond* mid Geatum   *ond* mid Suþ-Denum.

earth ; of good and evil there I made trial, from my race remote : afar
from my kindred, I served far and wide.
And so I may sing and tell my story ; declare before the company in
the mead-hall how men of great race were nobly liberal to me.

which have been most suspected of being late interpolations, his position
is untenable. See also Lawrence in *Mod. Philol.* IV, 335, 336, footnote.
   53. *folgade wide.* I followed, served as a retainer. Rieger reads *folgaðe wide*,
" far from my household," taking *wide* as equal to *feor*. But this is hardly
possible grammatically, and is certainly unnecessary. Equally unnecessary is
Klipstein's *folgathe wide* ' in a wide retinue.'
   57. *Hreð-Gotum.* See Appendix : Note H, *The term Hrædas applied to the
Goths.*
   58. *Geatum.* The Geatas of Beowulf. There must be some primæval connection between the names of the Geatas and of the Goths ; they stand in
ablaut relationship : *Gaut-* to *Gut* or *Got.* (See Bremer in *Pauls Grdr.* (₂) III,
817, 818 : Erdmann *Om folknamnen Götar och Goter*, Stockholm, 1891.) But
whilst the Goths were scattered over Europe, the Geatas (O.N. *Gautar*) have
remained throughout their whole history in the same locality : the country to
the south of the great lakes Wener and Wetter. Ptolemy is the first to locate
them definitely (II, 11, 16) καὶ κατέχουσιν αὐτῆς [Σκανδίας]...τὰ δὲ μεσημβρινὰ
Γοῦται [read Γαῦται]. Procopius knows them in the same place (*Bell. Gott.*
II, 15). Already in *Beowulf* the Geatas are engaged in strife with the Swedes
dwelling on the other side of the great lakes : the strife resulted in the absorption of the Geatas into the Swedish kingdom in prehistoric times (cf. Müllenhoff,
Beovulf, 22 ; *A.f.d.A.* XVI, 269). In the earliest definite accounts of Sweden,
those given by the Christian missionaries, we hear only of one kingdom. But
from the middle of the 11th to the middle of the 13th century warfare between
the two peoples was again constant, ending in the final absorption of the
Gautar. See Zeuss, 511–513 ; Bremer in *Pauls Grdr.* (₂) III, 833 ; Fahlbeck (P.)
Den s.k. striden mellan Svear och Götar, dess verkliga karaktär och orsaker, in
the *Historisk Tidskrift*, Stockholm, 1884, IV (pp. 105, etc.).
   This identification of the Geatas and Gautar is etymologically exact, and
agrees well with the data of *Beowulf* : it has been accepted by most scholars
(e.g. Ettmüller, Thorpe, Grein, Müllenhoff, Ten Brink, Sarrazin, Wülcker,
Earle, Brandl, Grienberger, Schück, Schücking, Holthausen, etc.) and seems
as certain as almost any of the ethnological data of the Old English epic.
   On the other hand Kemble wished to locate the Geatas in Schleswig, Grundtvig
in Gotland, and Haigh in England. The only other suggestion, however,
which need be considered seriously is that of Leo, who wished to identify
the Geatas with the Jutes. In this he was followed by Schaldemose, Bugge
(*P.B.B.* XII, 1 etc.), Fahlbeck, Gummere in *M.L.N.* IV, 421, and Gering (*Beowulf*).
The arguments in favour of this view will be found most fully in Fahlbeck's
Beovulfsqvädet såsom källa för nordisk fornhistoria in the *Antiqvarisk Tidskrift
för Sverige*, VIII, 2, 1. Fahlbeck points to a number of characteristics of the
Geatas as being more appropriate to Jutes than to Gautar : they are called
sæmenn, brimwisan, 2930, 2953 ; their land *ealond*, 2333–5 : the Swedes reach

59 Mid Wenlum ic wæs *ond* mid Wærnum　　*ond* mid
　　　Wicingum.

them *ofer sæ*, 2380; 2394, 2473. These arguments are inconclusive. The
strongest evidence in favour of the identification of Geatas and Jutes lies in the
use of *Gotland, Gothos*, for Jutland, Jutes by Alfred and Ethelwerd: and of
Reið-Gotaland for Jutland by the Icelanders: but this usage, though puzzling,
is not sufficient to establish Leo's hypothesis. See also pp. 237–241, 255.
　　Holt. adds *ic wæs* after *Sweom.*
　　59.　*Wenlum.*　The same tribe as that referred to in *Beowulf*, 348, where
Wulfgar, Wendla leod is mentioned as dwelling at the court of the Danish king
Hrothgar. These Wen[d]le or Wen[d]las have been generally identified with
the Wendilenses of Saxo (Book xiv: called also Wandali, Book xi), the
inhabitants of Vendill, the modern Vendsyssel, in the north of Jutland.
Whether there is any connection between this tribe and the great East Germanic
race, the Vandals of history, is doubtful (see Bremer in *Pauls Grdr.* (₂) iii, 818).
　　Müllenhoff, however, would explain both the Wenlas of *Widsith* and the
Wendlas of *Beowulf* as referring to these Vandals of Eastern Germany
(*Beovulf*, 89); he thinks that Saxo comes too long after the time of *Widsith*
and *Beowulf* to justify us, without further evidence, in putting a chief of the
Jutland Wendilenses at the court of King Hrothgar: Wulfgar is a champion who
has migrated from the distant Vandals to the court of Hrothgar, rather than a
tributary prince of the neighbouring Vendill. There is nothing impossible in
Beowulf containing a reference to these Vandals, though they had migrated
long before to the South. The stories recorded by Paul the Deacon of combats
between Lombards and Vandals far in the North-East prove that the Vandals
were long remembered in tradition as dwellers in Northern Germany.
(Müllenhoff, *Beovulf*, 89–90. So Bugge, *P.B.B.* xii, 7; earlier Bugge had
followed Grundtvig in equating the Wendlas with the Wendilenses.)
　　Much in *P.B.B.* xvii, 210–11 rejects both identifications, and supposes the
Wendle to be neither the Vandali of Tacitus nor the Wendilenses of Saxo, but
rather a people akin to the Angles, and to those Cimbri who are noted by
Tacitus (*Germania*, xxxv) and Ptolemy (ii, 11, 7) as inhabiting the north of
what is now Jutland. He supposes the name Wendle to have belonged in the
first place to these Cimbric ' Anglo-Frisian' people, and only later to have been
taken over by the Danish tribe who had ousted or assimilated them. Wulfgar's
people then are half tributary to Hrothgar, but not yet Danish. Much urges
that the Wenle are here grouped with the Wærnas, who were certainly a
non-Danish tribe akin to the Angles, and with the Vikings, a term which at
the time of *Widsith* would apply rather to Anglian than to Danish folk.
　　The trouble taken both by Müllenhoff and by Much to avoid identifying
the Wen[d]le of *Beowulf* and *Widsith* with the Danish inhabitants of Vendsyssel
is however quite unnecessary; for we can gather from Procopius that about
A.D. 510 the northern part of the peninsula had been already settled by Danes
(*Bell. Gott.* ii, 15). We know that later these Danes of North Jutland were
known as *Vendilfolk*; it seems clear then that the *Wendla leod* present at
Hrothgar's court must be their chief. The fact that they are mentioned here
in a non-Danish context cannot count for much: the poet wanted three W's to
alliterate (cf. Möller, *V.E.* 3, 4; Weiland, 15; Shück, 43).
　　There was a famous Vendil north of Upsala (cf. K. Stjerna in *A.f.n.F.* xxi,
77, etc.) but there seems no reason to localize our Wen[d]las there.
　　Wicingum. Vikings. See l. 47. Möller proposes *Wiðingum*, whom he would
identify with the *Nuithones* of Tacitus (*Germ.* xl), supposing the *N* to be
erroneous. These [N]uithones were a people akin to the Angles; Möller would
locate them in the neighbourhood of Schleswig and supposes the name of the
river *Widau* (older *Withā*) and of the district *Wiedingharde* to have been taken
from this folk by the Danish and Frisian stock who supplanted them, and
who now occupy the district (*V.E.* 6–7).
　　Against this conjecture of Möller's see Much in *P.B.B.* xvii, 211.
　　Possibly the line is to be taken in connection with v. 62 and 68: the last

60 Mid Gefþum ic wæs *ond* mid Winedum   *ond* mid
    Gefflegum.
Mid Englum ic wæs *ond* mid Swæfum   *ond* mid
    Ænenum.

name in each line not being the name of a tribe, but characterizing the preceding names: "I was with Vandals and Wærnas—Vikings: I was with Saxons and Sycgan—swordsmen : I was with Franks and Frisians—brave men." But this interpretation is very doubtful.

60. *Gefþum.* The Gepidae ; near of kin to the Goths, and originally their neighbours at the mouth of the Vistula. (See Jordanes, IV, XVII.) They migrated south in the third century, and founded a kingdom in what is now the S.E. of Hungary, which was overthrown after a protracted struggle by the Lombards in the sixth century (567). See Hodgkin's *Italy* v, 132. They are still known in *Beowulf*, though as a remote people (2404). The mention of them here together with the Wends, which is not necessitated by the alliteration, points to their position in the extreme east of Germania, bordering upon the Slavonic peoples. See Introduction, p. 163, *note* 2.

Winedum. The Wends. These are the Veneti of whom Tacitus knew (*Germ.* XLVI) though he was uncertain whether to reckon them as Germans or not. The name seems to have been given by the Germans to their Slavonic neighbours in the East. Jordanes (XXIII) mentions the Veneti as having formed part of the great empire of Ermanaric, and as pressing upon the German nations in his day. *Hermanaricus in Venthos arma commovit, qui, quamvis armis despecti, sed numerositate pollentes, primum resistere conabantur... Nam hi...ab una stirpe exorti, tria nunc nomina ediderunt, id est Venethi, Antes, Sclaveni, qui quamvis nunc ita facientibus peccatis nostris ubique desæviunt, tamen tunc omnes Hermanarici imperiis servierunt* (ed. Holder, 1882). The Wends pressed forward into the lands between the Elbe and the Vistula vacated by the Germans, where Wulfstan found them in the ninth century. (Alfred's Orosius, ed. Sweet, 1883, p. 20.) See Grimm, *G.D.S.* 171, 190, 322 ; Müllenhoff *D.A.*, 1887, II, 33 etc., 89 etc. For the correct form of the name see Collitz in the *Journal of English and Germanic Philology*, VI, 282 (1906–7).

Gefflegum. Unknown. "Nach Skandinavien möchten noch zu setzen sein die Geflegen, deren Name in Gefle, nördlich von Upsala, erhalten ist." (Lappenberg, 176.) A rather desperate guess.

61. *Englum.* See Introduction.

Swæfum. See l. 22 above.

Ænenum. L. Schmidt, *Zur Geschichte der Langobarden*, Leipzig, 1885 (p. 49), suggests a connection between the Ænenas and the *Anthaib* of Paul the Deacon. But this is *ignotum per ignotius*, for no one knows to what place or race Paul the Deacon was referring when he spoke of *Anthaib* ; neither did Paul himself, who took the word out of the *Origo gentis Langobardorum*.

Grimm (*G.D.S.* 510) would connect the Ænenas with a noble Bavarian race the *Aenbiená* or *Anniona* (see also *R.A.* 270) which is quoted in the Bavarian laws as enjoying a double wer-gild (*Leges Bajuuariorum*, ed. J. N. Mederer, Ingolstadt, 1793). Grimm sees in this line, which quotes together Angles, Swabians, and (presumably) Bavarians, proof of a connection which he is trying to establish between those peoples. See also Huschberg *Geschichte des hauses Scheiern-Wittelsbach* pp. 51–61, especially p. 55, "Das Adelsgeschlecht des Anniona war ansässig im Hochgebirge jenseits des Brenners" (between Botzen and Trient).

Grimm's interpretation does not suit the context, as we are dealing with the North Sea coast. Müllenhoff proposed to identify the Ænenas with some tribe of this coast [more particularly the Eowan] through the name of the Middle High German hero Enenum, who comes from Westenlande, i.e. North Friesland. This hero would be the last reminiscence of the forgotten Ænenas (*Nordalb. Stud.* I, 163).

Mid Seaxum ic wæs *ond* [mid] Sycgum   *ond* mid
Sweordwerum.

Mid Hronum ic wæs *ond* mid Deanum   *ond* mid
Heaþo-Reamum.

Mid þyringum ic wæs *ond* mid   þrowendu*m*
65 *ond* mid Burgendum,   þær ic beag geþah :

And I was among the Burgundians; there I received an armlet.

62. *Seaxum.* See Introduction, pp. 67–69.

mid. Not in MS. or K, Leo. Supplied by Ettmüller ($_1$) ($_2$) silently, followed by Thorpe and later editors ; though some (Thorpe, Grein, Rieger) are not aware that *mid* is not in the MS. Kluge retains the MS. reading.

Sycgum. See above, l. 31.

Sweordwerum. See note to l. 59. Lappenberg (178) suggested that we have to do with the Suardones of Tacitus (*Germ.* XL), a people neighbouring upon, and related to the Angles : though if the name is derived from *sword* as that of the Saxons from *sahs* we should expect in Tacitus * *Suerdones.* See Grimm *G.D.S.* 471; Much in *P.B.B.* XVII, 212 ; Weiland, 16 ; Seelmann *Die Bewohner Dänemarks vor dem Eindringen der Dänen,* in *J.d.V.f.n.S.* XII (1886) 28; Müllenhoff interpreted Suardones as Swordsmen (*Nordalb. Stud.* I, 119) but changed his mind later (*Z.f.d.A.* XI, 286).

63. *Hronum.* Unknown. A suitable name for a sea-folk : cf. *hron råd* (Müllenhoff *Z.f.d.A.* XI, 287). Apparently from the context a Scandinavian people. Grimm (*G.D.S.* 751, following Ettmüller ($_1$) 22) compares the *Granii* who are mentioned by Jordanes (cap. iii) among the inhabitants of Scandinavia.

The word of course means "whale" and, says Möller, "cannot be a real tribal name : people could only be called *whales* by friend or foe in jest." (*V.E.* 8.) Cf. Kossinna in *I.F.* VII, 304.

Deanum. Obviously not the Danes, "doch weiss ich solche Deanas oder altn. Daunir sonst nicht zu zeigen," Grimm *G.D.S.* 751. Müllenhoff proposed to cancel the D, which he supposed to have crept in from the *mid* preceding, and to read *Eawum,* the Aviones of Tacitus (cf. l. 26 above), or else "if any alteration is to be allowed" to read *Heahum* and to identify with the Chauci. But in view of the scantiness of our sources Müllenhoff doubts whether the reading may not be right, and preserve the name of some otherwise unrecorded tribe. (*Z.f.d.A.* XI, 287.) As the context makes it probable that they are a Scandinavian people, it is tempting to suppose that, by a mistake of an Old English or a Greek copyist, they are the same people as are mentioned by Ptolemy as Δαυκίωνες (II, 11, 16), and located by him in the south of Sweden, but whom it has been impossible to trace in any other document.

Heaþo-Reamum. Cf. *Beowulf,* 518, of Breca
        þa hine on morgentid
    on *Heaþo-Ræmas* [MS. Ræmes] *holm up ætbær.*

They dwelt near the modern Christiania. Jordanes (cap. iii) refers to the *Raumaricii* or *Raumariciæ* among the inhabitants of Scandinavia. The Norse form of the word is *Raumar* or *Haða-Raumar,* and the kingdom *Raumariki,* near *Haða land :* the modern Romerike and Hadeland. See Grimm, *G.D.S.* 751. Brandl (992) suggests Raumsdal in Western Norway.

64. *þrowendum.* The men of Drontheim (?), ON. *þrændir.* See Lappenberg, 176 ; Grimm, *G.D.S.* 751. The sudden jump from Thuringians to men of Drontheim is strange : but we have had the Scandinavian Heatho-Reamas just above (Müllenhoff, *Z.f.d.A.* XI, 288). Müllenhoff earlier (*Nordalb. Stud.* I, 165) tried to get over the difficulty by interpreting þyringum as referring to the Thuringians of the lower Rhine (see above l. 30) and by referring þrowendum to an Old Frisian *Thréant.* Brandl (967) identifies with the Treveri.

65. *Burgendum.* See note to l. 19.

geþah. MS. geþeah.

me þær Guðhere forgeaf   glædlicne maþþum
songes to leane;   næs þæt sæne cyning!
Mid Froncum ic wæs *ond* mid Frysum   *ond* mid
   Frumtingu*m*.
Mid Rugum ic wæs *ond* mid Glommum   *ond* mid
   Rumwalum.
70 Swylce ic wæs on Eatule   mid Ælfwine:

Guthhere gave me there a goodly jewel, the reward of my song. He was
no sluggish king! I was with the Franks and the Frisians and the
Frumtings, the Rugians and the Glommas and the Romans. Likewise I

66. *Guðhere.* Thought of, perhaps, as at Worms. See Introd. pp. 58–63.
67. *sæne.* Usually 'sluggish': here perhaps 'niggardly.' This sense is
not elsewhere recorded in O.E., but the M.H.G. use of *seine* as "too short" (of
a coat) has been instanced. (Eichler in *Anglia*, Beiblatt xxii, 164.)
68. *Froncum.* See note to l. 24.
Frysum. That these are the West Frisians, dwelling west of the Zuider
Zee, in the neighbourhood of the modern Amsterdam, is perhaps implied by
their being linked with the Franks, as in *Beowulf* 2912, 1207, 1210, where the
raid of Hygelac [who must have sailed up the Rhine] is repulsed by the joint
[West] Frisians, Franks and Attuarii. The *Fresna cynn* of l. 27, ruled over by
Finn Folcwalding, refers apparently to the main body of the Frisians, dwelling
east and north of the Zuider Zee. Heyne, in his index to *Beowulf*, notes that
the land of these North [or better East] Frisians, for they must not be confused
with the modern North Frisians of the islands, is called *Frysland* (1127), that of
the West Frisians *Fresna land* (2916). In *Widsith* the *e* and *y* are reversed.
See Introduction, pp. 66–7.
Frumtingum. Nothing is known of them. Grimm (*G.D.S.* 752) would
interpret the word as a scornful nickname. Müllenhoff (*Z.f.d.A.* xi, 288) would
make it an "epic fiction": to be taken here as an epithet of the Franks and
Frisians. Möller (*V.E.* 5) would make it equivalent to "pushing, brave folk."
69. *Rugum, Glommum.* See above, l. 21, where the same people are
coupled together. But whereas in the earlier passage they were mentioned in
connection with a sea story, and evidently thought of as dwelling on the Baltic
coast, they are here mentioned in connection with the Romans, and are thought
of, apparently, as dwelling on the borders of the Empire, perhaps in what is now
Austria, which the Rugii occupied during the middle of the fifth century, till
their overthrow in 488; or perhaps in Italy itself, which they occupied with
the Ostrogoths. See Hodgkin's *Italy*, iii, 169; Müllenhoff in *Z.f.d.A.* xi, 288–9.
Rumwalum. The Rome-Welsh, i.e. Romans. Möller (*V.E.*, p. iii) proposed
to read *Rumwarum*, but this is an unnecessary alteration. The compound is a
natural one (cf. *Wala rices* below, and *Gal-walum*, the "Welsh" of Gaul, in the
A.S. Chronicle, *sub anno* 660). On the Franks Casket we have *Romwalus* and
Reumwalus for Romulus and Remus: cf. Bugge, *Studier over de Heltesagns
Oprindelse*, p. 211.
70. *Eatule.* Leo (81) identified this as Italy. The identification is
certain: cf. the O.E. Bede, ii, 4 (ed. Miller, p. 108) *Ond he þa ðes ilca papa
[Bonefatius] seonoð gesomnode Eotolwara biscopa.* Müllenhoff (*Z.f.d.A.* xi, 289),
Möller (*V.E.* p. iii), Kluge and Holt. would read *Eotule* here. But *ea* for *eo*
occurs elsewhere in *Widsith*, cf. *Earmanrices* (l. 111).
The confusion of *eo* and *ea* is, of course, an Anglian, and more particularly
a Northumbrian peculiarity: cf. Sievers, *Angelsächsische Grammatik*, 3te Aufl.
1898, § 150 (3). The West Saxon transcriber has removed this peculiarity in
the common nouns, but left Anglian peculiarities in proper names, which were
perhaps unfamiliar to him.
Ælfwine. See Introduction, pp. 123–6.

se hæfde moncynnes   mine gefræge
leohteste hond   lofes to wyrcenne,
heortan unhneaweste   hringa gedales, ||
86 a   beorhtra beaga,   bearn Eadwines.
75 Mid Sercingum ic wæs   *ond* mid Seringum.
Mid Creacu*m* ic wæs *ond* mid Finnu*m*   *ond* mid
Casere,
se þe winburga   geweald ahte,
wiolen*a* *ond* wilna   *ond* Wala rices.

was in Italy, with Ælfwine: he had of all men of whom I have heard the readiest hand for deed of praise, a heart most liberal in the giving of rings, of shining armlets—the son of Eadwine! I was with the Saracens and the Serings. With the Greeks I was and with the Finns, and with Caesar, he who had rule over the towns of revelry, riches and joys and the realm of Welsh-land.

72. *wyrcenne. wyrceanę,* Holt.
74. *Eadwine.* See Introduction, pp. 123–4.
75–87. Brandl (*Pauls Grdr.* ii, 1, 966) supposes this passage interpolated by a half educated cleric who has drawn many of his names from Alfred's Orosius. But, considering that very much the same ground is being covered, the coincidences are certainly not striking. A heroic attempt has been made by Mr A. Anscombe to identify many of the names in this passage with those of tribes of Northern Gaul (in *Ériu,* iv, 81–90, *The Longobardic Origin of St Sechnall*). I am not able to agree with his conjectures.
For the character of this passage, see Introduction, pp. 7, 8.
75. *Sercingum.* Saracens (Lappenberg, 179; followed by Müllenhoff, *Z.f.d.A.* xi, 289; who compare O.N. *Serkir,* and the O.H.G. gloss *Sarzi, Arabes*). The ending *ing* is added on the analogy of English tribal names. Other instances are *Seringum* (Seres), *Lidwicingum* (Letawicion, Letavici), *Exsyringum* (Assyrians), *Idumingum* (Ydumaei).
Seringum. Seres (Lappenberg, 179). Syrians (Brandl).
76. *Creacum.* See above, l. 20.
Finnum. See ll. 20, 79.
Casere. Here probably the Emperor of the West. Contrast l. 20.
77. *winburga.* Holtzmann (*Deutsche Mythol.* herausg. Holder, 1874, p. 185) would derive this old epic word from *wyn,* joy. The uniform spelling *win-,* and the parallel *medo-burg,* leave us, however, no doubt as to the derivation from *win,* wine. Yet the spelling *wynburga* is followed by Leo, and Ettmüller (₁) (₂).
78. *wiolena ond wilna.* The MS. has *wiolane 7 wilna,* which was kept by Kemble (₁). J. Grimm (*D.M.* 1835, Appendix vi) recognized these words as common nouns; in this he has been followed by Kemble (₂), Ettmüller (₁) (₂), Müllenhoff (*Z.f.d.A.* xi, 289), Rieger, Möller (*V.E.* iii), Wülcker (*Kl. Dicht.* glossary), Grein-Wülcker, Kluge, Holt., Sedg.; Leo kept the words as tribal names *Velena and Vylna* translating "Der Walchen und Walchinnen und des Walchenreiches." The words are also taken as proper names by Grein, Thorpe (*Cod. Ex.* and *Beowulf*), Brandl (*Pauls Grdr.* (₂) 966–7) and Anscombe in *Anglia,* xxxv, 527: but no satisfactory explanation of them as such is forthcoming. The reading of the text, *wiolena,* is Rieger's.
Wala rices. See note on l. 69, above.
Bugge sees an imitation of ll. 77, 78 in the *Vinbjǫrg, Valbjǫrg* of *Guþrúnar-kviþa,* ii, 33. See *H.D.* trans. Schofield, xxii; *P.B.B.* xxxv, 241.

Mid Scottum ic wæs *ond* mid Peohtum   *ond* mid
Scride-Finnum.

80 Mid Lidwicingum ic wæs *ond* mid Leonum   *ond*
mid Longbeardum,

79. *Scottum, Peohtum.* Müllenhoff (*Z.f.d.A.* xi, 290) thinks that the
mention of these names proves this passage to have been composed in England.
But a bard dwelling in the old Angel of Schleswig might have known of the
Picts and Scots by repute, as well as of the Finns and Huns.

Scride-Finnum. One section of the widely spread Finnish race, dwelling
more particularly in the north of Norway, and equivalent to Lapps rather than
Finns in the modern sense. The Finns mentioned before (l. 20) are, to judge
by the context in which they occur, the more southern section of the people,
dwelling east and north-east of the Baltic. The Scridefinnas take their distinguishing title from sliding (Icel. *skrîða*) with snow-shoes as is explained by
Paul the Deacon. *Scritobini...qui etiam æstatis tempore nivibus non carent, nec
aliud, ut pote feris ipsis ratione non dispares, quam crudis agrestium animantium
carnibus vescuntur; de quorum etiam hirtis pellibus sibi indumenta peraptant.
Hi a saliendo juxta linguam barbaram ethimologiam ducunt. Saltibus enim,
utentes arte quadam ligno incurvo ad arcus similitudinem, feras adsecuntur.*
Paulus (i, 5, ed. Waitz, p. 50). Procopius gives an account of the Σκριθίφινοι,
whom he numbers amongst the inhabitants of Thule [not Iceland, but
Scandinavia]. They are clothed in skins, and live by hunting: the mother
suspends her newly born babe, in a skin, from a tree: puts a fragment of
marrow in its mouth, and leaves it whilst she goes hunting with her husband.
But Procopius cannot vouch for the customs of Thule from personal experience:
Ἐμοὶ μὲν οὖν ἐς ταύτην ἰέναι τὴν νῆσον, τῶν τε εἰρημένων αὐτόπτῃ γενέσθαι, καίπερ
γλιχομένῳ, τρόπῳ οὐδενὶ ξυνηνέχθη. (*Bell. Gott.* ii, 15.) Jordanes also mentions
the Scride-finnas among the inhabitants of the island of Scandia, but his scribes
have corrupted the name—*Screrefennæ, Crefennæ, Rerefennæ,* possibly confusing
the Scride-finnas with another great branch of the family, the Ter-finnas.
The Geographer of Ravenna similarly gets confused over the name. In the
9th century the Scridefinnas are mentioned by Alfred in his Orosius (ed. Sweet,
1883, p. 16), *be westannorðan him* [the Swedes] *sindon Scridefinnas and be
westan Norðmenn.* Saxo speaks of the *Scritfinni* or *Scricfinni* (ed. Holder, 1886,
p. 8). See also Zeuss, p. 684, and some notes by Dahlmann in explanation of
Alfred's reference to the Finns (*König Ælfred's Germania*), in his *Forschungen,*
i, 451-454 ; Bojunga in *P.B.B.* xvi, 547 ; Müllenhoff, *D.A.* ii, 44.

80. *Lidwicingum.* R. Michel in *P.B.B.* xv, 377, etc. regards this name as
merely a variant of *Wicingum* (cf. *Dene* and *Sǣ-Dene*); and Bojunga, in his
criticism of Michel (*P.B.B.* xvi, 545), gives a silent consent to this view; so
Grein, and Wülcker in *Kl. Dicht.* 129. But from the use of the name in the
A.S. Chronicle *sub anno* 885 we may be almost certain that the Armoricans, or
Letavici, are referred to. In that year is noted the accession of Charles the Fat
to the full domains of his great grandfather *butan Lidwiccium* (Parker ms.)
or *Lidwiccum* (Cotton Tib. A. 6). mss. Tib. B. 1 and B. 4 have, however,
Lidwicingum. The form *Lioðwicas* is found in a later entry (Tib. B. 4 *sub
anno* 915) but *Lidwiccas* is the more usual form (cf. years 910, 918). In view
of the other passages in our poem in which the termination *ing* has been added
it seems clear that the reference is to the *Lidwiccas.* [The popular etymology of
the word is given in certain mss. of the *Historia Brittonum*: the Britons who
settled Armorica slew the original inhabitants, and married their wives, having
first cut out their tongues lest they should corrupt the purity of their children's
speech: *acceptisque eorum uxoribus et filiabus in coniugium, omnes earum
linguas amputaverunt, ne eorum successio maternam linguam disceret. Unde
et nos illos vocamus in nostra lingua Letewicion, id est Semitacentes, quoniam
confuse loquuntur.* (*Historia Brittonum,* in Mommsen's *Cronica Minora* (*M.G.H.*),
iii, 167, note.) The story is also told by Borrow in his *Wild Wales* and in
Skene's *Celtic Scotland,* 1886, i, 201 ; iii, 96. See also Zeuss, 577-8.]

81 mid Hæðnum *ond* mid Hæreþum   *ond* mid Hundingum.

Leonum. Dwellers in what is now Östergötland, in the S.E. of Sweden. They are probably the Λευῶνοι of Ptolemy: καὶ κατέχουσιν αὐτῆς (i.e. Σκανδίας) τὰ μὲν δυτικὰ Χαιδεινοί, τὰ δὲ μεσημβρινὰ Γοῦται καὶ Δαυκίωνες, τὰ δὲ μέσα Λευῶνοι (ed. Müller, 1883, II, 11, 16). Ptolemy's account would thus put the *Hæðnas* in the west, the *Geatas* and the "*Dauciones*" in the south, and the *Leonas* in the middle. The identification of the Leonas and the Λευῶνοι has, however, been disputed : some would amend the latter to Συεῶνοι, and identify with the Suiones of Tacitus. (Bremer in *Pauls Grdr.* (₂) III, 830 ; see also 818.) It is fairly clear that we must identify the Leonas with the *Lio-thida* [*thida* = Goth. þiuda, people] mentioned by Jordanes together with a number of other obscure tribes dwelling in Scandia ; and that they are identical with the men of Östergötland, whose capital is Linköping, the old *Liongköpungr*, and whose common parliament was known as the *Lionga-þing*. See Collin u. Schlyter, *Codex juris Ostrogotici* (*Östgötalagen*) in their *Samling af Sweriges gamla Lagar*, 1831. Cf. also Lappenberg, 176 ; Zeuss, 506 ; Müllenhoff in *Z.f.d.A.* XI, 290. Müllenhoff, who regards the whole passage 75–87 as interpolated, notes as remarkable the interpolator's acquaintance with Scandinavian names, *Leonum, Hæðnum, Hæreðum*.

Longbeardum. See l. 32.

81. *Hæðnum.* Probably the Χαιδεινοί of Ptolemy II, 11, 16, quoted in the previous note (so Lappenberg, 175) ; the *Heiðnir* of Scandinavian history, inhabitants of the *Heiðmork* on the borders of Norway and Sweden. See Bremer in *Pauls Grdr.* (₂) III, 830 ; Much in *P.B.B.* XVII, 188 ; Zeuss, 159. Leo, Ettmüller (₁) (in his text, but not in his notes where he follows Lappenberg), Möller (*V.E.* 8) take the word as a common noun "Heathen," but that seems unlikely here. See also Bugge, *P.B.B.* XII, 10 ; Müllenhoff in Mommsen's Jordanes, 165 ; Heyne-Schücking, 120–316.

It is probably only an odd coincidence that what appear to be mutilated forms of these names occur together in *Beowulf* (1982–4), where *Hæreðes dohtor* bears the tankard *Hæ*[ð]*num to handa.* See Sarrazin in *Engl. Stud.* XLII, 17, 18.

ic wæs is added after *Hæðnum* by Ettmüller, Thorpe (*Beowulf*), etc., Holt.

Hæreþum. MS. *hæleþum*: the correction was made by Lappenberg (179) followed by Ettmüller (₁) (*Haroðum* in his notes, though he still reads *hæleþum* in the text), Grein, Rieger, Möller, Wülcker in *Kl. Dicht*, Holt. and Sedg. But Ettmüller (₂), Thorpe and Kluge retain the MS. reading. The Herethas occur in the A.-S. Chronicle (Laud MS.) *sub anno* 787, *On his dagum comon ærest* III *scipu Norðmanna of Hereðalande. Đæt wæron þa erstan scipu Deniscra manna þe Angelcynnes land gesohton.* The Herethas slay the king's reeve, who wishes to drive them to the town, because he knows not who they are. These Herethas are the dwellers in the Norse *Horðaland* on the Hardangerfiord. From their ravages *Hiruaith* comes to be the Irish name for Norway (Zimmer in *Z.f.d.A.* XXXII, 205–6). There seem, however, to be another people of the same name dwelling in Jutland : the inhabitants of *Horð á Jótlandi*, the later *Hardesyssel* or *Harsyssel.* It is probably with this Jutland branch that we must identify the Χαροῦδες of Ptolemy, who are clearly inhabitants of the present Denmark. Ptolemy traces the tribes along the sea-coast till he comes to the Cimbric Chersonese, where the Χαροῦδες dwell to the East, and the Cimbri to the North : ἀνατολικώτεροι δὲ Χαροῦδες, πάντων δ' ἀρκτικώτεροι Κίμβροι (II, 11, 7, ed. Müller, 1883). The same people are mentioned with the Cimbri on the *Monument. Ancyranum: Cimbri et Chariides et Semnones et ejusdem tractus alii Germanorum populi per legatos amicitiam meam et populi Romani petierunt.* (See Suetonius, ed. Wolf, 2, 375.) For other references to the Haruthi see Much in *P.B.B.* XVII, 203–5 : Zeuss, 152, 507, 519.

Hundingum. See l. 23.

Mid Israhelum ic wæs   *ond* mid Exsyringum,
mid Ebreum *ond* mid Indeum   *ond* mid Egyptum.
Mid Moidum ic wæs *ond* mid Persum   *ond* mid
   Myrgingum
85 *ond* Mofdingum   *ond* ongend Myrgingum
ond mid Amothingum.   Mid East-þyringum ic wæs

82. *Exsyringum.* Müllenhoff suggests Assyrians (*Z.f.d.A.* xi, 291 ; Grein-Wülcker, i, 401). So Brandl.
Holt. supposes a name to have dropped out in this line.
83. *Indeum.* Grein reads *Judeum* by a slip of the pen. Holt. adds *ic wæs* after *Ebreum.*
84. *Moidum.* Medes (Müllenhoff, Brandl as above). Holt. alters to *Medum* : but cf. note by Sarrazin quoted in *Viëtor Festschrift*, Marburg, 1910, p. 309.
Persum. This has always been taken as "Persians" and in the neighbourhood of *Moidum*, "Medes," it is impossible to render it otherwise. Mr Anscombe (*Ériu*, iv, 88) points out that *Perse* is used in the A.-S. Chronicle for *Parisii*, *sub anno* 660. It is just conceivable that here *Widsith* is not so much interpolated as corrupted ; that *Persum* and *Idumingum* may have stood in the original poem, and have referred to Celtic and Baltic tribes : that, then, the passage being imperfectly remembered or transcribed, someone proceeded to fill up the gaps with Biblical names, which were suggested by the (apparently) Biblical *Perse* and *Idumingas.*
Myrgingum. It is strange that the interpolator should place the poet's own people, twice, amongst these exotic semi-biblical folk. Hence Müllenhoff (in Grein-Wülcker, i, 401) suggests that the people really meant here are the *Myrce*; the *Ælmyrcan* and *Guðmyrce* of the *Andreas* and the *Exodus.*
85. *Mofdingum.* Müllenhoff gave up these people, and the *Amothinge*, in despair, as "undinge"—perversions of some originally non-Germanic names (*Z.f.d.A.* xi, 291). Later (in Grein-Wülcker, i, 401) he identifies them with Moabites and Ammonites. So also Brandl (p. 966). Grein suggested tentatively *mid Ofdingum* (=? the Ubii). Lappenberg (179) suggested the Germanic settlers of Moffat in Scotland !
Rieger reads *Mid Mofdingum and mid Ongendmyrgingum.*
ongend Myrgingum. Holt. suggests *Mid Mofdingum ic wæs ond mid Mæringum* : Sedg. adopts *Mæringum.* Cf. *Deor*, 19 ; but this epic name of Theodoric's retainers seems out of place in the same line with those of Biblical peoples. Rieger and Gummere take *Ongendmyrgingum* as a compound name. I should rather take *ongend* as a preposition (=*ongen*, cf. *Ongendþeow* above) and translate "I was with the Myrgings...and I was against the Myrgings" : an attempt of the interpolator to harmonize passages like 38–44, where the poet is apparently opposed to the Myrgings, with 93–6.
85, 86 are metrically defective. They have been rearranged in a number of different ways by the editors. The arrangement followed is that of Grein, Grein-Wülcker, Möller, and Kluge.
86. *Amothingum.* Grimm points out that the spelling (*th* for þ) is suspicious, and suggests *Amolingas.* The Amals were the ruling family among the Ostrogoths (*Vesegothæ familiæ Balthorum, Ostrogothæ præclaris Amalis serviebant*, Jordanes, ed. Holder, cap. v). Hence the title *Amulinga* under which Alfred refers to Theodoric. The name *Amelunc* remains in Middle High German as one of his titles ; more generally, however, it is used with reference to Theodoric's followers, and this is the meaning which Grimm would give to the word here (*G.D.S.* p. 598). Lappenberg (179) identified with the *Othingi* of Jordanes (iii, 21) followed by Ettmüller (₁) 24 and Thorpe (*Cod. Ex.* 520). Nothing is to be said in favour of this. Ettmüller rearranged the line *mid Amothingum ic væs and mid Eastþyringum*; similarly Holt., but reading *Amoringum*, "Amorites." See also above, l. 85.

87 *ond* mid Eolum *ond* mid Istum   *ond* Idumingum.
Ond ic wæs mid Eormanrice   ealle þrage,

And I was with Ermanaric all the time: there the king of the Goths

East-þyringum. The Thuringians, called East-Thuringians, either (1) to distinguish them from the people of the same name dwelling in Zeeland and North-Brabant (see above, l. 30), or (2) as indicating that portion of the Thuringians which in the sixth century was still dwelling east of the Elbe; as suggested by Seelmann (*Nordthüringen* in *J.d.V.f.n.S.* xii, 1886, p. 1). Müllenhoff's later interpretation of the name (Grein-Wülcker, i, 401) as a corruption of "Assyrian" is unlikely.

87. *Eolum.* The name cannot be identified, and is probably corrupt. Grimm, apparently by an oversight, offered two different conjectures in the *G.D.S.*: (1) he suggested (p. 598) the emendation *Eorlum*, interpreting the (H)eruli, Ἔρουλοι. Linguistically this would be quite satisfactory. Corresponding to Eruli we should expect O.N. **Jarlar*; O.E. **Eorlas*: the name is probably connected with the common noun *eorl* "lord": the "u" in the classical form Heruli is not original (Möller in *A.f.d.A.* xxii, 152, 160). This etymology is to be preferred to the derivation from *heru* "sword," supported by Grimm (*G.D.S.* 470) and Erdmann (77). (2) In *G.D.S.* 736, Grimm suggested *Eotum*; these would be identical with the *Ýtum* of l. 26 (q.v.). Müllenhoff (in Grein-Wülcker, i, 401) suggests that the name is a corruption of *Elam* or *Elath*, Brandl of *Eowland*, Holt. of *Aeoles*, Aeolians.

Grimm's first identification, with the Heruli, is the more probable. These seem to have been a Scandinavian people, southern neighbours of the Geatas. They also occupied at a very early date portions probably of the south coast of Scandinavia and of the adjacent islands, from which they were driven by the Danes. (*Dani...Herulos propriis sedibus expulerunt*, Jordanes, iii.) The Heruli seem to have wandered over Europe, and to have been engaged as mercenaries in many places. Jordanes repeatedly refers to their swiftness and value as light-armed troops. Procopius (*Bell. Gott.* ii, 14, 15) gives a less favourable account of them. Of old they had been accustomed to put to death their sick and aged, and to compel widows to commit suicide; and in spite of their becoming allies of Rome and nominally Christians, they remained ἄπιστοι καὶ πλεονεξίᾳ ἐχό-μενοι...πονηρότατοι ἀνθρώπων ἁπάντων. After their overthrow by the Lombards, a party of them returned to Thule (Scandinavia). They disappear from history in the sixth century: and the absence of any mention of them in *Beowulf*, the scene of whose actions is laid near what had been their territory, is noteworthy [but cf. Müllenhoff, *Nordalb. Stud.* i, 124–5]. Müllenhoff (*Beovulf*, 30–32) would identify them with the Heatho-beardan.

Note that Theodoric addresses together the kings of the Thoringi and Heruli (*Variæ*, iii, 3). See Seelmann, *Das Norddeutsche Herulerreich* in the *J.d.V.f.n.S.* 1886, pp. 53–7.

Istum. See Appendix, Note F.
Idumingum. See Appendix, Note G.

Ettmüller, Grein and Rieger (who transposes *Eolum* and *Eastþyringum* and assumes a gap after *Istum*) insert *mid* before *Idumingum*. Holt. reads: *mid Eolum ic wæs ond mid Istum ond mid Idumingum.* I follow the ms. closely throughout all this passage. The evidence which it shows of an unskilled hand may throw light upon the history of the poem, and should therefore be retained.

88. Thorpe suggested that *ealle þrage* should be taken in close connection with *gode dohte*, "all which time to me the Gothic king was bounteously kind." This gives sense: Eormanric was treacherous and hasty, and might well not have been *consistently* bounteous all the time Widsith was with him. The recognized punctuation would give "I was with E. all the time," the meaning of which is not clear; and if this punctuation is kept we must agree with Lawrence (*Mod. Philol.* p. 359) that the line does not follow well on the preceding line, nor yet make such a faultless connection with l. 74 as Müllenhoff

þær me Gotena cyning   gode dohte;
90 se me beag forgeaf,   burgwarena fruma,
    on þam siex hund wæs   smætes goldes
    gescyred sceatta   scillingrime ;
    þone ic Eadgilse   on æht sealde,
    minum hleodryhtne,   þa ic to ham bicwom
95 leofum to leane,   þæs þe he me lond forgeaf,
    mines fæder eþel,   frea Myrginga.
    ond me þa Ealhhild   oþerne forgeaf,
    dryhtcwen duguþe,   dohtor Eadwines.
    Hyre lof lengde   geond londa fela,
100 þon*ne* ic be songe   secgan sceolde,
    hwær ic under swegl[e]   selast wisse

was bounteous unto me. Lord of cities and their folk, he gave me an armlet, in which there was reckoned of refined gold, six hundred pieces counted in shillings. This I gave into the possession of my lord and protector Eadgils, when I came home: a gift unto my beloved prince, because he, lord of the Myrgings, gave me my land, the home of my father. A second ring then Ealhild gave unto me, noble queen of chivalry, daughter of Eadwine. Through many lands her praise extended, when I must tell in song, where under the heavens I best knew a queen

maintained (*Z.f.d.A.* xi, 291) : something has therefore in that case presumably been lost, as well as something interpolated. Thorpe's rendering appears to me forced, and I doubt if we can take *þær* with *ealle þrage*, as suggested by Eichler in *Anglia*, Beiblatt xxii, 164 : "alle die Zeit über, in der mich der Gotenkönig beschenkte." See Introduction, p. 21 *etc.*

91-2. The *sceatt* is sometimes a fixed sum : a subdivision of the shilling : but often its meaning is quite vague, "a piece of money." It is best so taken here, the value of the *sceatt* being then defined by *scillingrime*. See Appendix, Note N, *On the beag given by Eormanric.*

    gescyred ; reckoned, numbered, as in the *Pharao*, of Pharaoh's chariots

        þæt þær screoda wære gescyred rime
        siex hundreda searohæbbendra.

So here "in which there was reckoned of refined gold, six hundred pieces counted in shillings," i.e. the ring was worth six hundred shillings (so Koegel, *Ltg.* i, 1, 139). It is not necessary to press the passage further, or to suppose, with Clark Hall (*Beowulf*, 1901, p. 177) and Stopford Brooke (i, 3), that the ring was scored into six hundred sections, each of the weight and value of a shilling.

    beaghord for *beag*, the suggestion of Grein, and *on scillingrime*, the suggestion of Ettmüller (₁), are unnecessary alterations of the text.

    95-6. The land had not necessarily, as Koegel supposes (*Ltg.* i, 1, 139), been forfeited or lost : but on the death of the father it would have needed to be granted anew to the son (cf. *Beowulf*, 2607, etc.). This is all that is necessarily implied in Widsith's statement that his lord gave him his father's inheritance.

    96. Ettmüller (₁) places a full stop after *Myrginga*, rightly : Ettmüller (₂) a semicolon. See Introduction, p. 27.

    101. *swegle*. ms. *swegl*, followed by K., Thorpe (*Cod. Ex.*) ; *swegle*, Leo, *etc.*, rightly.

86 b

goldhrodene cwen ‖   giefe bryttian.
Ðonne wit Scilling   sciran reorde
for uncrum sigedryhtne   song ahofan,
105 hlude bi hearpan   hleoþor swinsade,
þonne monige men   modum wlonce
wordum sprecan,   þa þe wel cuþan,
þæt hi næfre song   sellan ne hyrdon.
Ðonan ic ealne geondhwearf   eþel Gotena,
110 sohte ic á [ge]siþa   þa selestan:
þæt wæs innweorud   Earmanrices.
Heðcan sohte ic *ond* Beadecan   *ond* Herelingas

adorned with gold giving forth treasure. When Scilling and I with clear voice raised the song before our noble lord (loud to the harp the words made melody) then many men cunning and great of mind said they had never heard a better song.

Thence I wandered through all the land of the Goths: I ever sought the best of comrades, that was the household of Ermanaric. Hethca I sought and Beadeca, and the Harlungs, Emerca and Fridla, and East-

102. *giefe.* Thorpe (*Beowulf*) suggests *giefa*: unnecessarily.
103. Ðonne. MS. *doñ*, followed by Kemble, Schaldemose. Later edd., Leo, Ettmüller (₁) (₂), Thorpe, Rieger have altered *d* to ð silently.
Scilling. The name survived in England till historic times. A Scilling *presbyter* signs charters in Wessex during the third quarter of the eighth century (Birch, *Cart. Sax.* I, 186, 200); as does a contemporary Scilling, *prefectus* (Birch, I, 224, 225), also in Wessex: a Scilling also witnesses a Mercian charter (Birch, I, 181) of approximately the same date.
106-7. Möller (*V.E.* 10) condemns these verses as " wooden," and supposes them expanded by an interpolator from the simple
           þonne wordum sprecan wlonce monige.
Granting the woodenness, we have no right to assume that authentic O.E. poets never wrote anything wooden.
107. *sprecan.* Leo, Ettmüller (₁), unnecessarily normalize to the W.S. *sprǣcon*; *ē* for *ǣ* is simply a survival of the original Anglian dialect of the poem.
108. *sellan.* *sǣlran*, Leo, Ettmüller (₁) : *sēlran*, Ettmüller (₂) : *sellan song*, Holt. for metrical reasons.
109. Ðonan, i.e. from the hall of Ermanaric. See Introduction, p. 53, *etc.* Möller (*V.E.* 2–3) supposes these lines in the first place to have followed immediately after ll. 88 and 89, and ðonan to refer to ðǣr. Widsith first visits the court of Ermanaric and there receives a ring: thence he voyages through the whole Gothic land.
110. *gesiþa.* The MS., followed by Kemble and Thorpe, has *siþa*, "of courses I ever sought the best," so Wülcker in *Kl. Dicht.*; Ettmüller (₁) *gesīðða*, followed by Grein, Rieger, Grein-Wülcker, Kluge, Holt., Sedg.
110 is clearly to be taken in close connection with l. 109: the semicolon inserted at the end of that l. by Grein, and followed by Wülcker, is better replaced by a comma, as suggested by Müllenhoff, *Z.f.d.A.* XI, 291.
111. *Earmanrices.* Kemble, Leo, Ettmüller, Thorpe, Grein and Holt. would alter *Ea* to *Eo*. But cf. *Eatule* for *Eotule* in l. 70.
112. *Heðca.* Unknown (Binz in *P.B.B.* xx, 153). Müllenhoff (in *Beovulf*, 7, 64) speaks as if *Heðca* came into the East Saxon genealogy. This however is not the case: only *Biedca, Bedca* appears there. Sarrazin (*Anglia*, IX, 202)

Emercan sohte ic *ond* Fridlan   ond East-Gotan,
frodne *ond* godne   fæder Unwenes.
115 Seccan sohte ic *ond* Beccan,   Seafolan *ond* þeodric,
Heaþoric *ond* Sifecan   Hliþe *ond* Incgenþeow.

Gota, sage and good, the father of Unwen. Secca I sought and Becca,
Seafola and Theodric, Heathoric and Sifeca, Hlithe and Incgentheow.

suggests that Beadeca and Heðca may be identical with the Bǫðvarr and
Hǫttr of the saga of Rolf Kraki. This seems an exceedingly improbable
conjecture.
  Beadeca was a well-known hero in England : his name is associated with
lea, well, and hill (see Binz in *P.B.B.* xx, 152–3), and, in the form *Bedca*,
comes into the East Saxon genealogy, as given by Florence of Worcester (ed.
Thorpe for *English Historical Society*, 1848, I, 250), and as *Biedca* into Henry
of Huntingdon (*Historiæ Anglorum*, II, § 19, ed. Arnold, 1879, Rolls Series,
p. 49). See also Grimm, *D.M.*, Anhang, *Patuhho.*
  The vowel is short ; not *Béadecan*, as Grein, Ettmüller (1).
  Herelingas, Emercan ond Fridlan. See Introduction, pp. 28–36.
  113. *sohte ic.* Müllenhoff (*Z.f.d.A.* xI, 291–293) regards the repetition of
sohte ic as due to interpolation. It certainly seems wrong here, for Emerca and
Fridla *are* the Harlungs, and the two words were therefore rightly deleted by
Ettmüller (1) (2). But Müllenhoff would also strike it out in ll. 112, 115, 117,
119, 123, on the ground that it overfills the line. This however would mean
that *sohte ic* would have to be understood in l. 123 from l. 110, in spite of a
parenthesis (119–122) of several lines intervening. To avoid this Müllenhoff
would take the names in 123, 124 not as accusatives after *sohte ic* [understood]
but as nominatives in apposition to *Hræda here* : altering *Wudgan* and *Haman*
into *Wudga* and *Hama.*
  East-Gotan. Bojunga and Wülcker (*Kl. Dicht.* glossary) have taken as
plural, " Eastgoths " : but there can be no doubt that this is a reference to the
hero Ostrogotha, for whom see Introduction, pp. 13–15.
  114. *Unwenes.* Jordanes (xiv, 79) has " *Ostrogotha autem genuit Hunuil :
Hunuil item genuit Athal,*" upon which Müllenhoff comments *Hunuil nominis
certe ultimam partem corruptam esse nemo non videt.* He suggests in view of
this passage in *Widsith* that *Unuin* should be read : *Unwin* stands for *Unwen* as
Thiudimir interchanges with *Thiudemer.* The name means a son born beyond
hope, cf. *Z.f.d.A.* xII, 253. Unwen must have been a famous hero to have
been remembered in England till after the Norman Conquest (see Appendix K).
Yet he does not succeed his father Ostrogotha in Gothic story : he was
therefore presumably cut off in his youth. Was it in this connection that
Ostrogotha, like Thurisind or Olaf the Peacock, showed his characteristic
patience ?
  115. *Seccan.* See Müllenhoff in *Z.f.d.A.* xI, 276.
  Beccan. See above, l. 19.
  Seafolan ond þeodric. See Introduction, pp. 40–44.
  Seafola probably signifies " the cunning one " from a root preserved in
O.E. *sefa,* " understanding," or Latin *sapere.* (Müllenhoff in *Z.f.d.A.* xxx, 240 ;
Much in *P.B.B.* xvII, 199.) The names of the traitors Seafola and Sifeca are
thus perhaps connected.
  For further notes on Sabene see Grimm's *Heldensage,* 235 ; Bugge, *H.D.
passim.*
  116. *Heaþoric.* Müllenhoff (*Z.f.d.A.* vI, 458) suggested that this hero is
the O.E. equivalent of the Frederic who in the continental German versions is
murdered by his father Ermanaric. But this is a quite unnecessary assumption,
as a *Freoþeric* is mentioned below.
  Binz (*P.B.B.* xx, 208) and Schütte (*A.f.n.F.* xxI, 37) would identify *Heaðoric*
with *Heiðrekr,* the ferocious king who is the half-hero of the *Hervarar Saga.*

117 Eadwine sohte ic *ond* Elsan,   Ægelmund *ond* Hungar

Eadwine I sought and Elsa, Ægelmund and Hungar and the proud

But the two names do not correspond, and though the Old English one may be corrupted, we can hardly regard this as more than a probable guess. Schütte would further identify *Heaðoric-Heiðrekr* with the historic Ardaricus (Jordanes, ed. Mommsen, L). Lappenberg in 1838 had suggested "Heathoric der Haidreck von Hunaland im Oddruasliede [*Oddrúnargrátr*] in der Edda sein kann" (p. 181). See also Much in *Z.f.d.A.* XLVI, 315.

Sifecan. Clearly the traitor Sibich, for whom see Grimm, *Heldensage*, 18, 19. Binz's conjecture seems improbable. See Introduction, p. 34, footnote.

Hliþe. Generally identified with Leth, the third king of the Lombards. See Introduction, p. 122 (first by Lappenberg : supported by Ettmüller (₁) 25 ; Müllenhoff, *Z.f.d.A.* XI, 278 ; Möller, *V.E.* 11).

It was pointed out however by Svend Grundtvig in 1856 that *Hliþe and Incgenþeow* probably correspond to the *Hlǫðr* and *Angantýr* of the *Hervarar Saga.* (*Danmarks gamle Folkeviser*, 4°. Kjöbenhavn, 1856, II, 637.) Hloth and Angantyr are half-brothers and foes ; but as they are both concerned in the great fight between Goths and Huns which is obviously connected with the struggle referred to in ll. 120–122, they naturally have a place here. See Introduction, pp. 46–48.

Incgenþeow. If this *is* Angantyr, we should rather expect *Onȝenþeow.* For the present form however compare *Ingceburne, Incgenæshám* in Kemble, *Codex Dipl.* 813 (IV, 157), 593 (III, 127). See *Ongendþeow*, above, l. 31.

117. *Eadwine* (Audoin) and Ægelmund, below, are very possibly Lombard kings. Möller (*V.E.* 11) regards the Lombard passage as an interpolation. This seems more likely than that it points to a contamination of Lombard and Gothic story, centering perhaps in the person of Ealhhild-Swanhild. See Introduction, p. 122.

Elsa. Coming between *Eadwine* and *Ægelmund, Elsa* ought to be the name of a Lombard hero, and it is frequently asserted that it is (e.g. by Binz in *P.B.B.* XX, 206, Lawrence in *Mod. Philol.* IV, 344). For this there is no evidence except that the name *Alisso* occurs in a charter drawn up at Beneventum under Lombard rule in (?) 752. (See Meyer, *Sprache der Langobarden*, 1877, p. 195 : Troya, *Codice diplomatico longobardo*, 1852–54, IV, 440, No. 668.) But there is no proof that this Alisso was a Lombard : he is a *Condoma*, and, whatever that word may mean (see Ducange, *Condamina*, where the charter is quoted), it is clear from this charter alone that many persons of this status were not Lombards, or even Germans. Even were Alisso a Lombard, it does not follow that he was named after an early Lombard king or hero. The statement that Elsa is a Lombard hero is therefore unsupported conjecture.

On the other hand the name has come down to us as part of the Gothic tradition of Dietrich von Bern, in whose cycle there occur two heroes of the name *Else*, father and son (*Biterolf u. Dietleib, passim* ; *Dietrichs Flucht*, 8313). There is also *Elsân, der alte, der guote* to whose care the young princes are entrusted in the *Rabenschlacht*, and who has to atone with his life for his neglect of his charge. Also we have an *Elsung* in the *Thidreks Saga.* Evidence would therefore point to Elsa being a Gothic hero. The name *Elesa* however occurs in the West Saxon pedigree as that of the father of Cerdic (for a discussion of the name see Kemble, *Stammtafel der Westsachsen*, 1836, p. 27) : whilst *Alusa* occurs in the allied Northumbrian pedigree, as given in the early ninth century genealogies (Sweet, *Oldest English Texts*, 1885, p. 170, and in Florence of Worcester, ed. Thorpe, 253). See Müllenhoff, *Beovulf*, 63 ; Grimm, *Heldensage*, 138, 192. For *Aliso* see Zacher, *Das Gothische Alphabet Vulfilas*, Leipzig, 1855, p. 106 ; for a possible derivation and cognates of *Aliso, Elisa, Ilsung* see Müllenhoff, *Ein Altsächsische Gott Wëlo*, in *Nordalb. Stud.* I, 36.

Ægelmund. See Introduction, pp. 121–3.

Hungar. Müllenhoff (*Z.f.d.A.* XI, 284) would identify him with Onegesius, the viceroy of Attila, who is constantly mentioned in Priscus' account of his

ond þa wloncan gedryht Wiþ-Myrginga.

Wulfhere sohte ic *ond* Wyrmhere : ful oft þær wig
ne alæg,

120 þonne Hræda here heardum sweordu*m*
ymb Wistlawudu wergan sceoldon

company of the With-Myrgings. Wulfhere I sought and Wyrmhere:
there full oft war was not slack, what time the Goths with sharp swords
must defend their ancient seat from the people of Ætla by the Vistula-
wood.

embassy (see Müller, *Fragmenta Hist. Græc.* ɪᴠ). It has been denied that
Onegesius was a Goth. Thierry (*Histoire d'Attila,* nouvelle édit. 1864, p. 93)
concludes that he was a Greek, whilst Hodgkin (*Italy,* ɪɪ, 74 note) argues that
he was a Hun, and orientalizes his name into *Onégesh.* Onegesius acts as
intermediary and apparently as interpreter between the ambassadors and Attila.
But in the *Acta Sanctorum* (Parisiis, 1868, July 29, p. 81) Attila's interpreter
Hunigasius [*sic,* not Hunigaisus] is mentioned. The two are almost certainly
identical, as Hodgkin admits (ɪɪ, 123). But Hunigaisus is a purely Gothic
name, and corresponds exactly to Hungar. As a victorious Gothic leader who
had overcome the Acatiri (Priscus, pp. 82–3, 86), sitting on Attila's right in
hall (91), μετὰ τὸν 'Αττήλαν παρὰ Σκύθαις ἰσχύων μέγα (85), Hunigais would be
very likely to have passed into Gothic saga. He may well be the Hungar here
referred to.

118. *Wiþ-Myrginga. wi𝑑 Myrginga,* Kemble, Leo, "the company against
the Myrgings"; *winas Myrginga,* Ettmüller (₁); *wine Myrginga,* Ettmüller (₂);
Wiþ-Myrginga, Thorpe (*Cod. Ex.* and *Beowulf*), Rieger, Grein, Wülcker in *Kl.
Dicht.,* Grein-Wülcker, Kluge, Holt., Sedg. Unless, as Heinzel (*Hervararsaga*
in *W.S.B.* xɪᴠ, 101) suggests, these are the Lombards, we must abandon the
name as inexplicable. The Lombards might possibly have been also called
Myrgingas, for in all probability they occupied Maurungani and its neighbourhood for three centuries (from the middle of the second to the end of the sixth),
"hovering about the skirts of the Carpathians, perhaps sometimes pressed
northwards into the upper valleys of the Oder and the Vistula" (Hodgkin,
Italy, ᴠ, p. 102). Müllenhoff (*Nordalb. Stud.* ɪ, 149) interprets *Wiþ-Myrginga,*
"Friends of the Myrgings," i.e. Lombards [the same interpretation had been
given by Ettmüller (₁), p. 25]. Müllenhoff comments, "There is a very close
connection postulated by the poem between the Lombards and the Myrgings."
So Gummere, " neighbor-Myrgings " (cf. Möller in *A.f.d.A.* xxɪɪ, 152).

To suppose any connection with the Icelandic *Myrk-viðr* (as Schütte,
A.f.n.F. xxɪ, 34, 37, and Sarrazin, *Engl. Stud.* xxɪɪɪ, 236–7) is surely impossible.
We should expect, if anything, the O.E. equivalent, not a dislocated Icelandic
word. But see also Schütte, *Oldsagn,* 63.

Wulfhere. Unknown, although both Ermanaric and Theodoric have, in
story, retainers whose names begin with *Wolf.* Cf. *Biterolf* and *Alpharts Tod,*
passim, and *Wolfram dietrich* in the Low German *King Ermanaric's Death, etc.*;
and see Grimm, *Heldensage,* 238 ; Symons in *Z.f.d.Ph.* xxxᴠɪɪɪ, 161 ; Matthaei
in *Z.f.d.A.* xʟᴠɪ, 55 ; and note on *Wulfingum,* above (l. 29).

119. *Wyrmhere.* "Le nom *Vyrmhere* répond tout-à-fait à *Ormarr* de la
Hervararsaga, tout comme *Gûðhere,* en ancien allem. Gundahari, répond à
Gunnarr "—C. C. Rafn in *Antiquités russes,* Copenhague, 1850, ɪ, 112.

This identification seems fairly certain, and supports, and in its turn is
supported by, the interpretation of *Hliþe ond Incgenþeow* as *Hlǫðr* and *Angantýr,* as suggested by Svend Grundtvig and Heinzel.

120. *Hræda.* Ettmüller, Holt. change to *Hreða,* unnecessarily, cf. Müllenhoff, *Z.f.d.A.* xɪɪ, 259, and see Appendix : Note H, *The term Hrædas applied to
the Goths.*

121. *Wistlawudu.* The Goths left the Vistula towards the end of the

ealdne eþelstol   Ætlan leodum.

Rædhere sohte ic *ond* Rondhere,   Rumstan *ond*
Gislhere,

Wiþergield *ond* Freoþeric,   Wudgan *ond* Haman:

125 ne wæran þæt gesiþa   þa sæmestan,

Not the worst of comrades were they, though I am to mention them

second century A.D. (Hodgkin's *Italy*, I, 40). These lines therefore preserve
a very early tradition, but we can draw no exact chronological argument from
the allusion except that we are here dealing with saga and not with history.
See Introduction, p. 163. The wood is probably to be identified with the
Mirkwood which, in later Icelandic story, separates Goths and Huns.

There is a mark in the *Exeter Book* over the *a*, like an imperfectly formed
mark of length : it is quite unlike the curved heavy horizontal stroke which
signifies *n* or *m*. Mr Anscombe's suggestion (*Anglia*, XXXIV, 526) that this
should be read *Wistlan wudu* is therefore impossible. Besides, the stroke over
the word is never used in the *Exeter Book* for *n*, which is always written in
full, except in the word þoñ (þonne), and in Latin words ; the stroke is frequently used, but in all other cases signifies *m*.

123. *Rædhere* and *Rondhere*. Müllenhoff (*Z.f.d.A.* VI, 453) would connect
them with the *Randolt unde Rienolt* who are mentioned in *Biterolf*, together
with the Harlungs and others, as retainers of Ermanaric (5723, 4604 etc.),
" denn die namen bedeuten ganz dasselbe." Possibly Rondhere is the same
hero as the Randver who in the Scandinavian versions is Ermanaric's son, the
equivalent of the Frederic of the southern versions. The second element in
proper names is particularly apt to be corrupted. See Introduction, p. 23.

Rumstan. Almost certainly, as was pointed out by Lappenberg (181) and
subsequently by Hertz (*Deutsche Sage im Elsass,* Stuttgart, 1872, p. 220), the
Rimstein who is mentioned in *Biterolf* as a retainer of Ermanaric, and more
particularly of the two young Harlungs :

— *Von den Harlungen*
Fritelen dem jungen
unde ouch Imbrecken,
den volgeten die recken
Wahsmuot unde Rimstein,
ez wæn der tac nie beschein
bezzer wigande.   *Biterolf*, 10673–9 (cf. 4771).

The name also occurs in the *Thidreks Saga*, 147–149, where Rimstein is a
tributary earl of Ærminric but rebels against him. Thithrek gives help to
Ærminric, and Vithga (Wudga) slays Rimstein in a sortie.

Rassmann in his translation of the *Thidreks Saga* (*Die deutsche Heldensage
und ihre Heimat*, II, 459, 1863) also pointed out that Rimstein is probably
identical with our Rumstan. See also Grimm, *Heldensage*, 3te Aufl., Anhang,
462 ; Jiriczek(2) 79.

Gislhere. See Introduction, p. 65.

124. *Wiþergield.* "Withergield ist dem Beowulfsliede angehörig," Lappenberg (181). If the Withergyld of *Beowulf* (2051) is the name of a hero (as it is
taken, e.g. by Gering and Schücking), and not a common noun, he would be a
leading figure in the combat between Danes and Heathobeardan, presumably a
Heathobeard.

Freoþeric. Probably the Friderich who is frequently mentioned in *Dietrich's
Flucht*, son of Ermanaric, who is at last destroyed by his father. (See Introduction, p. 30, *note*.) There is however another Friderich, a retainer of Dietrich
(*Dietrich's Flucht, Rabenschlacht*). The historic prototype of one or both of
these figures is probably to be found in Frederic, king of the Rugians, a
picturesque scoundrel of the later fifth century, who first joined and then
deserted Theodoric. (See Hodgkin's *Italy*, III, 164–209 ; and cf. Matthaei in

þeahþe ic hy ánihst   nemnan sceolde.
Ful oft of þam heape   hwinende fleag
giellende gar   on grome þeode :
wræccan þær weoldan   wundnan golde,
130 werum *ond* wifum,   Wudga *ond* Hama.
87 a   Swa ic þæt symle onfond ‖   on þære feringe,
þæt se biþ leofast   londbuendum,
se þe him god syleð   gumena rice
to gehealdenne,   þenden he her leofað." —
135 Swa scriþende   gesceapum hweorfað
gleomen gumena   geond grunda fela,
þearfe secgað,   þoncword sprecaþ,
simle suð oþþe norð   sumne gemetað
gydda gleawne,   geofum unhneawne,

last. Full oft from that company flew the spear, whistling and shrieking, against the hostile folk. Wudga and Hama, wanderers o'er the earth, ruled there, by wounden gold, over men and women.

So have I ever found it in my journeying, that he is most beloved to the dwellers in the land, to whom God giveth dominion over men to hold it whilst he liveth here."

So are the singers of men destined to go wandering throughout many lands: they tell their need, they speak the word of thanks: south or north they ever meet with one, skilled in songs, bounteous in gifts, who desires

Z.f.d.A. XLIII, 326). Jiriczek(2) 73 regards the identity of the Freotheric mentioned here with the son of Ermanaric as certain. But it is hardly so : cf. Panzer, *H.i.B.* 78. Yet I think that the balance of probability is in favour of all the names being connected : and that *Widsith* records a stage of the tradition, at which the king Frederic of history has come to be regarded as a retainer of Ermanaric, but not yet as his son.

126. *ic hy anihst. ic hivan nyhst,* Leo, Ettmüller (₁). "Obwohl ich's Hausvolk zunächst nennen musste" (Ettmüller). Holt. reads *aneist,* for metrical reasons. See Introduction, p. 173.

127. *hwinende.* ἅπαξ λεγόμενον. Cf. O.N. *hwína.*

128. *giellende gar.* Bugge sees an imitation of this line in *Atlakviþa* 15 : *meþ geire gjallanda at vekja gram hilde.* See *P.B.B.* xxxv, 245, and *H. D.* tr. Schofield xxiii ; cf. Neckel, 468, note 4.

129. *þær.* Where? We seem, just as in ll. 50, 88, to have a reference to something not explained in the extant poem. This, with the allusions to Ealhhild and Scilling, favours the view that either *Widsith* has been muti-lated, or that the background of legend was so familiar as to render the most obscure references intelligible. *þær* may perhaps refer to the stronghold of Hama, and may be identical with the *byrhtan byrig* to which in *Beowulf* he carries off the *Brosinga mene.*

wundnan golde. Leo, Ettmüller(1) took *wundnan golde* as qualifying Wudga and Hama "die Wackern walteten da, bewunden mit Golde." So Thorpe, *Cod. Ex.* But *wundnan golde* is instrumental ; see Introduction, pp. 167, 170.

wundnan was altered by Kemble (₂) to *wundum* [for *wundnum*]; *wundnum,* Ettmüller (₁) (note, not text), Ettmüller (₂) text.

140 se þe fore duguþe wile   dóm áræran,
    eorlscipe æfnan,   oþ þæt eal scæceð,
    leoht *ond* lif somod :   lof se gewyrceð,
    hafað under heofonu*m*   heahfæstne dóm.

to exalt his fame before his chieftains—to do deeds of honour: till all
departeth, life and light together: he gaineth glory, and hath, under the
heavens, an honour which passeth not away.

131–4. Müllenhoff condemns these four lines as an interpolation on account
of their silliness (*Z.f.d.A.* xi, 293, 4).
    symle onfond. onfond symle, Holt. for metrical reasons.
135–143. Widsith's discourse is ended, and these nine lines form an
epilogue, similar to the nine lines of prologue prefixed to it. Compare the way
in which the *Wanderer's* discourse is fitted with a Prologue and an Epilogue.
These in each case may well be later additions, but evidence is not as strong
against these closing lines as against ll. 1–9. These verses are somewhat
commonplace, but not faulty, or out of harmony with the rest of the poem.
Cf. Introduction, p. 151.
    Müllenhoff finds them "voll Schwung und Erhabenheit" (*Z.f.d.A.* xi,
293). Möller on the other hand finds in them "einfachste nüchternheit"
(*V.E.* 36).
    140. *fore duguþe*, before the assembled company. Cf. *Juliana* 256;
Beowulf, 2020.

APPENDIX.

(A) BIBLIOGRAPHY.

(1) PERIODICALS AND COLLECTIONS

Aarbøger f. nord. Oldk. Aarbøger for Nordisk Oldkyndighed og Historie. Kjøbenhavn, 1866, *etc.*

Anglia. Anglia, Zeitschrift für Englische Philologie, herausgegeben von R. P. Wülcker [Eugen Einenkel]. Halle, 1878, *etc.*

A.f.d.A. Anzeiger für deutsches Alterthum. Berlin, 1876, *etc.* (*Z.f.d.A.* XIX = *A.f.d.A.* I.)

A.f.n.F. Arkiv for nordisk Filologi udgivet ved G. Storm [A. Kock]. Christiania, 1883, *etc.*

A.T.f.S. Antiqvarisk Tidskrift för Sverige. Stockholm, 1863, *etc.*

(Herrig's) *Archiv.* Archiv für das Studium der neueren Sprachen und Litteraturen. Elberfeld, 1846, *etc.*
    Quoted according to the original numbering.

D.L.Z. Deutsche Literaturzeitung. Berlin, 1880, *etc.*

E.E.T.S. Early English Text Society.

Engl. Stud. Englische Studien, herausgegeben v. Eugen Kölbing. Heilbronn, 1877, *etc.*

Ériu. Ériu: The Journal of the School of Irish Learning, Dublin. Dublin, 1905, *etc.*

Folk Lore: a quarterly review. London, 1890, *etc.*

Germania. Germania, Vierteljahrsschrift für deutsche Alterthumskunde. Wien, 1856–92.

I.F. Indogermanische Forschungen, herausgegeben von K. Brugmann u. W. Streitberg. Strassburg, 1891, *etc.*

J.d.V.f.n.S. Jahrbuch des Vereins für niederdeutsche Sprachforschung. Norden u. Leipzig, 1876, *etc.*

Langebek. Scriptores rerum Danicarum, collegit J. Langebek. Hafniae, 1772–1878.

Litteraturblatt f. Philol. Litteraturblatt für germanische u. romanische Philologie herausg. v. O. Behagel u. F. Neuman. Heilbronn, Leipzig, 1880, *etc.*

Mod. Philol. Modern Philology. Chicago. University of Chicago Press, 1903, *etc.*

M.G.H. Monumenta Germaniae Historica, edidit Societas aperiendis fontibus rerum Germanicarum medii aevi. 4° Berolini apud Weidmannos, 1877, *etc.*; 4° Hannoverae, 1879, *etc.*

M.L.N. Modern Language Notes. Baltimore, 1886, *etc.*

M.L.R. The Modern Language Review, ed. by John G. Robertson. Cambridge, 1906, *etc.*

Morsbachs Studien. Studien zur englischen Philologie. Halle, 1897, *etc.*

Nordalb. Stud. Nordalbingische Studien, 6 Bde. Kiel, 1844–54.

P.B.B. Beiträge zur Geschichte der deutschen Sprache und Litteratur, herausgeg. v. Hermann Paul u. Wilhelm Braune. Halle a. S., 1874, *etc.*

Pauls Grdr. ($_1$). Grundriss der germanischen Philologie, herausgegeben von Hermann Paul. Strassburg, 1889, *etc.*

Pauls Grdr. ($_2$). [The same], zweite Auflage. Strassburg, 1896, *etc.*

Pertz (fol.). Monumenta Germaniae Historica, edidit G. H. Pertz. Fol. Hannoverae, 1826, *etc.*

Q.F. Quellen u. Forschungen zur Sprach- und Culturgeschichte der germanischen Völker, herausgegeben von B. ten Brink und W. Scherer. Strassburg, 1874, *etc.*

W.S.B. Sitzungsberichte der k. Akad. der Wissenschaften zu Wien. Phil.-hist. Classe. Wien, 1850, *etc.*

Z.f.d.A. Zeitschrift für deutsches Alterthum [und deutsche Literatur], herausgegeben von Moriz Haupt [K. Müllenhoff, E. Steinmeyer, *etc.*]. Leipzig, Berlin, 1841, *etc.*

(Zacher's) *Z.f.d.Ph.* Zeitschrift für deutsche Philologie, begründet von Julius Zacher. Halle, 1869, *etc.*

(2) Editions of Widsith (in chronological order).

Conybeare, *Illustrations.* Illustrations of Anglo-Saxon poetry, by J. J. Conybeare, ed. by his brother, W. D. Conybeare. London, 1826. pp. 10–27, Text, Notes, Latin Translation and English paraphrase.

Kemble, *Beowulf.* The Anglo-Saxon Poems of Beowulf, the Traveller's Song and the Battle of Finnes-Burh, ed. by John M. Kemble. London, 1833. pp. 221–233, Text.

Kemble's Text is reproduced in Latham's Germania of Tacitus, London, 1851. Kemble's second edition (1835) differs considerably from his first.

Guest, *Rhythms.* A History of English Rhythms, by Edwin Guest. 2 vols. London, 1838. pp. 78–93, Text and English Translation.

Leo, *Sprachproben.* Altsächsische und Angelsächsische Sprachproben, herausgeg. und mit einem erklärenden Verzeichniss der angelsächsischen Wörter versehen von Heinr. Leo. Halle, 1838. pp. 75–85, Text, Translation and Notes.

Appendix 227

ETTMÜLLER ($_1$). Scôpes vîdsidh. Sängers Weitfahrt. Æðhelstans Sieg bei Brunanburg. Angelsächsisch und deutsch von L. Ettmüller. Zürich, 1839.

THORPE, *Cod. Ex.* Codex Exoniensis. A collection of Anglo-Saxon Poetry, ed. by Benj. Thorpe. London, 1842. pp. 318, *etc.*
Thorpe's Translation is reproduced in Latham's Germania of Tacitus, 1851.

EBELING. Angelsächsisches Lesebuch von F. W. Ebeling. Leipzig, 1847. pp. 97–101.

SCHALDEMOSE. Beo-Wulf og Scopes Widsið, to angelsaxiske digte, med oversættelse og oplysende anmærkninger udgivne af F. Schaldemose. Kjøbenhavn, 1847, second edit. 1851. pp. 176–188.

KLIPSTEIN. Analecta Anglosaxonica. Selections, in prose and verse, from the Anglo-Saxon Literature, by Louis F. Klipstein. 2 vols. New York, 1849. Vol. II : Text, 299–307 ; Notes, 422–430.

ETTMÜLLER ($_2$). Engla and Seaxna Scôpas and Bôceras. Anglo-Saxonum poetae et scriptores prosaici, ed. L. Ettmüllerus. Quedlinburgii et Lipsiae, 1850. pp. 208–211.

THORPE, *Beowulf.* The Anglo-Saxon Poems of Beowulf, the Scôp or Gleeman's Tale and the Fight at Finnesburg. With a literal translation, notes, glossary, etc., by Benj. Thorpe. Oxford, 1855. pp. 215–227.

MÜLLER, Angelsächsisches Lesebuch. c. 1855. 22. Des Sängers Reisen.
I have not seen this edition, which was privately printed. There is no copy in the British Museum, nor, apparently, in any of the German University libraries.

GREIN, *Bibliothek.* Bibliothek der angelsächsischen Poesie, in kritisch bearbeiteten Texten und mit vollständigen Glossar herausgeg. von C. W. M. Grein. 4 Bde. Göttingen, 1857. pp. 251–255.

RIEGER, *Lesebuch.* Alt- und angelsächsisches Lesebuch nebst altfriesischen Stücken mit einem Wörterbuche von Max Rieger. Giessen, 1861. pp. 57–61.

WÜLCKER, *Kleinere Dichtungen.* Kleinere angelsächsische Dichtungen, versehen von R. P. Wülcker. Halle, 1882. pp. 1–6.

MÖLLER, *V. E.* Das altenglische Volksepos in der ursprünglichen strophischen Form, von Hermann Möller. Kiel, 1883. pp. 1–39, I–VI.

GREIN-WÜLCKER. Bibliothek der angelsächsischen Poesie, begründet von C. W. M. Grein, neu bearbeitet von R. P. Wülcker. 3 Bde. Cassel, 1883, *etc.* Vol. I, pp. 1–6.

KLUGE, *Lesebuch.* Angelsächsisches Lesebuch, zusammengestellt von Friedrich Kluge. 2te Auflage. Halle, 1897. pp. 123–126.

HOLT. Beowulf, nebst den kleineren Denkmälern der Heldensage, herausgeg. von F. Holthausen. 2te Auflage. Heidelberg, 1908–9.
Text of Widsith in vol. I : *Bibliography and notes in vol.* II.

SEDG. Beowulf, ed. by W. J. Sedgefield. Manchester, 1910.
Text of Widsith, pp. 139–142.

15—2

Comments or translations without text will be found in

LAPPENBERG. [A review of Leo's Sprachproben appeared in the] Jahrbücher für wissenschaftliche Kritik, August, pp. 169–182, by J. M. Lappenberg. Berlin, 1838, II.

MÜLLENHOFF in *Nordalb. Stud.* Die deutschen Völker in Nord- und Ostsee in ältester Zeit. In Nordalbingische Studien, Kiel, 1844, I, 111–174.

MÜLLENHOFF in *Z.f.d.A.* Zur Kritik des angelsächsischen Volksepos. 2. Widsith. In *Z.f.d.A.*, XI, 275–294.

SCHIPPER in *Germania.* Zum Codex Exoniensis von J. Schipper. In Germania, XIX, 327–339 (especially 333).

GUMMERE (₁). Widsith, a translation, with brief commentary, in Modern Language Notes, IV, 419 *etc.* (1889).

MORLEY'S *English Writers* contains a translation into blank verse: reprinted in Cook and Tinker's *Select Translations*, Boston, 1902.

VOGT, *Beowulf.* Beowulf, übersetzt von Paul Vogt. Halle, 1905.

pp. 100–103 *give a useful abstract of Widsith, with commentary.*

LAWRENCE in *Mod. Philol.* Structure and interpretation of Widsith, by W. W. Lawrence. In Modern Philology, IV, 1906, pp. 329–374.

SCHÜTTE, *Oldsagn*, 1907, contains a translation of Widsith into Danish.

GUMMERE (₂). The Oldest English Epic. Beowulf...Widsith, translated by F. B. Gummere. New York, 1909.

SIEBS. Wídsíð. In *Festschrift Wilhelm Viëtor.* Marburg, 1910.

ANSCOMBE. Widsith. In *Anglia*, XXXIV, pp. 526–7.

(3) *Other O.E. poems have been quoted from the edition of Grein-Wülcker. Holder's Beowulf* (1899) *has also been used. Editions of other works frequently quoted are:*

ABELING. Das Nibelungenlied und seine Literatur. Leipzig, 1907. (*Teutonia* 7.)

AGATHIAS. Agathiae Historiarum libri quinque ; B. G. Niebuhrius recensuit. Bonnae, 1828. In the Corpus Scriptorum Historiae Byzantinae.

ANDERSON. The Anglo-Saxon Scop, 1903. (Univ. of Toronto Studies.)

Antiquités Russes. Antiquités Russes [edited by C. C. Rafn, *etc.*]. Copenhagen, 1850. Published by the Kongeligt Nordisk Oldskrift-Selskab.

BARNOUW. Textcritische Untersuchungen. Leiden, 1902.

BEDE, *H.E.*, ed. Holder. Bedae Historia Ecclesiastica, ed. Holder. Freiburg, 1882. Holder's Germanische Bücherschatz, 7.

BEDE, *H.E.*, ed. Plummer. Venerabilis Bedae Historiam Ecclesiasticam ...Historiam Abbatum...recog. C. Plummer. 2 tom. Oxonii, 1896.

BINDING. Die burgundisch-romanische Königreich, von C. Binding. Leipzig, 1868.

BINZ in *P.B.B.* Zeugnisse zur germanischen Sage in England, von G. Binz. In *P.B.B.* xx, 141-223 (1895).

BIRCH, *Cart. Sax.* Cartularium Saxonicum, a collection of charters relating to Anglo-Saxon history, by W. de Gray Birch. 3 vols. London, 1885-93.

BLUHME. Die Gens Langobardorum und ihre Herkunft. Bonn, 1868.

BOER, *Ermânarich.* Die Sagen von Ermanarich und Dietrich von Bern von R. C. Boer. Halle, 1910. Zachers Germanistische Handbibliothek, x.

BÖTTGER. Diöcesan u. Gaugrenzen Norddeutschlands v. H. Böttger. 4 Bde. Halle, 1875-6. IV, 214-17, 224-9 *particularly helpful.*

BRANDL in *Pauls Grdr.* (₂). Geschichte der altenglischen Literatur von Alois Brandl. Strassburg, 1908. In Pauls Grundriss, II, 1.

BRANDL in *Archiv.* Zur Gotensage bei den Angelsachsen. In Herrigs *Archiv,* CXX (1908), pp. 1-8.

BREMER in *Pauls Grdr.* (₂). Ethnographie der germanischen Stämme von Otto Bremer. In Pauls Grundriss, III, 735-950 (Abschnitt XV). *This section is to be found in the second edition only.*

BUGGE, *H.D.* Helge-Digtene i den aeldre Edda : deres hjem og forbindelser, af Sophus Bugge. Kjøbenhavn, 1896.

BUGGE tr. Schofield. [A revised translation of the above.] London, 1899.

C.P.B. Corpus poeticum boreale : the poetry of the old Northern tongue, edited by Gudbrand Vigfusson and F. York Powell. 2 vols. Oxford 1883.

CASSIODORUS, *Variae.* Cassiodori Senatoris Variae, recensuit Th Mommsen. Berolini, 1894. In the Monumenta Germaniae Historica, Auct. Ant. XII.

CHADWICK. The origin of the English Nation. Cambridge, 1907.

CHADWICK in *Camb. Hist.* "Early National Poetry" in the Cambridge History of English Literature, vol. I, chap. III (pp. 19-40).

Chronicle, ed. Plummer. Two of the Saxon Chronicles parallel, edited by Charles Plummer on the basis of an edition by John Earle. 2 vols. Oxford, 1892-99. See particularly notes on the Genealogies, II, pp. 1-6.

CLARK. Sidelights on Teutonic History during the Migration Period. Cambridge, 1911.

DAHLMANN. Forschungen auf dem Gebiete der Geschichte. Altona, 1822.

Danmarks Riges Historie. Danmarks Riges Historie af Joh. Steenstrup, *etc.,* I. Kjøbenhavn, 1897-1904.

Edda, ed. Symons and Gering. Die Lieder der Edda, herausgegeben von B. Symons und H. Gering. 2 Bde. Halle a. S., 1888, *etc.* Zachers Germanistische Handbibliothek, VII.

Edda, ed. Detter and Heinzel. Saemundar Edda, mit einem Anhang herausgegeben und erklärt von F. Detter u. R. Heinzel. 2 Bde. Leipzig, 1903.

ERDMANN in *A.T.f.S.* Om folknamnen Götar och Goter, af Axel Erdmann. In *A.T.f.S.*, XI, 4.

ERDMANN. Über die Heimat und den Namen der Angeln von A. Erdmann in the Skrifter utgifna af Humanistiska Vetenskapssamfundet i Upsala, I, 1890.

FAHLBECK in *A.T.f.S.* Beovulfsqvädet såsom källa för nordisk fornhistoria af Pontus Fahlbeck. In *A.T.f.S.*, VIII, 2.

Fornaldar Sǫgur, ed. Rafn. Fornaldar Sǫgur Nordrlanda eptir gǫmlum Handritum útgefnar af C. C. Rafn. Kaupmannahǫfn, 1829. Bd I contains: pp. 1–109, Saga Hrolfs Konungs Kraka; pp. 113–234, Vǫlsunga Saga; pp. 409–533, Hervarar Saga ok Heidreks Konungs.

FÖRSTEMANN. Altdeutsches Namenbuch. 2 Bde. 2ᵗᵉ Auflage. Bonn, 1900.

GERING. Beowulf, übersetzt u. erläutert von H. Gering. Heidelberg, 1906.

Germania, ed. Church and Brodribb. The Germania of Tacitus, with a revised text, English notes, and map, by A. J. Church and W. J. Brodribb. London, 1903.

Germania, ed. Holder. Cornelii Taciti de origine et situ Germanorum liber, ed. A. Holder. Freiburg, 1882. In Holder's Germanischer Bücherschatz.

Germania, ed. Latham. The Germania of Tacitus, with ethnological dissertations and notes. London, 1851.

GIBBON, ed. Bury. The History of the Decline and Fall of the Roman Empire, edited by J. B. Bury. 7 vols. London, 1896–1900.

GOLTHER. Handbuch der germanischen Mythologie. Leipzig, 1895.

GREGORII *Hist. Franc.* Historia Francorum, ed. Arndt. Hannoverae, 1885. In the Monumenta Germaniae Historica: Scriptores rerum Merovingicarum, I; Gregorii Turonensis opera.

GRIMM, *Heldensage.* Die deutsche Heldensage von Wilhelm Grimm. Göttingen, 1829. Second edition, revised by Müllenhoff, Berlin, 1867; third edition, a reprint of the first, revised by R. Steig, Gütersloh, 1889.

    References to the first edition, the pagination of which is noted in the margin of the third.

GRIMM, *D.M.* Deutsche Mythologie, von Jacob Grimm. Göttingen, 1835. Second edit., Göttingen, 1844; third, Göttingen, 1854; fourth, revised by Meyer, 3 vols., Weimar, 1875. Teutonic Mythology, translated from the fourth edition, with notes and appendix by J. S. Stallybrass. 4 vols. London, 1879.

    References to the first edition, and to Stallybrass' translation.

GRIMM, *G.D.S.* Geschichte der deutschen Sprache, von Jacob Grimm. Leipzig, 1848. Second edit., 1853; third, revised by Müllenhoff, 1867; fourth, 1880. *References to the first edition, the pagination of which is noted in the margin of the fourth.*

GRIMM, *R.A.* Deutsche Rechtsalterthümer. Göttingen, 1828. Fourth edition, Leipzig, 1899. *References to the first edition, the pagination of which is noted in the margin of the fourth.*

HAIGH, *Sagas.* The Anglo-Saxon Sagas; an examination of their value as aids to history, by Daniel H. Haigh. London, 1861.

Heimskringla af Snorri Sturluson, udg. ved F. Jónsson. 4 vols. København, 1893–1901.

HEINZEL, *Hervararsaga* in *W.S.B.* Ueber die Hervararsaga, von Richard Heinzel. In the Sitzungsberichte der philosophisch-historischen Classe der k. Akademie der Wissenschaften zu Wien, Bd cxiv, 417 (1887).

HEINZEL, *Ostgotische Heldensage* in *W.S.B.* Ueber die ostgotische Heldensage, in the same, Bd cxix, Abth. 3.

HEINZEL in *A.f.d.A.* Das altenglische Volksepos, von Hermann Möller. [A review by Richard Heinzel] in the Anzeiger für deutsches Alterthum x, 215–33.

Heldenbuch. Deutsches Heldenbuch. 5 Bde. Berlin, 1866–70.

HEUSLER, *L.u.E.* Lied und Epos in germanischer Sagendichtung, von Andreas Heusler. Dortmund, 1905.

HEYNE-SCHÜCKING. Beowulf herausgeg. v. M. Heyne. Neunte Auflage bearbeitet von L. L. Schücking. Paderborn, 1910.

Historia Brittonum, ed. Stevenson. Nennii Historia Britonum, recensuit Josephus Stevenson. Londini, 1838.

Historia Brittonum, ed. Mommsen in *M.G.H.* Historia Brittonum cum additamentis Nennii, in Mommsen's Chronica Minora saec. iv, v, vi, vii. Berolini, 1898 (Mon. Ger. Hist.).

HODGKIN, *Italy.* Italy and her Invaders, by Thomas Hodgkin. Second edit. 7 vols. Oxford, 1892, *etc.*

HOOPS, *Waldbäume.* Waldbäume und Kulturpflanzen im germanischen Altertum, von Johannes Hoops. Strassburg, 1905.

Hoops Reallexikon. Reallexikon der germanischen Altertumskunde. Strassburg, 1911. *Bd. i, Lief. 1 (A—BA) so far published.*

JAHN. Die Geschichte der Burgundionen. 2 Bde. Halle, 1874.

JIRICZEK (₁). Die deutsche Heldensage, von O. L. Jiriczek. 3te Auflage. Leipzig, 1906. Sammlung Göschen, 32.

JIRICZEK (₂). Die deutsche Heldensage, von O. L. Jiriczek. Vol. i. Strassburg, 1898. *Vol. i deals with the stories of Weland, Ermanaric, and Theodoric of Verona.*

JORDAN. Die Heimat der Angelsachsen, in the Verhandlungen der 49 Versammlung deutscher Philologen, Basel, 1907, pp. 138–140.

JORDANES, ed. Holder. Iordanis de origine actibusque Getarum, ed. Holder. Freiburg, 1882. In Holder's Germanischer Bücherschatz, 5.

JORDANES, ed. Mommsen. Iordanis Romana et Getica, ed. Theodorus Mommsen. Berolini, 1882. In the Monumenta Germaniae Historica, Auct. Ant. v, 1. *Unless otherwise stated references are to the Getica.*

KEMBLE'S *Saxons.* The Saxons in England, by J. M. Kemble. 2 vols. London, 1849.

KER, Epic and Romance. London, 1896.

KER, The Dark Ages. Edinburgh, 1904.

KOCK, *Ynglingar.* Om Ynglingar såsom namn på en svensk konungaätt in the Historisk Tidskrift (Stockholm), 1895.

KOEGEL, *Ltg.* Geschichte der deutschen Litteratur bis zum Ausgange des Mittelalters, von Rudolf Koegel, I, 1, 1894; I, 2, 1897. Strassburg. Particularly I, 96–175; II, 191–219.

Kudrun, ed. Martin ($_2$). Kudrun, herausgegeben und erklärt von Ernst Martin. Zweite Auflage. Halle, 1902. Zachers Germanistische Handbibliothek.

LAPPENBERG, *Geschichte.* Geschichte von England, von J. M. Lappenberg. 2 Bde. Hamburg, 1834.

LAPPENBERG, trans. Thorpe. History of England under the Anglo-Saxon kings, translated from the German of Dr J. M. Lappenberg by Benjamin Thorpe, with additions...by the author. London, 1844–5.

MEYER. Altgermanische Religionsgeschichte von Richard M. Meyer. Leipzig, 1910.

MOGK in *Pauls Grdr.* ($_2$). Mythologie, in Grundriss, III, 230–406.

MORLEY'S *English Writers.* English Writers. An attempt towards a history of English Literature, by Henry Morley. 14 vols. London, 1887–95. Particularly vol. II, pp. 1–40.

MUCH in *P.B.B.* "Die Südmark der Germanen," "Die Germanen am Niederrhein," "Goten und Ingvaeonen," von Rudolf Much. In Paul u. Braunes Beiträge, XVII, 1–225 (1893).

MUCH. Deutsche Stammeskunde, von R. Much. 2te Aufl. Leipzig, 1905.

MÜLLENHOFF, *Beovulf.* Beovulf. Untersuchungen über das angelsächsische Epos und die älteste Geschichte der germanischen Seevölker, von Karl Müllenhoff. Berlin, 1889.

MÜLLENHOFF, *D.A.K.* ($_1$). Deutsche Altertumskunde, von Karl Müllenhoff. Berlin, 1870, *etc.*

MÜLLENHOFF, *D.A.K.* ($_2$). [Second edition, revised by Max Roediger.] Berlin, 1890, *etc.*

MÜLLENHOFF in *Nordalb. Stud.* Die deutschen Völker an Nord- und Ostsee in ältester Zeit. In Nordalbingische Studien, I (1844), 111.

MÜLLENHOFF, *Z.E.*, or MÜLLENHOFF in *Z.f.d.A.* XII. Zeugnisse und Excurse zur deutschen Heldensage von Karl Müllenhoff. In the *Z.f.d.A.* XII, 253 *etc.*, 413 *etc.* Subsequent additions by O. Jaenicke, *Z.f.d.A.* XV, 310 *etc.*

MÜLLER. Mythologie der deutschen Heldensage, von W. Müller. Heilbronn, 1886.

NECKEL. Beiträge zur Eddaforschung. Dortmund, 1908.

Nibelungen Lied. Der Nibelunge Nôt, herausg. von Karl Bartsch. 2 Bde. Leipzig, 1870–6.

OLRIK, *Heltedigtning.* Danmarks Heltedigtning, en Oldtidsstudie af Axel Olrik, I Rolfkrake og den ældre Skjoldungrække, II Starkad den Gamle. København, 1903, 1910.

OLRIK, *Sakses Oldhistorie.* Sakses Oldhistorie, af Axel Olrik. Kjøbenhavn, 1892–4.
    Pt 1 *appeared in the Aarbøger for Nordisk Oldkyndighed,* II, 7, 1; *Pt* 2 *separately.*

PANZER, *H.G.* Hilde-Gudrun. Eine sagen- und literargeschichtliche Untersuchung. Halle, 1901.

PANZER, *H.i.B.* Deutsche Heldensage im Breisgau. Heidelberg, 1904.

PANZER, *Beowulf.* Studien zur germanischen Sagengeschichte von F. Panzer. I Beowulf. München, 1910.

PAULUS. Pauli Historia Langobardorum, ed. L. Bethmann et G. Waitz. Hannoverae, 1878. In the Monumenta Germaniae Historica—Scriptores rerum Langobardicarum et Italicarum saec. VI–IX.

PLINY, *Nat. Hist.* C. Plini Secundi naturalis historiae libri XXXVII post Ludovici obitum edidit C. Mayhoff. Lipsiae (Teubner), 1906.

PROCOPIUS. Procopius ex recensione G. Dindorfii. 3 tom. Bonnae, 1833. In the Corpus Scriptorum Historiae Byzantinae.

PTOLEMY, ed. Müller. Cl. Ptolemaei geographia, recognovit C. Müllerus. Vol. I. Parisiis, 1883 (Tabulae, 1901).

RAJNA. Le Origini dell' Epopea francese. Firenze, 1884.

RASSMANN. Die deutsche Heldensage. 2te Ausgabe. Hannover, 1863.
    Contains a German translation of the Thidreks Saga.

RICHTER. Chronologische Studien zur angelsächsischen Literatur. Halle, 1910. (Morsbachs *Studien*, XXXIII.)

RIEGER in *Z.f.d.A.* Ingävonen, Istävonen, Herminonen von Max Rieger. In the *Z.f.d.A.* XI, 177–205.

ROEDIGER. Die Sage von Ermenrich u. Schwanhild. In Weinhold's Zeitschrift des Vereins für Volkskunde, I, 1891, pp. 242 *etc.*

SARRAZIN in *Engl. Stud.* Neue Beowulfstudien, XXIII, 221–67; XXXV, 19 *etc.*; XLII, 1–37. See also XXIV, 144–5.

SAXO, ed. Holder. Saxonis grammatici Gesta Danorum, herausgegeben von Alfred Holder. Strassburg, 1886.

SAXO, tr. Elton. The first nine books of the Danish History of Saxo Grammaticus, translated by Oliver Elton. London, 1894. Publications of the Folk Lore Society, XXXIII.

SCHÜCK. Folknamnet Geatas i den fornengelska dikten Beowulf. Upsala, 1907.

SCHÜTTE in *A.f.N.F.* Gudmund Schütte—Anganty-Kvadets Geografi. In the Arkiv för Nordisk Filologi, XXI, 30–44.

SCHÜTTE, *Oldsagn.* Oldsagn om Godtjod, med særligt henblik på Folkestamsagn. Kjøbenhavn, 1907.

SEARLE. Onomasticon Anglosaxonicum. Cambridge, 1897.

SEEBOHM. Tribal Custom in Anglo-Saxon Law. London, 1902.

SEELMANN in *J.d.V.f.n.S.* Abhandlungen zur Geschichte der deutschen Volksstämme Norddeutschlands und Dänemarks. In the Jahrbuch des Vereins für niederdeutsche Sprachforschung, XII, 1886, pp. 1–93.

SNORRA *Edda.* Snorri Sturluson, Edda udgiven af Finnur Jónsson. København, 1900.

STOPFORD BROOKE, *Early Eng. Lit.* The History of Early English Literature, by Stopford A. Brooke. 2 vols. London, 1892. Particularly Vol. I, Chapters I and VI, and Appendices A and B.

SYMONS in *Pauls Grdr.* (₂). Heldensage, von B. Symons. In Pauls Grundriss, vol. III, pp. 606–734.

TEN BRINK, *Beowulf.* Beowulf. Untersuchungen von Bernhard ten Brink. Strassburg, 1888. (*Q.F.* 62.)
 A review of Ten Brink's Beowulf, by H. Möller, will be found in Englische Studien, XIII, 247.

TEN BRINK, in *Pauls Grdr.* (₁). Altenglische Litteratur. Particularly pp. 510–608 of vol. II, pt. 1 of the first edition.

Thidreks Saga. Saga Điðriks konungs af Bern, i Norsk bearbeidelse fra det trettende Aarhundrede efter Tydske Kilder. Udgivet af C. R. Unger. Christiania, 1853.

Thidreks Saga. Þiðriks Saga af Bern, udgivet ved H. Bertelsen. København, 1905, *etc.*
 References to Unger's edition. Unger's numbering is given (in brackets) in Bertelsen.

UHLAND, *Schriften.* Schriften zur Geschichte der Dichtung und Sage, von Ludwig Uhland. 8 Bde. Stuttgart, 1865–73.

Vǫlsunga Saga, ed. Wilken. Die prosaische Edda, im Auszuge, nebst Vǫlsunga Saga und Nornagests-tháttr, herausgegeben von Ernst Wilken. Paderborn, 1877–83.

WAITZ. Forschungen zur deutschen Geschichte. I. Der Kampf der Burgunder u. Hunen. Göttingen, 1862.

WEILAND. Die Angeln. Ein Capitel aus der deutschen Alterthumskunde von L. Weiland. Sonderabdruck aus der Festgabe für Georg Hanssen. Tübingen, 1889.

Weyhe in *Engl. Stud.* König Ongentheows Fall. In *Engl. Stud.* xxxix, 14–39.

Wülker, *Grdr.* Grundriss zur Geschichte der Angelsächsischen Litteratur. Leipzig, 1885. Particularly pp. 244-346: Angelsächsische Heldendichtung.

Zeuss. Die Deutschen und die Nachbarstämme, von K. Zeuss München, 1837.

(B) "MAURUNGANI" AND THE "GEOGRAPHER OF RAVENNA."

The "geographer" divides the points of the compass into twenty-four hours, twelve northern (of the night), and twelve southern (of the day). Following this arrangement, we have first the land of the Germans (Franks) with Britain beyond: then the land of the Frisians, then of the Saxons, then of the Northmen or Danes, with the Elbe country in front (of old called *Maurungani*). Then come the Scridefinni, then Scythia. We have thus travelled through six hours, i.e. ninety degrees. The text runs :

Prima ut hora noctis Germanorum est patria quæ modo a Francis dominatur...cujus post terga infra Oceanum prædicta insula Britania.... Secunda ut hora noctis ex parte ipsa Germania vel Frixonum Dorostates est patria...Tertia ut hora noctis Saxonum est patria...Quarta ut hora noctis Northomanorum est patria, quæ et Dania ab antiquis dicitur, cujus ad frontem Alpes [*read* Albes] vel patria Albis : Maurungani certissime antiquitus dicebatur, in qua Albis patria per multos annos Francorum linea remorata est, et ad frontem ejusdem Albis Datia minor dicitur, et dehinc super ex latere magna et spatiosa Datia dicitur, quæ modo Gipidia ascribuntur, in qua nunc Unorum gens habitare dinoscitur....Quinta ut hora noctis Scirdifrinorum vel Rerefenorum est patria. Sexta ut hora noctis Scytharum est patria, unde Sclavinorum exorta est prosapia[1].

The second mention of [? *Maur*]*ungani* comes in Chapter iv, § 18, between the description of Saxony (§ 17) and Pannonia (§ 19).

Item ad partem quasi meridianam, quomodo a spatiosissima dicatur terra, est patria quæ dicitur Albis [......]ungani, montuosa per longum, quasi ad orientem multum extenditur, cujus aliqua pars Baias dicitur....Haec patria habet non modica flumina, inter cetera fluvius grandis qui dicitur Albis et Bisigibilias sexaginta quæ in Oceano funduntur.

Baias is apparently Bohemia. For the unintelligible *Bisigibilias*

---

[1] *Ravennatis anonymi cosmographia*, ed. Pinder and Parthey, Berolini, 1860, pp. 27, 28 (§ i, 11).

sexaginta it has been proposed to read *Visurgi et alia sexaginta*. Müllenhoff supposes it to be a corruption of *Bisila* and *Biaduas*, the Vistula and the Oder. (See his *Beovulf*, p. 100.)

The derivation of *Mauringa, Maurungani* must remain unsettled. It may mean the swampy moor land, from a root connected with O.H.G. *mios*, English *moss* and *mire* (quite distinct from English *moor*[1]). Other suggestions have been made, but they are mere guesses. Thus it is proposed to derive the name from the root *maur*, an ant, on the following grounds : Mauringa was in historic times left desert by its inhabitants : they must have left the land because they were uncomfortable, and presumably overcrowded, the land was therefore called derisively " the ant heap "[2]. Heinzel, after weighing this etymology and finding it wanting[3], proposes one, if possible, even more far-fetched. The Burgundians, according to a Roman historian, knew themselves to have been of old of Roman stock[4] : hence perhaps they were of darker hue than the West Germanic folk[5]. Now the Burgundians lived at one time east of the Elbe ; hence the land east of the Elbe may have been inhabited by darker people, and hence have derived its name from the Latin *Maurus*, a Moor, assuming this word to have been early known in Germany—for which evidence is lacking.

(C) EASTGOTA.

Against the historical existence of Ostrogotha may be urged:

(1) His name, which looks mythical and eponymous, like King Dan of the Danes, Hwicca of the Hwicce.

(2) The lack of satisfactory contemporary evidence.

But (1) On the other hand, we should expect Ostrogotha, if eponymous, to come at the head of the pedigree. Only his having been an historical character can account for his name coming so far down in the list. We cannot pronounce a German chief mythical because his name seems strangely appropriate to his career. It was intended that it should be so, when he was named. The names *Airmanareiks, Alareiks, Thiudareiks, Gaisareiks* exactly fit the conquerors who bore them. An heir to the throne, born perhaps when national feeling was running high, might well have been named *The Ostrogoth*. Theodoric named one of his

---

[1] Zeuss (p. 472), Bluhme (p. 23), and Müllenhoff (*Nordalb. Stud.* i 140–41) suggested this meaning : but they wished to connect with *moor* (O.H.G. *muor*), which is linguistically impossible. See Müllenhoff, *D.A.* ii, 97 ; *Beovulf*, 102 ; Bruckner, 107 ; and cf. Ettmüller (₁) 11.

[2] This etymology was hinted at by Müllenhoff, *D.A.* 97, and has been seriously adopted by Kossinna.

[3] *Ostgotische Heldensage*, 24.

[4] Ammianus, xxviii, 5, 11.

[5] A most perilous assumption : for even if the Burgundians did boast of a Roman origin, there is no reason for thinking that there was more ethnographical truth in this than in the Trojan origin of the British.

daughters *Ostrogotho*[1]. An historic Gepid prince was named *Ostrogothus*[2], which is more difficult to account for.

(2) Whilst Jordanes and Cassiodorus are late in date, they are remarkably consistent in their notice of Ostrogotha. Reckoning back the generations of the Amal pedigree, we should expect to find him where we actually do meet him, about the middle of the third century. There seems then every reason to accept Ostrogotha as an historical figure; and this has been done without demur by Gibbon[3], Dahn[4], Müllenhoff[5] and Hodgkin[6].

Schütte, *Oldsagn*, 152–3, should however be compared.

(D) THE JUTES.

Ytum [weold] Gefwulf.

Ýtum = Early West Saxon *Íetum*, corresponding to which the Anglian or Kentish form would be *Éotum*, *Íotum*. These *Ýte*, *Íotas*, *Éote*, *Ýtan* (corresponding to a Prim. Germ. *Eutiz*, *Eutjoz*, *Eutjaniz*) are identical with the *Iutae*, *Iuti* whom Bede mentions as conquering and colonizing Kent, the Isle of Wight, and the adjacent parts of Hampshire. This is shown by the fact that:

(1) The words *Ytena* (Corpus, Camb., MS.), *Eota* (Bodleian, Cotton, Corpus Oxf., and Camb. Univ. MSS.) are used to render *Iutarum* in the Old English version of Bede's *History*, IV, 16, *ea (gens) quæ usque hodie in prouincia Occidentalium Saxonum Iutarum natio nominatur, posita contra ipsam insulam Vectam.*

(2) The neighbourhood of the New Forest was known as *Ytene* [i.e. *Ytena land*] till at least the twelfth century. Florence of Worcester speaks of William Rufus as having been slain *in Nova Foresta quæ lingua Anglorum Ytene nuncupatur*, and again *in prouincia Jutarum in Nova Foresta* (Florentii Wigorn. *Chron.*, ed. Thorpe, II, 45; I, 276). Traces of the name are perhaps to be found in *Ytingstoc* (Bishop's Stoke near Southampton—Birch, *Cart. Sax.* III, 1054; cf. Binz in *P.B.B.*, XX, 185). It is clear, then, that the Hampshire Jutae were known as *Ýte* (or perhaps *Ýtas*, *Ýtan*): and we have Bede's evidence that these were the same race as the Kentish folk (I, 15).

(3) *Iotum*, *Iutna* is used to translate *Iutis*, *Iutarum* in the passage inserted in the *A.-S. Chronicle* (derived from Bede, I, 15).

On the other hand, in the O.E. Bede, *Iutarum* in I, 15 is translated by

---

[1] Jordanes, ed. Mommsen, cap. LVIII.
[2] Οὐστρίγοτθος. Procopius, *Bell. Gott.* IV, 27.
[3] I, 245. Gibbon does not mention Ostrogotha by name, but accepts as historical Jordanes' account of the campaign.
[4] *Könige der Germanen*, II, 1861, p. 54; *Allgemeine Deutsche Biographie*, XXIV.
[5] *Z.f.d.A.* IX, 136.
[6] *Italy*, I, 48.

Geata, which has led to the theory that the Jutlanders and the Jutish conquerors of England are to be identified with the Geatas of *Beowulf*. Fahlbeck, who holds this view, supposes the name *Yte* to be derived from *Vecta*, and to have been merely the name adopted by the Jutish settlers in the Isle of Wight and on the adjoining coast : it was only later, he thinks, that the word *Yte* came to be regarded as synonymous with all Jutae, and thus became applicable also to the Kentishmen (see Fahlbeck, *Beovulfsqvädet*, 46–48). This theory is hardly tenable ; we should have to locate Gefwulf and his Yte in England, and attribute to the catalogue of kings in *Widsith* a date and character quite different from that to which all the other evidence points. For the kings in this catalogue all belong to the continental hero cycles of the fourth to the sixth centuries, not to the insular English cycles of the seventh. The Yte of *Widsith* are almost certainly a continental people, as is shown by their being grouped with Wærnas, Eowan and Frisians.

Fahlbeck's view is unsatisfactory, for it is based upon one passage in the O.E. Bede, where *Jutarum* is rendered *Geata*, whilst it is refuted by the other passage in the O.E. Bede, by the *Chronicle*, and by Florence, where *Jutarum* is translated by *Ytena*, or its Anglian or Kentish equivalent, *Eota, Iotna*. Cf. too Schück, 16–18.

We may accept, then, as fairly certain, the identification of the *Yte*, *Eotas*, with the *Iutae* of Bede. They are probably also identical with the *Eutii, Euthiones* who are mentioned as having made some kind of submission to the Frankish kings[1] in the sixth century. That these Frankish references are to the Yte dwelling on the English side of the channel, rather than to those who remained in their original continental home, has been suggested by Weiland (p. 36) and Bremer (*Zachers Z.f.d.Ph.* xxv, 130), and is quite likely.

Where this original continental home was situated is not so clear. Bede places the old Anglian country *inter provincias Iutarum et Saxonum* (I, 15), he must therefore have regarded the Iutae as dwelling north of Angel, i.e., in the modern Jutland. It has been urged by Jessen (*Undersøgelser til Nordisk Oldhistorie*, København, 1862, 55), Möller (*V.E.* 88 ; *A.f.d.A.* xxii, 159), Weiland (36), Müllenhoff (*Beowulf*, 98), and more recently by Siebs (*Pauls Grdr.* (₂) I, 1158) and Heuser (Review of Bülbring in the *Anzeiger* to the *Indogermanische Forschungen*, xiv, 1903, 26–30), that the character of the Old Kentish dialect makes Bede's statement incredible, and that Old Kentish dialectal peculiarities

[1] '...*subactis Thoringiis...cum Saxonibus, Euciis, qui se nobis voluntate propria tradiderunt.*' Letter of Theudebert to Justinian, *Epistolae Merowingici Aevi*, I, 133 in *M.G.H.* (between A.D. 534 and 547).
Quem Geta, Vasco tremunt, Danus, Euthio, Saxo, Britannus
Cum patre quos acie te domitasse patet.
Venantius Fortunatus in praise of Chilperic, about the year 580. See *Carminum* IX, 1, 73, ed. Leo, in *M.G.H. Auct. Ant.* IV, 1881.

would lead us to look for the original home of Hengest's warriors rather in Friesland than in Jutland[1]. This assertion as to the close connection between Kentish and Frisian has grown to be a dogma. (See however to the contrary Chadwick (67) and Björkman in *Engl. Stud.* xxxix, 1908, 361.) The matter needs investigation, but the coincidences between Kentish and Frisian have certainly been exaggerated, and seem insufficient without further corroboration to invalidate Bede's statement.

It has further been objected that any connection between *Ýte*, *Éotas*, *Iutae*, on the one hand, and Old Norse *Jótar* (Jutlanders, the *Iuti* of Saxo), is phonetically impossible (Möller *V.E.*, 88). But this objection arises from the assumption that the original name began with a *j*. This should, of course, be dropped in Scandinavian and represented by a *g* in Old English (cf. Goth. *juggs*, Icel. *ungr*, O.E. *geong*). It was however pointed out by P. A. Munch as long ago as 1848 that the Old Norse *Jótar*, as well as the O.E. forms, can both be traced back to a primitive form beginning not with *Ju* but with *Eu*, and that the evidence of Latin writers is that this was the original form.

Admitting this, Möller urges, as a last objection (private communication quoted by Kossinna, *I.F.* vii, 293) that at any rate the modern Danish form *Jyder*, if a pure Danish word, must go back to a form in *J* such as **Jeutiones*: it could only come from a form **Eutiones* if it were a North Frisian loan word. Undue weight seems to have been attached to this objection : for *ex hypothesi* the mod. Danish *Jyder* would *not* be a pure Danish word, and the objection therefore falls to the ground. For it is not argued that Bede's Iutae were racially identical with the modern Jutlanders, who are of Scandinavian stock: but only that the latter adopted their name from the earlier "Anglo-Frisian" inhabitants of Jutland, whose country, after the emigration of Hengest to England, they settled, and the remnants of whom they assimilated. On the Danish development of the word, see Jordan, 139.

Assuming, then, that the original name of the tribe was *Eutiz* (or *Eutjōs*, *Eutjaniz*)[2], we should get in the West Germanic dialects through the influence of the front vowel in the second syllable, *Iutiz*, etc. (cf. Wright, *Primer of Gothic*, § 61). In Bede's time the *Iu* would still be preserved in Northern English (cf. Sievers, *Zur Geschichte der ags. Diphthonge*, in *P.B.B.* xviii, 411–416), and he would write, quite correctly, *Iutae*. *Iutiz* would give Anglian *Éote*, West Saxon *Íete*, *Ýte*; whilst, on Möller's own showing, the Scandinavian tribes, borrowing the

---

[1] The holders of this view admit the possibility of the Hampshire men, of whose original dialect we know nothing, having come from Jutland ; they only deny that the Kentish men can have done so (Möller, *V.E.* 88, footnote : Müllenhoff, *Beovulf* 98). Jessen argues that the settlers of the Isle of Wight were of Scandinavian stock.

[2] Ten Brink (204) and Stevenson (167) are probably right in supposing the word an i-stem. Much (*P.B.B.* xvii, 208) suggests a jo-stem, Munch an n-stem. *Euciis*, *Yte*, point to an i-stem : *Euthio*, *Ytena* to an n-stem. Perhaps both existed side by side, cf. *Seaxan* and *Seaxe*, *Miercna* and *Mierce*.

name from West Germanic sources, would naturally alter it to O.N. *Jötar*, Danish *Jyder*.

To sum up.   (1) There is no sufficient ground for doubt that the Yte are identical with Bede's *Iuti*, *Iutae*, the conquerors of Kent, and with the *Eutii*, *Euthiones* indicated by continental authorities.

(2) Möller's attempt to prove that the original tribal name underlying all these later forms cannot be identical with that from which the name of Jutland is derived has not succeeded.   As to the original home of these Yte, we are then left on the one hand with Bede's statement that they dwelt north of the Angles, and on the other with the contention that the close similarity between the Old Kentish dialect and the Frisian speech would lead us to put the ancestors of the Kentish men in the closest proximity to Friesland.   But in the fifth century dialects hardly distinguishable may well have been spoken on all the North Sea coast, from Friesland to Jutland.   Our knowledge of the mutual relations of these tribes and of their dialects is too imperfect for us to argue with certainty.

The subject is one on which agreement will, in all probability, never be reached.   The English historian, impressed with Bede's reliability, will probably continue to repeat *his* statement, without any doubt or hesitation (cf. e.g. Sir James Ramsay's *Foundations of England*, 1898, I, 120).   Many philologists, on the other hand, will probably continue to believe that linguistic evidence makes Bede's statement incredible.   Other philologists, however, have accepted it ; e.g. Zeuss (501), Grimm (*G.D.S.*, 738), Ten Brink (*Beowulf*, 204), Much (in *P.B.B.* XVII, 209), Bremer (in Pauls *Grdr.* (₂) III, 856), Bülbring (*Altenglisches Elementarbuch*, 1902, 5). Stevenson, in his edition of Asser, 1904 (pp. 166–70), seems doubtful, and doubt has been more strongly expressed by Sarrazin (*Beowulf-Studien*, 28) and Erdmann (*Heimat der Angeln*, 40)[1].   Among those who have argued against Bede's location of the Iutae in Jutland, mention should be made, in addition to the references to Jessen, Möller, Müllenhoff, Weiland, Siebs, and Heuser, given above, to Kossinna's *Ethnologische Stellung der Ostgermanen* in *I.F.*, VII, 276, etc.

The question cannot be settled, because it depends upon the relative weight of two quantities difficult to determine, (1) Bede's reliability in dealing with events which occurred more than two centuries before his birth, (2) the extent to which we are justified in arguing, granting the disputed similarity of Kentish and Frisian in historic times, that four centuries before those times the ancestors of these peoples must *necessarily* have been *immediate* neighbours.   To the present writer it seems that, whilst the evidence upon which Bede based his statement that the Iutae

---

[1] Cf. also Erdmann, *Om folknamnen Götar och Goter*, in the *A.T.f.S.* XI, 4, 19–24.

dwelt north of the Angles *may* have been insufficient, the evidence by which it is sought to refute this statement indubitably *is* insufficient, and that Bede's statement accordingly holds the field.

Those who would make the Jutes originally neighbours of the Frisians are not agreed whether to put them on the north-eastern border (Siebs in *Pauls Grdr.* (₂) I, 1157) or on the south-west, in the Netherlands (Möller, Heuser). Hoops' suggestion that the Jutes may have come from Jutland in the first instance, but may have settled temporarily in the Netherlands (*Waldbäume*, 585), is an ingenious compromise, which derives considerable support from the fact that there is some evidence that the Angles and Saxons attacked Britain from such temporary settlements in the Netherlands[1]. (See Note E : *The original homes of the Angli.*)

(E) THE ORIGINAL HOMES OF THE ANGLI AND VARINI (ENGLE AND WÆRNAS).

The current view, that the original home of the Angles is to be sought in and around the modern Schleswig, rests upon the assertion of Bede[2] that the Angles came from Angel, and the apparently independent, because slightly dissimilar, statement of Alfred. The A.S. Chronicle, Ethelwerd, and William of Malmesbury, depend upon Bede ; but the reference to the *Insula Oghgul* in the *Historia Brittonum* is probably independent and corroborative. As has been pointed out above, it is clear that the *Widsith* poet regards the Angles as a people dwelling in the neighbourhood of Schleswig. For the poem makes Offa king of Ongel defend his frontier at Fifeldor—the river Eider. If it can be proved that the Angles came, not from the neighbourhood of Schleswig, but from the interior of Germany, then we must abandon any belief in *Widsith* as in the main early or authoritative, although we might still hold that it incorporated early fragments.

It was Zeuss who first dismissed the connection of the Angles with Angel as a piece of false etymology, resting upon the gossip of sailors. Zeuss placed the home of the Angles on the lower Saale[3]. To this conclusion he was led, partly by the many undoubted traces of the existence of Anglian or kindred tribes in the Saale neighbourhood[4], and partly by

---

[1] In a discussion of the Jutes it is better to leave out of the question
  (1) the *Eudoses* of Tacitus. These *may* be identical with the Eutii, Iutae, Yte (as Müllenhoff supposed, *Nordalb. Stud.* I, 112–119, though he afterwards abandoned the view). But if they are, the *d*, *Eudoses*, not *Eut-*, remains inexplicable.
  (2) the **Eotenas* mentioned in the Finnesburh lay in *Beowulf.* Holder, in his *Beowulf* (128), and others have wished to connect these with the Eotas-Iutae. But this needs investigation.
[2] See above, p. 74.   [3] p. 496.
[4] Since strengthened : cf. Bremer in *P.B.B.* IX, 579.

the desire which he often betrays of making his geography square with that of Ptolemy[1]. In view of the authority of Zeuss, whose work on early German geography is still what Kemble declared it to be—indispensable— and of the fact that the most elaborate investigation of the origin of the Angles, that of Axel Erdmann[2], endorses his view, it ought not to be assumed without investigation that the location of King Offa given in *Widsith* is necessarily correct.

As to the arguments which led Zeuss to place the Angles in the centre of Germany: it is certain that there was a settlement, on the Saale, in the neighbourhood of the modern Merseburg and Leipzic, of a people at any rate closely akin to the Angles, speaking a dialect similar to that of the Angles and Frisians. The *Merseburg Glosses*[3] written down at the beginning of the eleventh century, and still preserved in the Cathedral library at Merseburg, show traces of the "Anglo-Frisian" peculiarities. So do the forms of the German proper names adopted by the local chronicler, Dietmar von Walbeck, whose history, compiled about the same time that the glosses were written, and extant in a MS. partly written, partly revised, by himself, is valuable evidence as to the dialect of the district in the 10th century. Further, the old names of the districts, *Engelin, Werinofeld*, near Merseburg, point, not merely to a general "Anglo-Frisian" element in the population, but to the settlement here, on the borders of Thuringia, of bodies of Angles and Varini. In two places in the neighbourhood of Leipzic the name *Wernsdorf* survives to this day[4].

But whilst admitting this settlement of Anglo-Frisian people in the inland districts, it would require the very heaviest evidence before we could agree with Zeuss and Erdmann in making this the original home of the Angles, from which they conquered England. Such a theory is, we have seen, opposed to the express evidence of Bede, Alfred, and the *Historia Brittonum*. To make the Angles an inland people is also opposed to the evidence of Tacitus, who makes them share in the worship of Nerthus on an isle of the ocean; as well as to the evidence of *Beowulf*, which places Offa I betwixt the seas, *be sæm tweonum*. Zeuss' theory is indeed, if we may say so without disrespect to the memory of so great a scholar, contrary to common sense. To give a radius of over two hundred miles to the area of marsh and forest which had to be covered by the car of the goddess Nerthus is surely grossly to over-estimate the powers

---

[1] Cf. Müllenhoff's criticism of Zeuss in the *Nordalb. Stud.* I, 112.

[2] *Ueber die Heimat und den Namen der Angeln*, Upsala, 1890. So too Steenstrup in *Danmarks Riges Historie*, I, 76–77.

[3] Edited by H. Leyser in the *Z.f.d.A.* III, 280; and again by Bezzenberger, *Z.f.d.Ph.* VI, 291. Heyne (*Kleinere Altniederdeutsche Denkmäler*) first noticed the close dialectal resemblance of Dietmar's proper names to the glosses; and Bremer (*P.B.B.* IX, 579) first identified the dialect as "Anglo-Frisian." See also Seelmann, *Thietmar von Merseburg, die Merseburger Glossen und das Merseburger Totenbuch*, in *J.d.V.f.n.S.* XII, 89.

[4] Schröder, *Lehrbuch der deutschen Rechtsgeschichte*, 3te Auf. 1898, p. 244.

of the primitive Germanic cow. Besides, it seems incredible that the men who sailed across the North Sea to conquer England should have come, not from the opposite coast, but from a district more than two hundred miles inland. Erdmann seeks to surmount this last difficulty by supposing that the Angles may have been accustomed to use the Elbe for communication (pp. 23–31). But can example be found anywhere of an inland folk, even if settled upon a great river, having chosen the calling of sea-robbers ? Erdmann[1] quotes the Heruli with their ravaging of the Aegean and Euxine coast. But this is not parallel, for whatever be the origin of the Heruli, they were probably in the first place a sea folk[2]. The nearest instance would be that of Gaiseric and his Vandals. They were certainly landsmen, yet, after their conquest of Carthage, they made themselves dreaded throughout the whole Mediterranean. But, in Carthage, Gaiseric had won one of the four great ports of the ancient world, with all its ships, docks, galley slaves and pilots[3]. The case is therefore not parallel ; for the men who conquered England had to rely upon their own seamanship ; and they needed more seamanship than was required to row a dug-out down the Elbe, before they could conduct a campaign across the North Sea.

Again, the character of the Anglian speech, with its affinities to Frisian and to Scandinavian, would be unintelligible on the hypothesis of Zeuss. (Cf. Jordan, *Eigentümlichkeiten des anglischen Wortschatzes*, 1906, 114 ; Jordan in *Verhandlungen*, 139–140 ; Möller in *A.f.d.A.* xxii, 147, *etc.*)

Yet the evidence for placing the original home of the Angles on the Saale, near Merseburg, so far from being of the overwhelming kind necessary to overcome difficulties like these, is of the very slenderest. It rests solely upon the words of Ptolemy :

"The greatest of the tribes dwelling in the interior are the tribe of the Sueboi Aggeiloi, who lie east of the Laggobardoi, stretching towards the north as far as the middle of the river Elbe ; and the tribe of the Sueboi Semnones, who extend from that portion of the river Elbe eastwards[4]."

By the Suevi Angili Ptolemy pretty clearly means the Angles (for the Angles, according to Tacitus, formed with the Langobardi and the Semnones part of the great Suevic confederation). The Suevi Langobardi have already been located by Ptolemy below the Sygambri on the Rhine : whilst the seats of the Semnones we know from abundant evidence. Ptolemy's *Sueboi Aggeiloi*, between these two, would still be fifty miles distant from the

---

[1] p. 32.
[2] *Dani Herulos propriis sedibus expulerunt*, Jordanes iii. See note to *Eolum* (l. 87).
[3] See Gibbon, ed. Bury, iii, 410.
[4] τῶν δὲ ἐντὸς καὶ μεσογείων ἐθνῶν μέγιστα μέν ἐστι τό τε τῶν Συήβων τῶν Αγγειλῶν, οἵ εἰσιν ἀνατολικώτεροι τῶν Λαγγοβάρδων ἀνατείνοντες πρὸς τὰς ἄρκτους μέχρι τῶν μέσων τοῦ Ἄλβιος ποταμοῦ, καὶ τὸ τῶν Συήβων τῶν Σεμνόνων, οἵτινες διήκουσι μετὰ ,τὸν Ἄλβιν ἀπὸ τοῦ εἰρημένου μέρους πρὸς ἀνατολὰς μέχρι τοῦ Συήβου ποταμοῦ.... *Geographia* ii, 11, 8.

district of Merseburg and Leipzig. This essential point is overlooked by Erdmann, who speaks as if the account of Ptolemy (and, indeed, of Tacitus) placed the Angles on the Elbe and Saale (p. 24). Yet nearer than fifty miles no amount of stretching of Ptolemy's words will bring them ; for the Merseburg district is south, not west, of the ancient home of the Semnones.

But, further, Ptolemy is here so confused and uncertain that he has puzzled generations of scholars. The explanation given by a recent editor, Müller, seems convincing[1]. Ptolemy, it must be remembered, accurate and well informed on the whole as he was, wrote in Egypt, compiling his notes of German geography from various more or less imperfect statements. He knew, and reported quite correctly, that the Angles dwelt N.E. of the Lombards : but as to the Lombards he failed to reconcile his authorities. Under the name of the Λακκοβαρδοι he placed them quite rightly "next to the Angrivarii," i.e. on the left bank of the lower Elbe. But meeting them, in some other record, described as the *Suevi Langobardi*—he did not recognize them as the same people. He could not put these *Suevi Lango-bardi* in their right place, which he was reserving for their shadows, the *Laccobardi*. Consequently they are misplaced, on the right bank of the Rhine ; and this, in turn, leads inevitably to a dislocation of the *Suevi Angili*, whose position is defined with reference to the *Suevi Langobardi*.

Yet just because in the second century a puzzled Egyptian geographer failed to unravel the truth from conflicting accounts, we must not give the lie to Bede and Alfred. When we adopt Müller's explanation, and perceive that the *Laccobardi* and the *Suevi Langobardi* are one and the same, the Angles drop at once into the right place, N.E. of the Lombards, and consequently on the sea coast, in conformity with the evidence of Tacitus, Bede, Alfred, *Beowulf*, and the *Historia Brittonum*.

But though Ptolemy's evidence for an original Anglian home in central Germany falls, on examination, to the ground, the linguistic evidence, as we have seen, and the evidence of place names proves that there *was* some kind of a settlement of Anglian and kindred tribes on the banks of the Saale, on the northern borders of the ancient Thuringia. How this settlement came about we do not know[2], but we seem to catch a glimpse of these

---

[1] See Claudii Ptolemaei *Geographia*, ed. C. Müllerus I, 1, 258. Paris, Didot, 1883. " E boreali illa regione Anglos in mediam Germaniam penetrasse, aut priscas eorum sedes ibi ad mediam Albim fuisse, e Ptolemæo multi collegerunt, quem ego hoc quoque loco falsa exhibere censeo. Recte quidem Ptolemæus Angilos a Langobardis ortum et boream versus collocaverit, sed quemadmodum Langobardi isti ponendi erant eo in loco ubi Laccobardos posuit, sic etiam Angli a Laccobardis s. Langobardis ortum boreamque versus inter hos et Saxones, collocandi fuerint." Cf. also Müllenhoff on Ptolemy in *Nordalb. Stud.* I, 112 ; and *Z.f.d.A.* IX, 233.

[2] The obvious conjecture is that of an immigration of Engle and Wærnas from the districts nearer the mouth of the Elbe, in perhaps the fifth century— hardly earlier, as the immigration must have taken place *after* the Anglo-Frisian idiosyncracies had become marked. See Bremer in *P.B.B.* IX, 579. Seelmann (p. 90) denies the immigration so far as the Angles are concerned,

"Thuringian" Angles and Varini once about the year 500, and again about the year 800.

(1) Amongst Cassiodorus' *Variæ*[1] there is extant a letter from Theodoric, the Ostrogoth, to the kings of the Heruli, Warni, and Thuringi, suggesting an alliance. Clovis, king of the Franks, was at this time pressing hard upon Theodoric's friends and allies, the Visigoths, and it was Theodoric's aim to bring about a coalition which should prevent him pursuing his aggressive schemes.

(2) There is also a code of laws, dating probably from the time of Charles the Great, three centuries after Theodoric's letter, which bears the superscription *Lex Angliorum et Werinorum hoc est Thuringorum*. This "Law of the Thuringian Angles and Varini" is said by students of comparative Germanic law to show traces of kinship with English, and particularly with Kentish law ; but in the main it has taken the form impressed upon it by the Frankish influence under which it has passed[2].

(3) Further confirmation of the settlement of the Varini (Wærnas) in ancient North Thuringia has been found in the frequent occurrence of place names ending in *leben* within that district. This form is not found elsewhere in Germany till we come to Schleswig, where it occurs in the form *lev*. This fact, when first pointed out[3], was taken to support the theory of an Anglian settlement in Thuringia. But it has been shown more recently that it is only in *Northern* Schleswig that the names in *lev* are found, and that they extend over all modern Denmark, and, in the form *löf*, over parts of the southern coast of Sweden[4]. In Angeln and the islands immediately adjoining these names are *not* found : and they are found only rarely in England. These place names then point, in all probability, to settlements, not of the Angles *proper* but of their northern neighbours, Varini and Jutes. The occasional occurrence of English place names in *lew, læw* is to be attributed to settlements of Jutes and Wærnas in England.

We, may, then, take it as certain that there was, from at least the early sixth to the early ninth century, upon the northern borders of Thuringia, a semi-independent kingdom of the Wærnas, and, adjoining it, settlements of the Engle and Heruli.

Unfortunately, the question of the home of these "Thuringian" Angli and Varini has been complicated by the fact that there were two Thuringias : the great kingdom in central Germany, and a smaller Thoringia near the

---

and regards the Saale-Angles as ancient inhabitants of the country, not immigrants from Schleswig. But this is contrary to probability, and rests merely upon Ptolemy's statement as to Angles in the neighbourhood (and certainly not the immediate neighbourhood) in the second century.

[1] III, 3.   [2] Chadwick, 81, 108.

[3] By P. Cassel, *Ueber Thüringische Ortsnamen*, Erfurt, 1856 (*Berichte der Erfurter Akademie*).

[4] See Seelmann, *Die Ortsnamenendung "leben," J.d.V.f.n.S.* XII, 7–27. It is conceivable, though hardly likely, that this type of place name cropped up independently in the different districts, as Erdmann suggests (p. 57).

mouth of the Rhine, in the neighbourhood of the modern Dordrecht[1]. Hence arose the theory that the Anglii and Werini referred to in the *Lex*, and the Guarni and Thoringi addressed by Theodoric, dwelt in the Netherlands[2]. A further development of this theory would make these Netherland Angles the source of the English name. According to this view, settlers from the Anglian nation at the mouth of the Rhine may have taken part in the invasion of England in sufficient quantities to have given their name to parts of the conquered country, and it may be to them rather than to any connection with the Angel in Schleswig that the name of England is due[3].

Now here we must discriminate carefully. That there were in the Netherlands settlements, small or great, of Engle and Wærnas, of Saxons and Jutes, is possible enough ; and from the shores of the Low Country many of the attacking fleets may have set out. But this does not help us with regard to the *original* home of the Engle and Wærnas, for the statements of Ptolemy and Tacitus make it quite clear that Angli and Varini were not settled in the Netherlands in the first and second centuries. These Angles of the Low Countries must then have been immigrants from an older home, wherever that home may have been. But that the Warni to whom Theodoric wrote, and the Anglii and Werini of the Lex, may have dwelt in the Netherlands, and that these may have been intimately connected with the settlers in England, is possible enough. Direct evidence, it is true, is wanting. For the Angles there is none, beyond a corrupt passage in Adam of Bremen[4], who in any case is an authority too late to count for much in the period we are considering.

---

[1] See note to *þyringum* (ll. 30, 86).

[2] This theory was first advanced by H. Müller (*Der Lex Salica und der Lex Angliorum et Werinorum Alter und Heimat*, 1840, pp. 120 and 121). Müller was followed by P. C. Molhuysen, *De Anglen in Nederland*, in the *Bijdragen voor Vaderlandsche Geschiedenis en Oudheidkunde*, III, pp. 50–72 (1842). Waitz tentatively approved this conjecture (*Das alte Recht der Salischen Franken*, 1846, p. 50).

Arguments against the theory of an Anglian settlement in the Netherlands will be found in a review of Müller's work by the Freiherr v. Richthofen in the *Kritische Jahrbücher für deutsche Rechtswissenschaft*, 1841, pp. 996–1018. See especially p. 1015, with its very reasonable warning against drawing any conclusion from the occurrence of small isolated places compounded with the name Engel. "In a district where the bulk of the population were Angles, a single spot would hardly be called by their name." Mr Inman has plausibly suggested that "the occurrence of *Aengil—Engel*—in relation to places in Belgium and Holland (Felwe, Ghent, Texandria, Texel, Tournay, Utrecht) is possibly in connection with Anglian missions of the 7th or 8th century."

[3] "Ved Rinmundingerne bode Angler med Varner, altså hærfølger udgåede fra Anglerne og Varnerne inde i Tyskland. Hövdinger herfra i ledtog med de egenlige Sakser (Friser) kunde flytte Angle-navnet til England." *Undersøgelser til Nordisk Oldhistorie* af C. A. E. Jessen, København, 1862, p. 51. But Jessen thinks it more likely that the name sprang up independently in England.

[4] *Igitur Saxones primo circa Renum sedes habebant* [*et vocati sunt Angli*], Adam of Bremen, I, 3, ed. Lappenberg in Pertz (fol.), *SS.* VII, p. 285. The words are wanting in the best MS. and were accordingly bracketed by the editor. Indeed "they can hardly be taken seriously" (Chadwick, p. 111).

For the Wærnas we have the statement of Procopius that the Rhine divides the Varini from the Franks[1]; but Procopius' ideas as to the geography of these regions are confused in the extreme. The strongest evidence is of an indirect nature. Thus, it has been urged[2] that the Old English loan words from the Latin are, on the one hand, of a kind which could not have been borrowed in the remote continental home in Schleswig, but that, on the other hand, they show such close relationship to continental loan words as to preclude the possibility of their having been borrowed subsequent to the settlement in Britain, and that consequently the Angles must have been settled for some time in a continental home subject to Latin influence. So that it is quite possible that those scholars are right who believe that there were large settlements of Engle and Wærnas in the Netherlands[3]: it is certain that there were also such settlements far inland, on the upper Elbe and Saale. But that neither of these could have been the original home of the Angles is clear from the evidence of Tacitus alone, had we nothing more. " We may boldly maintain that in these dark ages no similar fact is better attested than the origin of the English Angles from Angel in Schleswig[4]." In these words the controversy was summed up some twenty years ago ; and though in every generation some good scholar revives the heresy of Zeuss, and brings his Angles from the inland, none have yet succeeded in finding any satisfactory justification for this eccentric view.

Here then, as in every other point of old Germanic tradition where we are able to control him, we find the poet of *Widsith* to be well informed.

[1] *B.G.* IV, 20. See note to *Wernum* (l. 25).

[2] Hoops' *Waldbäume u. Kulturpflanzen* (esp. Kap. XIV, *Die kontinentale Heimat der Angelsachsen und die römische Kultur*, 566–589).

[3] Müllenhoff in *Nordalb. Stud.* I, 130–133, 1844, accepted Müller's view of Anglian settlements in the Netherlands : so did Möller (*V.E.* 18). Möller's arguments in favour of England having been invaded from the Netherlands will be found in *A.f.d.A.* XXII, 152. Bremer, in *Pauls Grdr.* (₂) II, 854, also places the *Lex Angliorum* in the Netherlands, and supposes the advance guard of the Angles to have had their base there, though the bulk of their later followers were drawn from Schleswig. On the other hand, that the *Lex* belongs to the Angles of the Elbe and Saale is urged by many scholars. Schroeder (*Lehrbuch der deutschen Rechtsgeschichte*, 1902, p. 248) regards this as the only tenable view. Though the *Lex* must belong to one or the other locality, there is nothing inconsistent in supposing that there were settlements of Engle and Wærnas *both* in the Thoringia of the Netherlands *and* in the main Thuringia (so Erdmann, *Heimat der Angeln*, p. 28). That the evidence of loan words points to Saxons and Jutes having invaded England from the lower Rhine has also been argued by Heuser, *I.F.* XIV, *Anzeiger*, p. 30 (1903).

[4] Weiland, *Die Angeln*, 1889, p. 18.

(F) ISTE.

The *Iste* are apparently identical with the *Aestii* of Tacitus. What were the linguistic and racial affinities of these *Aestii* is not certain, but their situation is fixed. They dwelt on the "Amber Coast" of the Baltic, which extends from the Frische Haff in East Prussia in a north-easterly direction over the frontier into the "Baltic Provinces" of Russia. Tacitus describes the Aestii as being, in their religious rites and dress, like the Suevi, and though he notes that their tongue resembles the British, he classes them among the Germans. They gather amber on the coast *sed et mare scrutantur, ac soli omnium sucinum quod ipsi glesum vocant inter vada atque in ipso littore legunt....Ipsis in nullo usu, rude legitur, informe perfertur, pretiumque mirantes accipiunt*[1].

In a letter of Cassiodorus (*Hestis Theodericus rex*[2]) the Hesti are thanked by the Gothic king for a gift of amber, and edified by his minister with much information as to its nature, which Cassiodorus has taken out of the *Germania*. The Aesti are also mentioned by Jordanes as occupying the sea coast a little to the east of the Vistula : he characterizes them as *pacatum hominum genus*, and mentions them as having formed part of Ermanaric's empire[3].

The correct form of the word in Latin writers is uncertain : the MSS. of Tacitus fluctuate : apparently we should read *Aestii*, the *Ae* representing, as often, a Germanic *Ai* (Kluge in Pauls *Grdr.* (2) I, 357). Einhard calls them *Aisti, Haisti* (*Vita Caroli* in Pertz (fol.), *SS.* II, 449). The Gothic form of the name would be probably **Aistjus*, pointing to a Prim. Germ. *Aisteyes*[4]; or perhaps Gothic **Aisteis*[5]. With these Gothic forms the Icel. *Eistir*[6] would agree : the corresponding English form would be **Æste*, which however is nowhere found.

Two forms of the word are found in the O.E. Orosius. (1) *Osti*, a form no doubt borrowed from the Germans of the Continent and due to false analogy with *ōst*, "east"[7]. (2) *Este*, the form used in the account of Wulfstan's voyage. It has even been supposed by some scholars[8] that

---

[1] *Germania*, XLV.   [2] *Variae*, V, 2.

[3] *Aestorum quoque similiter nationem, qui longissimam ripam Oceani Germanici insident, idem ipse prudentia et uirtute subegit* (ed. Mommsen, XXIII).

[4] Cf. Erdmann, p. 90 ; Müllenhoff, *D.A.* II, 13.

[5] Grimm, *G.D.S.* 719 (fourth ed. 500).

[6] But note that the *Eistir* of the sagas do not occupy the same country as the *Aestii* of Tacitus. These Eistir live far to the north of the "Amber Coast," in the modern province of Esthonia. That the O.N. *Eistland* is limited to Esthonia and did not include the neighbouring Courland or Livonia is clear. Cf. *Hjá Garðaríki liggja lönd þessi....Eistland, Lífland, Kúrland. (Annotations géographiques tirées du livre de Hauk Erlendsen* in *Antiquités russes*, II, 438.)

[7] Cf. Müllenhoff, *D.A.* II, 13. The Baltic is called in the Orosius the *Ost-Sæ*.

[8] e.g. Latham in his edition of the *Germania*, 1851, 166, etc. ; Bielenstein, 300, 373.

the word means "Easterlings," the Eastern folk ; but that there is any original etymological connection with "east" is impossible, in view of the Latin forms (*Aist-* never *Aust-*), and of the fact that the Icelandic sagas generally give the form *Eistland*, only exceptionally *Eystland* (see *Fornaldar Sögur*, 1829, I, 509). But that a popular etymology sprang up, connecting Esth and East, is clear ; such an etymology would be almost inevitable in view of such constantly recurring phrases as "Esthland in the East." (Cf. *Fornm. S.* IV, 162 ; VIII, 272.)

The same false etymology accounts, as has been stated, for the O.E. form *Osti*, and apparently for *Este* as well. It also accounts for our not finding the phonetically correct form *Æste* (< *Ástiz*), but instead the form in our text, *Iste* (< *Íeste* < *Éastiz*).

With regard to the racial affinities of the Aestii : Grimm, following Tacitus, supposed them to have been Germans, and claimed in support of his theory that in *Widsith* the Iste are mentioned together with German tribes. This argument, however, is based upon an interpretation of *Eolas* and *Idumingas* which is doubtful in the first case, and almost certainly wrong in the second. Erdmann also (p. 93) supposes the Aestii to have been *originally* a Gothic stock, whence the embassy to Theodoric the Goth[1]. Both Grimm and Erdmann admit that this German stock was later swamped by Finnish and Lithuanian elements, which appropriated to themselves the name of the original German tribe[2]. More generally, however, it has been supposed that the Aestii were from the beginning either Finnish or Lithuanian[3]. According to Bremer they were Finnish[4], but the greater number of scholars have agreed in regarding them as members of that Lithuanian family which to this day occupies the country where we first meet with the Aestii of Tacitus or Cassiodorus. "On this Baltic coast," says Zeuss, "has dwelt through the centuries a race which must be distinguished from both its neighbours (Germans and Slavs) and which, through all the great movements which have taken place around it, has spread but a little over its original borders. This race is commonly called, from one of its branches, the Lithuanian. Its true collective name is that of the Aestii[5]." Accordingly a certain group

[1] But, if such a kinship had existed, is it not likely that some reference would have been made to it in Theodoric's letter of thanks?
[2] It is clear that when Wulfstan visited the Este their language and customs were not German.
[3] As Tacitus can only have known the Aestii by repute, his statement that their speech was British is of little positive value ; yet it serves to show that they must have differed in speech from their German neighbours.
[4] *Pauls Grdr.* (₂) III, 753 ; cf. also Bremer's review of Müllenhoff's *D.A.* in the *Litteraturblatt f. germ. u. rom. Philol.*, 1888, 436 ; Kossinna, *Zeitschrift für Ethnologie*, XXXIV, 214, etc. Much (*Hoops Reallexikon*, 54) argues from the particulars given by Tacitus that the Aestii must have been Lithuanians, not Finns.
[5] See Zeuss, 268, and cf. Müllenhoff, *D.A.* II, 11–34.

of writers have used the word *Aistisch* as the general term for this
Lithuanian family. Yet it is not certain that the Aestii were not
Finns : and it *is* certain that in modern times, through the Norse
Eistir, the word *Esth, Esthonian*, has come to signify a non-Lithuanian
folk, more nearly allied to the Finns. *Probably* the name has been
transferred from the Lithuanians to those tribes north of them who are
now called Esths. But we cannot be certain.

If the word was at one time supposed by the Scandinavians to signify
"Eastern men" we can the more easily understand how it lost its racial
signification, and came to be transferred by them from one eastern people
to another, from the Lithuanians of the Amber Coast to the Finnish
tribes of Esthonia.

The problem of the racial affinities of the Aestii is necessarily bound
up with the larger question whether the present Baltic Provinces of
Russia were, in the early centuries of our era, inhabited by a Livonian
(Finnish) or a Lithuanian or Lettish (Indo-Germanic) people. A summary
of this controversy, with full references, will be found in Bielenstein, *Die
Grenzen des Lettischen Volksstammes*, St Petersburg, 1892, 348–378.

The probability is, then, that O.E. form *Iste* is due to false analogy
with East ; that it refers to the Aestii, and that the Iste, Aestii were a
Lithuanian people. But we cannot be certain.

(G) IDUMINGAS.

J. Grimm (*G.D.S.*, 500) suggested the emendation *Eodingum*, which he
interpreted as the Iuthungi, recorded by Idatius and other chroniclers.
(See Hydatii *Continuatio* in Mommsen's *Chronica Minora* [A.D. 430],
Iuthungi per eum [*Aetium*] *debellantur* ; and cf. Zeuss, 312–314.)
Grimm would further identify these *Eodingas* with the [N]uithones of
Tacitus. He abandoned this conjecture, however, preferring to identify
the *Idumingas* with the *Ydumaei* ("Idumingum rechtfertigt sich durch
die Ydumei bei Zeuss, 682," a MS. note of Grimm's, incorporated by
Müllenhoff in the posthumous edition of the *G.D.S.*, 1867).

These *Ydumaei* are mentioned in the Chronicle of Henry of Ymera
(cf. Henrici *Chronicon Lyvoniae* ex rec. W. Arndt, Hannoverae, 1874 ;
Heinrich's von Lettland *Livländische Chronik*, übersetzt von E. Pabst,
especially the footnote to p. 77). The identification of the *Idumingas*
with the *Ydumaei* had been made by Ettmüller in 1839 (see pp. 24–5),
and later, perhaps independently, by F. J. Wiedemann (see his Introduction to J. A. Sjøgren's *Livische Grammatik*, St Petersburg, 1861,
p. xxix), who was followed by Koskinnen (*Sur l'antiquité des Lives en
Livonie*, in the *Acta Societatis Scientiarum Fennicæ*, VIII, 2, 395, 1866).
But Koskinnen accepted other identifications of the *Ydumaei* incon-

sistent with a name beginning with *I*. Thus he supposed *Ydumaea* the same as Wulfstan's *Witland* (Alfred's Orosius, ed. Sweet, p. 20) and as the modern Lettish and Livonian names for Livonia, *Widsemme* and *Widumaa*.

Accepting these last identifications of *Ydumaea* with *Witland, etc.*, Müllenhoff pointed out that Henry's *Ydumaea* could in that case be only a Latinized corruption : that the name must have begun with a *W*, which Henry had dropped in order to bring the name into line with the Scriptural *Idumaea* ; and that these [W]idumaei could therefore have nothing to do with the *Idumingas* of *Widsith* (Müllenhoff *D.A.* II, 347). The O.E. *Idumingas* Müllenhoff regarded as simply the biblical reminiscence of a learned interpolator (*Z.f.d.A.* XI, 291 ; Grein-Wülcker, I, 401).

Müllenhoff's argument is convincing, but the premises accepted by him and by Koskinnen are probably incorrect.

The identification of *Ydumaea* with Wulfstan's *Witland* is locally and racially more than doubtful, and, even if *Ydumaea* is identical with the modern *Widseme*, the *W* in the modern word is apparently not original, and due either to corruption or false analogy. (See A. Bielenstein *Die Grenzen des Lettischen Volksstammes*, St Petersburg, 1892, 71–74, and a note by Prof. Vilhelm Thomsen in the *Magazin der Lettisch. Litterärischen Gesellschaft*, XIX, 3, 151 (1894) ; but compare also Bielenstein, pp. 466–470, and especially the arguments of E. Kunik in favour of Müllenhoff's theory and the originality of the *W*.)

Bielenstein supposes the original form of Henry's *Idumaea* to have been *Yduma* ; and in adopting this form he is not led by any desire to bring the word into line with the Old English, which he does not quote, but only by the etymology of the word, which he takes to be of Livonian origin signifying the north-east-land. Henry's corruption is therefore confined to the second half of the word, which is obviously corrupt also in the O.E. *Iduming* (cf. *Lidwicing*), whilst the first syllable of the word is identical in each case. Phonetically then the identification of *Idumingas* with *Ydumaei* is possible enough. But it cannot be accepted as certain, in view of the great lapse of time between *Widsith* and Henry's *Chronicle*. This difficulty is somewhat increased by the fact that the *Ydumaei* are a tiny tribe occupying a territory about the size of one of the smaller English counties. We should hardly expect so small a people to maintain itself throughout seven centuries in such vast regions. The identification of Henry's *Ydumaei* with the *Idumingas* of our text can, then, be accepted only with considerable reservation.

Ydumaea is mentioned in sufficient detail by Henry to enable us to locate it accurately (see Wiedemann, p. xxiv : A. Bielenstein's *Atlas der ethnologischen Geographie des Lettenlandes*, St Petersburg, 1892). It was

the smallest of the districts into which Livonia was divided, lying between
the Raupa (modern Brasle) and the Aa. The *Ydumaei* were in Henry's
day Livonians, with a sprinkling of Letts. The collocation of *Idumingas*
with the *Iste* (who are most probably Letts and Lithuanians) and of
both with the most eastern German tribes of the border, the Heruli and
Thuringians, certainly looks like a piece of genuine tradition accurately
preserved.

(H) THE TERM HRÆDAS APPLIED TO THE GOTHS.

This term is found in O.E. and in Scandinavian sources, but not elsewhere. The Scandinavian documents are confused. The Icelandic
geographers of the 14th century explain *Reiðgotaland* as a district
bordering upon Poland (*Antiq. russes*, II, 438, 447). Snorri equates it
with Jutland. He evidently had a false etymology in mind, connecting
the name with *reið*, "carriage," for he makes it apply to the mainland, as
opposed to *Eygotaland*, the islands (see Sn. *Edda*, udg. Jónsson, pp. 7,
143) : *Reiðgotaland* is referred to also in the *Heimskringla* (udg. Jónsson,
1893, I, 18). Again, in one of the redactions of the *Hervarar Saga*, *Reið-
gotaland* is explained as Jutland (*Fornaldar Sogur*, ed. Rafn, I, 526).
Other Icelandic interpretations will be found in Heinzel (*Hervararsaga*
in *W.S.B.* cxiv, 56). It is to be noted that in the fragmentary lay upon
which this portion of the *Hervarar Saga* is founded, the land of the Goths
lies north and west of the land of the Huns, with Mirkwood between.
This is the geography of *Widsith* : Goths and Huns facing, with the
Vistula wood between.

The origin of the name is equally uncertain: the Old English poets
certainly understood it to mean "the glorious Goths" (*hrēð*, glory) and
this etymology has been supported with more or less hesitation by Rieger
(*Lesebuch*, 286) ; Vigfusson in Cleasby's *Icelandic Dictionary*, *sub voce*
hróðr ; Kunik in the *Mémoires de l'Académie des Sciences de St Pétersbourg*
VII, xxiii, 1, pp. 381-4 ; Kern in *Cosijn's Taalkundige Bijdragen*, Haarlem,
1877, p. 29 ; Bugge (contrary to his earlier view) in *P.B.B.* xxiv, 445-6.
Kunik, Kern, and Bugge devise different methods of bringing O.E.
hrēð (from *hrōþi) and Icel. *hreiþ* (from *hraiþi) from one and the
same root.

The exact forms preserved are *Reiðgotaland* in Icelandic, both prose
and verse ; *Hraiþmarar* in the 10th century Swedish Runic inscription at
Rök, referring to Theodoric's realm ; *Hreðcyninges*, *Hreðgotum*, *Hræda*
(gen. from a nom. *Hrædas* or *Hræde*) in *Widsith* ; *Hreðgotan*, *Hreða*,
in the *Elene*. (For the shortened forms cf. *Wederas* for *Wedergeatas* in
Beowulf.) Ettmüller (1) was the first to point out that the metre demands
an *h* in the one passage where the word occurs in Icelandic verse, and that

Reiö is therefore a corruption of *Hreiö*; and this is confirmed by the *h* in Swedish and O.E. Ettmüller also pointed out that the Icelandic *ei* does not correspond to the O.E. *ē* (*Hrēö*-), but to *ǣ* (*Hrǣda*). This was further emphasized by Müllenhoff (*Z.f.d.A.* XII, 260). The fact that one of the forms in *Widsith, Hrœda,* supports the Scandinavian form (*H*)*reiö* leads us to regard this as original, and the O.E. *Hrēö* as due to false analogy. The true derivation of *Hrēd* (from *Hraiþi*) remains still to seek. Heinzel (*Ostgotische Heldensage* in *W.S.B.* CXIX, pp. 26–8) derives from Radagais (O.E. *Rædgota*) who was cut to pieces, with his Goths, in Italy in 405. The name would then mean "the Goths of Radagais." Gering (*Z.f.d.Ph.* XXVI, 26) suggests a connection with *hríþ,* "tempest," "The storm- or battle-Goths." Much (*Z.f.d.A.* XXXIX, 52) would connect with *hrains* pure, comparing *Beorhtdene* in *Beowulf.* None of these suggestions, nor others hazarded by Förstemann in Kuhn's *Zeitschrift für vergleich. Sprachforschung,* XIX, 367, are probable.

See also Grimm, *G.D.S.,* 446, 740–1 ; Jessen in *Z.f.d.Ph.* III, 72 ; Munch, *Saml. Afhandl.* I, 439, II, 105–10 ; Bugge, *Ueber die Insch. des Röksteins* ; Bugge in *P.B.B.* XII, 6, 7 ; Jiriczek (2) 127 ; Schütte in *A.f.n.F.* XXI, 37.

(I) ERMANARIC AS THE FOE OF THE HUNS.

It has recently been argued by Heusler (*Berl. Sitzungsberichte,* XXXVII, 925, 1909 ; *Hoops Reallexikon,* Attila, p. 138) that the story of Ermanaric as the typical foe of the Huns had no continued existence, but was first forgotten, and then invented again about the ninth century when, since Theodoric was represented as taking refuge with Attila, hostile relations between Ermanaric and Attila were imagined.

The historic fact of antagonism between the Huns and Ermanaric is recorded in the fourth century by Ammianus. It would be a strange coincidence had the poets in the ninth century reproduced this situation accidentally, and such coincidence can hardly be assumed without evidence.

But the evidence is all to the contrary. Jordanes in the sixth century represents Ermanaric as the foe of the Huns. In *Widsith* the grouping of Attila and Ermanaric

Ætla weold Hunum, Eormanric Gotum (l. 18)

might reasonably be supposed to be due to a reminiscence of their connection in story, precisely as in the exactly parallel Icelandic lines the contending parties are grouped together :

Ár kvóðo Humla Húnom ráða,
Gitzor Gautom, Gotom Angantý....

This of course is only an inference, but on the other hand it hardly admits of dispute that in *Widsith* (ll. 109–122) the *innweorud Earmanrices* is represented as combating the people of Attila. This is certainly earlier than the tradition which makes Attila the refuge of Theodoric; yet *Widsith* was popular enough to be still transcribed c. 1000, by which time Attila was widely known as Theodoric's protector. So that we have an exceptionally good chain of evidence for the continuity of the tradition of hostility between Ermanaric and Attila. I have accordingly assumed this continuity as proved (pp. 45, etc.).

(K) THE LAST ENGLISH ALLUSION TO WUDGA AND HAMA.

The following passage, discovered by Dr Imelmann in MS. Cotton Vesp. D. IV (fol. 139 b), is of the utmost importance for the history of heroic tradition in England :

> In dieb*us* illis imp*er*ante Valentiniano imp*er*atore uel pr*i*ncipe, regnum barbaror*um* *et* germanor*um* exortum est. Surgentesq*ue* po*p*uli et naciones p*er* totam europam co*n*sederu*nt*. H*oc* testant*ur* gesta rudolphi *et* hunlapi, Unwini et Widie, horsi et hengisti, Waltef et hame quor*um* quidam in Italia, quida*m* i*n* Gallia, alii in br*i*tan*n*ia ceter*i* u*er*o in Germania armis et reb*us* bellicis clarueru*nt*.

The MS. is late : but whatever be the source of the information, it seems clear that the stories of Wudga, Hama, Hrothwulf, Unwen, Hunlaf(ing), Hengest and Hors(a) were current till so long after the Norman conquest that it was possible for these heroes to be classed with *Waltef*. Dr Imelmann is to be congratulated on an important discovery, which compels us to alter our ideas as to the date when these stories may have become extinct. See *D.L.Z.* xxx, p. 999 (April 1909).

(L) THE GEOGRAPHY OF THE *OROSIUS* COMPARED WITH THAT OF *WIDSITH*.

1. The statement of *Widsith* that the realm which Offa won was the greatest of kingdoms is confirmed by the addition to the *Orosius* (ed. Sweet, p. 19). However we read this passage, it can hardly be interpreted otherwise than that the old Anglian home extended two days' sail (i.e. between one and two hundred miles) from its centre in Schleswig, and

embraced "many islands[1]." Apparently *Sillende* and *Gotland* are also
included in the old home of the Engle. *Sillende* may be *Silund*[2] (Zealand),
but it is possibly *Sinlendi*, a district in the south of Jutland[3]. *Gotland* is
almost certainly Jutland (*Reið-gotaland*). It is not quite the case (as
Björkman argues, *Engl. Stud.* XXXIX, 360) that there is no philological
difficulty in taking *Gotland* as Jutland : Ohthere would have said *Jótland*,
and this should have been written *Geotland*, not *Gotland* : but seeing
that this portion of the *Orosius* is extant only in one late MS., which is
full of misspellings, this error presents no insuperable difficulty. It looks
then as if the *cynerica mæst* of Offa might well have included the greater
part of the present Denmark, as well as Schleswig.

2. Only the larger tribes are mentioned in the Alfredian description
of Germany : there is nothing like the exclusive interest shown in *Widsith*
in the tribes dwelling on the Baltic, though the Baltic islands are carefully
enumerated. The difference is between the current knowledge of a well
informed man in the ninth century and a geographical knowledge, more
detailed within its narrower sphere, going back to earlier times.

3. Brandl has suggested that the "Biblical interpolation" is derived
from the Orosius. But the coincidences are not very numerous, and the
forms used differ. Contrast *Moidum* with *Mæðum, Meðum* ; *Istum* with
Estum, Osti.

(M) SCHÜTTE'S LAW OF INITIAL AND TERMINAL STRESS.

Oldsagn om Godtjod, by Dr Gudmund Schütte, has been frequently
quoted above with reference to details : one general point needs a fuller
examination. Schütte formulates the law that, in Germanic name-lists,
the first member is the one of greatest general importance ; the last the
one in which the framers of the tradition have the most special interest.
Dr Axel Olrik has emphasized the value of this law as "a test in cases
which have hitherto perplexed the student" (*Folk-Lore*, XIX, 353, 1908),

---

[1] See above, p. 72. In favour of the interpretation of *Denemearc* there
given, it should be noted that Adam of Bremen (in describing that same portion
of the present southern Sweden, which Ohthere is coasting) makes the Danish
territory stretch up to Norway : *primi occurrunt Nortmanni, deinde Sconia
prominet, regio Danorum* (Adam of Bremen in Pertz (fol.) VII, 373). Adam
regards Sconia as an integral part of Denmark : *Sconia est pulcherrima visu
Daniæ provintia.* To Adam the boundary between Denmark and Sweden is
not, as at present, the sea, but the forests and uplands of what is now the
interior of Sweden : *Sconia est pars ultima Daniæ fere insula, undique enim
cincta est mari præter unum terræ brachium quod ab oriente continens Sueoniam
disterminat a Dania.* This is exactly the geography of Ohthere.

[2] For the form and interpretation of *Silund*, cf. Much in *P.B.B.* XVII, 196 ;
Kossinna in *I.F.* VII, 281.

[3] Chadwick (104, *note*) ; cf. Schück (19) "*Sönderjylland.*" It can hardly
be, as Sweet thinks, Holstein.

and suggests that "Schütte's Law" may prove as efficient in folk-lore analysis as has Verner's Law in phonetic analysis.

That the law represents a widely-spread tendency of the mind seems clear : it will be found to apply very generally. I take the first two lists which occur to me. The list of David's mighty men of valour (II Samuel, xxiii) begins with Adino the Eznite, chief of the captains and hero of the greatest achievement ("he lift up his spear against eight hundred, whom he slew at one time")—clearly the one of greatest general importance. It ends with Uriah the Hittite—certainly the one of greatest special interest. So in Mallory's *Morte d'Arthur* : where the "hundred knights and ten" of the Round Table are enumerated, the first to search Sir Urre's wound is King Arthur, the last Sir Launcelot.

But I doubt whether in *Widsith* any such law is consciously operating. It is claimed that the Catalogue of Kings begins with Attila and ends with Offa (Olrik, p. 353). But is Attila, rather than Ermanaric, the king of greatest general importance ? And the list does not end with Offa. If we include the supplementary lines (35–49), it ends with Hrothwulf, Hrothgar and Ingeld : if we omit these lines, it ends with Alewih. The list of Gothic champions begins with Hethca, otherwise unknown. It ends with Wudga and Hama, who certainly seem to be of most special interest to the poet. But that he did not consciously regard the last place as due to those in whom he had a special interest is shown by his apology for so placing them :

> ne wæran þæt gesiþa þa sæmestan,
> þeahþe ic hy anihst nemnan sceolde.

(N) ON THE *BEAG* GIVEN BY EORMANRIC.

The *beag* is said to contain refined gold to the value of *siex hund sceatta scillingrime*. The *scilling* (not an actual coin, but a denomination of money value) was equal, in Mercia, to four silver *sceattas*. The *sceatt* was a current coin, but the term is also used generally in the sense of "money," and I take that to be its force here, "money to the quantity of six hundred counted in shillings," i.e. the *beag* is worth 600 shillings (=2400 *sceattas*, using *sceatt* in its narrower sense).

This rendering seems preferable to the alternative one, of taking *sceatt* strictly and *scilling* vaguely, "six hundred *sceattas* reckoned in money," because :

(1) It is easy to parallel the use of *sceatt* as equivalent to "money" generally, indeed this is its normal force, but it would be difficult so to explain *scilling*.

(2) If we take the Anglian reckoning of four silver *sceattas* to the shilling (Seebohm, 363) and allow twenty *sceattas* to the Roman ounce

(Seebohm, 443–455) and reckon gold to silver as 1 : 12 (Seebohm, 451) we find that a golden *beag* worth 600 *sceattas* would have weighed 2½ ounces, one worth 600 shillings ten ounces. Since the gift is mentioned as noteworthy, the latter interpretation is distinctly preferable, in view of the considerable weight of existing gold necklets and armlets. Cf. e.g. Odobesco (A.), *Le Trésor de Pétrossa*, Paris, 1900 ; Rygh, *Norske Oldsager*, Christiania, 1885 (especially Nos. 704, 705, 707, 708, 714 a) ; *Archaeologia*, XXXIII, 347 ; XXXIX, 505, *etc.*

On the other hand, to take the *beag* (with Holthausen) as worth 600 *gold* pieces would be to make it altogether too massive, and seems hardly possible linguistically, for though the *sceatt* is, exceptionally, a gold coin, the *scilling* is, as stated above, a denomination for the value of so many *silver sceattas*.

The dotted lines are drawn to connect different localities inhabited at different times by one tribe. No attempt is made to indicate the exact route taken by that tribe in its migrations.

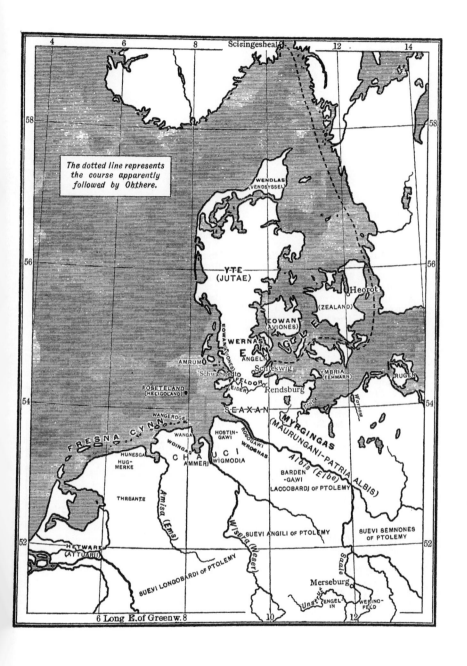

The dotted line represents the course apparently followed by Ohthere.

INDEX

CAMBRIDGE : PRINTED BY JOHN CLAY, M.A. AT THE UNIVERSITY PRESS.

For EU product safety concerns, contact us at Calle de José Abascal, 56–1°,
28003 Madrid, Spain or eugpsr@cambridge.org.